*The Realizations of the Future*

SUNY Series in Philosophy
George R. Lucas Jr., editor

# The Realizations of the Future

## AN INQUIRY INTO
## THE AUTHORITY OF PRAXIS

## George Allan

STATE UNIVERSITY OF NEW YORK PRESS

Published by
State University of New York Press, Albany

© 1990 State University of New York

For information, address State University of New York Press,
State University Plaza, Albany, N.Y., 12246


**Library of Congress Cataloging-in-Publication Data**

Allan, George, 1935–
    The realizations of the future : an inquiry into the authority of
praxis / George Allan.
        p.      cm. — (SUNY series in philosophy)
    Includes bibliographical references.
    ISBN 0–7914–0441–2 (alk. paper). — ISBN 0–7914–0442–0 (pbk. :
alk. paper)
    1. Ethics.    2. History—Philosophy.      I. Title.    II. Title:
Praxis.    III. Series.
BJ1012.A465    1990
128'.4—dc20                                        89–77404
                                                        CIP


10   9   8   7   6   5   4   3   2   1

For my daughter Karen
   whose virtuous aims and pragmatic accomplishments
   are what this book describes

# CONTENTS

All the higher, more penetrating ideals are revolutionary. They present themselves far less in the guise of effects of past experience than in that of probable causes of future experience, factors to which the environment and the lessons it has so far taught us must learn to bend.

—William James

# PREFACE

Alcibiades says that Socrates is an impudent satyr. His talk is as bewitching as the melodies played by Marsyus on magical pipes. His words bring tears to your eyes, a lump to your throat, and turn your whole soul upside down. Socrates, testifies Alcibiades, can draw you with him into a frenzy of philosophizing and make you feel ashamed for having neglected it for the sake of such trivial matters as family and politics. Diotima, however, seems to think that Socrates is more like an incarnation of Eros, the son of Resource and Need. He is a master of device and artifice, she suggests, but uses his talents in a tireless quest for truth and beauty. Barefoot, homeless, he wanders in the world in search of these ideals, importuning others to follow him. At least this is what Aristodemus reports that Alcibiades and Diotima said of Socrates, if Apollodorus heard him right and has told us and Glaucon the whole of it.

Meno is of the opinion that a more accurate image of this Socrates would be that he is a stingray who numbs the mind and lips of anyone foolish enough to try to talk with him. Socrates should be arrested as a wizard or a witch, and indeed would be were he ever to travel to a foreign city where people do not know him and are not so willing to forgive his idiosyncracies. Meletus is not prepared to be so forgiving, however. He argues that Socrates is a traitor to Athens, a corruptor of its youth and an atheist, a deceiver who makes the weaker argument defeat the stronger. But Phaedo says that of all those whom he ever knew Socrates was the bravest, the wisest, and the most upright.

These views are very different, yet each is a sketch of Socrates made by Plato, who hides godlike inside the silenus-figures of his dialogues.

Aristophanes sketches quite a different Socrates, and Xenophon another still. From then until our own day, the number of his philosophical portrayals has been immense. In addition, there are the myriad understandings written only in the minds and hearts of unnamed individuals who were chaste novices, most of them, to the wonder of Socrates until, like Alcibiades, they lost their innocence while in his arms.

If you would know Socrates, which account of him should you believe? Perhaps you might happen to begin as Meno did, inquiring of him how virtue can be obtained, until the stingray's prick shocks you into awareness of your ignorance. Here most definitely is a Socrates to know and under whose tutelage to grow. Soon, however, you would know enough to know that this is not enough. You need also to be a fellow soldier with the Socrates who fought steadfastly for Athens throughout the long campaign at Potidaea and who in the retreat from Delium calmed his frightened comrades and fiercely provided them protection until they had made good their escape. You need to become an intimate of the Socrates who defied the local authorities, deriding them for their arrogance of power and their fear of truth. And you need to know the philosopher who thought his soul immortal. Yet you need to know as well the one who thought it sufficient were he able but to glimpse timeless beauty, content if in its presence he might be quickened to create mortal images of its immortality.

Each of these is Socrates and yet none of them. Each gives you all of him but only from a point of view. Take another stance and you may well be greeted by some fresh, surprising vista to be puzzled about or to understand. The whole of the knowing of Socrates comes no other way than this: to move from Meletus to Alcibiades, from Meno to Diotima, and to find in the clamor of their accounts a deeper story, one that cannot be told but only known.

Plato in his exposition of the divided line makes this same point, although in a more general way. There are basically four sorts of accounts, he claims, by which to tell the truth of things. One is by means of images, another by the narration of deeds, a third through specifying formal relationships, and a fourth is dialectical. You must experience all four ways of looking at reality, of hearing the rhythm of its tendencies, each for its own sake and for the totality to which it contributes. Each level of the divided line is a embarkation point for a journey into understanding. Each adventure, if it achieves its destination, accumulates important truths along the way. But no journey ever garners for itself the truth wholly and complete. Yet if you are a patient enough traveler and steadfast in your determination, the four kinds of journeying will yield collectively the end you seek.

Robert S. Brumbaugh argues that the divided line should not be interpreted as a ladder for mounting up from ignorance to certainty,
from experiences that are fleeting and trivial to those that are timeless
and significant. Imagination is not a paltry way to know the world,
good only for fools and children to use, while monarchs, philosophers,
and other better folk have access to dialectic tools of the most exquisite sort. Instead, says Brumbaugh, each of the four ways of knowing is
needed, each point of view necessary to truth even though none is by
itself sufficient. The totality of the accounts given, grasped all at once
by the attentive listener, is alone what tells the tale of Truth.

I am concerned about the nature of social value: how values emerge
and how they manage to gain the authority they have over the beliefs
and practices of generation after generation of human beings. In an
earlier book, *The Importances of the Past*, I approached this question
from the perspective provided by imagination. Within the flux of momentary experience, you feel the past pressing in upon you, circum-
scribing your possibilities but at the same time filling you with a sense
that you are participating in a meaningful order of things. You come to
believe that there are enduring importances, regions of permanent significance, within the universe. By being present in the sacred places
where these are known, by repeating the practices by which they have
been evoked, by revering those who in the past have preserved this
relationship, you trust that you also will become a part of that awesome reality. Emotion, memory, and myth effect your participation in
the importances of the past. These are the tools of imagination, fashioning and sustaining the traditions of your society, extending their duration and hence their value back in time to the beginnings of your
people, beyond that to the origins of all humanity and even to the timeless foundations of the universe. Hence,

this church, this ritual, these friends and the land we share, are compatriots in a venture that includes predecessors and successors. My joint
venture with them reaches back to the beginnings of history and it
reaches forward to the end of time.... In becoming a part of this collective journey through time, sharing in the identifiable structures of
importance that sustain it, seeing the pillars of cloud by day and the
guiding fires of the night, I find a reason for my life. I am at once fulfilled and filled with hope, assured that there is an abiding worth to
who I am, to what I have done, and to what my life yet might mean. By
my origins and endings I am saved. [IP 152]

The authority of tradition, however, suffers from debilitating limitations. Its reverence for the past can far too easily slip over into unthink-

ing rigidities, the seemingly solid limestone of its myths are vulnerable to the skeptical acids of modernity, and the sheer vitality of life's chaotic spontaneities keeps breaking through. Imagination is unable to protect the importances whose protectiveness it celebrates.

In this present book, I shall begin anew the search for a foundation to the values fundamental for individuals and their societies. I will ask you to turn with me away from the past and toward the future. What has become tradition must previously have been a novel accomplishment. You can preserve only what you have first created. Surely, then, it must be possibilities for realization that are the genuine sources of what is valuable. It must be in human effort, the concrete actions involved in choosing goals and pursuing them effectively, where we would find what gives those sources their authority. Let us inquire, then, into these matters. Perhaps this new perspective will prove more fruitful than the last, for praxis can more easily account for imagination than imagination can account for praxis. By realizing the future through their own creative activities, human beings make concretely actual the values that fulfill them and that therefore they seek to preserve.

So I shall, within the confines of this book, struggle to tell the story of the human praxis that Socrates epitomizes. May my narrative have the ring of truth to it; may it weave the essential fabric of our human reality. But Socrates this time too will escape our grasp, for there will be more to do than what we can accomplish even with the help of some brash Alcibiades. Nonetheless, what we can do we will; it is formidable enough a task to keep us fully occupied. The challenge of other tellings of our tale should properly be postponed until this one has been unfolded to its end.

I have been helped in my thinking by many colleagues, some of them close friends and others known to me only through their writings. I would like to thank Robert Cummings Neville, George R. Lucas, Jr., and Frederick Ferré for their thoughtful and detailed comments on a draft of the whole manuscript. Phillip T. Grier and Joan M. Bechtel, in their quite differing ways, gave me needed assurances and suggestions for Chapter 6. Other kinds of timely advice were provided by Sandra Rosenthal and Vincent Colapietro. Margorie Fitzpatrick cast a practiced literary eye over early drafts and chided me for spelling errors as well as providing sage commentary on my ideas and their articulation. My copy editor, Betty S. Waterhouse, and production editor, Marilyn P. Semerad, were helpful in improving my prose and assuring consistency in my mode of presentation. My wife Betsy helped me with the page proofs and index, as well as reminding me of tasks and joys for which writing can never substitute. I would especially like to thank Dickinson College for offering me a yearlong sabbatical leave from my administrative duties to complete this project.

David L. Hall read a draft of the first six chapters and offered his not always deferential judgments on its truth. He said that what I had written was a lot of "Han-thought": a syncretic attempt at cultural reconstruction for the sake of reactionary political ends. He mused at the futility of the enterprise, calling it a desperate attempt to keep at bay "the advancing shadow of the postmodern phalanx." Perhaps his words influenced the somber ending to this book. And perhaps he is not yet fully aware of how his own thought is actually so close to mine.

# One

## THE NATURE OF PRAXIS

This book is about ethics. It is a way for you and me to inquire into the character of various recommendations about how we might best live our lives, how we might best carry on our common life so as to realize the aspirations most important to each of us. This book is simultaneously about morality, because these recommendations are linked to the various concrete individual and societal practices that occasion them and that they in turn influence. Finally, this book is about history, for morality and ethics are expressions of a human condition that is intrinsically temporal. Ethics, morals, temporality: what you and I aspire to be, what you are, what I am, and the darkling plain of time that continually evokes and then revokes all our deeds and all our hopes.

When you or I assert that the human condition is intrinsically temporal, we mean that we experience the world around us as constantly changing, constantly creating, combining, reshaping, eroding, destroying the orderings that give it a meaningful character. Human life as an element of that character is thus a meaningful order that needs constantly to be achieved and constantly to be rescued from becoming transformed into some other ordering, some other characterization of the flux. This achievement, this making and sustaining of things human, is a practice: the accomplishing within a tolerating context of a distinctive reality. It is the sustained realization by persons and their communities of selves and societies, a making real that is self-referential and open-ended, that is real only in the making, actual only in the actualizing, and therefore that must always be going on. Its being is its own

1

becoming. Its substance is the story of its efforts, intended or unintended, solitary or shared, and of their results, known or unknown, coherent or contradictory, extending on to further efforts and on to
further results and on and on. The being of our humanity is its history.

The history of these human practices, the genealogy of your morality and mine, reveals amid the vast perishing of things tremendous success in stabilizing and sustaining important structures of meaning.
These importances inherited from the past are what give human being
its definition, what makes you and me the creatures we are: selves
within social communities within a natural order possibly encompassed by transcending permanence. Preserving these importances is
the means by which you and I save ourselves from aimlessness and sin,
from losing our sense of purpose and our sense of place, from ceasing
to be who we know we are and could become.[1]

The heart of the matter, nonetheless, is a question not of the importances that need preserving but of how in the first instance to create
what deserves to be preserved. Your task, my task, the task of every
human creature, is to search first of all for a practice that we might
legitimately find worth perpetuating. Our task is to find an ethic authoritative enough to guide us in fashioning a morality good enough to
provide a worthwhile content to the story yet to be told of our common life as creatures of history.

Perhaps you are impatient to set about that task, to begin considering
questions of how best to do what must be done in order to live and,
living, to live still better. I share that impatience, for there is much for
us to ask and many voices ready and waiting to respond, to instruct us
and implore us and to point the way toward a brighter dawn. I would
suggest, however, that we begin this inquiry, this search for a worthy
practice, by first roughing in a working sense of what any practice involves. We need a map of practice, one that might serve to guide our
quest for a better practice and the best. How, we must ask, would you
describe the general character of any human activity, however inept or
excellent it might be thought to be? That such a generalization might
even be possible is problematic. But were there such, what would it be?

The answer seems obvious enough. If human being is its becoming,
then the shape of that becoming, the contour of human practice,
should itself exhibit the necessary conditions within which the substantive character of the ethical ends we seek are to be found. The
form of morality should provide a foundation for the ideal possibilities
it can then be exhorted to make actual. We cannot usefully begin our
journey until we have first peered as closely as we are able at the map
of the terrain which lies before us.

Let me propose the term "praxis" as a name for such a putative general framework of human action. As we begin to invest this word with an interpretation, you will soon realize that its meaning is partially a stipulative definition of my own but partially one justified by the history of its usage.

I want us to mean by praxis more or less what is conveyed by the words "practical activity" or "action." This is consistent with everyday uses of the term *praxis* by the ancient Greeks, although Aristotle restricted its meaning to a special kind of human activity.[2] For him, actions are of two sorts: practical action on the one hand, and on the other *theoria* or abstract reasoning. When someone theorizes, when you are engaged solely in contemplating ideas and exploring their interrelationships, the purpose of your activity is understanding apart from any concern for the usefulness or other particular relevance of what you are learning. Aristotle then notes that the practical activity contrasting with *theoria* is in its turn also of two sorts. One kind is *poiesis,* an activity whereby a person makes something in the sense of constructing or creating an artifact. The other kind of practical activity is *praxis,* which is what a person is doing when engaged in an activity the performance of which is its sole purpose, in which the practical significance of the activity lies in the doing of it rather than in some tangible outcome for which it is the means. Thus for Aristotle *praxis* has what one commentator calls an "immanently teleological structure": the means is itself the end.[3]

In sport, music, war, and politics you do something—you run a race, play a flute, fight a battle, vote in an election. What you are doing has consequences, to be sure, and these may be quite important: the crossing of the finish line may crown your brow with laurel, the winning of the battle may alter the course of your nation's history, the song concluded might spur you on to play another song, the ballots tallied may force a change in government. But your activities are not primarily, if at all, for the sake of such results. *Praxis* is the deed itself, and its significance resides in the whole of the activity. The value of a song is the music from its first note to its last, the reason for the race is the running of it, the meaning of the battle is in the fighting, and the democratic polity is the decision-making that goes on by secret ballot.

Today praxis has a somewhat different usage. This more recent sense of the term derives from Kant and is given clear expression by Marx. In their usage it loosens Aristotle's meaning so as to refer broadly to any human activity that effects a change of some sort in the concrete world, either the natural world or the cultural. An evaluative caveat usually accompanies this meaning: that the change be positive, advancing in some manner the "humanization" of humanity. Aristotle was concerned that deeds of every sort be done well, but especially those that constitute in their doing the moral end of self and society. It was virtuous *praxis* that he sought: *eupraxia.* Marx simply makes the honorific qualifier a necessary attribute of the activity. Virtuous action is not the highest expression of praxis but its very core. Marx was concerned with consequences, with altering the material conditions of life, with making the world a better place. That better place was for him one where human activity is at last everywhere fully human. The goal of revolutionary praxis is to liberate human activity from the forces that debase it, to realize a condition wherein the life of noble actions is available to each person because of the noble acts of every other person.

We must look more closely at the nature of this praxis of ours if we are to see what makes it the locus of change and excellence in human life, the fountainhead for the coming-to-be of better persons and improved societies. Let me put it this way: any instance of praxis can be described as an event having the following fourfold character. First, there is a condition, an entity, a situation that is characterizably deficient; it expresses negative value. Second, there is a possibility of the condition of deficiency removed, the possibility that there might be a range of possibilities that could be characterized as relevant to some such alternative condition; it expresses positive value. Third, there is the characterizing of some of these possibilities either as realizable instruments for or as realizable ingredients in a new condition characterizable as without deficiency; it expresses instrumental values. Fourth, there is the effort of transformation, the actual struggle to change the old condition into the proposed new condition; it expresses the realization of value. Condition, goal, procedure, effort. Together these four qualities comprise the essential elements in the totality of anything justifiably called a human action, an instance of praxis.

I claim that this fourfoldness is a totality and therefore that it resists restatement in terms of something else or in terms of just one or even just three of its constitutive aspects; that this fourfoldness is distinctively human, an expression of self-referential, self-interpreting capacities unique to our kind of nature; and that there is a genetic account to be given of this totality, an account of it as a temporally emergent achievement and not as a timeless transcendental fact. These claims cannot be defended in advance of the inquiry you and I have agreed to undertake, and at its end I do not expect them to need defending. For now let them constitute the assumptive landscape within which we shall work.

Yet this landscape is too abstract, seemingly too arbitrary, to be informative, much less convincing. Fourfoldness, indeed! What can that have to do with fulfillment and loyalty, with individual happiness and securing the common weal? Let us therefore give our inquiry a more concrete cast by considering the views of some thinkers whose varied perspectives box the compass of contemporary philosophy. As examples of their traditions, although not necessarily its exemplars, as paradigms but not paragons, these philosophers can be resources for fashioning a description of praxis specific enough to function as a helpful instrument of inquiry.

Before doing that, however, pause with me for a moment to take a look at another fourfoldness, one that Aristotle says we necessarily use in coming to know fully a thing or an event:

Knowledge is the object of our inquiry, and men do not think they know a thing till they have grasped the 'why' of it (which is to grasp its primary cause). So clearly we too must do this as regards both coming to be and passing away and every kind of physical change, in order that, knowing their principles, we may try to refer to these principles each of our problems. [*Physics* II.3 194b18–23]

To grasp the why of anything, or rather to grasp the what-how-why[4] of it, is to be assured we have an adequate answer to each of four questions.

First of all, what is its material cause: out of what *(ex hou)* is it made? What is the substratum from which this particular thing arises? What was the raw material with which you had to work in fashioning it? Second, its final cause: for what end *(hou heneka)* was it made? What is its purpose, its value? What good do you think it will do? Third, the formal cause: what is it *(ti esti)* that unifies this particular thing? What was brought to bear upon it so that it became one thing? What defines it, what gives it shape, makes it the kind of thing it is? How did you go about giving it its distinctive character? And fourth, the efficient cause: by what agency *(hypo tinos)* was it made to be? Wherein lay the source of the changes that took place? What empowered you to get this done?

If we are to know fully what praxis is we must ask of it these same four questions. The fourfold of praxis can be grasped only by the fourfold of Aristotelian query. Praxis is a human being being human. To understand praxis is to understand ourselves, myself, yourself, and other selves, better. You actually went and did that deed; you acted in that specific way. And puzzled, I ask you: Why? I want to know all about your action, and so I must inquire as to its material, final, formal, and efficient aspects. I will require answers to these questions: What was the context? What did you have in mind? How did you go about doing it? Where did you get the energy to get it done? Only as my queries are answered does an understanding of what you did at last fully emerge, an understanding of why you did it and therefore an understanding of who you really are. Each causal question involves a response in terms of an essential quality of praxis. Thus praxis is the essence of our humanity, the explanation of our history and the promise of our future.

This same fourfold quest for the causes of human being is the common motif of the contemporary philosophers to whom we shall now turn. Their quite varied attempts to understand some aspect of the human situation all reflect the same Aristotelian sense of what is required of them. And their answers, I contend, converge.

Jean-Paul Sartre defines human reality in terms that closely approximate Aristotle's fourfold characterization. This might seem surprising since the title of his book, *Being and Nothingness,* implies that his concern is with a twofoldness, a distinction between being and its negation, *l'être-en-soi* and *l'être-pour-soi.* But this, Sartre insists, does not imply a dualism of two separate kinds of reality. Being-in-itself and being-for-itself are not retreads of Descartes's two mutually exclusive substances, one unthinking and extended, the other thinking and unextended. Being-in-itself and being-for-itself are, rather, two modes of being that presuppose something more fundamental. If you begin as concretely as possible, with the totality that is given as experience, being presents itself as your own being-in-the-world. Human-in-the-world, *l'homme-dans-le-monde,* is a reality from which the facticity of your situation, your intentional consciousness, and the relation between them are all abstractions [BN 34]. Although Sartre writes in a style rife with abstract generic terms, the human reality to which he refers is always irreducibly particular. Human-in-the-world is always about the presence of a specific situation characterized as a specific world through the nihilation of a particular in-itself by a particular for-itself [BN 786]. The structure of human-in-the-world may be generic, but it is always and only concretely existing individual human persons that constitute its reality.

It is as though reality were the continuous weave of a fabric, broken through at one point by a hole. The hole has no reality apart from the fabric it partially negates, yet while the fabric is independent of the hole, while it obviously does not need it to be a fabric, the hole is what gives the material its present distinctive character, makes it a specific, determinate object; the hole makes it this tattered piece of cloth. The relation of the material to the tear in it is asymmetrical although mutually defining. Their unity is not a matter of stitching two different things together, the cloth and the hole, as you might sew the red and white stripes of a flag together or might embed a sliver of wood amid crisscrossing strands. Similarly the human reality that you are is not a single thing, a totality within which mind and body are complementary or at least compatible constituents. Consciousness is the negating of what is in-itself, not just another kind or mode or domain of it. The hole is not a transparent piece of material but the absence of any fabric whatsoever; your consciousness is not an invisible object but rather no object at all.

This means, according to Sartre, that there is something inherently unsettled about a person. Your whole self, the sum total of who you are, the totality of your self-identity, is not a varied bunch of separate experiences laced together by memory nor stripes of mind and body spliced together with the help of some sort of ontological binding tape. A human totality is always "detotalized" [BN 793]. In the case of a piece of cloth, the presence of the hole means that it is incomplete, the continuity of its weave fractured, its unbroken plenitude of materiality destroyed. But this problem is remediable: the hole can be stitched up or patched, the broken threads replaced or spliced, the seamless web of it restored. Not so yourself. The way in which for-itself exists is negatively, by disclosing its world in the light of the possibility of a world that might replace it [BN 614]. To be yourself is to know yourself to be somehow unfinished, in process of becoming something else, as a result of all the possibilities for change that lure and threaten you from every side. The damaged cloth carries the potential for its repair, but the hole does not grasp this possibility, does not disclose for itself its damaged condition as its given reality nor contrast this with a possible undamaged condition that might succeed it. The holey cloth is a complex relation of fabric and nonfabric. Its concreteness may not be simply a unity of two similar parts, but it has nonetheless only two constitutive dimensions, the weave of threads and the gap sundering its plenitude. The very nature of a person, however, is to be all of this plus the awareness of all of this, and plus the awareness of more than this and of the power to realize that more.

Two of Sartre's most characteristic claims are that "what we call freedom is impossible to distinguish from the *being* of 'human reality'" [BN 60] and that "for human reality, to be is to act" [BN 613]. Both are his naming of this distinctively human way of negation. Freedom is the capacity to negate what is by disclosing it not to be something else, to negate all other things by comparing them to what is not, to negate what is not by disclosing it as what could be, and to negate what could be by making it what is. Freedom is a mode of transforming the given: rejecting it, contrasting it with an alternative, preferring the alternative, seeking to actualize such as a newly given. These forms of freedom are all actions. The only way to be free is to act; the only way to be human is by dealing negatively with the given. To be human is to be active, to be a verb of the world, always to be doing something with respect to it: rejecting, comparing, choosing, shaping. Consequently human nature must be understood as essentially incomplete, untotalized, perpetually at work transformatively. The damage done to the cloth can be repaired; it can be made whole again, can become once more a proper cloth. But the healing of the rift in a human is its death, the overcoming of its being rather than the overcoming of a deficiency in its being.

Sartre makes clear that this freedom/action structure has a fourfold character in an analysis the vocabulary of which he subsequently all but neglects but which is nonetheless crucial for his argument [BN 133–146] and for the inquiry upon which we will soon embark. The unique kind of negation, which "appears in the world only with the upsurge of human reality," Sartre calls "the lack" *(le manque).* "It is only in the human world that there can be lacks" [BN 135]. This is the transforming power, the negating that is exhibited in the many senses just discussed. The lack is a human-making, world-making efficacy. It presupposes and entails two related further aspects. There is that which is incomplete, "the existing" *(l'existant),* and that which is missing, "the lacking" *(le manquant).* You perceive yourself to be hungry. The lack disclosed is a relationship between your stomach, which exists in its state of emptiness, and the food it is lacking. This relationship is not static but manifest as at work, transforming the existing condition into one that incorporates what is lacking. Hence it co-implicates yet another dimension of the human. To experience an existing object as incomplete may be to perceive it as missing something, but that contrast has no power except by reference to an ideal completeness, a totality, a situation where the incomplete is completed by what it lacks. This Sartre calls "the lacked" *(le manqué).* The relational power of the lack is thus a function of the power of the lacked, the one striving for what the other proposes. But without what is existing and what it is lacking there can be no ideal ordering nor any newly achieved one.

All four of these dimensions are at once present, composing the structure of human reality as freedom, as action; else none are present and the reality is not human after all. Only an "ex-isting" reality, a reality that negates what is given as its situation, that stands over against itself, can be for itself incomplete. Only such an existing reality can envision an ideal that is "lacked," that is absent from the world as it is but which could be that world as complete instead of incomplete. Only what can experience itself as possibly existing as what is lacked can identify something else as what it is "lacking," take it not just for what it is in itself but for what it might be to the reality that lacks it. Only a "lack" so constituted could be in the world in the form of a transformative power.

What gives Sartre's analysis its poignancy is that the totality sought cannot, he argues, be obtained. Were you a completed self, you would be a fully determined reality but also active. Nothing would be at issue because everything would be settled, secured, filled in. Yet you would nonetheless be conscious, thinking about future possibilities, striving after goals with no assurance of success. Thus a "complete self" is an oxymoron. "Human reality is a perpetual surpassing toward a coincidence with itself which is never given" [BN 139]. To be human is to apprehend yourself as condemned to fail endlessly in the endeavor to satisfy your desire for completion. It is to seek perfection but never to find it. Sartre calls this ideal, which is *le manqué* but now interpreted in terms of the impossibility of its realization, "value." It is "the unconditioned beyond of all surpassings" [BN 144], the goal of every exercise of human freedom, yet a goal that is not an outcome realized but rather the very condition for the freedom, the striving, that human being essentially is. "The being of human reality is suffering because it rises in being as perpetually haunted by a totality which it is without being able to be it" [BN 140].

This is the basis for Sartre's familiar argument at the end of *Being and Nothingness* that human being is the impossible desire to be God. The totality of *le manqué*, if realized, would be an entity both complete and active, both self-sufficient and yet a transforming power. Such a being would be its own foundation: "the *Ens causa sui*, which religions call God" [BN 784]. Sartre tags this "a useless passion" because it is a goal that cannot, for ontologically necessary reasons, ever be realized. But the significance of his point is not that such an impossibility is inutile but rather that it is inescapable.

Freedom, action, the praxis that is the reality of human reality, remains just so long as its fourfoldness remains. Sartre teaches that the structure of praxis is essentially a structure of incompletion; it is therefore the constant inventive source of value and of endless realizations of value. The disvalue of the given is that it is less than what it should have been and its value is as the foundation for what it might become, the emergence of possibility as functionally significant rather than merely abstractly true. With Sartre's help we can see how these co-imply an ideal that can be envisioned yet never realized. Yet this is no counsel of despair. As Sartre goes on to argue, precisely because *le manqué* is a value and not an accomplishment, human reality continues to manifest itself as struggling to transform the world. The "impossible vertical surpassing" of the self toward an unrealizable ideal is what "conditions the flat movement of consciousness" and gives it a temporal trajectory, just as the vertical attraction exerted by the moon on the ocean results in the horizontal displacements of the tide [BN 789]. Hence human reality, because it is incomplete, is the power that realizes worlds. Because it is a world-transcending hope, it is a world-creating reality. The essence of praxis is not any givenness that might result from its activity but the activity itself, the manifestation in being of factuality, value, possibility, and power as a single phenomenon.

Perhaps you can hear as I do the resonance of Aristotle's four causes in what Sartre says. The existing facticity to be negated is the material condition for the being of a human self; the possibility that is lacking contributes its formal conditions; the envisioned value is its final cause; the power of transforming actual and ideal conditions toward a realized outcome is the efficient cause of its being human. When applied to selves, the fourfold conditions of reality reveal a dynamic complex of relationships that are future-oriented, that are, indeed, the what and why and how of the future and of the praxis it co-implies. This is the landscape without which your quests and mine for happiness and security would make no sense. Sartre has surveyed that landscape in bold, brash strokes. We need next to take a more everyday, less abstractive look at it.

John Dewey, like Sartre, insists on the priority of a total context to the praxis that structures the human self. Dewey's approach appears to be quite different from Sartre's because his concern has to do with methods for knowing things rather than with their nature. He is making, as he frequently says, an epistemological not an ontological argument. But if the very being of a Sartrean self is its activity of negating the world, this approach is a close neighbor of the method of inquiry that Dewey claims to be the best expression of the human capacity for changing the world in accord with its purposes.

A situation, according to Dewey, is the natural environment, the complex transactional flow of things apart even from the distinction between organism and environment. Dewey quotes William James's description: a big, buzzing, blooming confusion. You experience it pre-cognitively, viscerally. Your response is equally immediate, fearing or enjoying its pervading texture, finding it attractive or repulsive, and so encompassing it or withdrawing from it or otherwise engaging in the flow of it. Yet were all that happened only this, life would be lived unconsciously, vegetatively, an ongoing exchange of chemicals constellating around states of natural equilibrium. This is Sartre's being-in-itself clothed in the many-colored raiments of biochemistry.

The problem is that sheer environment is too diffuse to experience. For there even to be an "it" to it, for there to be *a* situation, the flux of things requires some boundary. The dominance of a felt, pervasive quality implies a domain to dominate; although the domain manifests itself as indeterminate with respect to content and consequences, it is at least *this* present that looms up, *this* surrounding, doubtful situation in which you find yourself, *this* unsettled, uncertain, unavoidably questionable reality [LTI 105]. And there is you, situated thus, distinguished from it only by your awareness of it as yours but not as you. This situation of yours stretches off spatially to the edge of experience, a circumambient world that you sense as familiar and yet in certain ways as unfamiliar as well. Because it also encompasses your accustomed behaviors and beliefs, the repertoire of past experiences—remembered, repressed, habitualized—that lie behind those feelings of the familiar and the unfamiliar, your situation also has a temporal dimension. Enough selection has occurred to justify a distinction between you as subject and the unsettling objective world around you. But the specificity is vague. You feel inchoately the world's presence, the objective indeterminacy of what is felt and also, indeed, the objective indeterminacy of what feels.

Dewey's notion of "an indeterminate situation" thus echoes Sartre: that the for-itself always arises in relation to a particular in-itself which it negates. Consciousness is always of *a* situation, never of the sheer uninterpreted reality its interpretations presuppose. This is akin to Aristotle's material cause. Without a foundational indefiniteness no definite outcome can be fashioned. It is the resource from which inquiry begins, the "that" which is to be worked with, the existing factual world appearing to human awareness as incomplete. According to Dewey, an organism is conscious only insofar as it and its environment become a characterizing of the whole as separation, as a difference of inner and outer within the more primordial ongoing flow of life-processes.

The next phase of inquiry begins, and consciousness thereby takes on a distinctively human flavor, when the indeterminate situation becomes problematic. Criteria of relevance come to table as soon as the felt inadequacy of things is given some kind of focus. Inadequacy is relative; the sense of it requires a comparison between what feels deficient and a contrasting imagined experience of feeling adequate. The imagined adequacy is possibly without content, certainly without much clarity with respect to any of its characteristics except that by contrast with which the taste of the existing situation has proved flat. You have found a lure of contentedness at the heart of your discontent, and it impels the needed sharpening of your sensitivity so that vague, dispersed restlessness can be distilled into directional discomfort and brought to proof as conscious perception: this sound, that sight, those tastes and smells, that resistance and that absence of resistance that you finally take as accounting for what it is about what is that makes it so problematic.

For Dewey, therefore, the quality that is felt throughout what you experience is instrumental not only in giving that experience its unity but also in providing the grounds for sensing its inadequacy. For the quality of a given situation to perform such a function, it cannot be merely a tag, marking some given difference shared by all consituents of that situation. It must also be a value expressing the deficiency felt to be inherent in that difference. That is, the quality must point beyond itself to another situation that, if realized, would be both different and better than what is given. But it points to that other situation indeterminately, as a future that at some time in some way will, unlike the present situation, be pervaded by a quality of adequacy. This placeholder for a future realization is that which is lacked and which, once you can determine what is in fact lacking, will be filled, as best you can manage to do so, with actual content. It is an ideal, therefore, an end not yet in view but toward which you have turned yourself. It guides you toward an outcome by tantalizing you with the future. It allures you by hinting at a more that lies beyond the far horizon and by disclosing the nearer landscape to be well equipped with instrumentalities for transforming what is far into what is near, for transcending the given and attaining what is known to you only as a place of greater value. Dewey calls this the "good"; it is Aristotle's notion of final cause cut loose from the pre-determination of goals entailed in an ontology of natural kinds.

The third phase of inquiry is to propose a solution to the problem before you. Where habits will do, they suffice; thinking can simply never be put in gear. But when the problematic character of the situation provides no ready-to-hand solutions, mentality must begin to function rationally if a genuine solution is to emerge. For Dewey the application of reason to a problem involves a triad of moves. It means ascertaining the relevant facts, discerning what compose the settled, determinate constituents of the situation. It means developing relevant ideas by abstracting out the relational aspects of these facts, exploring those relationships, imagining further relations and relata. Finally, it means forming a cluster of such ideas and taking it as describing both a possible new state of affairs and the ways in which it might be related to the present problematic actuality [LTI 108]. Facts, ideas, hypotheses; observing, conceiving, imagining. Cognitive activity is the marshaling of these resources for problem-solving.

There are many ways in which you can abstract, many ideas you can derive from any particular fact. A given situation is luxuriantly tolerant of various relationships among its components, tolerant of various ways to delimit those components or to subordinate, link, and extrapolate from those relationships. The connections that will capture your attention are those you can construe to construct a plausible solution to your problem. You are interested not only in the particular formal linkages you worked out to suit the task at hand, but also, sometimes even more so, in the general patterns of linkage you and others can extract from the particular patterns and then use over and over again as trustworthy problem-solving tools. Rules of thumb, tried-and-true procedures, methodologies, theories, laws: all of them are creatures of inquiry, tools you have made or that others have made to aid you in the task of turning problems into solutions [LTI 11,102].

Ideas are general because they are abstractions from concrete particularity and because they can be expressed by symbols. They are general in a third sense as well: most of our ideas are cultural inheritances. Because you live in an environment that is predominantly a social artifact, your beliefs and activities are imbued with characteristics typical of your societal situation [LTI 45]. You walk along roads your ancestors built to walk along, and others around you do the same. You and they conduct your business according to established procedures, some of them hoary with tradition, others the result of recent legislation. Newspapers and neighborhood gossip point up the important issues of the day, and you think about them in terms of ideas and arguments culled from your school lessons or in imitation of the peers you take as role models. You speak in a language that pre-defines the basic objects, relations, and processes constituting what you take to be real. These general forms of life change, of course, because even an intention to replicate some given pattern will depart from it at least in some small way. But the changes are minuscule at any point; your individual deviance is always in contrast to the vast conformity of the whole. Even revolutions preserve far more than they alter. Nonetheless, over sufficient time the little changes accumulate; the Latin language becomes

French and Spanish, the grumblings of the nobility at the high-handedness of King John become the contemporary debates of elected parliamentary bodies.

Forms for Dewey thus have a history. They are to a significant extent the traditional, tried-and-true ways of conceiving of things and their interrelationships. They are how people typically deal with what they experience. Even *modus ponens* and the law of excluded middle are taken as a valid form of argument only because such ways of relating symbols have been shown over centuries to be trustworthy, to project conclusions that have proved to be warranted. Some of these forms change rapidly and seem very much tailored to specific circumstances; others change hardly at all and seem to have guided inquiry effectively forever. None are eternal verities, Platonic forms. They are only wide-spread habits; but the best of them are as everlasting as anything human can be.

Forms are the tools for transforming the given into something better, for constructing an imagined alternative and an imagined way to get to it. By their use, you fashion a preliminary content for the end at which your praxis aims. What is lacking takes on a shape; the lacked as a value beyond reach becomes a valued, graspable possibility. The end you have sought beyond the far horizon becomes now an end in view, a realizable objective rather than an idle hope. For instance, your unease was interpreted as thirst and its quenching taken as your hope; you envision satisfying your thirst by walking into the kitchen, turning on a faucet, filling a glass; unease has become a yearning for its cessation and then a plausible course of action to attain a specific sort of end.

But the route you take from a proposed to an actual outcome is not simply a matter of persistently and energetically following step-by-step a set of self-evident instructions. Even your habits are only dispositions to solve some kind of problem in a characteristic manner. The actual solution will vary depending on the peculiarities of your specific situation, its exigencies, the unanticipated importance of neglected factors. Where a problematic situation calls for more than routine response, where concepts, techniques, and proposed solutions need to be freshly wrought, their issue is even less certain, as both the means proposed and the end envisioned are vague. Because newly envisioned, the tools you have selected and sharpened to do your work are untested, their import not fully known, the outcome you propose still short on crucial details. Consequently the process of realizing your end has to be one in which the outcome will be made determinate only as you constantly redetermine what it will comprise and how it will be formed. The end result of your efforts will differ from your original proposal at least by having filled in its vagueness with specificity. But the result may also fall short of what was envisioned, or may fulfill it in unexpected ways. It may fit the original dream as snugly as your hand fills out your glove, or it may have so altered things that the original idea even with all its protean ambiguity bears little relation to what has come about. It all depends on how the relevant linkages were conceived, in what ways things were clarified, what opportunities were seized, and what ones overlooked.

As a result, says Dewey, inquiry is serial, a sustained sequence of proximate goals proposed, then actualized, the results taken account of, leading to newly proposed goals and a fresh effort at realization. In this sense each step you take is itself a short-term end, a determinate outcome of what was done. But it is also a means to a longer-term end, a clarification of its shape, a contribution toward its content, making more determinate what will not be fully settled until the series has been completed. As every means toward a given end is at the same time itself an intermediate end, so also this final end contributes itself as a means to still further ends, your own and those of others. The series is infinite even though it can be segmented into finite stretches where the internal linkages circumscribe a noteworthy unity, some praxis that you or others find useful, interesting, or significant.

Dewey's two most value-laden terms relate to assessments of this process. The method of achieving outcomes is "experimental" if it begins by treating material conditions as trial facts and formal conditions as hypotheses. That is, both things and ideas are made operational, made to function as proposals for action, as guides for organizing possibilities and marshaling resources, rather than being allowed to function passively as items merely to be observed or thought [LTI 113]. Each hypothesis is tested by the facts that have been tentatively put forward for the nonce as accurate and relevant renderings of what is; these facts are in turn tested by the cogency of the concepts they entail, whether these locate them coherently within systems of causal relationships and meaningful explanation. "Intelligence" is experimental reasoning of this sort: proceeding methodically, testing your ever step, taking nothing as settled until everything is settled, obtaining the best available version of a preferred potential outcome.

Thinking is thus the efficient cause in praxis. Sheer instinct at behavioral levels below that of praxis is replaced by habits or dispositions and, as required, by the organizing cleverness and imagination of thought, especially and preferably intelligent thought. At all levels the role of thought is the same, however: to effect an outcome. Inquiry, says Dewey, "is the controlled or directed transformation of an indeterminate situation into one that is so determinate in its constituent distinctions and relations as to convert the elements of the original situation into a unified whole" [LTI 104–5]. When guided by intelligence, when "directed" rather than being left "uncontrolled," the "unified whole" that results will be optimal (conditional, of course, on the limitations of the situation, that is, on the material, formal, and final causes informing the effort at realization).

Despite his claim that a theory of inquiry bakes no ontological bread, Dewey's labors have done just that. But the ontology is processive and not static, a matter of occurrences rather than substances. Inquiry is not merely *an* activity performed upon occasion by the animal *Homo sapiens.* It is *the* activity of that creature, its way of being in the world. Inquiry need not be intelligent; it need only be conscious, and habit may be overwhelmingly in control. But less than this, the going on of purely instinctive and metabolic processes, is what characterizes fetal and comatose humanity, undeveloped or degenerated personhood. So, according to Dewey's analysis, the dynamic fourfoldness of inquiry *is* human reality.

Sartre's notion of freedom and Dewey's notion of conduct are thus both renditions of the same song of praxis. The hole in the fabric of being-in-itself made by the negating upsurge of in-itself finds its Deweyan analogue in consciousness as the way of being that is manifest in the breakdown of instinctual processes. Self and object appear as structures of that breakdown, as situationally emergent factors in a dynamic oriented toward a reinstitution of the instinctual flow. Dewey's care in setting the biological context for the appearance of human forms of behavior gives him better resources than Sartre, however, for resisting both a dualistic ontology and a monism based either on subjects or on objects.

Dewey puts the flesh and blood of concrete purposings on Sartre's abstractly skeletal insistence that praxis is essentially open-ended. Its orientation is toward closure, toward rendering the indeterminate determinate. But every end is also a means to some further end; the episodes of inquiry are serially ordered. Dewey borrows James's image: life is like the flitting of a bird, a matter of flights and perches, a striving-toward, a moment of closure, then renewed flight and another branch on which briefly to alight. Sartre's "useless passion" misnames his similar analysis of how a fundamental project is expressed through a milieu of lesser projects: this act, that act, each with its own relative accomplishment, but each also a manner of accomplishing the person's fundamental way of being. Dewey is much clearer than Sartre regarding the longitude of this, the manner in which such strivings compose a career, a life-trajectory.

The disvalue of the given is fundamental for both. Even though Sartre insists that freedom is by definition ungrounded, and hence that actions are always unjustifiable and life absurd, this rhetoric belies his analysis of humanity-in-the-world as that from which both freedom and facticity are derivative notions. The given is given as incomplete, but as transcendable. This is how Dewey characterizes the indeterminacy of the situational context within which inquiry arises as a response. Humanity is thus precisely the incompleteness of the given expressed in terms of its primary quality, which is the value of its overcoming. Or, in a Sartrean image, value lies coiled at the heart of being: the presence of the past is the foundation of the future.

Dewey has also opened up an aspect of praxis not given much consideration by Sartre, an aspect that will be especially important for us as soon as we begin the quest for which this discussion is prolegomenon. The formal conditions of an action are not timeless, natural verities. They are pragmatic artifacts, fashioned by individuals in their struggle with the exigencies of daily life. Those that work tend to be retained that they might be used again, and those that are resilient enough to be adaptable to changes in exigency are likely to be longest retained. These ideas, techniques, modes of reasoning and doing, are habits of action insofar as they have become ready-to-hand instrumentalities for problem-solving. But such acquired characteristic behaviors are not biologically inheritable. They are thus passed on from generation to generation by their embodiment in languages, customs, institutions, rules. You learn them by emulation, by oral instruction, by the understanding of principles, by the ancient mnemonics of guilt and punishment. Your methods for doing things are never mere clones of a social practice. You are all the time confronting novel problems and dealing with them in your own inimitable way. Your individual invention, your deviance from tradition, nonetheless feeds at the breast of culture and cannot be understood except as its offspring.

We need to examine this more closely, and so I suggest we seek some help from Donald Davidson's analysis of praxis. According to Davidson, reality is made up of events occurring serially. Our knowledge of those events, our explanation of them, is in terms of some kind of a description. Two sorts of description predominate, says Davidson: physical and psychological. The former describes events as linked by physical causes and their physical effects; it involves "homonomic" generalizations, that is, abstractions made from various concrete descriptions that can then be evaluated and improved until they yield general theories and laws of nature. These laws are taken to be explanatory of particular occurrences because the particular sequences appear as instances of the general laws that, in conjunction with specified initial conditions, predict them. The second type of description is in terms of intentionality, which involves a reference to attitudes and beliefs; such events are thus described as being mental; generalization from these descriptions is "heteronomic" in that it does not lead to laws that predict what specifically will happen, nor is the critique and further refinement of any such laws a way to increase their predictive usefulness.

Both descriptive strategies, nonetheless, offer causal explanations. "Cause is the cement of the universe; the concept of cause is what holds together our picture of the universe, a picture that would otherwise disintegrate into a diptych of the mental and the physical" [EAE xi]. Let me then give Davidson's point an ontological turn and say that causally linked events are the foundational constituents of reality. Taking some of these events as composing networks related by laws of physical cause and effect is to select one route of access to that reality; taking them as related by patterns of intentionality is to select another. For Davidson, homonomic and heteronomic descriptions are derivative from the events they describe, just as for Dewey other and self are derivative from the natural situation, just as for Sartre in-itself and for-itself derive from human-in-the-world.

We need not linger over descriptions of events as physical. Such is the mode of explanation utilized in the natural sciences. It is applicable to human beings as much as to any other reality, and it may or may not be adequate when so applied. Were it to provide adequate descriptions of human events, however, it would then presumably be at least theoretically possible to formulate a general law of the human in which humans are taken as physical objects, and then to construct an instance of that law that would be functionally indistinguishable from human beings of flesh and bone. Because the laws embedded in physical description are homonomic, by replicating the causes you can replicate the effect. Whether adequate physical laws of nature can ever be devised and such a Frankenstein's dream realized, says Davidson, is an empirical issue.

Turn now to the other kind of description, where some events are interpreted as mental. Davidson calls these "actions": "an event is an action if and only if it can be described in a way that makes it intentional" [EAE 229]. Some intentions are "attitudes." These are the background of general, vague preferences an agent has for engaging in actions of a certain kind, ones characterized by some specifiable property. For instance, you may have a positive attitude toward occasions where you are eating apples. The occurrence of such a sort of activity is something you value. In Davidson's language, you have made a "prima facie judgment" that actions performed by yourself which would realize an apple-tasting quality are good. Attitudes are schemata; they don't entail any particular action nor imply any specific procedures or consequences. But they express values for the sake of which actions are taken. So a "pro attitude" or "prima facie judgment" is close to the notion of final causation that we have been developing. It is a place-holder for a valued outcome, sufficiently characterized so as to orient behavior but not to cause it. It is more an indication that an appropriate solution is needed than it is an indication of what that solution might be specifically and how it might most effectively be realized.

What is additionally required is a "belief": the conviction that a specific course of action will provide a genuine instance of the kind of occurrence sought. This is what Davidson calls an "all-out judgment" because it is one that finds a particular possible action unconditionally good. It is akin to Dewey's formal conditions of inquiry because it is your judgment that *this* action will meet all the conditions required to satisfy your pro attitude regarding apple-eating. It is a specific end come into view as a proper content for a desired kind of outcome. In your judgment this Jonathan you are holding in your hand will do the job nicely; it will be a tasty morsel, the munching of it a real pleasure.

Davidson contends that a pro attitude in combination with a belief constitutes a "primary reason" for an action, and that this reason is the cause of the action. For the moment, limit the scope of an action to what Davidson calls a "primitive action," the bodily movements that comprise the realizing of a specific event. If your primitive action is a behavior that by virtue of a specific belief you think would realize a particular quality, and if that quality is of a kind toward which you are attitudinally predisposed, then your attitude/belief is the reason for your action. Your mental state explains the action because it causes it.

The primitive action, the effective agency, is a behavior: it is a matter of bodily motions that have an impact upon the surrounding environment and also suffer its reactive motions. The primary cause of the action is a mental attitude in combination with a belief. You *are* this primitive action and this primary causal reason. But remember that we are speaking within the framework of a description. It is in order to make sense of your behavior that I have described it as I did, and my effort will be judged adequate only insofar as it fulfills its purpose.

What counts as the action may expand or contract as my purposes change. I may be interested in what you did at the picnic, that more extended activity of which the apple-eating was a part; or I may wish to focus on even some lesser portion of the primitive action, perhaps wondering why you grimaced when you took the second bite. That actions can thus expand and contract as you choose is understandable once we remember that an action is a function of a description and descriptions are for the purpose of providing an explanation.

Descriptions of actions are only generalized heteronomically, Davidson argues. This means that in order for me to understand one of your actions I shall not search for the general law of which it is an instance. Instead I shall attempt to trace the agreement and disparity between the primary reason you have given (or I have ascribed to your action) and your other beliefs and attitudes. The pattern of your intentions is what makes sense of your present purposes. The coherence and consistency of your previous reasons for acting with your supposed current reasons is what warrants them as an explanation of what you have done [EAE 221]. I end up knowing why you ate an apple at the picnic and why you grimaced after the second bite. But this does not lead me on toward some generalization about human beings at picnics from which I could predict what another person might do, nor even what you might do on another occasion.

This is close to what Clifford Geertz calls "thick description"[5] and is what is usually meant by "historical explanation" in contrast to "scientific explanation": moving from particular to particular, from this action, this intent, to that action, that intent, tracing out a coherent pattern of a person's practice until it is understood. It is telling a particular person's actual, specific story, not subsuming him or her under the covering laws appropriate to descriptions of physical processes. Davidson makes it quite clear, however, that telling a person's story is not a flat, horizontal movement from particular to particular. A study of the tides needs eventually to include some references to the moon. Although beliefs and all-out judgments are rooted in the particular moments they assess, a person's attitudes are schematic. They have to do with dispositions to act; they are judgments about kinds of qualities of possible things or of possible ways of proceeding. If I am to make your attitudes a part of my description of your primary reason for action, I will need to become familiar with your world. This involves understanding the language you use, the meanings you intend to convey by the sentences you utter, your gestures, your style of self-presentation. I will also need to understand the why and wherefore of the groups to which you belong, the social conventions to which you subscribe, your superstitions, prejudices, and ideologies. In short, I will need to know

as much as possible about the societal milieu of which your attitudes
are an expression.

Thus weaving an explanation of your actions in terms of the history
of your beliefs, attitudes, and behavior involves me in a consideration
of the characteristic features of the culture whose history you also are.
What Dewey called the background of inquiry, the inchoate feelings and
their ideational articulations that constitute the vague convictions out
of which values and purposes arise, is the same as the attitudinal background to which Davidson alludes. The material conditions of praxis
include an inheritance of cultural forms which come to awareness as
dispositional orienting attitudes; these attitudes then become modu-
lated through the particular contingencies of individual experience
into the formal conditions by means of which outcomes are realized.

But we do not simply "have" the attitudes that derive from our cultural milieu as though they were the ground for our beliefs in the way
a loamy soil is the ground for our plants, providing independently of
our involvement the nutrients by which specific forms can sprout and
grow luxuriantly. As Charles Taylor argues, these attitudes are fundamentally self-definitional. They are not just a tool-chest of ideas that
you or I may draw upon as needed in constructing usable beliefs. They
also compose the "moral map" of your sense of who you are, and my
sense of who I am, and our sense of the world we share. Basic cultural
attitudes have to do with the "worth" of our beliefs, and so contribute
indirectly to *how* we will use our beliefs in accomplishing our purposes [HAL 67]. Who you think you are has quite a bit to do with what
you think needs shaping and how you think that might be most appropriately accomplished.

You make what Taylor calls a "strong evaluation" of your situation
when your judgments are about the qualitative worth of your choices:
whether or not they are of the right kind, in keeping with the sort of
person you are, in touch with your fundamental purposes, your aim in
life, your sense of what you have done and what you want to be [HAL
26]. These are attitudes in Davidson's sense because they have to do
with kinds of characteristics rather than with specific characterizations.
But they are the most important of attitudes: attitudes about our self-
worth, convictions regarding the nature of the qualities requisite for
being fully and genuinely a person. These key attitudes thus compose
what is for each of us our self-identity. They are the essential ingredients in our sense of self.

The cultural forms of your self-definition preexist you, pre-
determining who you will take yourself essentially to be: "What is of
fundamental importance for us will already have an articulation, some
notion of a certain mode of life as higher than others, or the belief that

some cause is the worthiest that can be served; or the sense that belonging to this community is essential to my identity" [HAL 40]. But these forms are open to criticism and part of our way of being a person may include the project of calling these strong evaluations into question at either or both the personal and cultural levels. Crises in self-identity are a healthy part of the process of growing up and they may well recur throughout the whole of your life. The society to which you belong may also undergo the self-criticisms of reform, reaction, and revolution. These occasions put your fundamental attitudes in question, shift the problems that concern you from outcomes and how to attain them to assessing the presumptions that have guided you in discerning problems and solving them. With the basic form of your life thus at issue, you fall back upon your "deepest unstructured sense of what is important, which is at yet inchoate" and to which you are trying to give shape [HAL 41].

Inchoate importance is experienced as "emotional import," says Taylor: a feeling of a situation that points beyond itself to its grounds, its reason or meaning. You feel ashamed. There is something about what you just did or were intending to do, or about which perhaps you were merely fantasizing, that isn't congruent with what is most important for you, that is at odds with who you think you really are. Usually you have the proper articulations at hand, the cluster of attitudes that give form to your actions. In that case shame is the sense of having been out of line: acting improperly, forgetting yourself, being beastly. In times of self- or societal criticism, your shame has no ready response. You find yourself appealing beyond the customary to something deeper you then struggle to articulate, something to do with your "true" self or with a "transcendent" community that commands your loyalty but confounds your tongue.

Thus Taylor helps us understand the distinction Dewey was making between the indeterminate background of experience with its pervasive but uncognized qualities and a problematic situation in which emotion has been given a dispositional form, mere feeling channeled into restlessness, a discontent with the given transmuted into an urge toward a meliorated outcome. Final causation is a construing of your inherited given situation. Its facticity is not only the particular physical objects and artifacts of the surrounding environment, the sticks and stones, the roadways and buildings, that must be taken account of in developing plans for realizing your aspirations. The material conditions for your praxis also include an ideational dimension, a cultural stock of ways of experiencing that, congealed but not yet petrified, lie in coiled slumber at the heart of the hard physicality of the world. They are objects of feeling that, as they are cognized, will become the Davidsonian attitudes that schematize practical choices and efforts. But as felt, as still inchoate, they are nonetheless already present as the qualities initially pervading your experience. The surprising power of the given in human experience to unfold into a structure of final, formal, and efficient causes that give rise to a redetermined given lies in the culturally derived importances that it harbors as its import. The being-in-itself of human-in-the-world already possesses the power to raise up the being-for-itself that is its counterpart. Facticity is already a human artifact. Consciousness presupposes the work of consciousness.

There is more that must be said, however, about Taylor's notion of strong evaluation, and here Michael Oakeshott can be of help. Except for the vocabulary, much of his argument parallels what we have been attempting to adumbrate. As a human agent, says Oakeshott, your activities or mine are based on a "platform of conditional understanding" [HC 34]; they are its "adjectives" or illustrations. Your particular performance at any given moment draws upon a repertoire of preestablished understandings. Your beliefs regarding the character of your situation, your imaginative projection of future conditions, the utterances and choices and other means by which you strive to realize some intended outcome, are all particularizings of those basic understandings. Driving down the road, you understand it to be curving through a copse of trees. Consequently you imagine that during this upcoming stretch the sun will be obscured, the markings on the asphalt hard to see. So you turn on your headlights. The road as you understand it has been made into an illuminated road; your action exhibits itself as an adjective of your understanding.

Your conduct, says Oakeshott, is these understandings as performed: the specific actions you launch into an unsettled future along with the platform of understandings from which they are begun. You are what in your conduct you become. You are free because the understandings that define you are not a part of your genetic heritage. They are understandings, and to understand is to interpret, to grasp something consciously as this thing or those shapes or that occurrence. Understanding is not a condition that happens to you, that is imposed, that you can be forced to acquire. Persuasion, brainwashing, and intimidation may constrict what still lies within your power to decide, yet finally the "grasping as" is yours, your act of construing, your diagnosis of your situation as unsatisfactory or promising.

In this sense each of us makes the world that is our situational environment. But since this making is concomitantly the further fashioning of our understandings, you and I are making ourselves as well. Hence

actions are what Oakeshott calls "self-enactments" [HC 37]. Your diagnosis of the world as in some manner deficient, your reading of it as
needing a certain sort of remedy, your engagement with its constraints
and possibilities toward realizing a specific remedy are all concrete expressions of the conditional platform of the understandings that compose who basically you are. In acting you enact yourself. As Sartre
would say, you are the totality of what you have done along with the
freedom that is your power of doing it.

When Taylor suggests that this platform of understanding is built
of culturally inherited lumber, he is not gainsaying Oakeshott's point.
The planks may be inherited, but it is still you and I who must build
the platform. The importances of our past come as vaguely felt pres-
ences until we give them shape and make them constitutive of our essential self. This you do, Oakeshott adds, not by your explicit decision
to interpret emotions as expressions of this or that attitude but by acting in specific ways for specific ends. In thereby giving adjectival character to your inchoate understandings you create yourself in both the
concrete and schematic dimensions of who you are. You create yourself
as a novel version of an inherited circumambient culture, as an individual having both accidental and essential qualities.

Oakeshott is especially concerned with an aspect of praxis that we
have so far neglected. Action is not only self-enactment but also "self-
disclosure" [HC 50]. Your actions normally take place within a societal
context, among other persons who are the objectives of your activity
and who may well choose to react in some fashion to what you do.
Conduct *inter homines* seeks a response from these others; its intended outcome is an action by another rather than a follow-up action
by yourself.

But others cannot be expected to respond appropriately unless they
know what your action meant, unless they can catch its intent. You
open the door, inviting your companion by that gesture to proceed
you into the room. For her to respond appropriately, she needs to understand the physical rearrangement of the door, your posture, the look
on your face, as together constituting an invitation for her to respond
by stepping out ahead of you. If she takes your meaning correctly, this
episode of conventional politeness will spin itself out, and the flow of
your interactions will move smoothly on to some next phase. She may
not have gotten your point, however. She may have mistaken your action as a request to halt her forward progress until someone coming
from the opposite direction has passed through the door. Or she may
be a foreigner and have no sense at all of what your gestures could

possibly mean; she knows that you have something in mind but is befuddled as to what that might be.

The purpose of your action has thus been to do more than give adjectival substance to your understandings. It is one more act by which you define yourself as a courteous sort of person, but it is also your attempt to disclose to your companion who you are, to make it clear to her that you are courteous and so intend to open the door for her, to be polite in this particular way. Your action is also an attempt to persuade her to respond appropriately, to be herself polite, to enact the conventional responsive behaviors mandated by your gesture. You invite her through the door: your opening it for her functions as your way of persuading her to fill the role in this social drama to which your action has assigned her. But she too is free. Understanding your intent, she may choose to be persuaded by it. Or she may resist, refusing the conventionality because she thinks it foolish or patronizing. Or she may resist because she does not wish to be polite to someone who just a moment before had been rude to her; she sees your gesture as mocking, and her anger rises.

Utterances, like actions, instantiate our understandings. If your gesture fails to convey your intent, perhaps you can express it in words as well: "After you, my dear." Your sentence refers with unmistakable clarity to a meaning that merely opening the door had left ambiguous. You are explaining your action, supplementing the expected outcome that is its value, hence its meaning, by speech which discloses that meaning by another means. Conversely, your actions could explain your utterances: your companion doesn't understand what you mean by saying "Wait, let me get that door for you" until you grab hold of the door handle and pull it toward you while turning to look at her.

The efficient condition of praxis, therefore, is achieved through self-disclosure as well as self-enactment. Your understandings must be understood by me and by others like me, not simply by yourself, if you are to realize your ends. You cannot act except through an understanding of yourself that deploys a repertoire of schematic ways and whys for what you do. Self-understanding is a commitment to forms for defining yourself as situated thusly in the world, forms that guide the beliefs or choices by which your background sensibilities are translated into the ends and instrumentalities of change. But in a communal situation, located with others within cultures, you cannot act except when these others in that community understand you and you understand them as well. You act by disclosing your beliefs and choices, your motives and intentions, and thereby disclosing at least tacitly your underlying understandings. To those disclosures of meaning others are invited to respond; and you, to their disclosures. Your effectiveness as an agent, your power and your autonomy, depend on your ability to persuade and to be open to persuasion; self-enactment requires self-disclosure.[6]

Oakeshott, in agreement with Taylor, insists that a person's actions are intelligible to another only as they can be woven together into a coherent series, an unbroken longitudinal web of contingencies. This is done by interpreting them as exhibiting the same or consistent meanings from one occasion to the next, as exemplifying the self-understandings that by persisting give the serial sequence its unity. Such a weaving is the telling of a person's story. It involves no reference to general laws nor universal meanings, has no absolute beginnings nor final endings [HC 105, 176]. But it does involve a reference to attitudes and understandings just as much as to behaviors and beliefs, and to the cultural background from which they derive. By such complexly layered accounts, we come to know, appreciatively and proficiently, a given individual or group.

Every end, as Dewey noted, is a means to something further and every means an intermediate end. For human praxis, intelligibility is heteronomic. It is attained by attending to the vague foundational background of the processes of specification, by recurring to the pervasive values of the indeterminate, and then tracing the how of their transformation into realizable ends, identifiable reasons, specific methods. A single deed or a person's whole career are made intelligible by an inquiry that has the same structure as what it seeks to know. Both the inquiry and the deeds inquired of are actions. To know and to do are both praxes.

Oakeshott contributes one further insight into the nature of praxis: his notion of a "practice" as the things that specify for the members of a community useful procedures relevant to their actions and utterances. A practice does not tell a person what to do; it announces, rather, "conditions to be subscribed to in making choices," whatever they might be [HC 58]. It is, says Oakeshott, an instrument upon which to play, not the tunes which you and I play upon it. Every shared human enterprise has its house-rules, its regulations and guidelines. But a common language and a "moral converse" are what pervade the whole of a society. They are the most general of our human practices, the "*ars artium* of conduct; the practice of all practices; the practice of agency without further specification" [HC 60].

Oakeshott uses the term "civil association" to refer to that dimension of a society defined by its general practices, the agreements as to how to go about doing things, to which the members of a community subscribe apart from any common ends they might or might not pursue. He talks about particular actions within a community as "adverbial qualifications" of its accepted practices. This phrase has a more active cast that his parallel one regarding "adjectival qualifications" of an understanding, but the notions are closely linked. An understanding is a general attitude given specific form through the actions that concretize it. These actions, however, are constrained by practices that set conditions on how the understanding can appropriately be realized. But the practice is inherent in the understanding. Indeed, an understanding and a practice are closely related: they compose the parameters of action, the final and formal conditions of action set by a culture and accepted by its members. "Understanding" connotes the general values and positive ideals involved in such parameters whereas "practice" connotes the orderly and ordering structure that they provide.

As we have seen, ideals and attitudes functioning as principles of order are crucial to self-enactment. From your initial unease to your eventual achievements, they give a structure to how you act. They sketch the outlines of your way of being in the world, your form of life. But understandings functioning as practices are also parameters of self-disclosure. You justify what you have done by showing its conformity to accepted practice; you argue that your action has an objective significance because its meaning is embedded in a generally accepted way of going about things. It is obvious, you say, that a man should open the door for a woman; anybody would have done the same; there is no way in which she could have reasonably construed what you did as an act of ridicule.

But you are a free agent, and so the practices functioning for you do not determine what in fact you will do. They illustrate but do not instantiate your practice [HC 92]. Knowing that you accept the practices of social politeness, it does not follow that you meant to be polite in this instance. Yet this is what I should presume to be the case, given that the pattern of your behavior has been typically conventional and that there seem to be no contravening practices also at work.

Self-disclosure is an effort to explain for the sake of securing a sought-for response. It is not enough to communicate by deed or by utterance the meaning of what you do. You need also to persuade others to agree to your meaning and then to act in ways and for ends consistent with it. Your very intention already presupposes some broad agreement, some shared understandings and commonly accepted practices. As Jürgen Habermas argues, we live in a world that presupposes that our actions are ideally rational. This means that you and I presume that a person's choices are made for reasons that can be explained, that any such explanation is open to criticism, and that our disagreements over its validity can in principle be resolved by coming noncoercively to a shared understanding, to an agreement with respect to proper practices.

"Communicative action," which for Habermas is the "practice" of reaching consensus regarding the conditions of our common life,

takes place within a lifeworld that remains at the backs of participants in communication. It is present to them only in the prereflective form of taken-for-granted background assumptions and naively mastered skills.... It is an *implicit* knowledge that cannot be represented in a finite number of propositions; it is a *holistically structured* knowledge, the basic elements of which define one another; and it is a knowledge that *does not stand at our disposition,* inasmuch as we cannot make it conscious and place it in doubt as we please.[7]

Insofar as praxis is an essential characterization of human reality, it leads us from processes of self-creation to those of self-disclosure, both of which presuppose processes of reconciliation needed wherever creation and disclosure reveal divergent ends and meanings, reveal incongruities in underlying attitudes or practices. Praxis in all of these dimensions rests ultimately on, or more precisely is itself foundationally, a yet more general, uncognized but nonetheless directly experienced, shared background.

Alfred North Whitehead offers a model for drawing together the motley strands of our argument. What he calls an "actual occasion" is his proposal for describing the character of the basic elements of which our cosmos is composed. He explicitly rejected any attempt to use the actual occasion as a heuristic way to profile human action. But I propose we do just that, on the grounds that within the lesser cosmos of human being praxis is the basic element. An individual action is, as it were, a physical quantum-event writ large.

The origin of an actual occasion, says Whitehead, is in its experience of an "actual world" [PR 23]. A world is always relative to some experience, so in the originating of an occasion the world correlative to it also originates. That world is an already existing environment filled to the brim with determinate accomplishments but, for the new occasion that confronts it from a newly emerging viewpoint, it is multiple, incomplete, a "conditioned indetermination." Your world is a "datum" to be experienced, but at first in the sense of being made up of countless differing data distinctively experienced. The buzz of it is cacophonous; its bloom a riot of clashing smells and colors.

The world is thus the material condition for an occasion, for some one of the countless actions that compose your life. Your world has the solid facticity required of it by Sartre, but these facts are situated, that is, they are not solid with respect to their relevance. As Dewey makes clear, whatever may have been settled with respect to some particular outcome is always also a phase in some other still-unsettled inquiry. Experiencing, or "prehending," these facts, these data, means acquiring the past, the achievements of prior occasions, as the content of your own given situation. Because they are so varied and because your new perspective casts them unavoidably in a somewhat different light, your world constantly presents itself as an unfinished task. It reeks of the problematic.

The data prehended for their relevance to your new situation are in no sense protean, however. A past occasion was a particular determinate accomplishment; to perceive it as such is to feel the weightiness of its facticity. It is what it was. Although there are innumerable ways in which you can take account of it, you have no choice but to do so in *some* way. The brutality of brute fact lies in its power to command attention. You are what you have made yourself to be, says Sartre. Although you remain free to deal with that past as you choose, you are not free not to deal with it. You are "condemned to be free," not just by having always to make choices but also by having always to come to terms with the fruits of your previous choices *and* with the fruits of the choices of others and of societies of others. The weight of the past presses down hard upon the present. Whitehead calls this kind of experience "physical" to indicate its resistance to being ignored, its independence from the present that seeks to come to terms with it. The world is an object for consciousness and so is shaped by consciousness, made by it into a world. But the world made is made *ex rebus* and not *ex nihilo,* and so is suffered rather than invented.

This is to say, therefore, that the material conditions for praxis are genuinely conditions: they are the "ground of obligation" for an occasion because they demand to be taken into account [PR 29]. Their facticity is not sheer dumb givenness, however, as though facts were undigestible piles of grit somehow to be made into the day's nutritional diet. Each prehended past occasion is an example of a previous solution to some problematic situation. It implicates its original unsettledness in the unity it now presents, alludes to connections available in an initially diverse world and to the connectives by which that world then became this one occasion. These relations are part of what is given; prehending them is to sense not only their particular relevance for what had once happened but their potential relevance to what might lie ahead. Whitehead calls them "conceptual," because they are general rather than specific data in experience. They are more malleable than what they relate, more schematic, more adaptable to the changing needs of a changing situation.

Thus material conditions include the old achievements that constitute the solid ground upon which any new activity must rest, but they also include the vague cultural importances from which are constituted what Davidson calls attitudes, what Taylor calls the sense of self, and what Oakeshott means by practices. You need materials if you are to build a house; in a forested environment you might choose wood. But your choice implicates traditions that present the wood for you as lumber, as $2 \times 4$ studding and $1 \times 4$ tongue-and-groove siding, that immerse you in a sea of accustomed attitudes regarding what houses should look like and for what they might be used. It is this cultural inheritance that is especially rich in the relational relevances that give praxis room for innovation. Nevertheless, the salient character of what is given for experience, whether prehended physically or conceptually, is that it be acknowledged and perpetuated.

Whitehead speaks of an actual occasion as having a "subjective aim." From first to last any process of unification must be conditioned by an orientation toward some determinate outcome, however unspecified it might be initially. A process of unification must have unity as its value even when it is nothing other than an apparently incoordinate jumble of inheritance. Unless finality is present as what Dewey calls the "background quality" pervading the whole of even the most unformed situational experiencing, all will be lost. The world emerges functionally; it is apprehended in terms of its relevance for some end. Indeterminacy co-implies unrest. What is problematic is so because of some aim to overcome it.

This is what Sartre means by human-in-the-world. What has being-in-itself is for humans always in the mode of an object for some subject. Conversely, there can be no being-for-itself except as intending something, as having some objective that it values, which it stretches out toward, something to know or to make or to do. Object and objective, fact and value, go hand in hand. What-is is always a point of origin relative to an outcome sought but not possessed, and a goal is always relative to the actual situation it would replace. Whitehead's "ontological principle" is the claim that the reason for anything, in Davidson's precise sense of a reason, lies "*either* in the character of some actual entity in the actual world of that concrescence, *or* in the character of the subject which is in process of concrescence" [PR 24]. The conditions for praxis lie in the diverse, actual world it inherits and in its self-defining intended purpose. Material cause and final cause are why occasions have the character they do as processes begun in plurality and concluded in unity.

The formal conditions for actualizing an occasion detail the means by which that end is accomplished. An occasion is a process: its forms are therefore how it proceeds; they are the adverbs of its verbal reality. Whitehead calls them "subjective forms" because they are the formative ways in which the unifying intentionality of an occasion achieves its ends. They inform the process, formulate its strategies, deform and reform its transitional accomplishments, provide the recurrent change-orders and instrumental adaptations in terms of which the job gets done. The initial aim of the occasion is already an expression of the how, because a judgment regarding how to interpret the relevance of the physical and conceptual materials of experience is a judgment regarding the specific nature of the intended result. The intended outcome is then a continual reexpression of judgments of relevance. Your initial judgment lifts the goal of the process from deep obscurity by adumbrating slightly its likely shape. By taking these aspects of the past as more significant than those, by finding some relationships more potent than others, you imply their greater relevance to the end result and so imply something regarding the nature of that result. An end so sketched suggests further judgments of relevance for you to make, until coming to terms with the givens, some positively, some negatively. By valuing some givens significantly, some trivially, you cause your vague goal to emerge as an end-in-view and to come at last to be an end realized poorly or proudly relative to what you sought, realized conservatively or radically relative to your past, but realized nonetheless as a new actuality, *this* occasion, *this* one accomplishment, new among the vast multitude of entities comprising the universe.

The subjectivity of forms functioning as instrumentalities for realizing outcomes means that their reason lies as much in the determining occasion as in its inheritance. You learn the forms from your physical and cultural environment; what you find conceivable to do is constrained by the limitations of that learning. But your culture constrains you, and enables you, only insofar as you acquire it, only insofar as the reason for the form is transferred from a past occasion to your own present, active agency. This is why education for Dewey and strong evaluation for Taylor are so crucial, that we might wring maximal benefit from what is inherent in the funded wisdom of a people or even of the species.

But blinders are not blindfolds, and you can see even through rose-colored glasses. Inherited forms of life and forms for life-choices are not sufficient conditions for determining an occasion. By reference to the formal conditions at work in your praxis I can explain your action and trace its congruences with your past actions and with the culture you instantiate, even though I cannot predict that praxis. How you formulate your problem and how you go about resolving it are individuating processes; through knowing how you operate I can come to know who you really are. These adverbials tell the story of how you took generic, schematic forms for determination and came to actualize yourself through them.

Objectified data, subjective forms, and a subjective aim are the three factors of any prehension, and the sum of all the prehensions unified by a given subjective aim are the "concrescence" of an actual occasion, the becoming that is its being. Concrescence is thus the efficient condition of the occasion because it is its power to grow together. It is the efficacy of a process of becoming, its effectiveness in working its task through to specific completion.

Whitehead typically talks about the past as the efficient cause of becoming, but he speaks misleadingly. The power of the past lies in its unavoidability. Given an end sought and given available ways of seeking it, the past is what must be worked with for the ways to become functional and the end to be realized. But without the lure of an end, fact and form would lose their relevance; without a power already present and unsheathed, any vaguely valued outcome would be but an inconsequential fantasy. Whitehead's appeal is to "intuition" [PR 22] when he argues for efficacy as the unformed power at work amid the formative conditions for actualization. Hence he calls it the "ultimate" metaphysical principle, a category for explaining things that cannot itself be explained by reference to some yet more ultimate principle nor by analyzing it into its more fundamental component parts. The universe is efficacious, but how or why or from when and for how long are questions to which providing answers is not a proper response.

The Ultimate involves three notions: one, many, and creativity [PR 21]. It asserts that there are many different actualities in the universe, that any one of them arises out of the others, and that what arises is always something new. It is simply the nature of what-is that it everywhere recurrently concresces. But the unity achieved in a concrescence is at a particular time and place and so differs from the many entities that enter into it. Hence the many things that are turn out to be increased by their convergence into unity. They are used but not used up and so present themselves along with the new achievement as a new diversity requiring new efforts toward further complex unities.

The ultimate metaphysical principle is the advance from disjunction to conjunction, creating a novel entity other than the entities given in disjunction. . . . The many become one, and are increased by one. In their natures, entities are disjunctively "many" in process of passage into conjunctive unity. [PR 21]

Thus the "creative advance" of the universe is for Whitehead an indeterminate power canalized again and again into determinate outcomes. And so for us history is the story of how human achievements, remembrances, and hopes are canalized again and again into new achievements rich in cherished importances and fraught with newborn hope. The condition of human efficacy is that the what, how, and why of history should find its answer recursively. Dewey invests human action with a similarly indeterminate power manifesting itself in the recursive seriality of practical inquiry. Sartre views human beings as always projecting themselves toward outcomes that always turn out to be further expressions of yet more fundamental projects, endlessly chasing an ideal horizon that recedes as quickly as it is approached. For each philosopher, efficacy is the inexplicable power by which the constituents of being, human or otherwise, are made explicable.

Illustration 1.1 offers a summation of each philosopher's views. Now perhaps you can understand better what I hoped we might accomplish together in this preliminary chapter. I would like to live a good life and to help others do so. I suspect you share my aspirations. I would like to know how to go about doing this. At the same time I wonder why this should be a concern for me at all and why it is one shared by you and by others also, maybe by every person who has ever lived. As a way to begin this endeavor, we have turned to the Western philosophical tradition and assembled a few examples from its vast resourcefulness. We have interpreted these texts as contributing in their varied ways and differing vocabularies to a profile of human action that is invariantly illustrated on every occasion of human activity. Our activities in this inquiry should therefore be construed as a further illustration of that profile. Tradition has provided the material conditions for our inquiry, selective interpretation has constituted our way of giving them a useful form, our goal has been to create a model of praxis, and we have expended considerable time and energy in the deployment of appropriately efficacious arguments and explanations.

What we have accomplished in this first chapter will serve as a foundation for what follows. Our inquiry, however, is barely begun. The model of praxis is, after all, only a working model, still embarrassingly obscure, very much needing to be refined and perhaps considerably reworked. And our ultimate goal is not the model. As a formal element

**Illustration 1.1 The Fourfoldness of Praxis**

| praxis | condition | goal | procedure | effort |
|---|---|---|---|---|
| values | negative | positive | instrumental | realized |
| Aristotle | material | final | formal | efficient |
| Sartre | *l'existant* the existing | *le manqué* lacked/value | *le manquant* the lacking | *le manque* the lack |
| Dewey | indeterminate situation feeling | problematic situation imagining | ideas/ideals hypotheses conceiving | experiment intelligence thinking |
| Davidson | events | attitudes prima facie judgment | beliefs all-out judgment | behaviors primitive actions |
| Taylor | inchoate import | strong evaluation | weak evaluation | action |
| Oakeshott | societal givens | platform of understanding | practices moral conver | enactment disclosure |
| Whitehead | datum prehended | subjective aim | subjective form | concres- cence |

in this inquiry, the model is only a useful means to approach a resolution of the ethical concerns that perplex and plague us.

Thus this chapter in one way, and the whole book in another, are what Dewey loved to call an "inquiry into the nature of inquiry." Methodologically, therefore, it is incumbent upon us that what is studied and how it is studied be self-referentially consistent. Our undertaking should have the same character as what it seeks. And so the character of this chapter is as it is, and so the character of this book. And so, it may be hoped, this life of mine; and your life as well; and the human history and destiny we share.

# Two

## THE MOMENT OF DESIRE

A model of praxis is a silhouette, an outline indicating shape but saying nothing of content. To give it substance is to give it a history. That history may be coiled up inside the model like Leibniz's monads within their formulae, but if so it is only as an expected exemplification and not a necessity. Solely by living out your history, carrying forward the sum of your praxes from birth to death, is there any content to appreciate or to utilize. So we must turn from model-building to morality, from structures to trajectories. We must inquire about the course of human lives. Our concern is with how those lives are lived, but in order then to ask how they might best be lived.

All of your talk or mine about good and bad, right and wrong, justice and injustice, derives from the characteristics of some human action. Whenever any situation of moral significance occurs, it is the case that some deficiency has been discerned, a situation devoid of that deficiency has been proposed, possibilities relevant to its attainment have been derived, and means for its realization have been undertaken. No matter how problematic any of these four aspects of the situation might be, no matter how vague or false or in dispute, they together provide all that is required for discovering the moral values at issue. Whatever we understand the morality of the situation to be, of a deed done or one in the offering, whether to evaluate it or to perform it, our recourse must be to the fourfoldness of the praxis therein exemplified.

But it is the working out of the fourfoldness that we shall consider, not just its incarnation but how that incarnation is manifest concretely

35

across the days and years of a person's life, the decades and centuries
of a nation's viability. To do so, we must recast praxis in a way that
displays the seriality of its dynamic. The fourfold remains, but it is elon-
gated into a dipolarity. A life as morally described, as available for ethical assessment, is articulated in terms of desire. It is a tension between
desiring and desired.

Persons such as you and I are by our natures essentially creatures of
desire. You have needs, instincts, drives, the capacity for which, if not
always the actual content of which, are biological givens. These are
integral to your nature as a metabolic organism. As a result, the world
is always organized for you in terms of its resources, its ability to provide objects for satisfying your needs, instincts, and drives. You find
yourself all the time living out a tension between what you take to be a
deficiency in your current situation and what you take to be its possible remedy.

This tension between desire and its object rearticulates the four aspects of praxis dynamically. "Desiring" emphasizes the deficiency pole
of the tension: the interpretation of a currently existing situation as
inadequate and the active yearning to overcome its inadequacy. This
composes the material and final conditions of action. "Desired" emphasizes the remedial pole of the tension: the objective of desire, the array
of relevant possibilities and energies that are made operational as pathways for realization and that, as they are put to use, will come to constitute a reality adequate for the satisfaction of desire. These are the
formal and efficient conditions of action. The deficiency pole of the
tension lived out by personal existence is linked inherently to the remedial pole. The former is the ground of the latter, its expressive value,
the reason for its being. The latter is the expressed power of the
former, the reason for its having a history.

The dynamic of this polarity is toward its elimination. Your desire is
to desire no longer. That moment when the polarity will have been
dissolved is all-important to you: the occasion upon which the incomplete and the possibility for its completion are fused. If you will permit
me an old strategy for nomenclature, let us use a capital letter and call
every such moment an instance of the Moment. I take the notion of a
"moment" from Søren Kierkegaard's *Either/Or* where he uses it to characterize what he calls "the aesthetic." Some of the aesthetic forms of
life illustrated in his book will be commandeered to my own purposes
in what follows.

For desiring, the Moment is the sole locus of moral value. Whatever
is seen as possibly contributing to the content of a Moment, and whatever is taken as a pre-condition or instrumentality for attaining it, is

good in a derivative sense. Abstract possibilities and plans of action have value because of their promised relevance; the value of the end gives value to the means. Even the original situation, although bad because deficient, is derivatively good because it provides necessary conditions for the ideal and for the means of its realization. But only the Moment of actualization, only the Moment in which incompleteness vanishes and completeness is triumphant, only the Moment of the collapse of the desiring—desired polarity, the end of praxis: only this Moment is essentially, intrinsically, foundationally good.

When Sartre equates the elusive *manqué* with "value," he seems to be making precisely this point. But you and I might rightly object that it is a mistake to give final causation priority among the aspects of praxis. All four causes should be considered equally significant, equally possessed of intrinsic value, in accord with the biblical homily about the body needing eyes as much as feet or hands. All are necessary conditions; only together are they sufficient for an action to occur. But the Moment is not *le manqué*. "The lacked" for Sartre is the idea of the Moment, the end as envisioned. It is an expression of the desire for fulfillment. The Moment is that reality itself, not merely the dream of it. It is the collapse of the tension between the passion of desire and its desired objective. The Moment is not a yearning for the Good. It *is* the Good, and praxis is the means for its realization.

This is only a bit of descriptive psychology, however. It becomes an ethical theory as soon as you advocate the Moment. Yet if the desiring—desired polarity is an aspect of human nature, and if that polarity is dynamically expressed as an orientation toward its elimination, then for you to advocate the Moment is to advocate a natural process culminating in the fulfillment of your human nature. It is natural for you to seek the overcoming of your felt deficiencies, to desire to be no longer desiring but to be desireless instead. So be natural, do what comes naturally. Evolutionary processes have adapted our bodies to their environment such that we act best when we act in ways that lead to the fulfillment of our biological needs. Act in accord with your nature. In this way descriptive and normative discourse, cognitive and performative behaviors, turn out to be the same.

This claim about human nature, this proposal that we should seek to be what by nature we essentially are, is the ethical theory called hedonism. You are familiar enough with its ancient expressions. Aristippus of Cyrene is said to have argued that pleasure is the goal of life. In a material world where everything is atoms in motion, their "smooth" interplay is the physical experience of pleasure, which is to be sought, whereas "rough" interactions are the grating, painful ones to be avoided. Epicurus improves upon this basic hedonism by conceiving of pleasure as more than physical gratification, recognizing that such pleasures sometimes carry excessively painful concomitants or consequences. He expands the meaning of pleasure to include the absence of pain; he gives particular pride of place to mental pleasures which, although perhaps less intense, are also less likely to be accompanied by pain and are likely to last longer. Epicurus did his philosophizing within a private garden, away from the bustle of the Athenian marketplace. He preached the virtue of *ataraxia*, of what has been nicely described as "repose of mind and cheerfulness of disposition."[1]

Whatever their differences, however, both Aristippus and Epicurus agree that pleasure is an end and not merely the means to something else, that your energies are and ought to be directed toward the filling up of experience with whatever satisfies you. It is natural to be at peace with yourself and the world. It is thus both natural and appropriate to want to regain such a state of affairs whenever you have lost it. Only pleasure brings, or rather constitutes, that peace. Thus pleasure is your good and seeking it the aim and meaning of your life.

Thus for hedonists, ancient and modern, the desired is the desirable. The most straightforward way to express hedonism's recommendation for how you should live is by the admonition to seize the day: *carpe diem*. Make each moment the Moment, so that desire is never desiring, never separated from its object, so that the tension created by deficiency is always overcome. The Moment is all. Seek it unremittingly, say the hedonists, and in succeeding you will become what you truly are.

Sophisticated advocates of hedonism have had little to add to this uncomplicated claim. Their sophistication has to do more with matters of strategy than of basic goal. John Dewey, for instance, defines a *"de facto* enjoyment" as the quality of any immediate experience of desire's fulfillment. It is, in our terminology, the Moment. Dewey is concerned, however, with the question of how to improve the quality of that quality, how to identify experiences that will be optimally rich in their capacity for fulfillment, that are therefore genuinely worth pursuing. So he contrasts *de facto* fulfillments with those that are *"de jure,"* and it is these only that he calls "values" [QC 263]. Dewey means by a value an array of possible enjoyments for realization that are identified as such within the context of an experimentally sound analysis of a problematic situation.[2]

Dewey argues that you may find many experiences satisfying. But for them to be satisfactory as well, the satisfaction will need to be the consequence of an action involving intelligence, one in which the possibility you sought to actualize was chosen through a rational inquiry into your genuine rather than apparent needs, the relevant rather than merely familiar kinds of creatable remedies, and the pragmatically effective means for accomplishing the specific end thereby brought into view. There is a

difference between the enjoyed and the enjoyable, the desired and the desirable, the satis*fying* and the satis*factory*. . . . To declare something satis*factory* is to assert that it meets specifiable conditions. It is, in effect, a judgment that the thing "will do." It involves a prediction; it contemplates a future in which the thing will continue to serve; it *will* do. It asserts a consequence the thing will actively institute; it will *do*. That it is satisfying is the content of a proposition of fact; that it is satisfactory is a judgment, an estimate, an appraisal. It denotes an attitude *to be* taken, that of striving to perpetuate and to make secure. [QC 260–61]

Dewey thus seeks to focus your interest not on the Moment as such but on it as a function of the methods used in its pursuit. His argument is that this not only results in more overall satisfactions but also in better ones. There is an increase in the quality of a satisfaction that has been achieved intelligently. Dewey distinguishes mere enjoyment from enjoyment combined with an awareness of the conditions upon which its presence and hence its replenishment depends: "Enjoyments that issue from conduct directed by insight into relations have a meaning and a validity due to the way in which they are experienced. Such enjoyments are not repented of; they generate no after-taste of bitterness" [QC 267].

Epicurus turned away from the pursuit of physical gratifications and argued that pleasures of the mind should be sought; he found it was they alone that generated no bitter aftertaste. Aristippus sought the smooth but not the rough, as Bentham after him would advocate attending to the purity and fecundity of a pleasure as well as to its four intrinsic values as a way to be assured against bitterness [PML 4.2]. For them all, the central point was the same: the Moment of fulfilling experience is that for the sake of which all else is instrumental.

Yet whether in Dewey's sense your actions are spontaneous or intelligent, your quest for the Moment encounters a fundamental problem. The Moment is momentary. The completion it offers is fleeting, a transitory accomplishment that perishes as the present becomes past and your experience of fulfillment becomes merely a remembrance of that experience. You are hungry and so you reach out for something to satisfy this feeling of deficiency; the fulfillment is enjoyed but soon this gives way once more to hunger. Nor is this cycle mere happenstance. It is inherent in the metabolic process that the resource required by a creature such as yourself will be effective only for a short time. What is acquired gets used up and needs to be replenished. Put more generally, the experience of fulfillment is an event in time, constrained by time to fade quickly in the face of the upsurge of successor events. The Moment of present experience is durationally finite: neither the future from which it arose nor the past to which it is consigned is directly accessible to human experience. Any moment of completion is an achievement, the creation of a definite occasion for enjoyment. But in being enjoyed it vanishes. The products of praxis are perishable commodities, realities of the present moment only.

Its momentariness is not the only reason the Moment is a problem for hedonism. The quality of the experience it provides is also often poor. Your fulfillment in the Moment proves to be only partial rather than complete, its significance narrowly parochial rather than general. The sequence of the momentary opportunities that compose the present for your experience are obviously not all the same with respect to the perceptual sensations they stimulate nor with respect to the linguistic and conceptual meanings they invoke. But if the content of a specific fulfilling experience is the confluence of a specific perception with a relevant meaning, the variety of the world will give rise to unavoidable variation in the value of the Moment. Yet suppose your perception on some occasion should not be fortunate, your situation a desiccated resource for satisfaction. Or suppose the relevant concepts that might be brought to bear upon its interpretation prove inept and clichéd. How you and I experience the world and the extent to which that experience is fulfilling are closely linked. The partial, parochial, perspectival nature of experience renders any and every Moment to some extent deficient. The effort to overcome one deficiency might well result only in having substituted another in its stead.

The Moment is not merely a momentary and marginal atom of experience, however. Your present experience fades into an inexperienceable past, yet it is also felt and remembered in subsequent present moments as having once filled the present. These derivational feelings and remembrances are how the concerns of the predecessors of the present infiltrate it as somehow needing to be taken account of. This constraint erodes the purity of the present. Your experience is not as such but as it appears against an inchoately felt or consciously reconstructed backdrop of experiences that you are no longer experiencing. Similarly for the future, you anticipate its possibilities as realizations that you could seek. They invite deliberation and choice by filling the present with a concern for its successors. The constraint of what is likely but still avoidable is more gentle than the constraint of what is absolutely unavoidable, but it is nonetheless a constraint, stirring up and beclouding the pure waters of a self-contained enjoyment of immediacy.

Transitory, incomplete, and time-bound, the Moment is thus in its very essence a problem for hedonistic praxis. An ethic that tells us that the Moment is the sole nonderivative locus of Good and which recommends that possession of the Moment be our main purpose in life must solve the dilemma its claims create. If the Moment seems of necessity to destroy the very fulfillment it alone provides, then why should you or I seek it? But if it alone gives life meaning, how can we do other than seek it? At the root of hedonism lies a dilemma that threatens to destroy its plausibility.

Kierkegaard, in the guise of an unnamed young hedonist who authors the first volume of *Either/Or,* offers some models for us to emulate, models for how best to overcome the hedonistic dilemma. Let me show you three of these, in order of their increasing subtlety and effectiveness.

Don Juan, that grand eroticist celebrated in myth and in the incomparable music of Mozart, offers a quantitative solution to the problem of the Moment's perishing [E/O-1 43–134]. Fulfillment for him lies in the pleasures of lovemaking, in the sexual satiation of coitus. But these occasions rise to their climax and are then over; soon, all too soon, the restless urgings of desire reassert themselves. Don Juan's strategy is simplicity itself. He merely repeats the moment of fulfillment as often as required, making up by the constant repetition of instances for the brevity of any one of them. Without respite or preparation or artifice, Don Juan seduces. The objects of his desire present themselves in ceaseless sequence. And in Spain alone the numbers have already exceeded a thousand. As Mozart has Leporello say: "This is the list of the beauties my master has courted, a list I've made out myself: take a look, read it with me. In Italy six hundred and forty, in Germany two hundred and thirty-one, a hundred in France, ninety-one in Turkey; but in Spain already a thousand and three."[3] The importance of the thousand and three is not that it is a very large number but that it is uneven, hence open-ended, hence part of a project that is unfinished, ongoing, without beginning and without end.

Don Juan overcomes the partialness of the Moment by the essentiality of his passion. Each occasion of his pleasure, each woman seduced, is the particular reduced to its fundamentals, to its crux. Take Zerlina, for instance. She may be merely a peasant girl, simple, uneducated, smelling of the stables. But she is a woman and she possesses what all women have in common: the capacity to fulfill Don Juan's desire. For him, every woman shares in the essence of womankind, every particular instantiates the universal he seeks: "To Don Juan every girl is an ordinary girl, every love affair an everyday story. Zerlina is young and pretty, and she is a woman; this is the uncommon which she has in common with hundreds of others; but it is not the uncommon that Don Juan desires, but the common, and this she has in common with every woman" [E/O-1 96]. The absolute value of any moment is its objective power to bring a person to the Moment, and insofar as it has that power it is without deficiency.

Don Juan conquers temporal intrusions into the Moment by living fully and only in the present. He is not a reflective person who anticipates his actions, plans them, assesses them. It is even inaccurate, indeed, to call him a seducer, as he undertakes no projects of seduction. Don Juan's presence suffices to overcome whatever resistance any woman, every woman, might intend. In asking, he receives. Nor does the Don have any interest in remembering his past conquests. Each fills his present to the brim and then is, for him, no more. It is up to his colleague Leporello to tally the ledger of his past triumphs. It is you and I, not Don Juan, who wonder what tomorrow might bring and who treasure up or dread what yesterday had brought. For Don Juan there is only the present, and it is to be enjoyed.

Here you have the pure model for avoiding hedonism's dilemma. Take each moment as it comes, secure in the realization that moment succeeds moment in an unending procession of opportunities for fulfillment. Grasp that opportunity for what it is, ignoring everything but its essential capacity for complementing your need with its offering of satisfaction. Immerse yourself fully in the experience before you, never looking back in guilt or joy, never peering forward in anticipation or anxiety. Seize the day. Embrace it, couple with it, making of yourself and it one whole, so complete as to need nothing outside itself. These days, endlessly repeated, blur into one Day: the Moment rescued from its momentariness, divested of its partiality, its temporality transcended, the very distinction between desiring and desired, lacking and lacked, obliterated.

But the "erotic immediate" is an idle dream. Don Juan is a creation of myth and music. No human being of flesh and bone can sustain an absolute immersion in the present. Consciousness will not be denied, for memory and hope are fundamental to human activity. However much Zerlina might be taken as the embodiment of Womankind, she remains a particular peasant girl whose accidental qualities are essential to who she is. Nor do moments of opportunity march endlessly toward us like sheep willingly to the slaughter. The world is not always so generous as Don Juan presumes it to be. Only within the enchantment of myth can what you want and what there is be immediately one. Don Juan at last grows old and his desire no longer irresistably allures its object. The brevity of a moment's satiation is then underscored by the worry that there may not be another like it, that its successor might not be so satisfying. This worry throws us into the future anxiously seeking, into the past fondly recalling. The problems of the Moment are not solved by Don Juanian immediacy. His way is at best a tour de force, an act of bravado. It is at worst a cruel illusion.

The Rotation Method [E/O-1 279–96] offers a more realistic alternative. Its fundamental insight is that the natural order of things is profoundly repetitive and that repetition is the secret enemy of the Moment. You will find a fulfillment immediately repeated less fulfilling the second time than the first. Partiality is not merely an inherent quality of immediate experience but also one relative to its predecessors and its anticipated successors. Variation is thus crucial to sustaining the capacity of the world to provide adequate fulfillment. But since the necessary variation is not assured, since, indeed, the natural flow of things runs counter to it, you must devise a method for creating it yourself. The cultivation of variety is thus what a rotational method is all about.

Don Juanism, after all, is passive: it awaits each emerging present, confident that the new day will bring new satisfactions. But if this confidence is misplaced, then the proper strategy should be to have a strategy: to seek actively to make the world over into an environment capable of the role you have assigned it. This means taking advantage of the time-boundedness of what happens, utilizing both memory and imagination to enhance the quality of present experience rather than fleeing from them into a present over which you have no control.

A rotational approach is more selective than Don Juan's. By limiting the occasions for enjoyment, it affords you the opportunity to shape each of them into moments assuredly satisfactory. The more naive forms of rotation involve variations in external circumstance. If for a Don Juan it makes no difference whether the woman be a countess or a peasant, for a practitioner of the Rotation Method the differences are crucial precisely because they offer variations on an erotic theme. Different countesses are enjoyed for their differences from one another, and likewise the contrast of countess and peasant is savored. In addition, an effort is made to devise interesting, unexpected patterns of experiencing these versions of fulfillment. The erotic moment is approached in varied moods, on one occasion pensively, another angrily, first playfully then sorrowfully. The goal is variety; the technique, arbitrary alternation of the conditions and context of experience.

The Rotation Method is alert to the problems in this approach, however, and is most effective when it abandons "extensive variation" altogether. Control is crucial, and whatever is external always potentially eludes your control. The solution is to turn to "intensive variation," to withdraw from the present into memory and anticipation, to find the Moment in a union of desire with its own creations. An experience remembered is an experience over which you have control because it no longer depends on interaction with an external world that was parent to its initial creation. As remembered, it is an experience available for alteration, for embellishment.

Select some few moments for remembrance and forget the remainder; consign them to triviality or oblivion. Then through the play of your imagination, enhance these few remaining memories, mold them closer to your heart's desire. You hiked one afternoon along a mountain trail, amid stately oaks and past an occasional building. Select from all you saw and felt a few moments useful for remembering. Dress these up fancifully, enrich them with your artistry, turning the oaks into guardians of some primeval mystery and investing the buildings with a sacred history. Now you have something far more memorable, not merely more capable of being remembered but far more worthy of being remembered. It will enliven your otherwise boring afternoons to recall this adventure in the hills; it will give you companionship on lonely evenings and courage to face the dawn.

Such a technique of selective remembering and opportune forgetting works from a principle of limitation. Not only must the relevant experiences for embellishment be limited (since it takes time properly to enhance them), but their intensity must also be damped lest the experience be so emblazoned in consciousness as to be unforgettable. The Rotation Method thus requires disengagement: the world must be kept at a distance, so that we are never encompassed by its importances. You must never lose control of your situation; thus, you must never become so involved in something that its value could determine the nature and scope of your involvement. A nonserious attitude is required. Friendship, marriage, political office: these exemplify the serious relationships that endlessly spawn the intensities of exhilaration and sorrow, commitment and defeat, that are the bane of playfulness.

No moment must be permitted so great a significance that it cannot be forgotten when convenient; each moment ought, however, to have so much significance that it can be recollected at will. . . . One who has perfected himself in the twin arts of remembering and forgetting is in a position to play at battledore and shuttlecock with the whole of existence. [E/O-1 289–90]

It is a matter of social prudence that you should have in life no entangling alliances. If your aim is to maximize the Moment, to assure yourself of a life filled with pleasure and devoid of pain, disengagement from the world is the better valor.

In abandoning the spontaneous immediacy of Don Juan, the rotational strategy calls for a self that is temporally thick, one that has a past constituted by its rememberings and a future defined by its anticipations. Such a self is not simply a gaping void, an emptiness awaiting, demanding, that it be filled. It is a creative center of activity, purposefully able to take control of its environment, able to fashion through its own artistry the proper objects of its desire. The opportunities for filling in deficiency, the resources and pathways for satisfying desire's desiring, are not merely received passively but are actively selected, not merely selected but to some degree invented. As William James aptly put it, "The trail of the human serpent is thus over everything."[4] The Moment is transformed from an ideal that will without question be realized in the natural course of things to a product accomplished by human artifice. Desiring is freed from its dependency on the natural order.

Don Juan's hedonism is flawed because the object of his desire is radically external to his desiring; it is something he needs but must depend on nature to provide, whereas his strategy is to presume that the distinction between himself and nature does not exist. The Moment when desiring and desired are one is thought to be guaranteed by the power of the desiring, its necessary harmony with the world, whereas in fact it is only by virtue of the desired, by the grace of the natural flow of things, that the Moment emerges. Don Juan's world is Aristotelian, where final causes are natural givens and the task of a self-moved efficient cause is to actualize its predetermined form, to fulfill its natural destiny.

The Rotation Method sees this as a flaw, as a naive confidence in the relevance of the natural to our pleasures. We can repair the flaw by freeing our desires from such dependency. If what you want, the desired, can be limited to products of your unconstrained desiring, then the presence and the adequacy of the desired can be assured. For instance, if the material conditions can be sufficiently trivialized as factors constraining your praxis, then the final cause will be free to tailor itself to the efficacy of available forms so that its coming to realization will be guaranteed. Or, to say the same things in a Whiteheadian vocabulary, if the subjective forms by which a concrescence effects its satisfaction work with conceptual prehensions freed from their relevance to the physical prehensions from which they were derived, then the subject's aim can be freely chosen, freely formed, freely realized. The rotational approach is Epicurean in contrast to Don Juan's Aristippean style. It substitutes self-control for the world's control.

The price paid, however, is enormous. The self, in order to achieve control, has withdrawn from its immersion in immediate experience. The Moment is not the present rescued from its transitory incompleteness but an invention of memory or anticipation that is then substituted for the present. A rotational strategy poeticizes experience. Reality is overlaid with a veneer of fantasy; as it is impossible to distinguish the veneer from the reality the difference soon vanishes. The work of imagination becomes reality.

But the ideal is not the real. When you wall yourself off from the intrusions of the world, when you retire to the garden and the cultivation of *ataraxia,* you blind yourself to the real workings of the world and so leave yourself vulnerable to its inevitable negativities. The perishing of the Moment and its partiality are not addressed by the Rotation Method but merely avoided. Despite the effective use of time-boundedness, these two other factors in the dilemma of hedonism are ignored. Consequently, an illusion of success is all that is achieved. This will suffice only if the natural flow of things conspires fortuitously to sustain the conditions necessary for the illusion, if the tender bubble of fantasy never rubs up against the rough edge of fact. Yet this is precisely the Don Juanian situation: dependence on what lies beyond the self's control, dependence on the natural order of things, on a reality marked essentially by processes of rapid alternation, qualitative variety, and interdependence, processes inimical both to attaining and to sustaining the Moment of hedonistic fulfillment.

A third solution is possible, one that reconciles Don Juan with the Rotation Method by applying the creative artistry of the self to the real world, by actually transforming our environment rather than transforming it only in fantasy. *Either/Or*'s model for this is Johannes, whose diary records the details of a seduction paradigmatic of the way recommended for best attaining genuine fulfillment amid rather than apart from the real world [E/O-1 297–440].

Johannes replaces Don Juan's quantitative approach to fulfillment with a qualitative one, in this sense opting for the rotational strategy. He selects one object for his desire, one candidate for seduction: a young woman named Cordelia. Johannes's single act of seduction will take him six months to accomplish; in the meantime, Don Juan will have had nearly two hundred opportunities for fulfillment. Thus Johannes must so fashion things that the single moment of Cordelia's seduction will be a greater satisfaction for him than what composes the totality of the many erotic moments he would have enjoyed were he to have taken a Don Juanian approach. But this means that his fashioning must be such that Cordelia is genuinely the equivalent of a multitude of Zerlinas, that the intensity of his one Moment with her will objectively justify his selection of it and his ignoring of all other lesser opportunities. It must be a real accomplishment and not the figment of his imagination. Johannes must, in short, actually make Cordelia into an extraordinary woman whose seduction will be truly an extraordinary experience.

Johannes sets about cultivating Cordelia's possibilities. She is a late adolescent, full of the potential that is the dowry every girl brings to the nuptials of her womanhood. In keeping with the agricultural metaphor suggested by the Rotation Method, Johannes farms Cordelia. He labors in the springtime and through the summer of a certain year, nurturing the seeds of Cordelia's personal and social accomplishment so that in the autumn he might harvest the results for his private enjoyment. He is expert at his horticultural task: Cordelia flourishes. She becomes truly one of the most charming, intelligent, sensitive persons in their world. Johannes further enhances her increasingly delectable qualities by grounding them in her freedom. Cordelia is given autonomy, given the ability to choose, to accept or reject his advances, to be a fully flowered self with its own integrity, its own imagination and creative power. And it is this Cordelia whom Johannes seeks, whose freedom he attempts so to engineer that it will be she that in the end seduces him.

Johannes multiplies the intensities of the genuine qualitative superiority of this desired object by experiencing each step in his months-long seduction at multiple levels. He experiences each day's events for what they are, immersing himself fully in their immediacy. But each is also set in a context of what has preceded it and what he hopes will follow. Each is a step in a process, a station along the way from a beginning to an end, enfolding into itself the whole extended story which it embodies in a specific way, for which it is one of a number of unfolding perspectives. In addition, Johannes projects himself constantly into the future, imagining on any given day what it will be like in a subsequent day to occupy one of those future vantage points. He casts back in memory to past days, enjoying once again the view they provided, perhaps enhancing a bit the bouquet of each such occasion with a garnish of fancy and invention. Also, he keeps a diary, re-creating at the end of each day the story of its accomplishments, the summary of its rememberings, the plans composing its anticipations.

All of this then takes its meaning from the outcome toward which it contributes. Johannes's life had been an attempt to realize the task of living poetically. With a keenly developed talent for discovering the interesting in life, he had known how to find it, and after finding it, he constantly reproduced the experience more or less poetically. His Diary is therefore neither historically exact nor simply fiction, not indicative but subjunctive.... The poetical was the *more* he himself brought with him. This *more* was the poetical he enjoyed in the poetic situation of reality; he withdrew this again in the form of poetic reflection. This afforded him a second enjoyment, and his whole life was motivated by enjoyment. In the first instance he enjoyed the aesthetic personally, in the second instance he enjoyed his own aesthetic personality. [E/O-1 300–301]

Here we have poeticizing like that of the Rotation Method, but the poetry is woven into the fabric of the real world, transforming it and transforming its author as well.

The Moment is for Johannes not merely some moment in the course of things but a culmination of half a year's experiences, each moment of which includes the whole of the process from a perspective and in the triple modalities of diary, plan, and practice. The resulting valuational intensity is objective rather than fanciful, a real accomplishment within the real world, a transformation of a segment of that world into a characterization of one of its moments. It is this Moment that Johannes experiences in the act of his union with Cordelia. It is a Moment rescued from half a year's perishings, built up from half a year's partialities, utilizing fully the resources of half a year's temporal interdependencies.

Johannes's artistry differs from that of the Rotation Method because its raw material is the external world rather than a dream world. He differs from Don Juan in that his relation to the external is active rather than passive. The initial separation between the desiring subject and its object is acknowledged; it is then closed not by denying the object, that is, substituting a subjective creation in its place. Rather the object itself is infused with subjectivity, formed into a reality suited for desire. Sartre calls this the "practical-inert": a reality that is "inert" insofar as it is mere matter, "practical" insofar as it has been transformed into a purposeful, instrumental reality. It is neither materiality nor praxis because it is both at once [CDR 153–96]. Thus a gardener cultivates the natural wild flow of things into entities appropriate for human consumption, works them up into a form in which they can be used, makes them, as Dewey would say, operational. Johannes is the gardener, Cordelia the natural possibility he works upon until she is ready for harvesting.

Cordelia's value is solely in her use. In a flight of Hegelian pedantry, Johannes names the category under which she and any woman exists:

it is, he says, the category of "being-for-another." This she shares with Nature as a whole, for both find their meaning, their value, in the contribution they make to something other than themselves. Whatever has its being for another is, in itself, merely potential, a virgin resource that is unaware of itself and its relevance. It is the vocation of that other, of Johannes, of yourself or myself, to awaken this potentiality, to nurture it to the point where we can actualize the value it harbors. When all things are ripe, then this being whose reason for existing is wrapped up in what it has to offer another, can fulfill its role, realize its meaning, attain its purpose. Cordelia gives herself to Johannes, becomes the desired for his desiring, makes possible the Moment he has been preparing her for. She thereby serves well the purpose for which she was made.

Woman is essentially a being for another. Hence it is that the moment has here such infinite significance; for a being for another is always the matter of a moment. It may take longer, it may take a shorter time before the moment comes, but as soon as it has come, then that which was originally a being for another assumes the character of relative being, and then all is over.... The moment is everything, and in the moment, woman is everything; the consequences I do not understand. [E/O-1 427]

The consequences have to do with what for Johannes no longer has any value. The unimportance of anything is a function of its irrelevance to his concerns, which is to say its inability henceforth to play any role at all in his strivings for fulfillment. Cordelia fulfills her role in fulfilling Johannes's desires. As no longer a virginal resource, she is no longer a resource for his desiring and so no longer of value. Johannes's success requires, indeed, that his world be composed solely of means to his end and not include competitors who might interfere with his plans or drain off his resources. The being of the world for Johannes is its being for him. Its value is in its use.

In this manner Johannes attempts to give a natural foundation to his purposes. He needs to engage in artifice if the naturally given is to be transformed into something suitable for his needs. Just as the farmer takes wild grains and animals and domesticates them so that they might more readily and efficiently serve as food for his table, so Johannes cultivates his Cordelia. But if the flora and fauna of the natural order are essentially food sources for human beings, if Cordelia like them is essentially a being whose value lies in what she gives rather than in what she needs, if nature is in its very nature *le manquant* and not in any sense *l'existant*, then the cultivation process is not unnatural and inappropriate. It does not violate nature but completes it. Desiring and desired stand in a natural harmony with each other: it is fundamental to the one that it receive and to the other that it give. As Nietzsche puts it in one of his outspoken images, "That lambs dislike great birds of prey does not seem strange: only it gives no ground for reproaching these birds of prey for bearing off little lambs.... To demand of strength that it should *not* express itself as strength... is just as absurd as to demand of weakness that it should express itself as strength."[5] Thus in the Moment both what desires and what is desired attain to the realization of their truest self. In that Moment, it is as it should be: that this one consumes and that the other is consumed.

Yet surely you would agree with me that Johannes's arguments are highly suspect. If Cordelia's being is essentially her being-for-him, why must he deceive her into thinking his intentions to be otherwise? Why must he propose marriage as a stratagem to attain an evening of erotic pleasure for which there are to be no "consequences"? Johannes is a subtle craftsman, a genius in his techniques of seductive appropriation. But he has made himself an exception. He has bestowed being-for-itself upon himself as his own solitary possession, made himself the unique beneficiary of the largesse of the whole world. He has made himself God, who he is not at all and who Sartre insists no one can be. So Johannes's strategy turns out to be no different from the other hedonistic strategies in *Either/Or*: a method for denaturalizing the natural flow of things. It may be more effective than the others because it really transforms the world rather than merely pretending to do so. But it is nonetheless finally unnatural and so doomed to failure, a proposal for overcoming what cannot be overcome. The perishing, partial, time-bound aspects of the Moment are ineluctable characteristics of the way things are.

These three versions of hedonistic moral strategy can be generalized. The "aesthetic" characters in *Either/Or* are not merely role models whom we as separate individuals may embrace or reject. They are also metaphors for societal strategies. The natural flow of things for a group—a family, a community, a nation—is endlessly, relentlessly, cyclical. There is an arising of needs, of a deficiency in the conditions of existence; possibilities are glimpsed for remedying this deficiency; from them, methods come to be identified or fashioned as the best way to remediation; activity transforms the conditions of existence, closing the gap between the needs and their remedy, attaining fulfillment; needs once more arise. Needing-needed-Moment-needing-needed-Moment: the familiar desiring-desired cycle everywhere endlessly repeating itself throughout the social terrain. In this sense the group is an individual writ large.

Dewey pointed out that individual consciousness emerges as a factor in the natural process only when the metabolic cycle becomes problematic. The cessation of desire would simply be death, but life can go on thoughtlessly, instinctively, insofar as the two poles of the praxis polarity are in rough balance. Desire arises, but there is a method at hand for addressing its demands; consequently the desire subsides, although only for a moment. In like fashion, a community can function on the basis of its traditions, uncritically repeating the same practices generation after generation, as long as the results provide some kind of enduring subsistence and stability.

The resources for sustaining an accustomed quality of life, however, may become less and less adequate or the needs of the community may grow beyond the capacity of the available resources. An early frost may have nipped in the bud fruits and berries upon which the group depends, or a spate of births may have increased significantly the number of unproductive mouths to be fed. Or the problem might be caused by a breakdown in the normal means utilized for carrying on the work of the group, so that the resources remain adequate but their availability has been put into question. Thus dangerous animals may be newly lurking along the pathways from the village to the places where the fruit bushes grow. As the familiar routine of things becomes increasingly dysfunctional, customary ways come under scrutiny, although usually in neither explicit nor articulated ways.

The solutions suggested by *Either/Or* turn on solving the dilemma of a Moment that has become in its natural way insufficient by devising a strategy for denaturalizing it. Multiplying the natural Moment into a close-packed quantitative sequence, substituting a subjective aim that the Moment can readily satisfy, transforming the natural Moment into one specially enhanced to dovetail with one's needs: all three of these solutions, with varying success, aim at improving upon what has been given so that it will be more resistant to unsettling alterations in the accustomed equilibrium. The Moment is by nature a fragile accomplishment because of its triad of inherent limitations: this fragility is exacerbated by the fickleness with which its natural conditions recur. The creative advance is not only a constant coming-to-be and perishing, but one marked by incredible variety in the how, where, and why of it. The cycle of nature is endlessly repetitive but also endlessly surprising. Like death, taxes, and the poor, the cycle is always with us but the forms it takes, the ways by which it comes, the consequences it has, are difficult to anticipate. We must reach beyond the natural and its unpredictabilities if we are to find or fashion a Moment that can be counted on.

A quantitative approach of the Don Juanian sort, one that seeks to sustain the Moment through time by a replication strategy, is debilitated by the problematic character of the future. Don Juan presumes the world to be a cornucopia of female companionship. The communal version of this would be to assume that the trees will bear fruit every year, that the game will always be available to the hunter, that the fields will year after year bring forth grain. Don Juanism implies a nomadic society, one that adapts itself to the cycle of nature's resources, following the migration of the animals it hunts, moving with the seasons to where the fruits and grains are still available, but always presuming that what had worked before will work again. Rotationalism implies a way of life that deals with adversity by adjusting its expectations to what the world can in fact provide. Within the obvious constraint imposed by the requirements of bare subsistence, such groups are sedentary, accepting changes in what is available with a patience, a fatalism, that is often remarkable. Johannes recognizes that he must work to make the world his cornucopia, but he still presumes that the world has that potential, that it is a resource adequate to the demands he wishes to make upon it once it has been properly shaped by human purposes. His societal analogue is technological: a group organized to turn nature into its obedient servant.

The rotational method of mere accommodation we will set aside, and the Don Juanian method of blind confidence as well. What remains is the aggressive strategy suggested by Johannes. It is based on the assumption that the needing–needed cycle can be kept in balance, that an adequate supply of Moments of fulfillment can be secured through cleverly cultivating the natural order of things in a sustained manner over the long haul. All that is required is some reasonable ingenuity, some cleverness, some inside track to divine support, or, as Dewey recommends, the systematic application to social groups of the experimental method of the natural sciences. But this strategy remains vulnerable to the one fact that will not go away: the requisite abundance is finite in principle and not just contingently.

The Moment can be sustained for an ethic of abundance only in the absence of scarcity, only on the condition that the world's resources, natural or manufactured, will not run out. But wherever the conditions for something are not infinite, they are not necessary. Contingency lurks at the heart of every technological solution to the hedonistic dilemma. The remedies are always postponements of scarcity, not its eradication; they are tactical but not strategic victories.

If the supply of objects of satisfaction cannot be expanded indefinitely, one response is to curtail access to the supply. At the level of human community, this is what Sartre calls the defining of its surplus population [CDR 125–39]. You and I, along with our compatriots, pursue our various purposes within the constraints of commonly accepted practices. But one day it becomes evident that the resources for satisfying everyone's needs are running short. There is simply not enough food to go around, especially with more and more children being born and the fertility of the fields already diminishing. Increasing our trade, selling manufactured goods or minerals for grain and beef, may help. But we realize that in the long run even this will not suffice. Some of us will need to go hungry, ultimately to starve and to die, if others of us are going to survive. Who are to be those expendable ones, *les excédentaires*?

Within the environment of scarcity that constitutes our historical terrain, that is a given for every human situation, it is impossible for all the inhabitants to survive. Some must be sacrificed so that the others might survive. It would be more humane to settle the matter by a policy of nonreplacement: control the birthrate through contraception or sterilization or abortion, until deaths outnumber births and the population declines to a size commensurable with the available resources. Failing that, there is always infanticide or senicide as practiced so effectively by communities existing on the edge of subsistence. Neglecting to protect segments of the population, usually the poor, from disease, or allowing them to starve by failing to provide an adequate distribution of resources, also works. Or there is the time-honored war option, increasing our land at our neighbors' expense while at the same time depleting our own numbers. In this sense, the character of a community is disclosed through whom it considers expendable, whom it kills or allows to die, whom it sacrifices to the survival of the others.

Yet these solutions may well come back to haunt us. The natural workings of our world have been worked upon by ourselves and by others. They have been reformed into a world in which those others—those unborn children, those despised poor, or those ancient enemies—have been made expendable. But it is human praxis that has made the world with them as its expendables. That same praxis could just as easily make the world again, but this time expending you and me. Johannes denaturalized his surroundings, turning everything he could into instrumentalities for Cordelia's enhancement of his pleasure. Not just she but the whole world along with her was made expendable. But if Cordelia and her friends could be so cunningly manipulated, it is quite possible that another person might, unknown to Johannes, be manipulating him in turn, using his proud cunning to ends that when achieved will leave him the seduced rather than the seducer, leave him traduced, discarded, an expended being-for-another. How ironic it would be were Cordelia herself to be that more crafty strategist, deceiving her putative deceiver, using her own operationalizing of the world to turn his inside out. *Les excédentaires* is a category, a way of shaping things without specifying the content. What you specify can be re-specified by someone else. Hedonists are vulnerable to what Sartre calls the "commutativity" of their efforts to secure abundance against the ravage of scarcity. That you can make me expendable co-implies that I can make you expendable.

This should come as no surprise. The hedonist of Johannes's ilk has freely, creatively, invented new values for things, arranging the world so that there is only one being-for-itself and a vast plenitude of beings-for-another. But if every person is a hedonist, there will be a glut of beings-for-itself, an endless incommensurability of masters demanding that all the other masters be their slaves. The result will be Hobbes's infamous war of all against all, and life "solitary, poor, nasty, brutish, and short." Under conditions of scarcity, the hedonistic strategy for gaining control of the Moment by denaturalizing its brief, perishing, particularities ends up making a world inhabited by persons whose lives, brief, fragile, and dehumanized, are no better, indeed surely are worse, than under the regimen of nature's necessities.

The Malthusian problem where demand outruns supply can be seen as one way to articulate a social and economic version of this failure of hedonism. Where the available resources are finite, so must the draw upon them be finite. The number of mouths to feed in a society increases geometrically under conditions of relative abundance until supplies are inadequate. People starve, some of them die, and some of the others are unable or unwilling to produce more offspring. The surplus population declines and the food resources once more become sufficient to meet the demand. This Moment of adequation, however, spurs a new geometric rise in the number of mouths until once again their needs can no longer be met, which forces a reduction in the population until a Moment of supply–demand equilibrium is again momentarily obtained. This natural cycle can be overcome, the Moment of adequation sustained, only by tailoring the demand to the supply. The converse is also possible, of course, but it is the demand that grows geometrically; its control is far more easily accomplished than an attempt to keep the supply spiraling to meet demand. Given a certain pool of resources, therefore, it is a matter of social prudence to restrict accordingly the population with access to it.

Garrett Hardin gives vivid expression to this solution in arguments on behalf of a "lifeboat ethics." A rich nation has the capacity to sustain its own population in the lifeboat of resources under its control, but it cannot at the same time provide the support needed by people in the poorer nations, those clamoring to get into the lifeboat. Justice would require an equal distribution of the resources, but that would be to pull down the standard of living for everyone below subsistence level. Letting everyone into the boat will swamp it and everyone will drown. "Complete justice, complete catastrophe." Therefore a rich nation ought to conserve its resources so that its own people can survive, even though this is at the expense of the survival of others. "For the foreseeable future, our survival demands that we govern our actions by the ethics of a lifeboat, harsh though they may be. Posterity will be satisfied with nothing else."[6]

Moral egoism is where hedonism always seems to lead. You are, ultimately, an instance of desiring that has precedence over all other instances. You alone are essentially worthy of the available resources. Others insofar as they serve your pleasure share contingently, not essentially, in that worth. Within a societal context, this means that political power is to be seen as a group's exercising its ability to determine who the expendables are. The political expression of moral egoism is tyranny, the absolute ability of one group, one coterie, or even one single individual, to be defined as alone unexpendable.

Yet even this power is no solution. Desiring itself is inherently infinitizing. As the Rotation Method implicitly acknowledged, the adequacy of an object of desire is a function not only of its self-contained characteristics but also of its relational context. Fulfillment repeated and repeated decays into unfulfillment; appetite is whetted, not quenched, by its success. The Moment is addictive. Like any addiction it needs more and more of the same or the same of the different in order to sustain itself. It spirals toward ever-greater intensities. Like a raging fire, the very vigor of its success increases its demand for further resources to sustain and enhance that vigor.

Judge William, the voice of the perspective offered in the second volume of Kierkegaard's *Either/Or,* defines this spiral as "hysteria of the spirit" [E/O-2 189–94]. Your dread of emptiness, of the Moment slipping away from your grasp, spurs you to action aimed at its reattainment. But the fuller the fulfillment, the greater the resulting emptiness, and so the more frenetic the pursuit of some new and better fulfillment. Nero is the example offered, the supreme hedonistic ego, self-defined as the solitary unexpendable center of desire within the whole wide world of available resources. He is a compleat Don Juan whose presence suffices to effect what he desires, a Johannes who commands rather than seduces the world to suit his whim. He is sovereign of the known universe, ruler of an empire instrumentalized to serve his private needs.

Nero's quest for the Moment is not as simple as it seems, however. His successes breed new challenges. He finds himself continually in search of greater variety and increased intensity in the pleasures of his life. This leads him from simple erotic satiations to extravagant ones and then to horrific excesses, from private orgies to the burning of Rome, from gluttony to sadism and then eventually to nihilism:

Only in the moment of pleasure does [Nero] find distraction. He burns up half of Rome, but his torment remains the same. Before long such things entertain him no more. There is a still higher pleasure available, he would terrify men.... A woman approaches his throne, he smiles graciously upon her, and yet she becomes almost impotent with dread; perhaps this smile already singles her out as a sacrifice to his lust. And this dread delights him. He does not wish to produce awe, he wishes to terrify.... He is capable of having a child cut down before the mother's eyes to see if her despair would give passion a new expression which would entertain him. If he were not Emperor of Rome, he perhaps would end his life with suicide; for in truth it is only another expression for the selfsame thing when Caligula wishes that the heads of all men were set upon one neck so as to be able with one stroke to annihilate the whole world, and when a man puts himself to death. [E/O-2 191–92]

The intensification spiral cannot be constrained except by failure, therefore. Resources can be maximalized by the power of human inventiveness, and the demand on resources can be minimalized by restricting the kind and number of the unexpendables. But political domination, creative reconstruction, and technological enhancement—the strategies of Don Juan, the Rotation Method, and Johannes, respectively—all have an outer limit. Even Nero, who utilizes all three, finds them eventually insufficient. With the full power of an empire at his beck and call, his most fanciful and depraved notions able to be immediately realized, the transformation of the world by force of arms or by imperial edict or by conflagration his but to command, he must nonetheless confront eventually and inevitably the inadequacy of it all to satisfy his ever-spiraling needs.

The alternative to the impossible task of augmenting resources indefinitely, it was proposed, is to constrict need. But the totality of those in need has its lower limit in the single absolute self, and we have seen that it is precisely this self that has no limit to the spiral of its desiring. The hedonistic dilemma is thus irremediably Malthusian: desiring will always overwhelm the desired, and for essential not accidental reasons. Nero's desire is infinite but the world's resources merely large. As Descartes remarks, you and I as humans share with the divine an infinitizing will: "There is only volition alone, or the liberty of the free will, which I experience to be so great in myself that I cannot conceive the idea of any other more ample and extended, so that this is what principally indicates to me that I am made in the image and likeness of God."[7]

But in all other respects—our imagination, our power, our memory, our understanding, our goodness—we, like the world, are very finite. The incommensurability of desiring and desired is grounded in the essential nature of human being. All solutions are only adventitious: they work if you or I are lucky. But the chance of failure haunts each of our futures and haunts them the more so the more we have been successful in the past.

The cycle of desire desiring cannot be overcome by attempting to sustain the Moment through time, by making the world into a context for desire wherein its needs can be met now and forevermore. Desire cannot merely make up its satisfactions out of imagination; neither can it make the real world up into an adequate environment for satisfaction. If the natural flow of things cannot be denaturalized, made over into a beneficently manufactured flow of things, then the only remaining hope is to obliterate the flow of things itself, to conquer time, to transform it into eternity.

The Moment is the Good. The condition of completion it describes is the aim of all human activity, perhaps of all activity. Every other good gains its worth from being linked in some way to this one absolute value: as a resource, as an instrumentality, as an inevitable or contingent consequence. This Moment when experienced is a brief respite from the effort required to identify it and attain it. The flow of things within the framework of praxis is one of intentionality, a tropism from deficiency toward fulfillment. Time's arrow has a teleological directionality. It is a movement that has a goal, and the goal is the cessation of its movement. There is a sense, then, in which the Moment is a respite from time, a breaking out into calm waters after the turbulence of the rush and flow of purposive activity. Its self-contained, completed fullness contrasts with the incomplete, other-oriented striving of desire. The Moment and its pursuit, the noun of arrival and the verb of journeying, stand in sharp and poignant juxtaposition.

A world polarized into eternity and time is the result, the one a serene, settled region of maximal realized value, the other a chaotic, cacophonous realm characterized essentially by the deficiencies of striving and of loss. It is the contrast between a realm of the sacred and a region of the profane. As Mircea Eliade explains, the sacred is manifest in history as the power that organizes the chaos of the profane, that "ontologically founds the world" [SAP 21]. The gods make the universe in a primordial, originating act of giving shape to what was shapeless. The high-god Marduk slays Tiamet the chaos-dragon and forms its body into earth and sky; in the beginning "the earth was without form and void, with darkness over the face of the abyss, and the spirit of God hovering over the surface of the waters" [Gen. 1:2].[8] A particular place within the everyday world becomes a sacred space when people discover that this divine world-creating force has somehow become explicitly present there. Wherever the gods are present, that place is a microcosm of the whole cosmos, for divine power re-creates there what it first created, what it is always creating: the making real of a world from the unreal indeterminacy of primeval chaos.

The sacred is the absolute value that gives the profane whatever relative value it might possess. In this way of thinking, the Moment when desire ceases its desiring is taken to be a reality independent of its being desired, the ontological foundation for all such hoped-for experiences and for their preservation. The question, therefore, is how to gain access, preferably permanent access, to the sacred. The answer is that human praxis can evoke the presence of the gods by shaping its mundane spaces in imitation of the divine; to use Eliade's word, by "cosmicizing" them. For example, when a wandering people settle down in a new land they will lay out their community in ways and along lines that echo their understanding of how the gods laid out the cosmos. The cosmos has a center, an axis around which it revolves; the body of the world has a navel that is the seed from which it grew. The new community must also have its *omphalos,* its center-pole around which the major artifacts and institutions of the group will be clustered, with streets and neighborhoods, each harboring functionally defined persons and their activities, extending out from there rank after rank to an edge, an outer boundary beyond which is the profane, the wilderness, the place of outcasts, aliens, and enemies. So constructed, this community is a copy in miniature of the world. At its center are the religious objects and the structure that houses them, the sanctuary where the divine resides and from which its creating, redemptive powers emanate. The gods reside there because what is "homologous" to the transcendent realm must therefore reflect its qualities and thus be invested with its powers. To make a home for the gods is to invite them to dwell among us; as they draw near to us we draw near to them, to the Moment, to the absolute reality which they are essentially.

Not only space but time as well must be homologized. The explicit reenactment of a past event gives it new life, makes it present once

again. Oedipus is once more caught in his tragic web of pride and circumstance when you watch the actors performing Sophocles. The brav-
ery of those who long ago stood at Marathon is palpably in the air for
you to breathe, to make your own, when their tale is told to you and
your compatriots around campfires the night before a crucial battle is
to begin. By the telling of myths and the performing of rituals, by the
careful observance in word and deed of traditional modes of activity,
the separation of past from present is overcome. Time is made "indefinitely recoverable, indefinitely repeatable" [SAP 69].

And where the tale told, the ritual enacted, is of the originating act
when world first emerged from chaos, then we who are present in
that hearing or that doing are brought into the presence of the power
that founds all powers. In those moments, you are made new, made
anew, reborn and revitalized. And so also your society, drawing vitality
from the "strong, fresh, pure world that existed *in illo tempore*" [SAP
94]. It is now as it was in that time, on that first morning of creation
when there was not yet any perishing, when sin and death were still
unknown. The Moment is what is now, the eternal present come down
among us full of grace and power.

This imitation of the gods, and of those whose previous imitations
have proven successful by the fruits of the individual and communal
fulfillment they have harvested, needs to be a part of everything we do,
especially of those key moments in life: birth, puberty, marriage, death,
seedtime and harvest, winter solstice and midsummer night. When we
marry, our union is a reflection of the union between the sky and
earth. That is why we must both be of different families, that our min-
gling might be as that of cosmic differences which, by becoming one,
give rise to new and valued realities. When we farm the land, we are
like the sky god impregnating the earth goddess with our seed. We
offer the first fruits of our cooperative labors as a burnt offering at the
temple, as our ancestors once offered the first-born of their seed in
propitiation of the gods.

So in these ways the sacred touches all of life. Humans have an "ontological thirst," says Eliade, for "being." We crave access to permanent
realities, to a condition where the terror of chaos, of the momentary,
partial, perishings of creaturehood can be overcome. You take this Moment to be a place as well as an event, because it is the event that
made it possible for there to be places, because it is the place where all
events are at once. You thirst for the sacred because it carries you away
from change, imbues your history with the presence of eternity.

Thus it is argued, not propositionally but performatively, that since
some persons, heroes, and divinities have in the past attained perpetual

fulfillment, as a quality of their lived experience and thus also as the assurance of a condition that will be their existence beyond the pale of death, then for you to emulate them, to become at one with them by mirroring their praxis in your own, is to gain access to that very same fulfillment, that very same assurance. The mirroring occurs not only when you echo the actions of these special ones but also when you are present yourself in the places where they performed those crucial, fulfilling deeds, or at least when you are present in places where others since them but before you have successfully accomplished the crucial mirroring activities. Such a harmony of place and practice constitutes you and those others who share such experiences with you as a community. It is a community linked together through structures of enduring importances that are as thick as blood and as sturdy as bone. You and they are thereby also linked, in the ways by which culture becomes biology, to the original practitioners who are the founders of that community and who serve as the guarantors of its tethering to eternity.

The similarity to Johannes's project is perhaps startling at first. As God shaped the elemental chaos into heaven and earth, so Johannes shapes the youthful Cordelia. As he places himself at the center of things as its only intrinsic reality, so divine power is at the center of the universe as its absolute reality. As the Eliadean farmer intrudes his plow into the soil in order to plant seeds that will fructify and yield an eventual harvest, emulating the copulation of the male god with mother earth, so Johannes tills the unformed girl until she is ripe for the harvesting. Thus Johannes, the consummate moral egoist, functions as though he were a god. He acts within his world just as a god would act, fashioning value, securing an order for things, working up the Moment as creature to his creativity. Those who would imitate the gods in the way Eliade describes differ from Johannes only in that they submit their praxis to a higher authority. They strive to be like gods in the sense of asking that the divine draw near to them. They ask not to create the Moment but to be re-created in its presence, to mirror its glory, and ultimately to dwell in it.

By believing that what is experientially out-of-time can break into the profane strivings of humanity, you are offered access to genuine Moments of fulfillment. Yet these moments are only anticipations, the first fruits of something far better. Striving humanity can find unending fulfillment by being drawn totally into the sacred, by entering irrevocably that ontological region wherein the Moment is the only kind of experience supported.

But there's a rub. The problem with ritual is that it is still hostage to contingency. Human praxis still frames the process by which the Moment is secured, even though that Moment may have become a place to reach rather than a deed to do, and even though a model may have been provided for how best to instantiate that praxis so as to assure the fulfillment sought. Freedom is essential to praxis, but freedom means an excess of possibilities beyond what can be actualized. It entails the risk of error, of selecting an inopportune possibility, of willful repudiation of the Good. In the ritualized allegiance to a tradition that promises access to timeless truths, lasting fulfillments, eternal goods, the Moment has been rescued from contingency, but not the process by which it is attained. Fulfillment is eternalized, but the striving after it is still racked by incurable uncertainties.

Some kinds of mysticism and idealism attempt to resolve this remaining problem by denying the relevance or the reality of the striving. Zen Buddhism, for instance, celebrates the ontological identity of the individual self and the world's totality. The *tathata* particularly of a "this" and the *sunyata* universality of the whole of Being are not two kinds of reality nor even two instances of one kind, but one. Yet they are one without either of them being reducible to the other, without either being less real or less fully what it is.

The task is not to bring your life into accord with that of the transcendental, to make *tathata* a mirror that reflects back the perfect image of *sunyata*. Indeed, the very striving to attain such a relationship, the very desiring of it, is already to have gone astray. For Zen there is no task; or rather, the task is to give up having tasks, to quit trying to bring self and sacred into harmony. What you only need do is open your eyes and see what has been true all along, that the two are one. *Sunyata* is *tathata*, *tathata* is *sunyata*, even though their unity does not deny that you are a distinct individual and the totality of things is a totality. As one commentator says,

Pure subjectivity is pure objectivity, the *en-soi* is the *pour-soi;* there is perfect identity of Man and Nature, of God and Nature, of the one and the many. But the identity does not imply the annihilation of one at the cost of the other. The mountains do not vanish; they stand before me.... The mountains are mountains and yet not mountains. I am I and you are you, and yet I am you and you are I.[9]

Or as another puts it, "One particle of dust is raised and the great earth lies therein; one flower blooms and the universe rises with it."[10]

For other forms of Buddhism, and for Hindus also, this same unity is affirmed but by denying the ultimate reality of the "this." The undifferentiated One is the truly real against which the apparent differences of

experience and time are set. The particular self, not merely in its surface plurality but even in its deepest significance as *atman,* is illusion
insofar as it is taken as itself fundamental. For *Brahman* alone is real;
*atman* is real only insofar as it is grasped as *Brahman.*

You *are* eternity, if you will but realize it. Your task is not one of
creating but one of appreciating, of recognition rather than actualization. The desiring of desire attains its goal not by filling up the void it
creates but by not creating the void in the first place. To learn that
your true self, you in your essential being, is not the deficiency of desiring but is already the very perfection desire desires: this is wisdom,
joy, salvation. What is natural need not be overcome after all, because
the truly natural is not the incessant flow of things but rather a timeless completeness. The goal of striving is discovered to be not goal
but given.

Yet this is the Rotation Method reappearing in only a slightly altered
guise. The self need not go outside itself to find fulfillment. It is its own
sufficiency; it is the Good if it will but recognize this fact and construe
its aims accordingly. These mysticisms have solved the contingency inherent in rotational strategies by giving the sought-after sufficiency ontological status: there is no need to invent the objects of fulfillment as
these are the self itself. The notion of the sacred raised the goal of
praxis to the level of an ontological necessity, a timeless realm. The
notion of *atman/Brahman* raises the essence of praxis to that same
status. The material and final causes having been rescued from contingency by being identified as the same, the formal and efficient causes
collapse into irrelevance. The stretching out from what is toward what
could be is not the foundation of selfhood after all, nor the possibilities
for change a necessary condition of success. The striving-after of desire
and the coming-to-be-and-perishing of temporality have no meaning
when the Moment is not an achievement but a given. The price that
has been paid, however, is the same one that the Rotation Method paid.
Praxis has been rendered meaningless.

But are we willing to purchase security at such a cost? My fundamental intuition about the world, and I hope yours as well, is that time
is real, that selves are essentially incomplete, and that the natural order
is characterized by the striving of those selves through time to overcome both their deficiency and the temporal flow that continually re-
instantiates it. The task is to overcome time, not to deny it; to explain
it, not to explain it away. By insisting that the natural flow of things and
all its contingency cannot be swept aside as illusion, we need not mean
that the Moment is unavoidably at risk. Let us continue to accept the
ontologizing of the Moment, claiming that it is a timeless locus of ful-

fillment immune from the chanciness of the temporal flux. The time-less need not be the truth of time in the sense of being its foundation but rather in the sense of being its destiny. It is not that time is unreal but that it is finite.

Apocalypticism makes precisely this shift in how you should under-stand your relationship to a fulfillment that is able to break you free permanently from the endless circle of your strivings. It offers an as-surance of the ultimate victory over time without denying time its pen-ultimate reality. The cycle of desire's desiring, its momentary transcen-dence, its remorseless reemergence, is taken as itself transitory. The natural cycles of temporal contingency are temporally contingent. They need not go on endlessly. The timeless will at some time replace the temporal. The apocalyptic vision thus inverts the hedonistic di-lemma and thereby overcomes it. For hedonism the cycle of desire was endless, the Moment transitory. For the apocalypticist it is the cycle that is momentary, partial, time-bound and it is the Moment, once truly possessed, that is endless.

The most influential statement of apocalypticism is found in the bib-lical book of Daniel. "In the second year of his reign Nebuchadnezzar had dreams, and his mind was so troubled that he could not sleep" [Dan. 2:1]. Daniel reconstructs this portentous dream, which the king says was of a "great image," and he provides him with an interpreta-tion. What is Nebuchadnezzar to make of the fearful dream-image with its head of gold, chest and arms of bronze, midsection of iron, and feet part of iron and part of clay, this creature so fearful and yet so dra-matically destroyed by a great stone "hewn from a mountain, not by human hands" [Dan. 2:31–35]? Make this of it, says Daniel: that Neb-uchadnezzar is to see himself and his authority as the head of gold, and the other portions of the creature as lesser kingdoms that will each in turn succeed his own, the last a divided kingdom, "partly strong and partly brittle," an unstable time of troubles that will be destroyed in the end by the great stone. For by the intervention of "the God of heaven" there shall arise after all of these events "a kingdom that shall never be destroyed; that kingdom shall never pass to another people; it shall shatter and make an end of all these kingdoms, while it shall itself endure for ever" [Dan. 2:44].

Later, in the first year of Nebuchadnezzar's successor, Daniel himself has a dream [Dan. 7:1–27] in which he sees a sequence of "four huge beasts coming up out of the sea." The first is a lion with eagle's wings; it is followed by a bear crunching three ribs in its mouth; next comes a leopard with bird's wings; and lastly there arises a beast with iron teeth, bronze claws, and ten horns. The last beast is the worst of them all, and from among its horns springs up another horn, with "eyes like the eyes of a man, and a mouth that spoke proud words." These Daniel interprets as a sequence of empires, and they too in the dream are finally swept away by a divine act, in this case that of "the Ancient in Years," who calls into being "an everlasting sovereignty which should not pass away."

The commensurability of the two dreams can be readily established by a concerned reader, and the kingdoms in the sequence identified with real historical kingdoms. Babylonia, Nebuchadezzar's kingdom, is the first, and the only one explicitly named by Daniel. It is the kingdom currently and proudly ensconced in power; its glory and importance are identified by the nobility of the metals and animals that signify it: gold, a lion, and an eagle. The successor kingdom is inferior to Babylon, as indicated by the lesser nobility of its metal, silver, and by the lesser majesty of the animal, a bear. The reader is quite confident that the references, therefore, cannot but be to Media, especially since the three ribs held by the bear correlate with the three nations Media will subdue in its rise to domination. The Persian empire with its four great kings—Cyrus, Darius, Xerxes, and Ataxerxes—must be referred to by the bronze and the four-winged leopard. This means that the fourth portion of the image and the fourth beast from the sea would have to be the empire of Alexander, the creature's ten horns his Seleucid successors, and the king who shall follow these ten none other than the despicable Antiochus IV Epiphenes, whose destruction shall usher in a God-authorized sovereignty that shall have no end.

The writings that comprise the book of Daniel were not written, of course, at the beginning of the period about which the prophecies speak, at the time when Nebuchadezzar reigned in Babylon. Their author lived instead at the end of that period, at the time when Seleucids are flourishing, when Antiochus is on the throne and the Jews in an uproar over his desecration of their temple. It is the worst of times. The cycle of desiring and desired has been for the author of the book of Daniel and for those he addresses one marked by few if any moments of fulfillment. Hedonism's sanguine call for strategies to maximize one's pleasure would seem to those suffering people bizarrely inadequate. The oppression of kings has turned the fleeting partialities of the Moment into permanent impossibilities. The presumption for the hedonist is that control is a reasonable goal for a person to have, that the scarcity of resources provided by the natural flow of things can be overcome by deploying the appropriate techniques. And so it can be sometimes—for some people. For the rulers, the Johanneses of this world. But for the Cordelias, for those who find themselves defined by others as *les excédentaires,* wherein does their fulfillment lie?

Note first of all how the significance of the hedonistic dilemma alters when your vantage point is that of weakness. The separation of the desiring self from the possible objects that might assuage it becomes a chasm. The objects of desire are snuffed out like stars overwhelmed by the first light of dawn. But this separation is not simply the result of a natural gap in things for which you might be able to devise some astute remedy. It is instead the work of a malevolent agency that seeks with still greater astuteness to prevent your remedies from working. The societal environment, not the natural one, is what is at fault. It is kings taking the fruit of your labors in taxes and murdering your children in war; it is Antiochus destroying your sacred places and demeaning your traditions. Against a triumphant hedonist, how can those he has defined as having their value only in the value they give him find any value of their own? Hedonism is an ethic for the victor; you require an ethic for the victim.

Daniel's solution involves a double move. First he re-naturalizes the encountered flow of things, wrests its cycle of strivings out of the hands of purposeful tyrants and places it under the aegis of an historical necessity ordained by God. Events thus retain their purposive structure, but they are not controlled by human agents. Secondly, Daniel re-situates the Moment from the present now being experienced to a future anticipated to be someday present. You find yourself living within a time of great suffering. The chance of your own fulfillment and that of those you love is at its nadir. Once, in a golden time, when the likes of Babylon was in ascendancy, your opportunities for fulfillment might have been better than they are now (although even then Israel was in captivity and Daniel not free but suffering under the yoke of an alien and selfish king). Yet since then things have only gotten worse. In this present day, your weakness has become unbearable, your moments of fulfillment all but nonexistent.

Take heart, however, says the author. Realize that this down-going path is a necessary one, a course of things that the prophet Daniel from long ago could foresee. His foretelling is trustworthy because you can see how each period from his time to yours has come to pass just as he said it would. This means that your suffering is not as a result of some other human being's willfulness. You are not the victim of an unnatural act. You are not someone who has been defined by another as expendable. Your abysmal situation is not the result of bad luck but of destiny, not due to Antiochus's will but to God's.

The author of the book of Daniel thus rescues you from the despairing negativity of your situation by claiming that what has been happening is actually natural, is part of the way things were meant to be. Your powerlessness would make it foolish to hope that those in power might change their minds, that once having defined you as expendable they might miraculously redefine you as one for whom others are to be expended. The malevolence of the hedonists toward those who threaten their fulfillment is not likely ever to disappear voluntarily.

But suppose the real control over the situation is not that of a malevolent purpose after all, but of a benign one. Suppose God, not Antiochus, is the intentionality shaping the course of things. Then whatever happens does so for a purpose that you can know with confidence is directed toward the ultimate satisfaction of your desires. You may not understand the how or why of God's method, but the result is not at issue. A moment shall come which is the Moment you desire, and in that moment "the kingly power, sovereignty, and greatness of all the kingdoms under heaven shall be given to the people of the saints of the Most High. Their kingly power is an everlasting power and all sovereignties shall serve them and obey them" [Dan. 7:27].

What the mystic seeks as an ontological given, as something already characterizing reality even though we might in our ignorance deny its truth, is claimed by the follower of the book of Daniel to be a future reality, the realization of which is assured. It is part of the divine intentionality and so is as certain as the past is certain. Only our ignorance prevents us from recognizing this truth. The Moment of fulfillment is a given for you and me if we will but open our eyes, but it is given as necessarily coming rather than as already present.

This givenness of the future is conveyed by both the political and moral character of the historical structure envisioned in the dreams of Nebuchadnezzar and Daniel. The sequence of kingdoms is the set of milestones marking progress along a temporal pathway leading up to the Moment. By locating yourself in reference to these markers, you can know how long it will be before your tribulations shall have an end. The gold, silver, and bronze portions of the journey already have been made. The realm in which those of us live who are hearing Daniel's prophecy is thus the last kingdom before the kingdom of the saints is to be realized. Political periodization is the method by which to give hope its confidence. History is a countdown to the apocalyptic Moment promised.

This journey has a moral content as well. The sequence of political hegemonies is from better kingdoms to worse ones. The saints have never suffered so greatly as they do right now, here in this last instant

before the cessation of all suffering. The fourth beast, unlike its predecessors, "shall devour the whole earth, tread it down and crush it"
[Dan. 7:23]. The king who shall arise as the last manifestation of this
beast shall be the worst of all; he will "hurl defiance" at God, "wear
down" the saints, and attempt "to alter the customary times and law"
[Dan. 7:25]. But the worst of times is evidence that the best shall soon
be manifest. The extreme of deprivation heralds the extreme of fulfillment that will supplant it. Those from whom much is expected are
those to whom much will be given.

The Christian counterpart to the book of Daniel is the apocalyptic
account recorded in the book of Revelation. Its scenario is somewhat
different but only with respect to the details. The sequence of creatures is no longer clearly fourfold and their interpretation seems more
cosmic than political, but the movement is definitely sequential. If you
are a careful reader you can readily find your location along a pathway
from origin to ending.

You begin with Satan's fall, with the beginning of the times when
human life became entwined unavoidably with suffering and loss, when
powers of deprivation were able to wreak havoc on even those "who
keep God's commandments and maintain their testimony to Jesus"
[Rev. 12:17]. A beast then emerges from the sea. It has the characteristics of Daniel's creatures: a lion's mouth, a bear's feet, a leopard's body.
It dominates the world because of the power ceded it by Satan. The
beast flourishes briefly, blaspheming God and waging war on God's
people. It is "granted authority over every tribe and people, language
and nation" [Rev. 13:7], and so also another beast that rules on the first
beast's behalf, and so also the great whore Babylon who comes riding
upon a scarlet beast. This last is the worst of all, and her beast is the
only one given an explicitly political interpretation. It has a number of
heads, symbolizing various kings, the one now reigning being the sixth
of seven [Rev. 17:10]; its horns stand for still further kings who have
not yet come to power.

The book of Revelation goes on to trace an esoteric scenario in
which cosmic forces led by a White Rider destroy the beasts and chain
up Satan, ushering in a thousand years of earthly fulfillment: "happy
indeed, and one of God's own people, is the man who shares in this
first resurrection" [Rev. 20:6]. But Satan is then let loose. Terrible
forces, the hosts of Gog and Magog, are mustered to do his bidding,
and God's people are once more threatened. Soon fire comes down
from heaven, however, and all the powers of evil are destroyed or cast
into endless punishment. Every human being that ever lived is judged
as worthy or not of participating in the new heaven and new earth that

is then created. This cosmic order is the final one, for its distinctive characteristic is the absence of the sea, the triumph of settled, determinate perfection over the turmoil of restless change.

And in that time, the coming to be and passing away of things will have itself passed away, and forever and forever more will God dwell with his saints in peace. No more the endless cycle of the polarities of desiring and desired. Instead, the ideal *le manqué* realized and made endless, an everlasting Moment become the new nature of the cosmos.

I offer in Illustration 2.1 a comparative summary of the solutions to the desiring–desired dilemma presented in this chapter.

**Illustration 2.1 Solutions to the Desiring–Desired Dilemma**

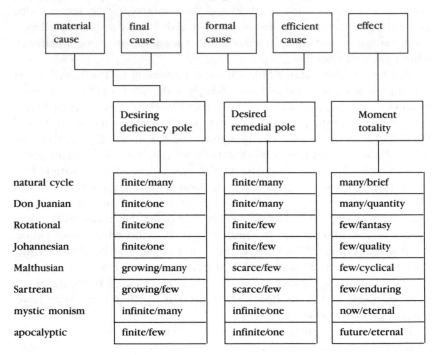

| | Desiring deficiency pole | Desired remedial pole | Moment totality |
|---|---|---|---|
| natural cycle | finite/many | finite/many | many/brief |
| Don Juanian | finite/one | finite/many | many/quantity |
| Rotational | finite/one | finite/few | few/fantasy |
| Johannesian | finite/one | finite/few | few/quality |
| Malthusian | growing/many | scarce/few | few/cyclical |
| Sartrean | growing/few | scarce/few | few/enduring |
| mystic monism | infinite/many | infinite/one | now/eternal |
| apocalyptic | finite/few | infinite/one | future/eternal |

# Three

## THE DISCIPLINING OF DESIRE

The Hellenistic and Roman periods were a time of tremendous social turmoil. Tracts like the books of Daniel and Revelation were written to provide people with much-needed reinterpretations of what they were experiencing. The cycle of desiring and desired is tolerable only if you and I have some expectation that moments of fulfillment will recur with reasonable frequency and that there is a possibility that their quality or quantity might somehow be increased. A middle way between the ideal of our fulfillment being endless and the anti-ideal of its unending absence is enough to make hedonism a workable guide for life. The ideal of sustaining fulfillment carries us beyond praxis, however, for with its coming the fourfold structure of action collapses. Our goal becomes the actual, possibilities and procedures for attaining it are no longer relevant, and efforts on its behalf are no longer required. Final, formal, and efficient causes become one with the material cause. But the same is true if you or I were to experience the anti-ideal. Here also praxis is transcended, because the end, if unattainable, renders the possibilities for its attainment irrelevant and the quest for its realization futile. Our goal thus becomes only a dream, a subjective phantasm that is an expression of the given facticity of our situation but no longer in dynamic contrast with it. The tension constitutive of action collapses into a fatal acceptance of the given.

Hence for those whose world seems to them a permanent incarnation of the anti-ideal, apocalyptic meaning has a special urgency. It restores the viability of their praxis, gives their actions significance. But as their situation improves, the urgency fades. For Augustine, writing at a time when Christianity was showing signs of outlasting the political order within which it had been engendered, the heritage of apocalyptic interpretation needed to be reshaped into a form more suited to the requirements of faith. Political concerns need no longer be limited to questions of determining a proper periodization, your energies and mine consumed in patiently counting off the milestones that lead inexorably to a promised perfect Endtime. Nor need the sufferings of our generation be accepted resignedly as the unavoidable means for attaining the joys of that hoped-for perfection. Such passive comforts could be dispensed with in the resurgent optimism of the age. But the naive confidence that desiring could by itself attain its desired end had been properly chastened by centuries of martyrdom. Divine grace in addition to human praxis was still thought to be necessary for attaining the Moment.

In *The City of God*, Augustine retains only the vaguest echo of Daniel's four-stage history of the world, noting that Assyria—with Babylon at its head—held political dominion in the time of Abraham and that Rome was its successor in the time of Christ [CG 16.17]. These and all the lesser realms that compose the earthly city, in contrast to the heavenly city of God, are dismissed as relatively unimportant: "For, as far as this life of mortals is concerned, which is spent and ended in a few days, what does it matter under whose government a dying man lives, if they who govern do not force him to impiety and iniquity?" [CG 5.21]. Some nations flourish for centuries and others are crushed before their aims have been even partially realized; some political leaders are morally upright and others tyrannical abominations. God bestowed "the blessings of the earth" on Persia, whose people worshiped gods the Romans rejected, and then bestowed power on Rome. God gave temporal authority to Augustus but also to Nero, to the Christian Constantine and also to the apostate Julian. Most certainly, argues Augustine, it is only the true God who could have made possible these individual and societal fulfillments. But it is obvious that they have been bestowed without reference to the moral virtue of the recipients, without any consideration of their religious faithfulness. But why this should be, how the good fortune of evil men could be tolerated much less caused by a just God, makes no sense. "It is too much for us, and far surpasses our strength, to discuss the hidden things of men's hearts, and by a clear examination to determine the merits of various kingdoms" [CG 5.21].

What is important for us to recognize is that the earthly city was founded by the fallen angels, creatures who are "good by nature but by will depraved": proud, bent upon "subduing and hurting" others, "tempest-tossed with beclouding desires" [CG 11.33]. It is willfulness not nature that governs the rise and fall of empire, that guides the virtues and vices of individuals. So Augustine cuts the linkage the books of Daniel and Revelation had forged between the natural flow of things and the flow of history. Both nature and history are under divine control, to be sure, but the periodization of historical events, in particular the sequencing of kings and empires, provides no clue to that control. That your desires are frustrated by oppression and misfortune cannot be taken as evidence for the timing of when an end to that frustration will occur. The rise of a king is not a checkpoint on the straight road that leads to the Endtime but merely one more mysterious, unpredictable lurch in a meandering process permitted and constrained by God but defined by the contingencies and arbitrariness of selfish human will.

We are returned to the problematic situation apocalypticism sought to resolve, but with one important change. The city of God, in contrast to the earthly city, has a definite structure for Augustine. It encompasses a history of the saints that begins with Adam and proceeds by five clusters of "days," each of which lasts about fourteen generations or a millennium, to the coming of Christ. This sequence is expressed developmentally by means of a metaphor of human growth. The first cluster of generations after Adam composes the infancy of God's people, while Noah and his successors exemplify its childhood. From Abraham its puberty begins, the period of its suffering under the yoke of the earthly city. Beginning with David, the community of God's people attains its advanced youth, and the period from the Captivity to Christ marks its transition to full maturity [CG 16.43]. There follows a sixth thousand-year cluster of generations stretching from Christ to the end of history and then, as the seventh period in this progression, there commences the eternal sabbath of the second resurrection.

The movement of the city of God is developmental, from childhood to flourishing adulthood, from the creation of history in a very ancient time, lost like one's infancy in oblivion, to the dying of history in an event that will bring new life and endless fulfillment to the saints. But Augustine refuses to be specific about the chronology. A thousand years is not a literal measurement but rather a rhetorical trope, referring to one of the seven broadly conceived distinctive segments of history, but sometimes meaning the value of such a segment or its salient aspect. Hence the reference in the book of Revelation to a thousand-year rule of the saints is to be understood by synecdoche as referring to that portion of the sixth "day" which still lies in the future, or, by "employing the number of perfection to mark the fulness of time," as referring to the anticipated End that brings that sixth day to a close [CG 20.7].

Thus even though the city of God has a history divided into specific units that you can mark off, revealing your own times as the last before that final Moment which will have no end, this history is nonetheless, pragmatically speaking, no different from the history of the earthly city. Both are shrouded in divine mystery. All you can do is behave as it is appropriate for a good citizen to do, and leave in God's hands the questions of the why of historical change and the when of its eventual cessation.

What you can do, meantime, is to be sure your love, your passions, your purposes, conform to the love of the heavenly city. Augustine provides the list of virtues appropriate to that love and contrasts it systematically with the love practiced by those who love not God but themselves. We are assured that during this period from Christ to the Endtime Satan is bound. He is at work, trying to seduce you and me to follow him, but his power is resistible: "For the Almighty does not absolutely seclude the saints from his temptation, but shelters only their inner man, where faith resides, that by outward temptation they may grow in grace" [CG 20.8]. God protects those whom He has predestined to eternal life, and He protects "the nations from which the Church is gathered." Hence although your temptations are real, you know in confidence that you have through God's grace the power to resist, to keep your love fixed on God rather than upon yourself.

The earthly kingdoms thus provide the environment within which the saint lives. The specific fortunes of these kingdoms have no relevance even though their reality is crucial. They are the proving ground for faith, an arena in which our love is tested constantly. You are rescued from the despair that grips the oppressed and unfulfilled, however, because you know that God always gives you the power needed to meet any such test. You grow in faith and thus in virtue by living amid the earthly city in a way that is defined by the values of a heavenly city. If you and I so live, then even the actions of those who love only earthly things can assist us. The best of the citizens and leaders of the nations can teach something to the saints by their example. Their loyalty, even though only to momentary ideals, is a lesson in selflessness: "So also these despised their own private affairs for the sake of the republic, and for its treasury resisted avarice, consulted for the good of their country with a spirit of freedom, addicted neither to what their laws pronounced to be crime nor to lust" [CG 5.15]. They have been rewarded by God in ways appropriate to the object of their loyalty: honor among the nations while they lived, their deeds celebrated in literature and history after their deaths. "But the reward of the saints is far different," and so the fact that such nobility could be achieved for the sake of merely earthly rewards is an admonition to us to persevere in the efforts required to achieve the reward God has in store for all His saints.

It was not only for the sake of recompensing the citizens of Rome that her empire and glory had been so signally extended, but also that the citizens of that eternal city, during their pilgrimage here, might diligently and soberly contemplate these examples, and see what a love they owe to the supernal country on account of life eternal, if the terrestrial country was so much beloved by its citizens on account of human glory. [CG 5.16]

Thus Augustine hangs an ethical content on a framework of teleological necessity. You are admonished to develop a moral character that is selfless in its desirings and able to resist all the lures that would tempt you to pursue self-willed ends. Yet the moral course of individual lives and of human history is foreordained. This oxymoron works because the specifics of it are quite unknowable. You do not know if you are among the saints, hence it is unclear whether your effort to resist temptation will succeed. It is even unclear whether you in fact desire to resist temptation. But you can believe that you are a citizen of the heavenly city. If so, you know that this requires from you acts of loyalty, courage, steadfastness, selflessness that are at least as excellent as those performed by the heroes of the earthly city. Endless fulfillment is promised as the reward for a praxis the final cause of which is obedience not only to a will other than your own but to a will unknown to you except by faith.

Hedonism offered you effective selfishness as a solution to the perpetual perishing of the Moment, but foundered on the aggrandizing character of the ego, the infinitizing dynamic of desiring. Unless the desired were itself infinite, desire must eventuate in unfulfillment and the Moment thus always recede from your grasp. Mystical monism proposed identifying the infinity of desire with the infinity of the desired, self with cosmos. But this was to reduce the natural and historical flow of things to illusion and thus to render your desiring meaningless. Apocalypticism tried to put the unity of self and cosmos back into history by locating it not as a timeless truth but as an eventual result. Thus the willful efforts of the hedonists to fulfill themselves at your expense could be taken in stride, as your deprivations were soon to be ended, replaced by a time when the faithful would be the ones fulfilled and that for evermore. Yet because the process was inevitable, it might as well be illusory; you only waited out the inexorable march of time, counting on the ticking of the Doomsday clock to bring closer the Moment you were destined to possess.

Augustine seeks a middle ground between denying history in order to secure fulfillment and affirming the reality of the concrete flow of things by denying the possibility of fulfillment. His Moment lies beyond history but history is the environment for its attainment, the context without which the heavenly city cannot develop its citizenry. As sacred history is developmental so also is the career of an individual. Without the challenges of adversity, without tempting and testing, not even God's chosen can grow up to be His saints.

Desire is crucial, but for Augustine its natural end is not what its environment would shape it toward. Desiring, in order to attain the truly desired, must resist what it is constantly tempted to desire. If your selfishness were natural, then resisting it would be unnatural foolishness (although even Aristippus and definitely Epicurus knew that pleasure-seeking meant sometimes foregoing a satisfaction now for a greater satisfaction subsequently). Johannes was a wiser hedonist than Don Juan. But if your selfishness is unnatural, then its pursuit is what is foolish and fulfillment requires that your desire be reoriented from loyalty to your own will to loyalty to nature's will, to the will of nature's creator and master, God. Augustine thus agrees with the best of hedonistic thought in claiming that history is where you must work out your dream of realizing the Moment and that success depends on attuning efficient with final cause, of bringing your desiring into harmony with an ideal for desiring that you have not made up but that is an objective given. Augustine differs from the hedonists only by locating the finality of desiring in God's will rather than your own, in a city of God rather than in a citadel of subjectivity.

How is this possible? How do you and I ever make the transition from self to city, from solitary fulfillment to a happiness achieved only within community? Augustine's answer is to posit the community as predestined but to obscure its presence among us. The city is drawn from the world's population but at no time in history does that city show itself, even to the eyes of faith. You may hope that you are among the saints, but they remain a secret society known only to God. Your striving is as solitary as that of the most unredeemed hedonist. You act by faith on the basis of a characterization of your natural community that you cannot know to be correct or mistaken until it is too late to change where you have invested your loyalties, if indeed such a self-chosen change makes sense at all. The contradiction of being urged to discipline yourself to the point of self-sacrifice without knowing if this is really the natural and thus the right thing to be doing is obvious. The Moment remains for you always a promise and never a reality. As with the selfish hedonist, it is thus always receding, never possessed except beyond history. So the dilemma reasserts itself: either the unity of for-itself and in-itself is impossible or the concrete flux of things has no intrinsic value. Each horn of the dilemma impales a solitary self.

I suggest that we turn back to the purely secular world with which we began, branding mystical and religious transcendentals as illusions to be avoided. What we have learned is that the single self will trap itself in a Malthusian environment of its own making unless it can re-orient itself to an end other than itself. We need a community that like the city of God serves as a natural environment, that will define the meaning of our desiring, will set us appropriate goals for which to strive and proper means by which to reach them. But unlike the city of God, this must be an earthly city, a reality fully present in history, a thing of flux and flow, of concrete time-bound orderliness. Yet like the city of God it must be no mere creature of some human will or wills; it must be natural, an appropriately human foundation for a human praxis. The paradigm for such a city is, of course, the *polis*; its apologist, Aristotle.

The Moment of fulfillment, the experience of no longer being dependent on what is both absent and beyond your control, is a goal that no individual can achieve alone. Happiness, which is what Aristotle says we call this experience, is thus the same as self-sufficiency. It is what you and every human being wants, the one goal sought solely for its own sake and never as a way station toward something else. But we do not mean by a self-sufficient man one who "lives his life in isolation, but a man who also lives with parents, children, a wife, and friends and fellow citizens generally, since man is by nature a social and political being" [EN 1.1097b9–11]. Acting on your own, you might attain some momentary fulfillment. But for this fulfillment to last and for it to be of the quality appropriate to your humanity, for it to be happiness and not merely satiety, other persons are required. Only in community can you give concrete expression to your distinctively human capacities, and thus only in community can you become fully human. Happiness is the condition of being rather than yearning to be human, and of being human rather than a beast or a god.

Why is this so? Because unlike all other things and creatures, human beings are free. You have capacities that can be realized in differing ways and which in being realized can frustrate rather than fulfill your desires. Most of Aristotle's *Nicomachean Ethics* is taken up with advice regarding how you might best act so as to fulfill rather than frustrate your quest for happiness. Excellence in any activity is a matter of sensible effort, avoiding the sorts of extremes that exhaust or atrophy our capacities, aiming not only for this personal balance but also for one that brings our activities into concord with those of the others with whom we share a world. This effort is difficult to realize: there are a multitude of ways to miss a target but only one trajectory by which the arrow will find its center [EN 2.1106b28].

There is no formula for excellence, not in the art of making things, nor even less so in the affairs of life. General principles can and should be learned, but practical activity concerns itself with particular situations. The question is how best to express the general in the specific. It is not difficult to know in general what to do. The problem is to know when to do it, in what manner, with whom, for how long, and for what end. Hence, for example, Aristotle summarizes his discussion of courage in this way: "Accordingly, he is courageous who endures and fears the right things, for the right motive, in the right manner, and at the right time, and who displays confidence in a similar way. For a courageous man feels and acts according to the merits of each case and as reason guides him" [EN 3.1115b18–21]. This sensitivity to context, this skill in adjusting abstract general principles so that they provide suitable guidance for dealing with the peculiarities of concrete particularity, cannot be learned from books but only from experience. Action becomes right action, *praxis* becomes *eupraxis,* only under the tutelage of right experience.

Your untutored desires will be immediately drawn to momentary pleasures, and your fear of pain also directly shapes your choices. Look at the way children behave, and animals, and those whose self-indulgence makes them no more than animals or children. So powerful are these desires that it is by their means that children are taught to obey; they are the "rudders" we use to "steer them straight" [EN 10.1172a21]. Desiring is of the essence of our humanity. It is your nature to seek the pleasure that comes with desiring's satiation. But the propensity to find that pleasure in the satisfaction of your appetites, in the immediate slaking of your bodily thirsts, is to express your nature in an extreme form. An excess of such desiring distorts rather than fulfills your nature, and excessive interest in the appetitive pleasures gives disproportionate importance to your animalistic aspects at the expense of what is distinctively human about you: your power to think, to reason, to be self-aware.

You are acting in a human way when you are aware of yourself and your place within a society of humans, when you are doing the things that make that community possible, when you are carrying out the functions defined by your place within a family and your membership as citizen of the state, and through these activities also satisfying your basic appetites, exercising your physical skills, and testing your ability to think and to understand. This full range of activities must be harmonized: your sexual urges and your intellectual desires, your individual health and the well-being of your family and nation, the demands of courage and those of gentleness, of magnificence and of candor. The principles that make this harmony possible must be fully grasped, their applicability in this instance and that instance confidently realized. The best way of carrying on each of these various activities is in such a manner that they are in themselves moderate and that they harmonize effectively with your other actions and those of your family and compatriots. The excellences with which the many deeds are done compose the excellence of the whole, of the virtuous individual who attains that happiness which is alone the end of life.

It is a pleasure to do something well [EN 1.1099a7–15]. To find no joy in a deed done courageously or magnanimously or with self-control, to be pained by the flourishing of a friend or the success of the state, is not natural. Although the capacity for finding pleasure in excellence is natural, however, its exercise needs to be nurtured. You can easily grow accustomed to doing things immoderately and so find pleasure in excess or deficiency. A child's spontaneous emotions, lacking yet the proper nurture, are typically immoderate. Because both what is proper and the love for it are learned only through experiences in which such attainments are first of all possible and then in some appropriate manner realized, the way to make you virtuous is through habituating you to choices that are in fact excellent and to the satisfactions that accompany those choices and their consequences. The sapling grows straight and true only if it is trained to do so. For this it has a natural capacity, but it requires the tending of a gardener to make it into a reality.

Thus the main task of a community is "to engender a certain character in the citizens and to make them good and disposed to perform noble actions" [EN 1.1099b30–32]. The requisite habits of excellence cannot be inculcated by just anyone, not even by parents; only the state has sufficient authority. Its laws have the scope and even-handedness needed to serve as a standard for harmony and concord; its rulers have the power to punish those who seek less noble ends or less effective means. Both strong rulers and good laws are the gardeners of the individual trees and of the collective forest which if properly cultivated grow to full maturity, magnificent in their paradigmatic realization of all that they can be. "A man must receive a good upbringing and discipline in order to be good," and this can only be achieved "by living under the guidance of a kind of intelligence and right order which can be enforced," that is, under the guidance of law that has "the power or capacity to compel, being the rule of reason derived from some sort of practical wisdom and intelligence" [EN 10.1180a14–22].

Aristotle has thus dramatically reshaped the dilemma of hedonism, offering a whole new approach to the problem that the Moment of fulfillment is fleeting, incomplete, and not self-contained. First of all, he denies the value of mere immediacy, of making fulfillment an absolute immersion in the present moment. Happiness arises only across a sustained, consistent way of acting. Habits of excellence, not the good fortune of a random act, are the means for attaining lasting fulfillment. Where Don Juan sees the repetition of fulfillment as how its brevity can be circumvented, Aristotle finds fulfillment only through the repetition. Brevity does not fulfill. A single swallow does not a summer make nor one instant's joy the apotheosis of desire. Consistency of habit not spontaneity of impulse is the wellspring of happiness.

Second, like Johannes the Seducer, Aristotle would overcome the inadequacy of what is merely given using a strategy honed to bring out the best potential in an occasion. Quality is crucial, not merely quantity. The goal is not just to pull back the bow and let fly an arrow, but to send it straight and true to its intended target. But for Johannes quality is at the extremity; his aims lack moderation, his reasons are blind to just proportion and balance, his emotions are wrapped up solely in his own fulfillment. His friendships can only be based on utility or pleasure; the friendship Aristotle thinks so crucial to the good life is beyond his comprehension. People of like excellence, concerned with the well-being of one another, and with their own well-being only insofar as self-love is friendship applied to oneself, share the goal of attaining well-being. Friendship "consists in community" [EN 8.1159b32] and within a community of friends the proper goal is not an "advantage of the moment" but what is advantageous "for the whole of life" [EN 8.1160a28]. Quality finds its highest expression in actions that are excellent both in what they aim at and in how they are pursued, which means that qualitative fulfillment is a shared and lifelong quest. Happiness is the Moment writ large enough to be able to provide genuine sufficiency.

Third, only because there is a wisdom of the past that can be taught by abstract admonition and by tales told about the legendary heroes of old, only because there exist contemporaries able to exemplify and enforce its lessons, and only because there is an honor to be won by acts sustaining and extending these truths: only because of these things is it reasonable to claim that this good does not perish with the perishing of the moment or the dying of the self. The Rotation Method recognizes these linkages but recommended divestiture. Its "theory of social prudence" warns against friendship, marriage, and public office, for "to play at battledore and shuttlecock with the whole of existence" requires avoiding entangling alliances. Freedom is the highest virtue and obtaining it means not "sticking fast in some relationship of life." Friends, for instance, provide "mutual assistance in word and deed," they "form a close association in order to be everything to one another." But, says the rotation expert, "it is impossible for one human being to be anything to another human being except to be in his way" [E/O-1 291].

Aristotle's quite different strategy is rooted in his insistence that human nature is fundamentally social, that self-sufficiency is a collective not an individual possibility. Friendship, marriage, and public office are not to be sought solely for what they bring. Their value lies not simply in their utility as instruments for attaining some higher end nor in the pleasure that such commitments might bring, although they have utility and bring pleasure. It is rather by being a friend, by carrying out your familial role, and by accepting the responsibilities of citizenship, that you express the excellence that is the fullest realization of your humanity. The good life is essentially entangled in those alliances.

Augustine has helped us realize that the problem with hedonism is the primacy it accords the individual. Desire is always your own desire and everything and everyone else are the opportunities or obstacles defining the landscape within which you are seeking its fulfillment. But if you are fundamentally related to me and to others through a larger, encompassing reality, if our mutuality is an aspect of who we are, then you cannot fulfill yourself except that you fulfill as well that aspect of who you are that is your mutuality with others. The city of God defines you; its realization is what you mean by "I." By then turning to Aristotle we have found a way to rescue this notion of the essentiality of community from its hiddenness. The city that defines us is the one tangibly encompassing you and me right now, although we soon discover that its scope far exceeds the horizon of present tangibility. Its self-sufficiency derives from the interactions of its several members, the rightness of their moderated concord, the enduring consistency to which these give rise. Desire thus communalized has lost its infinitizing drive; it has been disciplined by the requirements of mutuality to find fulfillment through contributing rather than controlling. It has received the endurance, intensity, and autonomy of satisfaction for which it longed.

Yet Aristotle's strategy soon discloses debilitating limitations. The community he celebrated was radically elitist, a few privileged men fashioning their good life at the expense of eight times their number of other humans who were conveniently determined by them to be incapable of the higher forms of action and therefore of the excellence that is alone the mark and content of happiness.[1] The citizen of the *polis* is Don Juan writ large. These friends, this band of comrades, are the desiring that demands of the world its natural right to be fulfilled. Women, children, slaves, and barbarians are Cordelia to its Johannes, those whose being is only for another, whose excellence is only instrumental and whose end therefore cannot ever be happiness. Aristotle regards these noncitizens like Augustine regarded the earthly city. The members of the worldly *civitas* were at best instrumental, an occasion for the testing of those virtues given by divine grace to only a few. They were people cut off since the beginning of the world, cut off essentially and not by bad luck or self-regarding choice, from the beatitude that is Augustine's name for happiness.

Aristotle has the further problem that excellence can only be sustained by habit. The excellence of your *praxis* entails that you are free, able to deliberate about proper goals and the best means for their attainment, able to make choices. "Man is the source and begetter of his actions as a father is of his children" [EN 3.1113b18]. But habits form your character, create your disposition to act in certain ways, become all but indistinguishable from natural capacities. You are responsible for your habits, says Aristotle, because they were initially voluntary as is any action arising from choice. As dispositions they are no longer voluntary; they can be changed, as indeed your nature can in fact be changed, but only with great difficulty [EN 7.1152a29–31]. This is the whole point, of course: habits of excellence are what save you from the allures of extremism. They are how you cure desire of its infinitizing proclivity. But this means that you become a slave of your habits and thus of the state that has trained you to behave that way and to find pleasure in doing so. How then do you differ from household slaves except that your master is the state rather than the head of the family? Is a noble deed done from habit really noble? It would seem that Aristotle has lost his end by his choice of means.

This, at least, is the problem he has bequeathed his successors, those who like him and often under his inspiration have seen human fulfillment as a function of social order. Take Jeremy Bentham, for instance.

He understands happiness in a rather simplistic way, as equivalent to "benefit, advantage, pleasure, good" [PML I.3]. What is in a person's interests is whatever adds to the quantity of these pleasures; the interest of the community is "the sum of the interests of the several members who compose it" [PML I.4]. The role of political government is to recognize that pleasure and pain, happiness and its denial, are our natural masters. Government therefore has a natural mandate to "rear the fabric of felicity by the hands of reason and of law" [PML I.1], which means by effectively implementing the principle of utility:

By the principle of utility is meant that principle which approves or disapproves of every action whatsoever [whether individual or governmental], according to the tendency which it appears to have to augment or diminish the happiness of the party whose interest is in question: or, what is the same thing in other words, to promote or to oppose that happiness. [PML I.2]

Bentham's community is less elitist than Aristotle's, its members related in merely additive fashion rather than organically, and its origin conventional rather than natural. But despite the differences, Bentham agrees with Aristotle that "felicity" involves a community in which government functions to enhance the opportunity of individuals to attain the best possible life, one marked by maximal fulfillment. "The business of government is to promote the happiness of the society, by punishing and rewarding" [PML VII.1].

Individuals are to be "made" to fashion their behavior in accord with this goal. Their happiness is achieved not only by their own natural pursuits of their own several pleasures but also by the hand of government. Pleasure is the final cause of human action. But it and especially its ever-present companion, pain, are also the efficient cause, the means by which that end can best be obtained [PML III.1]. In this instrumental role of shaping actions for the sake of obtaining happiness, pleasure and pain are termed "sanctions." The natural workings of our natural masters function as physical sanctions regulating our behavior. But when these natural workings are "purposely modified by the interposition of the will of any human being" [PML III.3], the sanctions are termed political, moral, or religious. The reason why you failed to do a certain thing may not be that the physical obstacles were too great but that a sermon on the wages of sin gave you pause or you were worried about public opinion or a court injunction restrained you. The results, however, are the same: pleasures or pains occur and you alter your behavior accordingly. The "powers of nature" can be reshaped by human purposes to serve human ends. These sovereign masters are thus readily made the docile servants of government, which means that government becomes the master of its citizens through its control of the powers of nature.

For every action or intended action, says Bentham, there is a motive that gives birth to it. No matter how complex the motives involved, they are always reducible to the desire for some prospective pleasure or the fear of some prospective pain [PML X.9]. All actions can therefore be catalogued in terms of the kinds of pleasures and pains people expect to experience by performing them; these actions in turn come to be associated with the sanctions appropriate to them. For instance, sexual activity is motivated by a desire to gratify the senses, but within the constraints delimited by physical sanctions; the desire to have a good name is motivated by the pleasures of social honor, which is formed by the moral sanctions effective in a given society.

Bentham's four sanctions, appropriately enough, are similar to the four dimensions of praxis. The physical sanction relates to the material substrate of action, your body and its organic functionings. The religious sanction has to do with final causes, with the ultimate end of attaining eternal salvation that underlies all the more proximate ends in life. The moral sanction is related to formal causation, to the formative societal attitudes and practices operationally at work in an actual life-situation. The political sanction has to do with efficient causes, with the edicts and enforcement powers required for the management of institutions. Each sanction thus shapes the contour of our praxis by directing its influence to a specific one of the fourfold conditions of that praxis. The four sanctions are stops that a government pulls out or pushes in on the organ of state to assure an ongoing harmony to the social fugue it is composing.

No motive is in itself good or bad nor therefore any action correlate to it. A given motive or action is compatible with or disrupts a society's aim at the happiness of the greatest number depending on its effects, which can vary tremendously from context to context. But if you develop the habit of engaging in actions that appear typically to have socially pernicious tendencies you can be said to intend them, to be motivated by the pleasures you find in those socially disruptive consequences. You have what Bentham calls a "mischievous" disposition. In contrast, if these intended tendencies are beneficial, your disposition is a "meritorious" one [PML XI.2–3]. "Standing tutelary motives" are thus those that tend "to restrain a man from *any* mischievous acts he may be prompted to engage in" [PML XI.30]. Chief among these motives are good will, the love of reputation, and a desire of amity.

Clearly, therefore, it is the task of government to encourage you in the exercise of standing tutelary motives, to help you develop a meritorious disposition. This is done by applying the available political sanctions, and the moral and religious ones as far as government can influence their application. These sanctions are applied whenever your actions have painful consequences for others but not for yourself, and where you might be tempted to their repetition and hence to a pattern of actions motivated by pernicious ends. The exercise of the sanctions causes pain and so is an evil, but if the result is "to augment the total happiness of the community," and there is no other less painful way to achieve that end, then it is justified [PML XIII.1]. Furthermore, the moral and religious sanctions, and obviously the physical, are too indeterminate. They cannot be depended on in specific situations to give the timely and appropriate penalties needed to inhibit pernicious and encourage beneficial motives. The political sanction of law alone is able to be "meted out in number, quantity, and value" with requisite specificity [PML XIV.26].

In ways that echo Aristotle, Bentham has characterized human beings as motivated by a wide range of desires, some physical some intellectual, some narrowly self-serving, some wide-visioned and altruistic. You have the capacity to draw your pleasures from any point or points on this spectrum and therefore to develop a disposition to act consistently out of motives conducive to the common weal. It is the "art of government" to educate the nation's youth to find their pleasures in socially beneficial ends and to exercise the political sanctions under its power so as to channel adult behavior in similar fashion. For Bentham, pleasure has become both the efficient and final cause of individual intentions and actions. Aristotle says that happiness, which is the final cause of human actions, differs from the accompanying pleasure, which can be at times a useful efficient cause but never a proper target at which to aim. But if excellence is a more noble ideal than felicity, nonetheless for both Bentham and Aristotle the ideal of a citizen's praxis requires nurture and sanction. It is a natural capacity that, to be realized, must become a social habit constantly subject to positive and to negative reenforcement. Societal law is both the pedagogue and policeman of virtue.

What Bentham implies John Stuart Mill in *Utilitarianism* makes explicit:

As between his own happiness and that of others, utilitarianism requires him [any agent] to be as strictly impartial as a disinterested and benevolent spectator.... As the means of making the nearest approach to this ideal, utility would enjoin, first, that laws and social arrangements should place the happiness, or (as speaking practically it may be called) the interest, of every individual, as nearly as possible in harmony with the interest of the whole; and secondly, that education and opinion, which have so vast a power over human character, should so use that power as to establish in the mind of every individual an indissoluble association between his own happiness and the good of the whole ... [so that] a direct impulse to promote the general good may be in every individual one of the habitual motives of action, and the sentiments connected therewith may fill a large and prominent place in every human being's sentient existence. [U 418–19]

Whatever the results of each individual's free, unregulated pursuit of happiness, it is not likely that the sum of these over the long run will be optimally advantageous to the community as a whole. Government will need through its laws and political arrangements to set limits on what is done, to herd the pursuits together in a manner sufficient for the creation or preservation of community harmony. Even more effectively, it will need to encourage the forces of education and social opinion to play an active role in nurturing persons of good will, in developing people whose disposition is to seek the good of the whole as their own good. To be assured of citizens loyal to the security and well-being of the state, government will also need to exercise directly its propaganda skills and its control of educational policy.

Mill recognizes both the necessity and the limitation of the use of these sanctions. The fear of punishment and the attraction of tangible and intangible rewards can shape behavior significantly. You can pass laws against racism, prohibit Jim Crow or apartheid practices, and the result may be a society in which people of all races are treated fairly. In the absence of the threat of sanctions, however, the racism would soon resurface. It would be far more effective were these external levers of influence to be internalized, made into "a feeling in our own mind: a pain, more or less intense, attendant on violation of duty," made, that is, into a conscience [U 431]. It is the function of government to assure that its citizens have developed a conscience that if present throughout the commonwealth would obviate the need altogether for external sanctions.

Mill is quick to note that a socially acquired conscience is nonetheless natural:

It is natural to man to speak, to reason, to build cities, to cultivate the ground, though these are acquired faculties. . . . [Likewise] the moral faculty, if not a part of our nature, is a natural outgrowth from it; capable, like them, in a certain small degree, of springing up spontaneously; and susceptible of being brought by cultivation to a high degree of development. [U 433–34]

But because what can be cultivated can be cultivated for ill as well as for good, and since the "force of early impressions" is a crucial instrument of cultivation, the acquiring of the right kind of conscience is fundamentally important. Governments, whole civilizations, can be evaluated by the measure of their effectiveness in educating citizens whose desire for "unity with our fellow-creatures" is primary. This feeling has a natural basis; therefore its development is not for the sake of an arbitrary, merely conventional, end. But the mandate to nurture this feeling is clear and imperative. That government governs best which governs by creating citizens whose acquired social conscience allows it to govern least.

Bentham by implication and Mill explicitly are rebelling against the sanguine belief of Adam Smith that individuals in the pursuit of their own several pleasures will produce results that are over the long run and for the most part beneficial to them all. A belief in the invisible hand, the wisdom of the free market, or a Leibnizian preestablished harmony is a belief that the natural flow of things can suffice to create social commensurabilities parallel to the ones extant throughout physical nature. The shipwreck of this belief upon the hard shoals of historical fact is what leads to the Utilitarian alternative, echoing Aristotle: nature must be perfected for this desired unity to emerge out of the cacophonous pluralism of desires, but it is not unnatural for that perfecting to take place.

Yet Utilitarianism only replaces one naive sanguineness by another. Is human nature really as tractable as Mill asserts? Are the flickering feelings of good will really capable of being fanned into the flames of good citizenry? Those rocky historical shoals give this claim no more harbor than the one it purports to replace. Even if this shaping of communal character were possible, what assurance do you or I have that the shapers will have the good of the whole in mind? Unless society has already trained leaders of good will, how can it have a government whose schools, laws, and *ethos* function to breed citizens of good will? "Who guards the guardians?" is a question that neither Bentham nor Mill can answer, nor for that matter Aristotle, who inherited the dilemma from Plato without resolving it.

It would seem the better course to fall back upon a more realistic, chastened strategy. Acknowledge the spiral of individual desiring, but acknowledge also that it can be controlled to some extent. Refrain from making anything normative out of this malleability. Grant that it is a natural capacity of the self to be so molded; were it not, the molding would be impossible. But there is given no special authority to any molding that might occur, for whatever anyone does is as natural an act of nurturing as what someone else might do. The security and well being of a community require social controls, imposed and internalized. It can function only if it has a centralizing agency with both the power and the authority to realize the general harmony necessary for that community's existence. But it is the effective praxis of that agency that makes it good or bad and not any appeal it might wish to make to a natural basis, end, mode, or means. The material, final, formal, and efficient causes at issue are, to put it candidly, artful and arbitrary. They are human artifacts for which their creators alone should be held responsible.

So argues Machiavelli. Desire always runs ahead of the resources available to it. Those who are benefiting by a given social arrangement "are inclined to think that they cannot hold securely what they possess unless they get more at others' expense." Those at whose expense were gained not only these further appropriations but the initial ones rise up against them either out of revenge or in the hope that they might "share in those riches and honours in regard to which they deem themselves to have been badly used by the other party" [D I.5].

Nature has so constituted men that, though all things are objects of desire, not all things are attainable; so that desire always exceeds the power of attainment, with the result that men are ill content with what they possess and their present state brings them little satisfaction. Hence arise the vicissitudes of their fortune. For, since some desire to have more and others are afraid to lose what they have already acquired, enmities and wars are begotten, and this brings about the ruin of one province and the exaltation of its rival. [D I.37]

This wickedness, this pursuit of one's own advantage, out of insecurity, fear, revenge, or whatever the motive, at the expense of others, is to be "taken for granted" in deciding what best to do in fashioning or enforcing societal rules. "Men never do good unless necessity drives them to it; but when they are too free to choose and can do just as they please, confusion and disorder become everywhere rampant" [D I.3]. The task of government, therefore, is to create the conditions that lead people to think they must of necessity do good, must act for the benefit of society instead of for their own benefit.

Machiavelli's strategies are no different from Bentham's or Aristotle's except that he presumes his goal to be an unnatural one. People are naturally and incorrigibly wicked, which is to say self-interested. This selfish desiring can be controlled but it cannot be eliminated; the cancer of divisiveness can be put into remission but it cannot be cured.

Machiavelli's notoriety rests on his advice to governments that are in the control of a single individual, a prince, and that are functioning in situations where "confusion and disorder" is most unfortunately "everywhere rampant." Under such conditions he recommends extreme measures for the sake of reestablishing social order and then seeing to its stable continuance. But Machiavelli prefers a republic to a tyranny, and yearns amid the hard realism of his counsels for a leader who might be able to fashion the conditions under which republican rule can flourish. Were they to have the leadership of prudent and just elected leaders, working within the embrace of laws designed to prevent pernicious and wicked behavior, the people could attain to a quality of life that is its own justification [D I.3]. But such governments, such societies, arise by chance and not by natural necessity; they flourish by the skill of their members and by good fortune; they perish when things go awry or when they are overtaken by natural calamities.

In the absence of a natural proclivity to desire the good of others, and in the absence of even the belief that community is a natural condition for humanity, the arts of government are free to function unconstrained. Neither the ruled nor the rulers can appeal beyond their existing effectiveness to some ideal in contrast to which that effectiveness can be judged inadequate or wrong. If it is the end of government to govern, by the sanctions at its disposal to effect a practical unity among the centrifugal pluralism of individual desires, then success is the sole authority. That government governs best that governs totally. Hobbes expresses it well:

The final cause, end, or design of men, who naturally love liberty, and dominion over others, in the introduction of that restraint upon themselves, in which we see them live in commonwealths, is the foresight of their own preservation, and of a more contented life thereby. . . . Which is not to be had from the law of nature. For the laws of nature, as justice, equity, modesty, mercy, and, in sum, doing to others, as we would be done to, of themselves, without the terror of some power, to cause them to be observed, are contrary to our natural passions, that carry us to partiality, pride, revenge, and the like. And covenants, without the sword, are but words, and of no strength to secure a man at all. . . . The only way to erect such a common power, as may be able to defend them from the invasion of foreigners, and the injuries of one another, . . . is, to confer all their power and strength upon one man, or upon one assembly of men, that may reduce all their wills by plurality of voices, unto one will.[2]

Bare unadorned power, exercised for the sake of social unity as its own end, is vividly described by Sartre in the *Critique of Dialectical Reason*. Groups, he says, are formed in response to external threats, a multiplicity of persons finding in their common danger a commonality of purpose. The problem is how to sustain that unity in the absence of the threat [CDR 428–44]. You and I and these others, as comrades sharing in the same attempt to secure our lives and our well-being against an encroaching enemy, have resolved to act as one. Our loyalty to one another, our promise to subordinate individual purposes to the one larger purpose that has brought us together, is evoked and concretized by the exigency of our situation. We covenant[3] with one another, implicitly or explicitly, to remain the group we have become, recognizing that not to do so would mean the loss of the power our commonality provides to resist what threatens us. But as the exigency dissipates, this resolve seems to be revealed for what it truly is: merely the good intentions of a moment, merely promises that become irrelevant with the passing of the occasion that inspired them.

A covenant, however, is not merely a good intention. It is a commitment that you make to all the others that you will remain loyal to them as they, reciprocally, have agreed to remain loyal to you. When you pledge your loyalty to me and to these others, you find we have anticipated you by already pledging to you our own loyalties. Consequently in the moment when you freely offer to remain loyal, you find yourself confronted by the demand that you do so [CDR 428]. Any social covenant must assume a coercive form in order to assure its members that no one of them will renege on a commitment to which all of them must be faithful if they are, each of them, to survive.

Everyone's freedom demands the violence of all against it and against that of any third party as its defence against itself (as a free power of secession and alienation). To swear is to say, as a common individual: you must kill me if I secede. And this demand has no other aim than to install Terror within myself as a free defence against the fear of the enemy (at the same time as reassuring me about the third party who will be confirmed by the same Terror). [CDR 431]

The freedom of each requires the violence of all against each.

Sartre's notion of the Terror is Hobbes's Sovereign not yet concretized in a given individual. Sartre teaches us what the real basis of the authority is that a sovereign or a prince or a legislator has. The authority of government is its mandate to be the instrument by which society enforces the implicit recognition by its citizens that their individual fulfillment depends upon the simultaneous fulfillment of their fellow citizens. It is through the praxis of those others that the capacity of the individual to be genuinely fulfilled has been given the resources that make its realization possible.

You have chosen this group as the general reality within which you can then select one or another specific route to your own individual ends. In choosing this group, you have chosen to accept the conditions under which those individualizing options are possible, including the constraints inherent in them and including the ultimate constraint that the social reality itself must be preserved. Community is not only a tool for you to use in obtaining the objects of your desire, it is also the source of the context that makes them possibilities for desiring.

Oakeshott echoes this insight in his discussion of civic association as the implicit covenant of a people regarding the ground rules under which they will conduct their actions *inter homines.* Pursuing differing and even incompatible goals, they nonetheless agree to do so in a common manner. Although disagreeing on ends, they agree in regard to acceptable means. The practices, the subjective forms of interaction, are what give a society its functional unity. Oakeshott proposes this understanding as an alternative to the modern totalitarian state in which functional unity requires control of ends as well as means, turning the state into an "enterprise association" [HC 114] that, like a business corporation or an army, is organized for the sake of a common end, in these instances financial profit or military victory.

But Sartre, like Hobbes, thinks of groups as arising out of conditions of extremity in which one common end takes precedence over all the others: that of survival. So the practices of the civic association permit its citizens the freedom to pursue their private ends, but on the condition that practices which secure the continued existence of the group are always preemptive.

In wanting the opportunity to follow our own ends, you and I have committed ourselves to the authority of what makes that opportunism possible. Therefore we have acknowledged its right to do whatever is required to assure its continuance. The Terror is an hyperbole for the legitimate use of power against even those who give it its legitimacy. As Hobbes made clear, the power of government is absolute so long as it functions as a government, as the means by which the condition for all your means to happiness are realized. The formal conditions of praxis, we should not forget, are specifications of the underlying material conditions that are composed most importantly of uncognized cultural habits and attitudes. The right of the Terror is the claim made upon the ends and energies of individuals, upon the exercise of efficient causative agencies to achieve sought-after determinate outcomes, upon the traditions and prejudices of a culture as they function to delimit the means available to individuals to form ends and to form strategies for their realization.

We had thought that the inherent self-aggrandizement of desiring could be rescued from its self-destructiveness by disciplining it, and we found the agency of that discipline in community. But discipline is intrusive. Even though the noble and good-willed citizen is a possible expression of human nature, an ideal to be sought above all others, that result is no more natural than many another product of the cultivating arts. Excellence is a highly problematic quality; for it to bloom everywhere among a nation's citizenry depends on who does the cultivating. We soon came to realize that these cultivators must themselves exemplify what it is their task to make.

And so we find ourselves mired in the Platonic conundrum of who guards our guardians. How can the absolute authority needed to do the work of creating good citizens be made commensurable with the finite, fallible individuals who must necessarily be its agents? Plato dreamed of philosophers become kings and Machiavelli hoped against hope that a magnanimous monarch might arise who would then create the conditions for a genuine republic. For both, as for Aristotle and the Utilitarians as well, the guardian who would not need guarding was not a *deus ex machina.* Society itself would train leaders with the requisite skill. But neither Syracuse nor Macedon, nor Florence nor England, could manage to rear a leader who was both wise and effective, both willing and able to act unselfishly, nobly, fully for the good of the whole. Even if the education of a candidate for this role might promise an eventual flowering of virtuous leadership, the conferring of the power was sure to nip the virtue in the bud. In Lord Acton's chilling observation, power would corrupt them and absolute power would corrupt them absolutely.

Sartre insists that, whether you like it or not, the social good must be grounded in some absolute. Contemporary raptures regarding the liberating experience of polymorphous creativity and the joyful conversation of guileless relativists are naive. Either the group by covenant creates its own absolute source of unity or the group fragments into factions vulnerable to the encroachments of another group. Either we are our own source of our Terror or others will impose it upon us from without.

External imposition is the best that the hedonists can offer, but either the absolute authority turns out to be some Nero imposing his arbitrary narrow ends upon a world instrumentalized for his benefit, or the arbitrary will is that of a god, the Ancient in Years or the White Rider bringing down fire from heaven, a harrowing of the world differing from absolute totalitarian subjugation only by the assurance that the savior is divine and benevolent rather than merely human.

Sartre points a way out of this blind alley in which we find ourselves entrapped, this impossible choice between a tyrant acting like a god and a god acting like a tyrant. The Terror is not about a government imposing its coercive will upon the general populace, nor is it about some individual Johannes doing so. The Terror is not an external imposition but instead an imposition of its creators, a free choice constraining freedom in the very act of realizing it: freedom disciplining itself. To understand this we must turn away from the static ahistorical standpoint into which we have slipped. It is not enough that we should juxtapose claims and arguments from a variety of different philosophers as though they were contemporaries in a timeless, situationless conversation. We must ask a historical question. How do communities arise such that the Terror comes to them as a discipline they freely embrace? It is only in the historicity of communities that we can hope to find what we are looking for: a praxis fashioning a cooperative, enduring, self-sufficient form of human fulfillment.

In the beginning, says Ibn Khaldûn, there was the Bedouin.[4] These desert nomads, living at a bare subsistence level, must eke out their existence in accord with three natural human necessities: the need for food, for aggressiveness in its pursuit, and for defense against the aggressiveness of animals and other persons also seeking that food [M 1.1]. Under desert conditions, all three needs require cooperation if they are to be fulfilled. So the regimen of bare survival is not a Hobbesian state of nature, the war of all against all. Instead, it is communal, the banding together of individuals to achieve mutually what they cannot achieve separately. Society in this minimal form is not the result of a social compact but a natural given; the banding together is that without which there would be no Bedouin, no human existence whatsoever.

These factors—an end in view, the willingness to strive after it, and a strategy for doing so—combine to procure success. The feedback is positive; success breeds success. The Bedouin praxis results in an improved way of life, one that involves more than minimal fulfillment of needs and thus involves the control of territory to improve defense and the development of agriculture to improve the supply and certainty of food. Hence towns and cities are founded; civilization emerges out of barbarism [M 2.1].

For Ibn Khaldûn, the soil and sustaining nutrient for this growth is what he calls "group feeling": the affection members of the Bedouin group have for one another, their emotional solidarity, their sense that glory is a common property they share, their willingness to fight and to die for one another [M 3.1; 3.11]. This feeling is religious in its intensity, presumably divine in its origin and ascetic in its disregard of self-interest or material gain. Without its "religious colouring," group feeling is merely family loyalty. With it, individual envy and jealousy disappear, hearts are united in the quest for a single objective, the many become as one [M 3.5].

Remember that Bedouins are creatures of the desert, accustomed to adversity. Their desert toughness, their habits of rapacity, their unruliness and lack of restraint [M 3.11–12], when put at the service of a group inspired by a common aim, make them seem to opponents as a beast of prey [M 2.2]. Under a leader who is a model for them of these qualities, claiming nothing for himself exclusively but always seeking the benefit of the whole [M 3.15], the group is unstoppable and its success assured. And so "Man seeks first the bare necessities. Only after he has obtained the bare necessities does he get to comforts and luxuries. Therefore urbanization is found to be the goal to which the Bedouin aspires" [M 2.3].

Ibn Khaldûn differs from Aristotle in finding the *polis* to be a natural outcome of the desires of pre-civilized peoples rather than the given form of human community. But this temporal difference makes all the difference, because this means that for Ibn Khaldûn societal unity precedes both logically and historically its political rationalization into laws and classes and the other institutionalized differences characteristic of sedentary communities. And that unity is emotional: impassioned, revolutionary, self-sacrificial. You learn right practice by doing things and by emulating what others do; on this Ibn Khaldûn and Aristotle agree. But for Ibn Khaldûn the desire to act and to imitate must come first, and so the love of the group by its members must precede their education as its citizens. That love cannot be taught but only given shape. The selfishness of an individual and the self-interest of an elite, which plague the efforts of a society to secure its members' well-being, are symptoms of something lost, not something needing to be attained. Civic loyalty is not the result of disciplining selfish passions. Natural, untamed passion is what is communal; its taming is what gives rise to selfishness, jealousy, and all the other dangers to the *polis.* Group feeling is rooted deeply within the material subsoil of a community. How human beings naturally and spontaneously express themselves is in a cooperative manner; it is only within the milieu of that expression that civilizations can arise. It is selfishness that is unnatural. Natural passion is the mother rather than the enemy of society.

Sartre is after the same point in his account of how groups emerge [CDR 345–404]. His paradigm is the revolutionary moment in human affairs when a new group is forged by the white heat of a situation in which the passivity of many separate persons is being hammered by an external power they each perceive as threatening their own existence. Groups comes to historical presence incrementally, accidentally, by stealth, and in a thousand ways other than cataclysmically. Yet the apocalyptic urgency of social crisis, the intensity of revolutionary fervor, provides a concrete approximation to a pure instance of group formation. Both the emotional power and the contextual opportunities necessary for the creation of a new societal reality, one able to transform existing pluralities into a fresh and decisive unity, are immediately visible for analysis in such times of crisis. As in geology, so also in cultural analysis: the more intense a process the less it is determined by other processes, and therefore the more its fundamental characteristics become transparent to inquiry.

This was Ibn Khaldûn's approach also, but Sartre's paradigm makes the challenging adversity human rather than inanimate, an opposing purpose rather than a material condition. We can follow Toynbee in noting that the former challenge is more primordial and the latter more difficult to transcend, but what is important about both is that they are the occasions but not the sufficient causes for what arises to confront and master them. Sartre no more than Ibn Khaldûn can predict the emergence of social novelty, but he can describe it and offer it as the evidence we seek that the emergence of community serves as the reality wherein a belief in the possibility of human fulfillment is first born.

Sartre's revolutionary paradigm is the set of events that culminate in the storming of the Bastille, events that mark the emergence into history of a social reality powerful enough to disrupt fundamentally the cultural fabric of eighteenth-century France and Europe and to offer the world a new hope of how happiness might be attained. The crowds of Paris until July 1789 were mere clusters of individuals, restless and angry over the conditions of their existence but powerless to do anything except suffer a repression seemingly inexorable. When outbreaks of violence lead Louis XVI to deploy his troops around the outskirts of Paris, however, the social situation begins to alter. The appearance of a force directly threatening the safety of any Parisian requires from each of them simultaneously some kind of response. Each citizen acts to save himself from the encircling troops, but since the goal of any one citizen is precisely that of all the other citizens, similarity of purpose blends into identity of purpose. The recurrently same common enemy spontaneously evokes a common response. The I becomes We, and in the fall of the Bastille the We steps forth into history as a new reality newly to be reckoned with.

An analysis of this complex event discloses two conditions necessary to the formation of new groups. The first derives from the basic characteristic of individual praxis, the radical self-interest that comprises its desiring—desired polarity. The object of your desire is always relative to your quite specific desiring, its value is of your making and all else is valued insofar as it serves the attainment of that desired end. Different individuals thus have what seem to be unredeemably differing purposes, and so the multifariousness of the ends they pursue entails a seemingly unavoidable cacophony in their actions, a clash of uncoordinated and incompatible efforts. Even a single individual displays considerable virtuosity in the aims and ends of daily action, aims often at odds with one another and pursued over time with conspicuous inconsistency. The sin of incommensurability would seem to be an original sin from which there can be no salvation.

Occasionally the aims of a number of people prove to be similar, however, usually by accident but occasionally by design. The result is actions that are momentarily coordinate and compatible with each other. Yet these parallelisms soon vanish, for the purposes that create them are ever-changing, routinely compromised by other aims, constantly obscured or thwarted under the influence of the aims and actions of others. As a result, it is clear that a challenge to the accepted, familiar patterns of behavior and purpose within a social milieu will require uncustomary responses if it is to be mastered.

If the challenge is widely spread throughout that milieu, a masterful response must be widespread as well. In a situation of social crisis such as that posed by Louis' military encirclement of Paris, not only is there a challenge demanding of every Parisian some sort of response but the challenge poses an immediate, inescapable threat to the well-being of each of them, even to their very continued existence as individuals. Other concerns, other plans and pursuits, fade in importance before the preemptive intensity of this one threatening event. Just as iron filings are rearranged in the presence of a magnet, so the chaos of social diversity is transformed by the power of this external force. The divergent purposes of a hundred thousand Parisians are aligned in a common orientation due to conditions created by one king's purposes. Each individual is consumed single-mindedly with the task of finding some way to remove the danger threatening him or her. Everywhere throughout the magnetic field of the threat this same single-mindedness appears, everywhere the same desperate purpose seeks the same outcome [CDR

353–54]. So individual passions, brought into parallel, compose the social conditions prerequisite to the emergence of new social realities. The bridge from I to We is constructed from materials milled into uniform components by the hard-edged blade of danger.

The immediacy of the danger, the way in which it calls into question all habitual responses and purposings, invests the situation with emotional intensity. Action is required, and the social structures ready-to-hand for action are quite naturally the resource most likely to be utilized. Whether your action is to stay and fight or to flee, to resist or to surrender, you are likely to find in those around you the model for your own response. The urgency of your situation requires that you do something and yet precludes the habitual responses appropriate to routine times. Unable to think out what to do, you turn for help, unreflectively and gratefully, to the behavior of others. You imitate your contemporaries, take flight on the heels of their fleeing feet, stop and stand your ground as their turning turns you with them to face the pursuing enemy [CDR 369–71]. The intensity resulting from this drastic disruption in the familiar landscape of everyone's praxis requires immediate inventiveness and so fosters openness to whatever implicit or explicit guidance others might provide.

This intense need for help puts into play the second of the factors crucial to the emergence of new groups. In turning to others for guidance, you find their actions recommending that you do what you are already doing. You take your cue from those who are taking their cues in turn from you. Each of you discovers yourself obeying commands from others before they have even been uttered, proclaiming orders already carried out by those you would command [CDR 379–81]. In this manner, parallelism resolves into mutual role modeling. What is similar becomes interchangeable, the actions and purposes of each sensed as incarnations of the aims and deeds of all. Everyone is everywhere throughout the environment of response. What you individually are doing is how we collectively are at work; what we together are seeking is the goal toward which you are single-handedly struggling. In the spontaneity of immediate and free responses to crisis, if carried out within a terrain aligned by similarity, one purpose emerges that many individuals hold in common, and their actions are coordinated into one concerted effort as they attempt together to resolve their crisis by eliminating its cause.

The transforming of similar into same is the alchemical formula we are searching for. According to Sartre, the birth of a group involves a reordering of experience in which what we experienced once as separate realities is henceforth experienced as a single reality, in which independence is reinterpreted as interdependence and in which connecting ties rather than distinguishing ones are emphasized. This shift occurs because in the charged atmosphere of crisis nothing can be taken for granted: everything must be accounted for and understood with respect to its relevance for the resolution so fervently sought.

Sartre, following Malraux, characterizes these occasions as apocalyptic [CDR 357]. He provides more than a vivid metaphor. Experience is radically defined by its ends whenever established purposes are swept aside and new ones struggle for our allegiance. With accepted forms in disarray, we are thrown back on unformed feelings and the urge toward finality to which they give rise. Final causation is radicalized and becomes the overweening source for a meaning to your praxis. Except by reference to some envisioned Moment when desire's fulfillment will be securely grasped, you no longer know how to act or what will work. In moments of crisis when the hopes for fulfillment which you have been taught from birth and have come to accept by habit as sufficing for your practices are collapsing all around you, you recognize this fact of your human nature clearly. Your way of dealing with the world becomes suddenly and forcefully one in which you explicitly characterize things solely in term of their relevance to your newly emerging purposes. All your needs are defined by the ends they would hope to accomplish, all objects by the deeds for which they can be instruments, all persons by what they do for the group or fail to do.

As a Parisian citizen threatened by the king's encircling army, your world has now been defined by one overwhelming purpose: the eradication of the royal menace to your safety. If you flee down some street, you take this deed as being a defensive measure against the threatening enemy. If you hide behind an overturned cart it is because you take it as a barricade from which to initiate a further move in the strategy of defense you are engaged in pursuing. If you interact with me, helping me or receiving my help, it is because you see me as assisting the success of this venture. The streets of Paris are redefined in terms of the degree of access they provide the soldiers advancing toward us. Walks in previously familiar sectors of the city are transformed from recreational excursions into reconnaissance missions. The mere contiguity of persons is made over into the solidarity of a new-formed group.

People who were previously no more than contemporaries, who shared the same world but with no sense of this having any significance beyond temporal juxtaposition, have quickly and dramatically become confederates in a common enterprise, collaborators for the sake of a common end. A new purpose for action has cleared away all the old lines of confluence and fusion that once had given meaning and direction to the present. The contours of the map have been completely redrawn. Things have new names appropriate to their new uses, and possibilities have become visible in the light of this new sunrise which before, because invisible, were thought not to exist at all.

The reorganization of the present requires that past and future be reorganized as well. The genealogy of the emergence of the present needs tracing. Its explanation and therefore its meaning resides in the account of the events that gave rise to it. Until this present emerged there was no need for anyone to take seriously your hopes and dreams or mine. They were mere fantasies, private daydreams, our opiates. Now they are the skein of raw possibilities from which we are weaving the fabric of this new world, the strong fibers of explanation and significance by which what we weave is woven into the long-enduring tapestry of human history. Insofar as our present is truly new, its emergence a surprise and a wonder, to that extent the weaving could never have occurred in advance. Nor could friends have been anticipated and enemies warned against, sacred places protected and the habits of victory practiced. Old friends and ancient enemies, hallowed shrines and folk heroes, are fashioned by the present as it makes for itself its own appropriate past. Our traditions are retroactive creations. The predecessors of the present are thus not merely those *Homo sapiens* who have lived and died at some earlier point in time's progression, but persons whose acts have made possible that present and the values it embodies or who have opposed it. Those who are irrelevant cease to have a proper place within the intelligible scheme of things.

In like manner the future is defined in terms of successors: those whose deeds will fashion a line of perpetuation beyond present achievement and perhaps even beyond present purposes. This person and that may vie for the right to lead us into that future, but both know it as their and our future, a region of real possibilities distinct from the daydreams and hopes of those whose lives and purposes have been rendered irrelevant.

Your immediate intuition of brute fact is, as Whitehead says, the appeal to Caesar [PR 174]. It provides the court of last resort in any dispute regarding truth or value. The sense you have of what is true or false, right or wrong, accurate or appropriate, useful or graceful, rests in this confidence. But the brutality of fact does not reside in its transcendence to human concerns. Facts are always artifacts, fashioned by the actions of persons who for the sake of some transcending aim have shaped the protean fluidities of their experience into a world of feeling and thought, of past realities, present challenges, and future opportunities for which those facts are unforgivingly essential.

In the apocalypse of history, human praxis is a *poiesis.* Our doings make a world and that world defines the environment that interprets, constrains, and lures forth our further doings and makings. Everything important, everything fundamental, everything intractable is born along with the groups whose purposes fashion for us the very notions of facticity, importance, and possibility by which we live. The act by which a new group steps onto the stage of history is simultaneously the creation of a new stage and a new history. The apocalypse for which Daniel longed is now. The new heaven of your desiring, in which what you want is what you have, has come down to earth to dwell among us. And the sea shall be no more.

Yet this Moment, too, is only momentary. Ibn Khaldûn gives a Bedouin group four generations from its triumphal emergence to its collapse [M 2.14]. The reasons, moreover, are not fortuitous; the Moment does not fail to be sustained because of some unfortunate historical accident, some miscalculation by a leader or some natural calamity. It is not even that the accidental is necessary, in that a society like any organism is obviously difficult to sustain and so the eventual collapse of its complex accomplishment all but inevitable. Rather, argues Ibn Khaldûn, we must realize that the reason why a society perishes is its success. The Moment of fulfillment undermines itself; it creates the conditions of its demise. Fulfillment as a communally achieved and permanently secured reality is not accidentally but essentially an impossibility.

The achievement of the group is to have created conditions for existence that go beyond the constraints of bare subsistence.

When a nation has gained the upper hand... , its prosperity and well-being grow. People become accustomed to a great number of things. From the necessities of life and a life of austerity, they progress to the luxuries and a life of comfort and beauty. They come to adopt the customs and enjoy the conditions of their predecessors. Luxuries require development of the customs necessary to produce them. People then also tend toward luxury in food, clothing, furnishings and household goods. They take pride in such things and vie with other nations in delicacies, gorgeous raiment, and fine mounts. Every new generation wants to surpass the preceding one in this respect, and so it goes right down to the end of the dynasty. [M 3.10]

Luxury is what you were seeking: a milieu of assured objects for your desirings. Having gotten what you sought, your enjoyment of it becomes routine. You become accustomed to having your wants readily fulfilled. With the change of generations, this way of life has become habitual; the people do not even remember that it had been otherwise.

The accustomed becomes custom and then becomes the natural order of things. The skills needed to overcome the obstacles to satisfying desire are not those needed to exploit the possibilities of that satisfactory situation once it has been attained. Indeed, how can the skills of adversity be developed and polished except under conditions of adversity? In the urbanized, sedentary world of the victor the qualities of the Bedouin are not simply out of place: they are impossible.

The habits of luxury are not those of desirelessness, however. New conditions breed new needs, needs for more and also more subtle luxuries. At the same time, management of the stable community now made a reality requires a leadership cadre that exercises authority for the wider group. Power gravitates to that cadre, which uses it, while still serving the general good, to further its own interests as well. The experience of endless luxury thus involves a double spiral. First, the people generally become lazy, expecting as their natural right what their parents struggled to wrest from the resistances of nature or of a prior regime, and expecting more and more of it. Second, a power elite authorized to acquire these resources is separated from the mass of people; in attempting to meet the general demand, it manages to give its own demands priority. To satisfy this double demand, the territories of the community must be expanded as its immediately available resources are expended, and the people must be taxed more and more to equip the elite to carry out its mission and to permit it to satisfy its own increasingly special needs. Taxation, imposed by a few to their own benefit, is resented; the authority of the elite is increasingly in its armies and not in its dreams.

One other thing is happening as well. The second generation is at least aware by its own direct experience of those powerful group feelings that gave energy and vision to the founding heroes of their community. The sons may not be possessed by that same savage fervor; they are too civilized to display such untamed emotion. But they grew up surrounded by it; it was the atmosphere of the burgeoning culture in which they learned to be adults. The sons of the sons, however, know of these founders and their passionate purposes only by hearsay. It is for them solely a matter of tradition: stories told to them by bards who had the story told to them by those who were its firsthand witnesses. The third generation is loyal to its origins only by an imitation of an imitation of the original. And as for the fourth generation, any member of its leadership

is inferior to the preceding ones in every respect. Its member has lost the qualities that preserved the edifice of its glory. He despises those qualities. He imagines that the edifice was not built through application and effort. He thinks that it was something due his people from the very beginning by virtue of the mere fact of their descent, and not something that resulted from group effort and individual qualities. For he sees the great respect in which he is held by the people, but he does not know how that respect originated and what the reason for it was. He imagines that it is due to his descent and nothing else. [M 2.14]

And so collapse comes inexorably. The group feeling that gave solidarity to the people and thus their power to effect change has been repudiated, taken to be an embarrassment or even to be the enemy of their virtues. The society is thus divided into interest groups that give more credence to their parochial desires than to the good of the whole and are willing to use force to secure those limited ends. They have exhausted their resources in attempting to meet their ever-increasing demands for luxury. They have lost their sense of purpose, taking their goals as givens, replacing vision and hope with self-satisfied complacence. Efficient, formal, material, and final causes have all been transformed from the sufficient conditions for desire's triumph to those for its demise. Unwittingly, the desert Bedouins have become decadent city persons, their nation defenseless in every sense against the upsurge of some new Bedouin group seeking to realize the mutual fulfillment of their quite different dreams.

The various failed attempts to discipline desire that this chapter has explored can usefully be summarized by Illustration 3.1. They have all led to the same cyclical result. That civilizations rise and fall is an obvious if dolorous truth. That they fall because they rise, that their virtues become their vices, is an ironic reading of human history. The gods destroy those whom they favor by granting them their wishes. This is the argument championed by Oswald Spengler in his distinction between culture, the originative and creative phase of a people's history, and civilization, the phase of mechanistic stultification and decline. Susanne Langer also argues along these same lines. Every culture is uniquely defined by the form of the questions it asks, the way it determines what are to be the problems it must address. The "generative ideas" or "motive concepts" [PNK 8] that give rise to this way of seeing things, to this *Weltanschauung,* are expressions of the deepest of human emotions. How a person is related to others, to the circumferencing world, to his own birth and death, are the great, terrifying questions of life. A culture's generative ideas formulate those questions in some way, offering thereby an orientation toward meanings that will answer the curiosity and concern.

**Illustration 3.1 Conditions of Self and Society**

| | material | final | formal | efficient |
|---|---|---|---|---|
| | material | final | formal | efficient |
| **Augustine** | earthly city | heavenly city | faith: moral | selflessness |
| **Aristotle** | | | | |
|   individual | health, money, good family | happiness | excellence, virtue | desire for excellence |
|   society | male elite | self-sufficiency | good laws | good govern-ment educa-tion |
| **Bentham** | | | | |
|   individual | pleasure need nonpain need | felicity maximum/ minimum | meritorious disposition | tutelary motives |
|   sanctions | physical | religious | moral | political |
|   society | all persons | most happiness most number | principle of utility | sanctions |
| **Mill** | all persons | qualitative | educated | conscience |
| **Machiavelli** | all persons | stable republic | clever leader (monarch) | selfish desires |
| **Sartre** | | | | |
|   en fusion | incommensur-able pur-poses | apocalyptic new group | threat from externals | spontaneous role models |
|   group | all persons participants | sustained old group | covenant | Terror |
| **Hobbes** | state of nature | Leviathan stable state | social contract | Sovereign |
| **Ibn Khaldûn** | | | | |
|   Bedouins | subsistence necessities | civilized sufficiency | group feeling | aggressiveness asceticism |
|   cities | luxuries | increasing luxuries | elite/mass conflicts | complacence no discipline |

The formulation, however, is not in words, at least not at first. It is in activities, in gestures and behaviors that function as "presentational symbols" able to express primary felt values. A bodily movement associated with an event felt to be important, perhaps because of its impact on an individual's or group's survival, becomes associated with that feeling; in making the movement, the event and the feelings it evoked are recalled and re-felt. The movement thus becomes a symbol for something of special significance. The action does not simply point to or represent that event in question or those feelings, although it does both. But it takes hold of the reality once felt as significant, and thereby brings to presence the meanings that give answer to the terrors of the unknown, uncertain universe. Such gestures, formalized and extended, become ritual. Images function in the same way as actions; extended into fantasies and stories they eventuate in myths.

Says Langer,

A rite regularly performed is the constant reiteration of sentiments toward "first and last things"; it is not a free expression of emotions, but a disciplined rehearsal of "right attitudes." ... [And, similarly, myth] is a recognition of natural conflicts, of human desire frustrated by nonhuman powers, hostile oppression, or contrary desires; it is a story of birth, passion, and defeat by death which is man's common fate. Its ultimate end is not wishful distortion of the world, but serious envisagement of its fundamental truths; moral orientation, not escape. [PNK 153,176]

The generative ideas of a culture, in short, are ways of organizing experience in a meaningful fashion, expressed in myths and rituals so that the very asking of the question of meaning reaches through the most profound human emotions to grasp the ultimate realities that ground that meaning.

This portion of Langer's argument is akin to Eliade's. A culture senses itself through such symbolic orderings as specially rooted in the nature of things and specially oriented toward what is of primary significance. It is thereby empowered to activity: intellectual, artistic, and practical. Its quest to understand more fully, to express more profoundly, and to fashion more permanently is an effort to find increasingly adequate forms for symbolizing its sense of these fundamental realities and the relation of individuals and the culture to them. And so it flourishes.

But, Langer argues, any generative idea has its limits since it is just one way of seeing, just a partial ordering of things. As the culture gains a more and more explicit, a more "discursive" or scientific articulation of reality, it will begin to bump up against those limits. In recognizing its symbols to be partial, the culture will become sensitive to the difference between the language of understanding and the objective world it seeks to represent. It will increasingly encounter "unanswerable puzzles" that threaten its confidence in the certainty and clarity of its basic assumptions. It will then seek to substitute "reasoned belief" for uncritical feeling as the test of truth. Facts, not feelings, will be taken as the proper referent for symbols. People will know more than they ever knew before and they will be able to articulate it with far greater precision, but this knowledge and this speech will be increasingly trivial because divorced from their feelings and so cut off from the sources of life's meaningfulness.

Because Langer sees this rationalization of symbols as a "natural tendency" for humans [PNK 270], she concludes that cultures by means of their own vital quest for adequate symbolic transformation of experience destroy that vitality by creating modes of symbolization that separate people from the realities that, as felt, are the sources of their vitality. Formative instrumentalities for action must be hewn from the material bedrock of a culture if collective ends are to be secured, but in doing so the techniques are separated from the feelings of shared significance that give them their authority. The society is left with techniques no longer constrained by the foundational collective values of tradition. The will of the gods no longer controlling the conditions of their use, the wills of tyrants serve as substitutes and an uncaring populace acquiesces. A culture dies of its own success.

In the contemporary idiom of a science fiction novel, A Canticle for Leibowitz, Walter Miller expresses this vividly in a story of the future rise of a successor civilization to our own, its flourishing, and its eventual destruction. Religious faith, incarnated by us as love, lived out in lives of humility and service to others in a time racked by widespread suffering and political instability, fosters the qualities requisite for the emergence of genuine community. Cooperation among persons, their concern for one another, for their common well-being, is a powerful milieu for improving the conditions of their existence. Experience is coordinated and found to be mutually enhancing, specialized skills developed and their fruits shared, and all of this preserved as knowledge passed on by informal and formal modes of education. Love is the womb of community and of knowledge. And knowledge brings power, the power to master the resources of nature, to sustain and augment the achievements of community. Peace and prosperity are at last obtained. But this well-being secured by power breeds greed. It sets loose the germs of self-glorification, envy, divisiveness, as people place their own welfare ahead of all other virtues. Their sense of community dies and then their society is destroyed as factions use their powers for selfish ends.

From need through faith to love, and thereby to knowledge and to power, which leads to the satisfaction of need: and thence to the destruction of love in the firestorm of self-love; consequently, since this means the destruction of community, to the loss of knowledge and power also. Amid these ruins faith can once more sow its seeds of love. Desire, disciplined by love and so succeeding, destroys love and so destroys itself.

"Are we helpless?" questions one of Miller's characters,

Are we doomed to do it again and again and again? Have we no choice but to play the Phoenix in an unending sequence of rise and fall? Assyria, Babylon, Egypt, Greece, Carthage, Rome, the Empires of Charlemagne and the Turk. Ground to dust and plowed with salt. Spain, France, Britain, America—burned into the oblivion of the centuries. And again and again and again. Are we doomed to it, Lord, chained to the pendulum of our own mad clockwork, helpless to halt its swing? [CL 245]

The answer is yes, the clockwork is inevitable:

To minimize suffering and to maximize security were natural and proper ends of society and Caesar. But when they became the only ends, somehow, and the only basis of law—a perversion. Inevitably, then, in seeking only them, we found only their opposites: maximum suffering and minimum security. [CL 305]

So the hedonistic dilemma reappears. The shift from an individual to a communal context, from the rampant desiring of a solitary individual to desire pursued within the disciplining limits of the group, has not given us a way off the horns of desiring's dilemma. You and I as individuals were caught in a cycle of desiring-desired. The Moment so strenuously sought would, no sooner gained, slip through our fingers, perishing in the very act of being possessed. The tasks of replenishment recurred endlessly. The Moment was always ahead of us or behind us, a goal or memory, never more than fleetingly the full, overflowing content of an enduring present.

The only practical solution seemed to be one that privileged a few, or a single self, at the expense of others. The world of other selves and things could be instrumentalized to your or my own advantage. But even such selfishness proved ineffective, for the satisfaction of needs resulted not in satiation but in the creation of needs of a different kind. Desiring's desire proved to be infinitizing, insatiable, inevitably outrunning in Malthusian fashion the capacities of the world to satisfy it. The desired was always inferior to the demands of what desired it. Mysticism and apocalypticism sought to resolve this particular difficulty by infinitizing the world either through identifying the self with its totality or by replacing its mundane resource with a new earth as resourceful as Eden in its power to match need with needed.

But we are not the Whole and the Endtime is not our time. We thus redirected our efforts, searching for a solution in the regions of temporality to a dilemma posed by temporality. You and I sought the disciplining of desire's insatiability in and by the community. Yet discipline required a disciplinarian, and we found that this seemed to mean that some elite would need to be authorized to create, apply, interpret, and inculcate the rules in terms of which the untamed inclinations of the desiring self could be canalized into the other-regarding virtues of civilized existence. Separate is never equal, however, and therefore the identifying of an elite seemed to mean only a new version of the rejected idea that a few might be satisfied at the expense of others. The only way for the guardians not to need guarding, for a special role not to become special privilege, was for that leadership to be already virtuous, already paragons of the qualities that community requires. But only a perfect community could foster such counsels of perfection. The guardians needed, impossibly, to be products of what they were commissioned to make possible.

The one route out of this dead end seemed to be to find in the history of a community precisely that requisite ideal situation. Perhaps the division into the few and the many is a corruption of community and not its prerequisite. The deduction of such a originating solidarity proved elusive and illusory, however, for even were it to have existed its nature would be inherently unstable, its virtues also its vices. The devolution of a spontaneous group into an organized society with rules and powers for imposing what had once been spontaneously given was inherent in the very nature of its success. Bedouins become rich tyrants; generative ideas degenerate into discursive edicts. Societies just like individuals seem to be trapped in a cycle of endless repetition. Striving, achieving, losing, striving once again: the cycle repeated, world without end.

So at both the individual and societal levels the conditions of fulfillment are at the same time the conditions that destroy fulfillment. The Moment is both Eden and the Fall. In this sense the *polis* is the *psyche* writ large, the soul a microcosm of the state. Both are driven by an urge to overcome their inherent deficiencies and both for the same built-in reasons are doomed to fail. Hedonism, whether individual or collective, cannot solve the dilemma of the Moment. Its ethic, its analysis of the nature of things and its recommendations for the best way to live amid that nature, is a failed ethic. Essentially so: irredeemably. Hedonists, egoists, millenarians, ethnic loyalists, utilitarians, revolutionary romantics: none of them offer us any foundation for a meaningful life.

# Four

## THE CREATING OF SELF

The problem with hedonism is that it contradicts itself. The Moment is not a dimension of praxis but a consequence; its attainment means the end of action. Insofar as human nature is the praxis it expresses, the Moment is an ideal that cannot be possessed except through the loss of human nature. This is Sartre's point in saying that *le manqué* is an impossible, unrealizable ideal, that the passion of human being is in vain. Whitehead concurs, arguing that a process of concrescence perishes in the attainment of determinacy, that a satisfaction is not enjoyed by its creator but only by successors. The resolution of a process is not a part of that process; the goal as realized is external to it as pursued. Therefore to make the outcome of human activity your Good, as hedonism does, is to root value in something that transcends human activity. For Dewey the transcendence is in the form of a reinstitution of what is less than human, the animalistic and vegetative behaviors of habit and instinct and the workings of the genetic code. For Sartre the transcendence would seem to be in the form of becoming a god, which is impossible, or of death, which is the deliverance of passion into the hands of natural necessity. Hedonism reveres a Good that is essentially anti-human.

Judge William, the stalwart critic of hedonism whom Kierkegaard makes the author of the second half of *Either/Or,* is especially trenchant in exposing the ontological quicksand on which hedonism attempts to build. He begins by noting the externality of its source of value: "But he who says that he wants to enjoy life always posits a condition which

107

either lies outside the individual or is in the individual in such a way that it is not posited by the individual himself" [E/0-2 184].

You might argue that what you want out of life is good health and the satisfactions which that makes possible. But no matter how regularly you exercise, no matter how carefully you satisfy the nutritional requirements for a well-balanced diet, no matter how prudently you manage stress and avoid unnecessary risks, your goal remains vulnerable to what lies beyond your control. Hereditary factors may make you prone to certain diseases or to excessive cholesterol; you might succumb to a viral infection for which there is no known preventative or cure; you might be the victim of an automobile accident in which you were not at fault or caught in a natural disaster beyond any effective human ability to predict or control.

What is true of the natural conditions for happiness is all the more true for societally based conditions. If you believe that wealth or fame or power over others is a necessary means for attaining fulfillment, your goal will be a perpetual hostage to fortune and to the praxis of those who might find your goals inimical to theirs. Even the development of your natural capacities, the talent you might have to make or to perform or to express something, is at the mercy of external conditions. Your golden-tongued orations will fall silent when an invading soldier cuts out your tongue or an invading cancer destroys your larynx; your reputation as a gifted flutist will suffer when arthritis cripples your fingers; your skill as a cabinetmaker will end when your eyes grow too myopic or your tools are arbitrarily confiscated.

But Judge William tells us nothing new in singing this old litany of risks. Aristotle, for instance, admits that your happiness depends on the contingent presence of precisely these external conditions, although he advises them in moderate amount and thinks that some measure of happiness is possible even in their absence. Good health and attractiveness, an adequate income, respectable ancestors and the respect of friends, political influence and the opportunity to play a meaningful role within your community: these are the soil in which happiness best grows [EN 1.1099a30–1099b8, 10.1178b32–1179a9]. Judge William's argument, however, is not just that the externality of these conditions makes them uncertain and thus requires that the quest to make them certain be all-consuming. He goes further, arguing that it makes them worthless as the foundation for value.

Let us suppose, he says, that all the conditions you need to attain a sustained and complete fulfillment are present. Everything goes right, nothing untoward ever happens to you. You live to a ripe old age surrounded by dear friends and loving children, you become inde-

pendently wealthy and gain a deserved reputation in your workplace
and in the community as a leader whose achievements are valuable and
enduring. We would all then agree that you have lived the good life,
that you attained the Moment and found it to be an enduring satisfaction. But now suppose that for you and for all other happy people like
yourself the exact opposite transpires.

Nothing of all this comes to pass. What then? Why, then, they despair. . . . Let us see now why they despair. Is it because they discovered
that what they built their life upon was transient? But is that, then, a
reason for despairing? Has any essential change occurred in that upon
which they built their life? Is it an essential change in the transitory
that it shows itself to be transitory? Or is it not rather something accidental and unessential in the case of what is transitory that it does not
show itself to be such? Nothing has happened which could occasion a
change. So if they despair, it must be because they were in despair be-
forehand. The only difference is that they did not know it. But this is an
entirely fortuitous difference. [E/O-2 196]

For you as a hedonist, the Moment is essential. It serves as the standard by which you judge the worth of everything. This object or person or choice or consequence is worthwhile only insofar as it
contributes to or is a component in some fulfilling experience of yours.
If there were no such Moments being experienced, or at least remembered and hoped for, your life would be unmarked by value. It would
be an endless desert of valueless experiences, pointless occurrences
following one another in unrelieved monotony. There would be no final
cause to orient your energies, no relevance to the play of your imagination among possibilities. There would be only deficiency, felt but
not correlated to any prospective remedy. There would be unfocused
energy dissipating helter-skelter any difference between itself and
its world. Your self would dissolve into a mere instance of the surrounding environment.

This is what Judge William means by "despair." As a hedonist, you
would be in despair were it to happen that all of the conditions for
your fulfillment should vanish. You have therefore made those conditions essential to your sense of self-worth and to your view of the
world as a meaningful order of things. But, says Judge William, those
conditions are in fact thoroughly contingent. They might be present,
they might not, depending on what happens to happen. Yet if what is
essential for you is actually contingent, then your life is founded on an
ontological mistake. Moreover, you are aware of this mistake. The strat-

egies of hedonism are all aimed at making the Moment objectively as well as subjectively essential. But that is impossible, because the Moment is essentially contingent. Insofar as you persist in your attempt to secure for desiring an object that is necessarily tailored to its subjective demands, you live not simply in ignorance of your true condition. You live out a lie to yourself. Ironically, you begin by justifying your deception of others as a legitimate means for securing your aims; you end by deceiving yourself as well, making yourself a mere means to an end you dare not acknowledge as illusion. Johannes becomes his own Cordelia. Hedonism is founded on despair. The self is a desiring that has no value except by luck. Its praxis has no essence, no foundation. The distinctive fourfoldness of human activity is degraded by hedonism into only a fleeting, insignificant variation on a nonhuman theme, a flash of difference making no real difference to the ongoing flow of natural necessity.

Judge William proposes an alternative. The fourfoldness of praxis need not be construed as hedonism construes it. The value it expresses need not be instrumental to its demise but instead can be intrinsic to its ongoing dynamic. Human nature as an intentional process can be the foundation upon which your life, your purposes, your doings and sufferings, are meaningfully lived. For praxis is essentially yourself, and so it encompasses conditions for value that are under your control, that in being essential to your subjective purposes are also essential to your objective nature as a human being.

Take yourself as your goal, which means taking selfhood as something normative rather than descriptive. Your self in its truest, fullest sense is an achievement not a given. It should be your aim to become what initially you have the capacity to be, to realize your potential, to attain the fullest possible measure of human excellence. Let us call that goal attained a Self. Not the Moment but the Self: this is the Good. Self is that which gives all other realities their value, which defines our world, our place within it, our purposes and their significance. Unlike the Moment, however, the Self is not an outcome external to the praxis that values it. The goal is in this case the process itself. The Self which is sought is a qualitative expression of the activity of the seeking. It is an instrument seeking its own perfection as an instrument.

Kierkegaard calls this approach "ethical" in contrast to the "aesthetic" character of hedonism. Thus to be ethical is to strive to become a Self and to become a Self is to strive for an ideal within a temporal terrain. But whereas the task of the hedonist was to overcome time, to find a way to rescue the Moment from its ravaging power, the task of an ethicist involves using time as a supportive resource, as a necessary

condition for succeeding. The momentary, marginal, time-bound character of moments, their contingency, needs therefore to be reinterpreted as an opportunity rather than an obstacle.

In this moment you make a choice, decide to do one thing rather
than another. The next moment you are faced with another choice, and
so on endlessly. Each decision makes a difference for subsequent decisions because it changes the conditions by which the new choice is
made. You come to a fork in the road and decide to go left; your next
decisions have to do with the situational character of the leftward pathway rather than the rightward. A decision cuts off some possibilities
while bringing others to realization. Once done, this is henceforth the
way it is, the way it was. The new fabric once woven can be unraveled
but it can never be woven again for the first time. Hence the momentariness of the Moment is always a unique opportunity for making a
difference, for giving a shape to things, for influencing what is to come.

But now suppose that you do more than make those several choices.
Suppose you also take responsibility for them. Your action then not
only makes a difference to the world; it also makes a difference to you.
It becomes a way by which you are characterized: you are the one who
decided you should go to the left rather than the right and who ac-
cepts that fact as true of you. Subsequent choices also become true
of you, over time a very large number of them. You become the conjunctive unity "$a + b + \ldots + n$" of the differences being made, the
durational identity of an agency leaving its imprint upon the shifting
sands. Your self is thus a one emerging from the many, because the
several choices each in turn proclaim themselves a continuation of preceding choices.

Hedonists are always starting afresh, the fading of their current enjoyment thrusting them out toward some new object of desire, the old
object now used up, no longer relevant to the task at hand. But as an
ethicist you are always redefining a new action as the current expression of a power and purpose and form of acting that in the past has
expressed itself and now does so once again. You characterize yourself
as all those choosings, as the sum of the differences they represent. So
the uniqueness of the Moment, its unrepeatable opportunity for making
a difference, is the womb from which an enduring reality can be born,
your Self understood as the persisting agency creative of and responsible for the uses made of those brief perished moments.

Your Self as Judge William helps us see it is a moral unity, but a unity
of actions not of an underlying substance. You are not, however, just a
summation of choices as Hume's self is a bundle of impressions. To take
responsibility for a choice is not only to acknowledge yourself as its

cause but to remain loyal to the values it realized or intended. Responsible decisions are those made in response to previous decisions, conforming with them. As time passes a choice made, confirmed, built upon, becomes a constant aspect of who you are. The choice elongates. It becomes a thread of continuity, a repeated characteristic of the series of your actions, a quality distinctively present whenever you are at work. Your initial choice, built up over time into an enduring presence, becomes a part of your character, an element crucial to any adequate account of what you are like, a part of any adequate definition of yourself. It thus becomes explanatory as well: you acted that way and probably will go on doing so because of your character. What is essential about you is that center of consistency that gives integrity, self-referential identity and predictability, to your various activities.

Once you decided to attend a neighborhood reception for a political candidate. It was a very spontaneous thing to have done: a choice of the moment, an exercise of your freedom. But you gave it more significance than that by deciding subsequently to contribute to her campaign and later to set aside an afternoon for calling prospective voters on her behalf. A marginal, very contingent choice soon became more central to who you are. The thread of consistency this introduced into your behavior came to be something worth mentioning about you, an insight into the sort of person you are: one who gets involved in politics, an activist, a person committed to making democracy work. Eventually the weight of these decisions bore down into the surface of your life and gouged a distinctive shape. You are a person whose character it is to be politically active, who could not be thought of apart from that way of doing things, that sense of how best to spend one's time. When the elections roll around again, I will not be surprised to find you knocking at my door with a petition to sign for a candidate. And I can fairly well guess how you stand on the issues of the day. Your obituary will probably be headlined: "Noted Community Leader Dies." You *are* that way of life, that kind of a Self. You have become a leader; you were not born one. Yet although these qualities are achievements, it is impossible any longer to imagine how you could ever have been otherwise, as though even in the cradle your babblings were inchoate political advisories.

Aristotle, as we have already seen, emphasizes character as key to the good life. A consistent love for and pursuit of noble ends, he said, is what frees you from being victimized by your own proclivities to excess and makes you into a person concerned not primarily for your own long-range advantage but for the good of your friends and of the community to which you belong. You were critical of his arguments because they seemed to make good character a means to an end, a surround designed to blunt the edge of raw selfish desire and to canalize it in socially acceptable ways. Habits of excellence make tame citizens of wild boys, and the systematic applications of societal sanctions are what make those habits. The justification lies in the results.

This is quite a different sense of character than the one Judge William suggests. But our hedonistic interpretation of Aristotle might not be fair to two important aspects of his thinking. First, he carefully distinguishes happiness from pleasure, notes that pleasures are momentary and so reduces them to a benefit but not a constitutive element of virtue: "Pleasure completes the activity not as a characteristic completes an activity by being already inherent in it, but as a completeness that superimposes itself upon it, like the bloom of youth in those who are in their prime" [EN 10.1174b32–34]. Happiness, similarly, might be taken as completing virtuous activities. Rather than being their justification, it is their crowning glory, the special bloom that gives radiance to life, overflowing with goodness what is nonetheless already intrinsically good. When Aristotle says that "happiness is activity in conformity with virtue" [EN 10.1177a12], and gives as his reason that happiness is an activity desirable in itself and that the performance of noble and good deeds are also desirable in themselves [EN 10.1176b5–8], he might mean that happiness and deeds done excellently are the same thing. But it would make more sense for him to mean that such deeds are fulfilling in and of themselves, and that happiness is the experience of those fulfillments severally and collectively, a satisfaction that those actions make possible but that is not required for them to be justifiable actions.

This latter interpretation fits well with Aristotle's comment about happiness being a quality not of a single action but of a complete life [EN 1.1098a18–19]. It comes as a fulfillment beyond all particular fulfillments, one sufficient but not necessary to motivate and complete the value of noble deeds. To make happiness a result of virtue and not its necessary motive also illuminates Aristotle's claim that a person can still live a noble life, a life that is its own justification because composed of actions all intrinsically valuable, even though his life might not be happy because deprived by ill-luck or fate of some of the conditions requisite for happiness. A low-born, physically deformed, indigent, childless, friendless person "cannot be classified as altogether happy," even less so one who had those goods and then lost them [EN 1.1099b1–6], who like Priam of Troy has through "great misfortune" lost all the conditions for happiness and "come to a wretched end" [EN 1.1100a5–7]. And yet, "nobility shines through even in such circumstances, when a man bears many great misfortunes with good grace not because he is insensitive to pain but because he is noble and high-minded" [EN 1.1100b30–32].

So there are hints in Aristotle of support for the claim that a person of noble character will live a good life if conditions are favorable, but if they are not he can still be said to have acted in ways that are intrinsically valuable. Although happiness is an outcome you seek for your life, it is noble to have fulfilled that aspect of the pursuit of happiness which is totally under your control: to have done well at least those things that circumstances permit. To have developed a noble character, the virtues of which will shine through even the worst storm clouds of adversity, is the necessary condition for happiness and all that a person can be held responsible for accomplishing.[1]

There is a second aspect of Aristotle's argument that can be interpreted as helping carry us beyond hedonism. Virtuous actions are those in which the functions proper to an agent are being fully realized. The horse is running swiftly and strongly, the eye sees clearly and distinctly. For human beings, the capacity to reason is of all functions the highest, the one distinctively human; its effective exercise is thus essential to a human agent doing anything virtuously and thereby essential to him being virtuous [EN 2.1106a15–24]. Reasoning in a practical sense involves making judgments based on rational principles; reasoning excellently means setting high standards for what you expect to accomplish [EN 1.1098a7–9] and deviating as little as possible toward either extreme. "We may thus conclude that virtue or excellence is a characteristic involving choice, and that it consists in observing the mean relative to us, a mean which is defined by a rational principle, such as a man of practical wisdom [*phronesis*] would use to determine it" [EN 2.1106b35–1107a1].

The good life, understood practically, is an expression of good actions, which are those performed by a person of good character, a person able even under adverse conditions to choose consistently by reference to rational standards of appropriateness. Such standards are not abstract universals from which specific courses of action can be deduced. They are norms relative to human beings and their unique situations, by the practical use of which their natures will be best realized. A good person is one who exemplifies norms of proper human functioning, and that proper functioning includes the reasoned identification and use of those norms for the sake of achieving that exemplification. The excellence of the acting not of the consequences, the exercise of character not the enjoyment of its fruits, is the test of virtue.

Look at what is happening once you have shifted your attention away from the endpoint into which a desiring–desired polarity seeks to be absorbed and have focused instead on the tension itself. The capacity to sustain an aim becomes as important as whether or not the aim is realized. This is in part because you recognize that an effective strategy for life is a generalized one, one able to adapt constantly to external vicissitudes. A good method, a good way of going about things, one to which you are committed and which you utilize consistently, will over the long run serve you better than an unthinking use of whatever means might happen to be readily at hand. A worthwhile end, one you can reaffirm even amid your constant reassessments of its meaning and the nature of its relevance, will over the long run serve you better than an unthinking pursuit of whatever fulfillments might seem the best and brightest opportunities of the moment. These consistencies become important as you begin to see yourself there in that process, begin to sense in the repeated affirmations of goal and means, the repeated effort for the sake of a persisting need, the emergence of the enduring singularity of your Self. And this you find to be the more fundamental reality, the greater good. The Self, not the Moment, is the foundation of goodness.

By being led from the immediacy of activity to the agent rather than to the result, we have been exploring the inside of praxis rather than its outside, its essence rather than its fortuitous consequences. We have found there two salient features: self-identity and character. Both speak of selfhood, for character is the proven capacity to define what is important for you in terms of a consistent style of pursuit, and a character is the measure of that style by reference to its effectiveness in expressing an ideal of consistency, of a sustained integration of past and present, of an enduring self-identity.[2]

Charles Taylor was referring to character in his notion of "strong evaluation." Judgments about the worth of the kinds of activities in which you engage are judgments about your life-style. They have to do with character insofar as your concern is about responsibility and consistency. You spent your time yesterday distributing election leaflets rather than catching up on your paperwork. You are prepared to accept the consequences: the praise of the political candidate, the annoyance of your employer. In doing this you not only express your solidarity with the agent of yesterday's deed but you identify the agent as yourself. To be a Self is to have a self that endures throughout an extent of time. An enduring self is not given, as though it were an extensive substratum preexisting various activities it then performs. Quite the contrary, an enduring self is like a Sartrean group: it is created in acts of identification, in decisions to conform new ends and means to old ones, to interpret present choices as extensions rather than merely repetitions of prior choices.

A character is to the enduring self what that self is to momentary choice. Your self as a specific praxis becomes an enduring self when it claims identity with a serial grouping of praxes unified by a shared common quality. You say of those activities that they have integrity because each grows out of the others, and by making your choice now as a continuation of them you grow your new praxis from them as well. The character of that past is a standard by which you work out the conditions under which you are to act, by which you determine what you should now do. In so doing, you merge your present action with its standard. You try to live up to your character. Your praxis identifies with the enduring self to which you were attempting to conform, and it in turn becomes more enduring a self than it was before.

But more even than this is involved in the development of Self. As a person of character, as someone who acts consistently and responsibly, you assess the quality of your achievements overall, the worth of your labors and of your life, by reference to a cultural standard of acceptable behavior. You have a sense of what it means in your society to be a responsible adult, to be someone who deserves the respect of friends and the love of family, who has earned a reputation as a good neighbor, colleague, and citizen. As you seek to conform your character to this societal standard, you are identifying yourself with its more enduring and extensive reality. Conversely, you are instantiating an enduring cultural tradition of normative human character in your own character.

Your individual character is an ideal expression of the underlying unity of your various specific actions, not merely all those actions compiled and compacted into a convenient package but rather their tendency. Just as the mathematical curve by which a physicist defines a missile's trajectory is a best approximate resolution of the data points that have plotted it, so your character expresses the trend of your actions, their ideal pattern. You can do something that is out of character without ceasing to have that character, although too many exceptions do not prove a rule but refute it. Similarly, the societal traditions you take as normative conditions for living are not merely a compilation of your characteristics along with those of the other members of your culture. You can do something immoral without ceasing to be a good person and there can be persons whose whole life is a repudiation of traditional values without our having to draw the conclusion that their society is essentially corrupt and deserves to be destroyed, its people put to the sword and its fields sown with salt.

We recognize the discrepancy between general cultural norms and individual forms of life as endemic. You may be chastised for not being the sort of person your parents had expected you to be but you would probably not be punished for it, not accused of being immoral or a traitor. We would expect your individual actions, however, to approximate much more closely your character. We expect you to be consistently yourself, to live up to your own expectations even if not to ours. But this is surely only a happenstance of contemporary society. In a highly structured culture with traditionally ascribed social roles, living up to the character pre-assigned you by others would be a primary and arduous task. For revolutionary groups such as Cromwell's Puritans and Robespierre's Jacobins, personal conformity to the standards of a saintly people was to be expected and failure to meet the standard meant expulsion from the community or death.

Shame, to take Taylor's excellent example [HAL 54ff], is an emotion that involves reference to a standard. You have done something; to feel ashamed of having done so, you need to interpret your action as deficient in comparison to some other possible action which you could have done and which you know it would have been better to have done. Why it would have been better is that you take it to more fully exemplify your character or to be a more adequate expression of some essentially cultural expectation. You are ashamed of having shouted angrily at a friend because you are an even-tempered sort; it was not like you to get so upset. Nor was that very civilized: people just don't go around yelling at one another like wild animals.

Your shamefaced feeling has what Taylor calls "import." You refer your deed to a context of norms, of expectations for how you behave or how "one" behaves, and you then compare your action to those norms with respect to fit. The shame may simply be felt or it may be articulated with considerable sophistication. But in either case you are evaluating your actions in terms of more than desires and satisfactions. You have set your deeds into a framework of fundamental criteria of worth, a framework that defines who you are and what your world is like.

It is because you have this sense of self-identity and because you believe that you have a human nature integrally reflected in it that you perceive yourself as a particular career of approximate achievement, both as this self rather than some other self and as a civilized being rather than some other kind of being. Your various actions are characterized as consistent expressions of one self with a definable character, and your character is characterized as a specific expression of a tradition, different in specifiable (although usually not specified) ways from other expressions of that tradition and from an ideal of civilized self-hood as such.

In our exploration of the nature of praxis, I interpreted Taylor's discussion of "strong interpretation" as involving comparisons to a standard of human worthiness that is ultimately cultural. Taylor, however, is studiously vague about this. He rejects any understanding of selves that ignores their "deepest unstructured sense of what is important, which is as yet inchoate" [HAL 41], but he is equally hostile to "Cartesian" claims that such standards are clear, distinct givens imposed upon individuals from some culturally transcendent source.

"Unstructured" feelings must be structured; what is "inchoate" needs definition. So what counts in your society as civilized is a matter for debate. You are constantly struggling to articulate what it means for you to live up to ideals, to have character, to be fully human; you are constantly debating with others about what it means to live nobly, to be a good citizen, to fashion a just society. Clearly the formal conditions of this "ontogenesis" of self and society are a matter of specific choices constituting the story of our species. But what of the material conditions, the unstructured background of experience that is felt vaguely as needing shape and articulation, and that then provides the resources for doing so? Is tradition the foundation for the standards by which we are Selves? Are yet older no longer operative traditions the foundations of these now-living traditions, and so on back into the obscurity of our human origins? Or do the material conditions of praxis, the importances of the past that assure us of who we are and why, reach even deeper than tradition?

The problem with hedonism was not only that it founded values on external contingencies but also that it made them a function of individual or societal will. The contingency of any Moment was as much due to the contingency of the human purposes that had made it a value as it was due to its perishability once attained. George Lucas has criticized moral theories that rest on culturally defined values, even when these have shifted the locus of value from ends sought to the character of the persons seeking them.[3] Virtue in the sense discussed by Aristotle, and more recently defended by Alistair MacIntyre, is a quality of personhood. Making yourself virtuous by developing effective habits of excellence, or being made so by your culture, is how your life comes to be good. Virtue has to do with how you live, not with what you achieve in life. It is a practice rather than a product. This is in accord with Judge William's admonition about developing a responsible Self. However, argues Lucas, culturally inculcated habits are effective only under normal conditions, only when what the habits presuppose can in fact be taken for granted. But:

the normal aculturated situations and recognizable paradigmatic cases do not always suffice in times of stress, ambiguity, or unclarity. Such a model [e.g., Aristotle's] of embodied cultural reasoning thus, on occasion, needs to be supplemented by recourse to a *minimal ensemble of governing principles* for the practice or procedure in question.[4]

Lucas thinks these principles can be discerned through an analysis of the moral situation as such. What do persons do when a cultural consensus breaks down or when cultures themselves come into conflict? Bereft of your familiar recourse to habit, do you feel or think yourself nonetheless still "minimally constrained" with respect to what you might do or how you might do it? Is there a sense of self, of yourself as a human being, that sets limits upon and points directions for your praxis, that is presupposed in the very notion of self, agency, culture, and not merely in the notions you habitually work from regarding your own particular self and its character, your own chosen purposes, your own specific culture and its traditions?

Having advocated this "transcendental turn in moral theory," Lucas is tentative about what might be appropriate candidates for inclusion in the "minimal ensemble of governing principles" he is sure are awaiting our discovery. He mentions the interchangeability or equality of selves, along with such implicates as fairness, nondeception, and noncoercion. Others have made arguments that are more closely attuned to the fourfold nature of praxis. Erich Fromm, for instance, attempts to find normative principles in the very nature of human desiring. He argues that fulfillment as the union of desiring and desired (in his language the "at-one-ment" found in love's overcoming of separation) is possible only if the loving is of a certain sort. Or, more accurately, only if it is of certain sorts.

Fromm understands love as an activity, a praxis, that has a generic structure. Loving is a distinctively human activity, and its excellence, the how of its practice, has four necessary dimensions. All four must be actualized for the self to be fully expressed, for the self to attain the highest harmony available for human being. A loving praxis must express a genuine, non-self-regarding concern for the life and growth of other selves. It must be responsive to their needs, accepting them for who they are, and as accurately informed as possible about the conditions relevant to those needs and their fulfillment [AL 22–27]. A caring, responsive, respectful, knowledgeable praxis is thus normative. To act in any other way is not to act virtuously; habits of such a quality of loving compose a character worthy of the highest human aspiration.

But love not only has a necessary structure, it has modalities as well. Fromm argues that for your love to be fully expressed it needs to be both inclusive and exclusive in scope. Its inclusiveness can be in the form of an unconditional acceptance of those who are dependent upon you: as a mother loves her children simply because they exist as entities in the world, loves them by assuring their survival and nurturing their growth into adult persons [AL 41–44]. Inclusive love can also express itself as a love for all other persons, for humanity as a whole. This means treating everyone as your peers, as persons whose value is equal to yours, whose needs include the need to be loved by such as you and, reciprocally, who meet your needs by such as them loving you [AL 39–41].

Love is also exclusive, however. You need to love a single other person, to appreciate and contribute to the precious uniqueness of self that has been achieved and is still being developed by that person, to find in one other a complete fusion of selves without loss of your separate uniquenesses [AL 44–48]. And, insists Fromm, love must also involve self-love, for others cannot be loved in any of the ways mentioned unless you can love yourself as much [AL 48–53].

So Fromm identifies four modes of love: motherly love, brotherly love, erotic love, and self-love. In the absence of motherly love, relations of dependency degenerate into ones in which the dependent persons are tyrannized by those who have power over them. As with Johannes, in the absence of your concern that others develop into independent selves, your love will find expression in terms solely of your own development. The power to nurture, to shape another life, can be readily turned into the power to instrumentalize it, to make of those dependent on you beings whose value is for you and not in any sense for themselves. Likewise in the absence of an encompassing love for all humanity, the circle of your concern will separate some from others, creating we/they distinctions, breeding conformity among the we and animosity toward the they. Self-love becomes parochial and selfish in a sense reminiscent of Don Juan when it is not expressed as an inclusive love for selves, among the totality of which your self is but one. In the absence of the intensity of erotic love for a single other, exclusivity becomes focused upon your isolated self, turns in upon itself in an orgy of self-absorption, pursues the general strategy of a rotational method by escaping from the intrusions of the world.

Fromm's fully functioning lover expresses a self that is not culturally defined. These modalities of love share many interesting and important features with Aristotle's modalities of the noble citizen who expresses excellence through his family responsibilities, his friends, his communal loyalties, and his sense of personal dignity. But Aristotle finds the measure of these excellences in a *polis* that is historical in origin and fragile in its capacity to stave off natural and human threats to its survival. Fromm finds them in our biological makeup. They are culture-transcendent truths about the human condition. Yet they are only capacities, and it is only within a social order that will foster their emergence that they avoid becoming truncated. You may be fully human only by expressing Fromm's fourfold praxis of love, but an unloving society can and does quite readily fixate your development at some halfway point along the scale of human fulfillment. Both persons and societies stand under the judgment of a biological standard of human excellence that it is their task to realize concretely.

To be fully what you are biologically constituted as capable of being, you need to love yourself and one other with exclusive intensity, and you need to love everyone else with an inclusive generosity, both those dependent upon you and those who are your equal. You need, in other words, to become a unique, *sui generis* self and at the same time a member of wider groups including, crucially, the whole human species. Fromm helps us realize that a Self is at the same time its unique self, one among its societal peers, and an instance of the human. Thus the levels of standard are enlarged by Fromm from two to three: an individual's character as a standard for particular actions, a societal norm for assessing the character of individuals, and human nature as providing the normative measure of societies.

Jean-Paul Sartre, in his popular but nonetheless important essay "Existentialism," also makes the sort of transcendental turn George Lucas has called for, doing so even while proclaiming his rejection of all such attempts. There is no such thing as a normative sense of human nature, he says: no set of *a priori* values to which you ought to measure up. Humans are radically free, positing their own values as functions of their desirings, inventing themselves through their own *sui generis* choices: "First of all, man exists, turns up, appears on the scene, and, only afterwards, defines himself. . . . [A]t first he is nothing. Only afterward will he be something, and he himself will have made what he will be. Thus, there is no human nature. . . . Man is nothing else but what he makes of himself" [E 15]. A person is "nothing else" than a power of choosing and the results of the exercise of that power, a self-making energy and the self that is made.

Sartre's version of the fourfold of praxis was *le manque* stretching out from *l'existant* in search of *le manquant* so that it might attain *le manqué*. But the project was useless: *le manqué* was an ideal of completion that would never be attained. In "Existentialism," however, Sartre's focus is no longer on that goal. If the goal is impossible, a denial of the human condition, then being human has to do with the striving and not its goal, with the human self and not the dream of its overcoming. Sartre asks that you attend to the conditions under which this striving goes on, and to realize that of those conditions three are necessary to its being genuinely a human striving. Sartre elsewhere speaks of an "authentic" act as one that affirms as normative this triadic fundamentally human mode of being. These three conditions are always exhibited in your actions, but you can deny that they are or you can deny their importance. You can deceive others and yourself into pretending that they do not characterize your every word and deed. But an authentic praxis is self-referentially consistent: it preaches what it practices. It affirms the moral worth of the conditions necessarily expressed in every instance of its praxis.

The first of these is "forlornness" or the recognition of the centrality of freedom. "If existence really does precede essence, there is no explaining things away by reference to a fixed and given human nature. In other words, there is no determinism, man is free, man is freedom" [E 22–23]. If we take this reiterated copula seriously, we are affirming an essence for human being but one that has to do with process rather than product, with efficient causation rather than final. There may be no preestablished end for you to strive to realize, the attainment of which makes you fully human, the falling short of which characterizes you as sinful, ignoble, or in some other sense imperfect. But the striving, after whatever the end, is such as to make you fully human. Striving is freedom at work, and expressions of freedom are therefore the actualizing of the human.

It follows from this that you are attempting to deny your humanity if you act in a way that denies that you are free. The waiter who insists that he is no more than his job, that he is only an instrument for serving people their food, denies that he is free to do other things, not to be a waiter but instead a diplomat or a reporter [BN 101–3]. In Sartre's play *The Flies*,[5] the people of Argos claim that their guilt as co-conspirators in the death of Agamemnon is a condition they can only suffer, that they are not free to repudiate. Authentic praxis rejects such forms of self-denial. You must affirm this freedom as unavoidably expressed by, presupposed in, every human action, even the act of repudiating it. The waiter need not be a waiter and in fact freely chooses to be one, freely chooses to define himself as unable to be anything else. The citizens of Argos have defined themselves as sinners; they may at any point define themselves otherwise.

But freedom is not simply a necessary condition of your praxis. It is the necessary condition of any praxis whatsoever. Whatever comes to characterize your way of being human does so through choices you make, and because this is true for every human being, something essential to being human is manifest whenever freedom is manifest. Freedom is how the human gets its definition. So you express more than yourself whenever you express yourself: you concretely realize an essentially human quality, a quality essential to having human qualities. Likewise, even if you attempt to deny another person's freedom, by word or act, by treating her as dirt or by putting him to death, you are thereby denying what is essential to yourself as well. This is quite literally self-contradictory. Hence a respect for freedom should characterize all the particular expressions of your own freedom. You cannot be free, cannot be what it is to be human, except that you acknowledge freedom as such as an unconditional value.

Sartre next considers "despair," which is the inverse condition to forlornness. Despair "means that we shall confine ourselves to reckoning only with what depends upon our will, or on the ensemble of probabilities which make our action possible" [E 29]. To "reckon with" what lies outside yourself and beyond your control is to rely on something besides your own free choice as a causal source for assuring your aims or as a reason for their failure. But if you are indeed radically free, this is not the case at all: rather, it is the case that you are the sole source of who you are and of the value of what you achieve. Despair means taking responsibility for the consequences of your actions. You cannot blame your heredity or upbringing for what you have become; you cannot expect to be anything other than what you make of yourself, given the range of possibilities you find available. You must act without the hope that your choices are guaranteed to get you to the right outcomes, and without the excuse that someone or something other than yourself is really responsible for what happens. Instead, you need to affirm yourself, to take upon yourself the credit and blame for being what, concretely, you have become through your own choices.

The homosexual who refuses to acknowledge his pederasty does so by explaining his previous actions as due to circumstances beyond his control or at least as not constitutive of who he really is [BN 107]. In *No Exit,* Garcin thinks of himself as a revolutionary hero only by refusing to admit that what he has done day after day, year after year, is to act the coward, to betray in a thousand petty ways the ideal to which he says he is committed. The Orestes of *The Flies* has no past to affirm, having been taken from Argos while still a baby. He has done nothing for which he can be responsible; he is freedom devoid of any real results. For you to repudiate what you have done by blaming it on external conditions or by disowning its relevance to who you are is to be in the same condition as an Orestes who takes his rootlessness as meaning his life is all ahead of him, that he has no past. But of course you have a past. Freedom is taking action, and actions have consequences that without your having chosen to act as you did would not have come to be. To affirm them as yours, to define yourself as the totality of the ways in which you gave concrete shape to things, is logically entailed by your affirmation of yourself as free.

Despair like forlornness must be respected wherever it is found. Your expression of it in your every act, and your affirmation of it insofar as your praxis is authentic, are an expression and affirmation not only of your own responsibility for deeds done but of facticity as essential to any human reality. Thus other persons as well as yourself must be held responsible for what they do, must be taken as having a moral identity over time that can become the object of our praise or blame. Even when you do otherwise, when you impose your will upon others, patronizing them or subjugating them, treating them as though they were not your peers, not able themselves to be responsible for what they have done, when you approach others in blithe disregard of the historical dimension of their selfhood, denying them their personal and cultural difference from yourself, when you belittle their achievements and their responsibility for those achievements, you deny in them the despair that is of the essence of who they are. Yet your very act of denial is an exercise of a freedom that has consequences for which you must be responsible, and their acceptance or refusal of your denial of their freedom is a reaction for which they in turn are responsible. So praxis, whether authentic or inauthentic, discloses a human reality that is always and everywhere ineluctably a facticity as well as a freedom, and it discloses this reality in each instance as an expression of a unique individual self.

Sartre's third condition of selfhood is what he calls "anguish," and it is an implicate of the other two. If your actions express your own freedom and at the same time proclaim human being as free, if they express your own facticity and simultaneously declare human being as factual, and if you define yourself by means of those expressions, then it must be that you also define human being by means of those same expressions. Your choices contribute to the definition of human beings as the kind of entity that in making choices chooses to become this sort of a choice-maker rather than that. The consequences you affirm as yours contribute to the definition of human beings as the kind of entity that has constituted itself as this selfsame reality rather than that. Both as a free and as a responsible self, your praxis has implications for what it means to be a human self. A person

who realizes that he is not only the person he chooses to be, but also a lawmaker who is, at the same time, choosing all mankind as well as himself, can not help escape the feeling of his total and deep responsibility.... I am responsible for myself and for everyone else. I am creating a certain image of man of my own choosing. In choosing myself, I choose man.... In creating the man that we want to be, there is not a single one of our acts which does not at the same time create an image of man as we think he ought to be. [E 18, 17]

You decide to be a waiter and then continue to ply that trade for fear that in changing jobs you might lose the financial stability it affords and which you think important. Insofar as this is your praxis, even though it is your quite idiosyncratic, unrepeatable act of self-expression, you have nonetheless contributed thereby to a profile of the human species as preferring stability over risk, as a species with a proclivity for developing habits rooted in arbitrarily chosen patterns of action. Furthermore, claims Sartre, you are implicitly recommending to others that they act likewise, that they take you as a role model, which if everyone did would eventuate in it being true of the human species, a given truth of its history, that it loves the familiar and fears the unknown.

But on what authority do you hold yourself up as a role model for others? On no authority at all, says Sartre, and hence the anguish:

At every moment I'm obliged to perform exemplary acts. For every man, everything happens as if all mankind had its eyes fixed on him and were guiding itself by what he does. And every man ought to say to himself, "Am I really the kind of man who has the right to act in such a way that humanity might guide itself by my actions?" And if he does not say that to himself, he is masking his anguish. [E 20]

Orestes affirms Argos as his city, takes responsibility for its history of regicide, then acts to rid his city of its tyrants. His praxis defines him as a bold and courageous leader, recommends to the Argive populace that they too should take action against those who would enslave them and subvert their heritage, and thereby makes his small contribution toward defining humanity as a species capable of the sort of excellences that would have made Aristotle proud.

The apparent contradiction in Sartre's arguments, that there is no normative human essence although authenticity is an affirmation of normative conditions of human action, is only apparent. Existence precedes essence only if an essence is taken as a descriptive summary of the actual choosings and their actual consequences, which together make up the biography of a given individual. That person is essentially that trail of facts, that totality of purposes and achievements. But essence precedes existence, or rather is its condition, where an essence is understood as what is expressed in every instance of human praxis, what is essential to any event being a praxis at all. The latter sense of essence is formal, having to do with the structure of a process, with the how of any human doing whatsoever. The former sense of essence is material, having to do with what is created in the crucible of that process, its factitious products. The products of praxis are historically contingent, delimited by the workings of culture and nature, by the massive inherited givenness of the settled past and the fortuitous interplay of the varied ephemeral choices of free individuals. But the process of the praxis that results in contingent products has itself an essential structure, which for you to deny means to deny your essential humanity.

Judge William had already made the point that existence precedes essence when he defined a self as creative of its own essence. It was across your choices, made freely and their results affirmed responsibly, that your self was said to emerge, a claim of identity extended over a temporal range of acts and consequences. First comes existence, the existence of a power of momentary decisiveness; then arises in time and through the use of time's special qualities, a selfsame durational power which is the essence of a you, a self. But if the good judge affirms the Sartrean notion of essence as product, as the what of selfhood, perhaps he also can provide insight into the notion of essence as process, as the how of selfhood.

Judge William explains the intertwining of the two:

Only when the individual himself is the universal is it possible to realize the ethical.... He who regards life ethically sees the universal, and he who lives ethically expresses the universal in his life, he makes himself the universal man, not by divesting himself of his concretion, for then he becomes nothing, but by clothing himself with it and permeating it with the universal.... Hence, when the ethical individual has completed his task, has fought the good fight, he has then reached the point where he has become the one man, that is to say, that there is no other man altogether like him; and at the same time he has become the universal man. To be the one man is not in itself anything so great, for that everybody has in common with every product of nature; but to be that in such a way that he is also the universal man is the true art of living. [E/O-2 260–61]

You create yourself, defining the essential features of your personality across the choices of a lifetime. But it is not enough, says Judge William, for you to become a unique self. You also are to undertake the task of becoming the universal person, a Self as well as a self. There should be dimensions of your personality that only you could have ever realized; there should be dimensions that every human being should realize, yourself included. But these are not different dimensions, as though one sector of your self were your private, idiosyncratic accomplishment and another sector the public and generic. Your choices, the unique self with its specific character which they construct, are to be at the same time choices that make what is unique also universal.

"Duty is the universal, what is required of me is the universal; what I am able to do is the particular" [E/0-2 268]. If "doing your duty" means performing universal actions, then this is an impossible request, a counsel of perfection, as though Sartre were to say that it is your duty to become God. You cannot do this because it would require you to become the norm for human action. But you are a concrete particular individual with a finite perspective and finite capacities, whereas the norm transcends precisely those limitations. Your limited perspective means that you are biased and ignorant; your limited capacities mean that you are weak and ineffective. If it were your task to enact a universal moral rule, you would be attempting to overcome your limitations as far as possible, to shrink the scope of your private self, to expand your generic self, to see and feel things *sub specie aeternitatis,* to sacrifice your individual self for the sake of the universal.

But this is to make ethical norms external impositions, realities to which you can conform only by denying your self. It seems to be a new version of the structure of hedonism: finding value in something external to human selfhood. This separation of particular self and universal self is pernicious, says Judge William, for the generic and the specific are not two sides of a Self. You are not yourself and a human self. Rather, in becoming a human self you become fully your own unique self and it is only through the fashioning of a specific individual self that human selfhood can be realized. Your task is to become *this* human being: not to become humanity as such nor to become a bare particular but to become a Self. The universal can only be expressed in its instances and each instance of a universal is a unique expression of it.[6] To be genuinely, fully a person—to have what Judge William calls a "personality"—is to express in your praxis the unity of the universal and the particular.

It isn't the content of the doing but the how of it that makes a deed expressive of the essentially human. Sartre agrees by making authenticity have to do with how freedom is exercised. You cannot help acting freely because any expression of freedom is an action and every action an expression of freedom; they are co-implicates. But only insofar as you take full responsibility for your choice and its consequences does your action also acknowledge what it in fact expresses: namely, its distinctively human structure of intentionality and facticity. An authentic act need not otherwise be different than an inauthentic one. As a waiter you can go about serving my meal whether you take yourself as condemned by an unjust world to this subservience or as only playing at the role but in no way defined by it, or whether instead you authentically affirm your actions as your way of being human at this particular point in your life and the world's history. There is no way to be human except in some particular way, just as there is no way to deny your humanity except in some particular way. And those ways are each indefinitely many, although you might agree with Aristotle that the ways to deny your humanity are more obvious and more likely to occur than are the ways properly to affirm it.

Judge William proposes three duties, three ways by which a person in living might gain a human personality. The first is stated thusly: "It is every man's duty to work in order to live," for "the duty of working in order to live expresses the universal-human, and it expresses the universal also in another sense because it expresses freedom. It is precisely by working that man makes himself free, by working he becomes lord over nature, by working he shows that he is higher than nature" [E/O-2 286–87]. For a hedonist, for anyone who finds the heart of value to lie in the Moment of fulfillment, work is at best a valuable means to an important end, at worst a "dolorous necessity" for those not fortunate enough to be able to obtain the objects of their desiring straight off and easily. If nature has favored you with a plentiful environment or if your culture has been organized to your advantage, then you have no need to work. The mangoes are there at your fingertips for the eating or a servant can be ordered to bring them quickly.

But if the heart of value has to do with creating a Self, then work is how it finds expression. You should not take Judge William's reference to lordship over nature as a hedonistic ideal. The point is not taking control but gaining freedom. The burden of natural necessity, the endless cycle of desiring and desired, is acknowledged in the act of labor. The "conflict for daily bread" is an unavoidable fact from which no metabolic organism can flee. For an exceptional few, the burden of that necessity might be avoided for a moment, or with luck for a lifetime, but for most human beings the quest for satisfaction is ongoing, a constant struggle against the relative parsimony of the world. For you to take upon yourself the task of laboring, of struggling to reshape your environment so that it provides you with the resources you need in minimal if not optimal amount, is to cast your lot with the vast majority of humanity and not with the exceptional few. Working is an act of humility, saying that you are no better than anyone else, affirming that if the struggle for survival is a biological given then you too must struggle, that nature doesn't owe you your existence, that you have no grounds for claiming your own benefit at the expense of others.

Yet to acknowledge this fact is to transcend it. If you take labor as a real but not a "dolorous" necessity, as an expression of your humanity and not an impediment to its realization, then you can recognize it as the way by which you gain a measure of independence. By your laboring you break free from the natural course of things, cease to be passively dependent upon nature. When you earn your bread, you transform the givenness of things into a medium for your fulfillment. You therefore take initiative in the face of necessity. You do what it requires, but in your own distinctive way. In some fashion all your own, you humanize the givenness of things. A hedonist seeks to overcome necessity. Your goal, in contrast, is to give it a human face, to leave upon it the marks of your self-chosen activity.

There is dignity in this celebration of a necessity that can be forced to make room for freedom, this celebration of a reality that is both free and necessary. Such a reality is what human reality is. To celebrate this intentional facticity is to celebrate the human. And the human is of greater worth than what is not human, for the Self is the greatest worth there is:

It is beautiful to see the lilies of the field (though they sew not neither do they spin) so clothed that even Solomon in all his glory was not so magnificent; it is beautiful to see the birds without anxiety finding their food; it is beautiful to see Adam and Eve in Paradise where they could get everything they pointed at; but it is still more beautiful to see a man earning by his work what he has need of.... Man is great, greater than any other creature, for the fact that he can provide for himself.... It is an expression of man's perfection that he can work, it is a still higher expression for it that he must. [E/O-2 287]

By working you affirm yourself as no different from any other human being; your labor exemplifies a human nature that is both free and determinate; this nature is of highest worth. But Judge William now asks you to go further and to recognize that affirming your equality with others is not enough. You do not earn your daily bread in solitary praxis but in relation with others. Your labor can benefit them as well as yourself. The unique way in which you shape nature produces benefits of value to others, perhaps benefits upon which they in whole or part depend for their own labor. You have a special contribution to make even in the act that affirms your commonness.

And so: "It is every man's duty to have a calling," to exercise your special talents for the good of all. Some people are more talented than others; some talents are more socially important than others. Your talents are thus what makes you different from others, and to call upon you to exercise your talents is to ask that you accentuate your uniqueness. But

in all the differences there is the common factor left that each is a calling. The most eminent talent is a calling, and the individual who is in possession of it cannot lose sight of reality, he does not stand outside of the universal-human, for his talent is a calling. The most insignificant individual has a calling, he shall not be cast out, not be reduced to living on a par with the beasts, he does not stand outside of the universal-human, he has a calling. [E/O-2 296–97]

What you have in common with others is that you are different from them. Nonetheless, or rather precisely because of your difference, they can benefit from what you accomplish and you from what they accomplish. A calling is an individualized talent seen as socially relevant.

Judge William adds, of course, that what is important is that you seek to exercise your talents as a contribution to the good of the whole. Whether the actual fruits of your praxis are as valuable as might be hoped is not important. To be sure, in one sense it is indeed very important: without a minimum of beneficial results, the members of your community and yourself among them will suffer impoverishment and, in the extreme, a loss of their life and of the viability of their society. In an ethical sense, however, in respect to what it is your duty to do, the actual consequences are beyond your control and for them you cannot be held responsible. It is your responsibility to carry out the role you have taken up within society, to exercise your talents as best you are able. Your task is to accomplish this: to exercise your distinctive capacities, to actualize what that exercise permits, and to recognize that in doing so you contribute your difference to the confluence of differences, the reconciliation of which gives rise to the complex pluralism requisite for any viable community: "So every man can accomplish something, he can accomplish his job. The job may be of very various kinds, but we are always to hold fast to this, that every man has his job, and that all men are reconciled by the expression that each of them does his job" [E/O-2 300].

And third, says Judge William, "it is the duty of every man to marry." Remember that this is a universal command; its instantiation in the particularity of your life will be unique. The duty doesn't tell whom you should marry nor does it predetermine whether the conditions of your life will be such that marriage is possible or appropriate. But what is appropriate is that your relationships with others have the characteristic that marriage normatively provides. As Fromm argued, a human self cannot fully mature except that it shares itself fully with another. The trust this requires, the vulnerability it risks, the responsibilities it imposes, expand the scope of selfhood. Whereas a calling discloses your relevance to others and whereas work discloses your mutual equality, marriage exhibits your identity with others. It is that experience wherein the intrinsic value of other selves is directly experienced; not your usefulness for them and they for you, but your oneness with them.

Yet this is not to be taken as a momentary passion, a special experience of two selves becoming one, as might be found in sexual climax or *satori* or any of the other "mountain-top experiences" that are rare precisely because extraordinary. Those are forms of the Moment and they suffer all the problems entailed by the hedonistic dilemma. The salient quality of marriage for Judge William is that it lasts over time, and what it teaches is the value of that endurance. Not just that what endures is valuable but that the enduring is what is valuable, the "filling up of time," the ordinary comings and goings of routine that compose the vast majority of our hours and days. It is this that you cannot do alone, or which if you try produces only empty, time-denying rather than time-affirming, gestures. You would be like the young aesthete grown old; hoping at best in your despairing and solitary days to learn to play the flute or "to invent an ingenious instrument for scraping your pipe" [E/0-2 313].

Judge William tells the story of a scholar who becomes excited by the discovery of a vowel-pointing in the oriental text he is studying. It is both a puzzling discovery and one startling in its implications. The scholar is so distracted by this extraordinary fact that he fails to come to dinner. His wife seeks him out in the study; he shares his excitement with her. She is appreciative of the importance of this event, but she also tries to help him put the matter in perspective, to recognize that it is also important to eat one's dinner. While engaged thus with her husband, the scholar's wife happens to sneeze and the vowel-point blows away; as it turns out it was only a grain of snuff which had fallen onto the page.

A person whose relationship to others was such that he visited them "only when his soul was rich and strong" would never have shared this concern of his solitary praxis, this expression of his special talents, with another. He might never have been saved from a lifetime of wasted effort, having never had a "helpmeet who came in and called him at midday, no wife who could blow the dot away" [E/0-2 315]. It is not that the scholar's wife played a useful role in brushing away the snuff, although she did so, but that the mundane, ongoing openness of their relationship made possible this service, one not even intended, yet an accident not possible except given two souls whose relationship turned far more than only their "rich and strong" surfaces to each other.

Aristotle speaks of friendship in these same terms. It is through such intimate, enduring relationships that you learn the intrinsic value of others and of lifelong commitments. The condition of true intimacy is time, a developed interdependence of purpose that enlarges and completes your individual aims. It opens up a dimension of selfhood midway between the individual and the communal, a dimension in which others are more than useful but still other than yourself. Sartre's category of anguish hints at this dimension, for it is your openness to others that is meant by your being their mentors and they yours. But Sartre's existentialism is too radically individualistic, his fictional and his philosophical heroes too solitary, for anguish to unfold the full meaning to which Judge William points.

We are ready now for Kant. As soon as it was suggested that selfhood involved more than self-creation, more than making yourself anything you might choose to be, the smell of Kant was in the air. The method we have been using was clue enough: to explore the necessary conditions for human selfhood, to inquire into the determinants of qualities that any self would have to possess for it to be judged, for it merely to be thought, human. We have been finding that such categorical necessities do in fact emerge, and in our consideration of Fromm, Sartre, and Kierkegaard's Judge William they have been strikingly similar.

Kant's categorical imperative commands that you and I do what a good will would do without the need of a command. A good will is his way of referring to an ideal self, to the Self as a fully human praxis. The necessary conditions for such a praxis are therefore fully expressed in the actions of a good will. You are a creature who ought to be human, a creature for whom the realizing of human being is a capacity. You are commanded to exercise that capacity, to realize your Self. Thus the categorical imperative demands that you act so as to express in your action the conditions necessary to that action's being a human one, and to affirm those conditions as the reason for your action. For Sartre and Judge William, these conditions have been three (and also for Fromm, if self-love is taken as a dimension of each of the other three). It should be no surprise that the categorical imperative therefore has three expressions as well, each making salient one of the necessary features of genuinely human praxis.

Kant explicitly rejected grounding ethical principles on human nature. Insofar as your knowledge of human nature is derived from empirical evidence, any such principles would lack the universality and necessity that are required for a rule devoid of any caveats whatsoever, a rule to which you could never make yourself an exception. Such principles would therefore lack the authority requisite of a command not owned by any special interest even though that be the interest of the human species *en toto*. Since the only alternative to basing moral principles on human nature is to ground them on what can be determined by reason alone, Kant insists that a rationally determined morality must apply to every rational entity and not just to human beings. The philosophies we have so far been exploring begin in one manner or another with human nature, so Kant's approach would seem to set them all aside as methodologically unsound. Kant's rational method begins with the question: "What must an act be to be good?"; our question is a more limited one: "What must you be to be a Self?" Yet both questions have the same answer, for your self is its actions, and a good will as the agency of actions is what an ideal Self would be. So our question is at least entailed by Kant's. A good person is a good will even if the converse need not be true. We will not, therefore, in a "dream of sweet illusions," have embraced a miscegenated "bastard" in place of virtue by limiting our concern to the conditions of a human being's self-completion [GMM 426]. Kant can be of help to us even if his arguments are more generic than we require, designed to assist various angels, Martians, and higher primates as well as persons like you and me.

The first expression of the categorical imperative, the second one as Kant presents them in his *Grounding for the Metaphysics of Morals,* emphasizes what he calls the material aspect of action: "Now I say that man, and in general every rational being, exists as an end in himself and not merely as a means to be arbitrarily used by this or that will. He must in all his actions, whether directed to himself or to other rational beings, always be regarded at the same time as an end" [GMM 428]. But what is the basis of this "now I say," this bald assertion that persons are always ends, always the goal and reason for an action, insofar as it is moral, and never merely useful means to a goal justified for other reasons?

The end of an action is the value for the sake of which it is done; for a hedonist, this would be the outcome sought. The worth of that action can thus be measured by what it would take to call off the effort, the conditions under which the value of the project would not be worth the time and energy spent on it. For a hedonist, the pain involved in the effort might exceed the pleasure to be found in the results. If your incentive to act is the value you attribute to that action, then you will act differently if a greater value should be substituted in its place or a disvalue introduced so that the value of this activity would no longer be competitive with that of available alternatives. Each end has a price. Its value can be compared to other values and hierarchically ranked. The price of a given end is its location on the resulting scale, where anything of equal price can be indifferently substituted for it and anything of greater price will be preferred to it.

This is the language of hedonism and of the marketplace, of the Moment as defining value and of the Utilitarianist control of behavior through manipulating the quantities of positive and negative value that constitute the actional context. Kant adds only one further thought: that there are some ends that have no price, that have a value so great that nothing could be substituted for them. Such a value would have to be infinite, and because infinities are not equivalent but incommensurable numbers, two such values would not be substitutable one for the other. What has infinite value has dignity [GMM 434–35]. Now every person, says Kant, is a natural hedonist. They act on the presumption of their own dignity; they take their own intrinsic and absolute worth as the unquestioned presupposition for all they do [GMM 429]. The loss of their own fulfillment is the one price they would never pay to attain some other value. But how do you break loose from this uncritical self-evaluation, as Kant requires, and come to know that all humans have dignity and that the truth of this claim is an *a priori* necessity for moral action?

A good will must be free in order for it to be good; a rational will must be free in order for it to be rational. You can do nothing praiseworthy or blameworthy unless the cause of your action be your own uncaused will. To remove your freedom from an action is for it to collapse into merely a natural phenomenon illustrating some general law of nature. The value of the action, its worth as a goal intended by a purposing agency, would vanish. There would be no agency. Hence human freedom is a necessary condition for praxis, not only yours but any praxis, every praxis. To act so that another human being is treated as merely a means to the attaining of your own aims is to deal with that being as though its value were less than infinite, as though its value were measurable by its usefulness. But this is to treat that being as though it were not a person, not an agent: it would be to deny its freedom. Yet other persons nonetheless are agents. They express their freedom in their every deed, even in the final deed of resisting (or, indeed, even of inviting) your denial of that freedom. Consequently freedom as the necessary condition for human praxis must be acknowledged in each action you perform and in each action you encounter:

Rational beings are called persons inasmuch as their nature already marks them out as ends in themselves, i.e., as something which is not to be used merely as means and hence there is imposed thereby a limit on all arbitrary use of such beings, which are thus objects of respect. . . . The practical imperative will therefore be the following: Act in such a way that you treat humanity, whether in your own person or in the person of another, always at the same time as an end and never simply as a means. [GMM 428–29]

"It is precisely by working that man makes himself free," said Judge William, "by working he shows that he is higher than nature." The dignity of human being lies in its freedom to make choices, to create values, which it does necessarily. Sartre says, "We are condemned to be free," because "man is freedom," because freedom is what we essentially are. You are praxis and freedom is its necessary condition. Any expression of praxis therefore expresses the infinite worth of its agent as the sole source of whatever finite worth might be achieved. Love, claims Fromm, must nurture in others and in yourself the independence, the dignity of creative autonomy, without which there can be no human self. Whatever you do is limited by human freedom. To respect yourself and other selves is to be aware that you share with them a nature the foundations for which must be reaffirmed in everything you do. Failure to obey categorically the imperative to respect human dignity is self-referentially inconsistent. It is denying the truth of your selfhood, a truth exhibited even in that denial. Like the Cartesian *dubito,* the denial makes plain the freedom it would suppress.

Freedom has consequences, the choosing of which both separates you from other people who have made other choices and unites you with them through the widened benefit of your shared accomplishments. Kant's way of expressing this is through envisioning a kingdom of ends. If your freedom is exercised in a way that respects the dignity of all humanity, then whatever you did would intend the disadvantage of no one and the benefit of all. In not pursuing your own interests at the expense of the interests of others, you act in a way uniquely your own but in a manner that takes everyone else's ways of acting into account. You are creating yourself, fashioning the practical maxims for living a life that fully realizes your potential as a self and that fulfills as far as appropriate your desire for pleasures and your hope of happiness. You are, as Kant prefers to put it, your own autonomous legislator. But what you choose, if done out of a respect for others, will be at the same time also compatible with and, you hope, contributory to the well-being of others. You provide for their realization of selfhood, and for their pleasures and happiness, in providing for your own. Kant emphasizes the dignity of selves in a kingdom of ends. That is, each human being

is bound only to act in accordance with his own will, which is, however, a will purposed by nature to legislate universal laws. . . . [And so] it will be possible to think of a whole of all ends in systematic connection (a whole both of rational beings as ends in themselves and also of the particular ends which each may set for himself); that is, one can think of a kingdom of ends that is possible on the aforesaid principles. . . . A rational being belongs to the kingdom of ends as a member when he legislates in it universal laws while also being himself subject to these laws. He belongs to it as sovereign, when as legislator he is himself subject to the will of no other. [GMM 432, 433]

Kant doesn't mention the subjective incentive for acting as though you were a member in such a community, but John Rawls in *A Theory of Justice* offers a contemporary instance in his notion of "the veil of ignorance."[7] You are asked to imagine a moment in which a community is being created in Lockean fashion by a band of rational humans sitting around a conference table. You would expect each of them to be seeking his or her own self-interest, for this is what we humans do in all such situations. But Rawls lowers a moral curtain that veils from the participants any information about their own likely role in the community they are creating. They know not even their age or gender, much less their jobs, their status, their political affiliations and ethical commitments. Deprived of those individualizing facts, they are forced by their self-interest to act in a manner neutral to any possible self-interest. The society that would be fashioned under such a general ignorance, says Rawls, will be just and can thus be taken as normative for the ethical assessment of any actual form of social order.

What for the Rawlsian paradigm is a matter of enlightened self-interest, and for Fromm would be a self-love extended without limit to encompass all persons as though brothers and sisters, must for Kant be lifted to the level of duty by showing that it is a necessary condition for human ethical action. "Despair," says Sartre, is "reckoning only with what depends upon our will," acknowledging your past choices as parenting the particular self you have now become. That is precisely how an autonomous legislator acts: without excuse, without any attempt to avoid responsibility for your deeds. One salient feature of

Rawls's hypothetical community is that its agents are free. They have been stripped stipulatively of all possible excuses for their actions in that originating moment. They are without question going to be fully responsible for the society they will have created and for the good or evil that founding action might subsequently entail. Their heritage has been put into neutral: the present is completely theirs to enhance or degrade as they choose. They have no place to hide from the consequences of their actions. Your present is complicated by the intrusion into it of the sins and virtues of your ancestors. But this past inheritance is in fact irrelevant with respect to the right or wrong of your own present deeds. It is not the consequences of what you do that exhibits your authenticity, but whether you acknowledge your authorship of your actions and of the distinctive personal character that emerges as the pattern of the way of your intending them.

In the kingdom of ends, you are to acknowledge in others what you acknowledge about yourself. They too are autonomous legislators; they too are responsible for what they do. Because they are therefore free from the constraints of passion, interest, and partisan habit that motivate people to seek their own advantage at the expense of others, you can trust them to be exercising their freedom in a manner that intends the general good. A Rawlsian legislator acts for your benefit lest when the veil of ignorance is lifted your role in life should turn out to be his. A Kantian legislator has your interest in mind because no other interest has grounds for being put ahead of yours, and because your infinite value is at all times respected. Although the Rawlsian motive is subjective and the Kantian objective, the result is for both the same: you respond to the legislation of the other as you would to your own autonomous legislation, for the benefits you give and those you receive both intend the good of the whole, which includes the just and equitable good of each member and thus of yourself.

Judge William asserted that you should actualize your special talents in some appropriate way, recognizing that "in all the differences there is the common factor left that each is a calling." The kingdom of ends would not be a community if it did not expect its autonomous legislators to act in distinctively different fashions, according to their unique abilities and social roles, although in an harmonious rather than divisive manner. A collection of clones, all doing the same thing, would not be a community. Kant's legislator wills from his or her particular perspective procedures for social interaction that dovetail with what others from their different perspectives would have thought appropriate. They do not will that each do the same thing or even that each will the same rules, but that what their several actions and rules are be com-

mensurate, that "all maxims proceeding from [each person's] own legislation ought to harmonize with a possible kingdom of ends as a
kingdom of nature" [GMM 436], which is to say as a well-ordered, fully
concrete, complex and enduring totality.

The command to treat all persons as ends in themselves makes the
value of each absolute, and hence incommensurable with the value of
any other. They are as free moral agents each an incomparable good.
By itself, however, this would permit a kind of radical individualism,
selves too precious to be brought into any kind of moral relationship to
one another. The command to be responsible for the fruits of your free
moral agency, to knit your efforts together with those of others by recognizing that their actions are determinative for you and yours for
them, insists that incommensurables can be harmonized. The incommensurability of the hypotenuse of a right triangle with the other an-
gles does not unsuit it for its role as an essential member of the
triangle. Indeed, it is its difference that contributes to the figure attaining geometric completeness. A Self is both free and responsible for its
freedom to others; you are autonomous but within a community.

Still more is required, however: "Act only according to that maxim
whereby you can at the same time will that it should become a universal law. . . . Act as if the maxim of your action were to become through
your will a universal law of nature" [GMM 421]. The formal, abstract
character of this command seems to conflict with the respect for difference just discussed: you are to do only what you want everyone else
to do as well. But the imperative is about rules not actions: you are to
act in accord only with moral maxims that you think everyone else
should also follow. Their actions might be different but the rules by
which they act should not be. Your deeds are moral only when they
instantiate ethical rules incumbent on everyone. Insofar as you act
morally, you hold yourself up as a role model for others to emulate.
You are doing the kind of thing that anyone should do; consequently
the sort of way you behave is how everyone ought to behave.

The Sartrean anguish of being "responsible for myself and for everyone else" seems to be mitigated for Kant because the form of life that
for Sartre your actions implicitly recommend, like it or not, is for Kant
guided by maxims you have explicitly judged worthy of being recommended.

What I recognize immediately as a [moral] law for me, I recognize with
respect; this means merely the consciousness of the subordination of
my will to a law without the mediation of other influences upon my
sense. . . . Respect is properly the representation of a worth that
thwarts my self-love. [GMM 401; footnote]

What calls forth your respect for a moral maxim that might serve to guide your action is your recognition that it does not privilege your standpoint. It treats you as morally equal to anyone else and so advises you to act in a way no different than it would advise someone else to act. You are led from a possible action to its maxim and thence to its universal applicability. Yet this is precisely what happens in Sartrean anguish. The deed you would do is one that you know will be automatically generalized as a deed recommended to all others for their doing. Insofar as you are authentic in your actions you would so act only if that universalization disclosed itself to be in accord with the necessary conditions for fully human praxis.

In keeping with Judge William's discussion of marriage and Fromm's description of erotic love, take this command therefore as affirming the moral identity of agents. The harmonizing of differences is here intensified into interchangeability. You have a way in addition to legislative coordination by which your free choices are integrated into the social order. By undergoing the self-enlargement that comes through mutual mentoring, through offering your praxis as exemplary and identifying another's maxims as suitable for your own praxis, you weave aspects of the purposes and styles of others into the fabric of your own life. The coordination of your purposes with those of others within a single legislative framework achieves harmonic breadth, but emulating the principles of others by integrating them into your own purposes achieves harmonic depth. The one assures consistency and compatibility; the other adds coherence and interdependence.

These role models, however, are not esoteric others whose personal quirks and accomplishments have attracted your attention. You do not emulate them for their idiosyncracies but as examples of how any person should go about the affairs of life. They are role models because of the universal import of how they act. Your actions recommend themselves to others as instances of what it means to be human in a world where good will is never more than an ideal. The moral identity of agents is in virtue of their shared humanity.

Kant does not actually make this point, but it is a distinction he requires. The intensity of mutual self-reflection and the harmony of divergencies are two different dimensions of community, one as integrating as the other is encompassing. The ideal imitation of others within a kingdom of ends would be a togetherness in which breadth and depth are fully isomorphic, in which the intensity of your respect for those with whom you identify is applied so widely that its scope includes the whole of humanity. Fromm plunges into an obscure mysticism in attempting to articulate precisely such a togetherness. It is difficult to affirm this sort of total oneness without obliterating the differences of the many that compose it. It is fitting, therefore, to retain an interme- diate region between the sanctity of the individual and the absolute worth of the harmonized totality. The family or neighborhood, the re- gion or the nation serve well to provide that middling status, remind- ing us that there are three modalities for genuine Selfhood that we have been tracing, all of which must be expressed in and affirmed by your praxis and by mine for our lives to be fully human, for each of us authentically to instantiate the Self.

And so to summarize the arguments of this chapter. We have said that a Self has three modalities (See Illustration 4.1). The first of these is individuality, yourself or myself as a center of freedom, each of us creating ourself as an unique presence in the world. Your selfhood is the essence of your individuality, the signature with which you sign your every deed. It is an achievement, accomplished in time by making choices and taking responsibility for them such that a durational iden- tity emerges as the foundation for a welter of interdependent aims and serial outcomes. Your self emerges, binding the many things you have done and would hope to do into one unrepeatable reality, into a self- sameness of which you and I and others are aware. But you or I also have a sense of standard, a character, by which we measure the quality of our enduring selfhood. You judge yourself by reference to an ideal, your actual praxis by comparison with what you think yourself truly to be. Your deeds have import because they are taken by you, by me, by others, as expressing or denying criteria of excellence, of what it is best for you or me to do and to become.

A second modality of Selfhood then emerges. Society sets standards of expected attitudes and practices that should become a part of our

**Illustration 4.1 Modes and Levels of the Ideal Self**

| level \ mode | (efficient)<br>self | (formal)<br>society | (final)<br>world |
|---|---|---|---|
| standard:<br>ideal | character | tradition | human nature |
| identity:<br>enduring | life-style<br>form of life | a societal<br>practice | human behavior |
| particular:<br>momentary | actions<br>choices | forms of life | many societal<br>practices |

character as well as an external obligation imposed upon each of us by the others. The free citizen accepting the will of other free citizens as a duty, a responsibility, concomitant with the rights of autonomy is an idealized expression of how the residue of the choices of others, including the residue of your own choices as one among them, is the first of your responsibilities. Making it yours, owning up to it, merging it with your choices, is how what was a cultural legacy becomes as well your form of life. We internalize the traditions of our community. Conscience is how our ancestors become immortal.

Even this is not enough, however, for there are occasions when a society can be thought to betray its heritage, to forget its destiny. Our culture has a social character, a tradition; there are universal standards to which it should adhere and by which it can be judged. But because the achievements and failures of our community are yours and mine who are its living expression, these standards need to inform our individual actions and be integrated into our individual characters. We have found that such overarching criteria for action can be discovered by attending closely to the very nature of praxis. You and I deny our humanity when we act as though what is necessary to our action were not. You deform your character, debase yourself into less than a human creature, when day after day you fail to affirm the conditions of authentic selfhood. A society abrogates its right to exist as a form of human togetherness insofar as the patterns of interaction made essential over the generations to its functioning do not affirm the dignity of individuals and the value of their mutuality.

This third modality of the Self thus takes a transcendental turn (See Illustration 4.2). It discloses, we argued, three transcultural conditions for praxis, qualities expressed universally and necessarily in every human act. These were (1) its freedom, the irreducibility of the choice of aim and mode, of end sought and style of seeking; (2) its individuating consequence, the stamping of that unique choosing into a determinate facticity for it and others to utilize; and (3) its generalizability, the availability of each choice and consequence to be copied by other selves. Variations on this triune theme were heard: love, authenticity, duty, the categorical imperative. They all agreed that there are ways of acting that are exhibited as realizable in every human action, therefore in yours and in mine, and so serve as measures of the extent to which our actions achieve full human expression.

The threefold transcendental conditions of Selfhood find expression in each of the three temporal modalities of Selfhood. A Self exhibits its freedom, its uniqueness, and its commonality in its own individualized character, in its social roles, and in its ways of being human. Your life

Illustration 4.2 Transcendental Conditions of the Ideal Self

|  | material | efficient | final | formal |
|---|---|---|---|---|
| Fromm<br>love<br>[material] | biology<br>self-love | motherly<br>develop-<br>mental | brotherly<br>peers, all<br>humanity | erotic<br>intimate<br>partner |
| Sartre<br>authen-<br>ticity<br>[efficient] | agency<br>conscious<br>facticity | forlornness<br>freedom | despair<br>responsi-<br>bility | anguish<br>recommend<br>defining all |
| Judge<br>William<br>duty<br>[final] | society | work<br>equality<br>humility | calling<br>unique<br>contribu-<br>tion | marriage<br>inter-<br>dependent |
| Kant<br>imperative<br>[formal] | humanity | dignity<br>treat as<br>end only | autonomy<br>kingdom<br>of ends | universal<br>role model |
|  |  | selection | individuation | generalization |
|  |  | chosen | determinate | available |

or mine is genuinely a human life to the degree that our various actions each make real such an ideal Self. Because we are free, we are not prevented by any externality from choosing to realize this ideal. Because our choices are efficacious, this ideal can be concretely realized as an intentional community within which you and I and others engage the world. Because our engagement has no natural boundary, this ideal can give temporal expression to the essence of human nature, making human history the moving image of its eternal truth.

Unlike the Moment, the Self is a practical, obtainable ideal. It does not project us beyond our humanity toward some impossible overcoming of its necessary conditions. Instead it calls you and me to embrace that humanity, to make real its ideals by affirming rather than denying the necessary conditions for being human.

# Five

## THE COMPLETING OF SELF

What is desirable need not be desired. Genuine humanity might be within reach of our human praxis without you or I making an effort to grasp it and possess the prize. Kant mentions a "gouty patient" who knows that he probably needs to control his drinking and his diet in order to regain his health but who chooses "to enjoy what he likes and to suffer what he may" on the grounds that "the enjoyment of the present moment" should not be sacrificed to "some possibly groundless expectations of the good fortune that is supposed to be found in health" [GMM 399]. This is not a person who has been overcome by overweening desire, the steady voice of reason commanding duty but the impulsive cry of passion shouting it down. Instead reason has become confused, "led astray" by desire into "a propensity to quibble" with the commands of duty, to find ways to bend duty's strict laws into a form "more compatible with our wishes and inclinations" [GMM 405]. Self-deception, it would seem, is endemic to the human condition.

The frailty and impurity of ordinary, actual human praxis thus contrasts with the strength and purity of the rational principles upon which it rests. The empirical self contrasts starkly with the normative Self. Your self is a noble enough reality to be able to grasp the principles upon which its moral worth is judged and to know how to act by reference to them; it takes no special expertise to know what is your duty. But because your self is a reality that is more than its rational capacities, because it is of flesh and bone as well as thought, it can easily become befuddled. What may be clear to the pure light of your

143

reason may be ambiguous when you are making actual choices within a concrete historical situation. Consequently it may well be that neither you nor anyone else has ever done as they ought, never for even one brief moment exemplified the Self. Good will may be the ideal, but all you or anyone in fact ever encounter as the real motive for action is "the dear self," its needs and desires.

The problem is not with our reason but with its innocence. The power of our desires is their ability to deceive reason, and the deception is possible because a rationally informed praxis can easily be lured away from attention to the principles by which it should set its course. The solution is simple enough to state: stiffen the resolve of reason and it will be freed from the siren song of our desirings. Having learned to resist the extraneous "empirical inducements" that draw it off its course, reason will lead you truly to your destination. You should not think that this true course is something inherently repulsive that you must grimace and bear with. Neither should you imagine that the true course is merely a matter of indifference. The rational ideal of Self-hood, the pure sound of the completeness it offers, would have its own sufficient allure if only the static of desire could be tuned out.

For the pure thought of duty and of the moral law generally, unmixed with any extraneous addition of empirical inducements, has by the way of reason alone ... an influence on the human heart so much more powerful than all other incentives which may be derived from the empirical field that reason in the consciousness of its dignity despises such incentives and is able gradually to become their master. [GMM 410–11]

Is able to become their master, that is, if and only if the self does not have its ears so stoppered up with desiring that it is unable to hear the call of reason.

Aristotle has reminded us that reason is at its most innocent in the very young, and that therefore their inclinations tend to be expressed without constraint. Unless someone intervenes, habits of preferring self-interest to the common good will become fixed early and then will be nearly impossible to overcome. Education, the educating of the self to attend to the inner voice of its reason, is what you require if you are to prevent a spontaneous child from turning into an irresponsible adult. Aristotle noted that parents are not well equipped to provide the sort of education needed, but you were not very sanguine about his suggestion that the *polis* play that role. Governments, indeed, are too often expressions of the desires of an individual or an elite; they can be as corrupting an influence as are the natural passions.

After having followed Judge William and his compatriots to their climactic celebration of the categories of Self expressed in Kant's categorical imperative, are you and I then left only with an empty ideal, with
regulative principles that can never be constitutive? Is Sartre correct in
claiming that the end of praxis is incapable of being realized, that it is
an ontological impossibility? We have found a norm by which to guide
our actions and to judge their rightness. But does it offer only vain
counsels of perfection? Is it a stern taskmaster, always condemning our
actions as selfish and never as good? If so, the norm is something external to each of us and not under our control. It is not a goal that you
can strive toward by making concrete choices, a goal that comes to be
realized as your character, your citizenship, your human nature. The
ideal of Self would seem to lie beyond the horizon of your possibilities;
you would have to overcome your humanity in order for it to be constitutive of your reality.

This is not the conclusion that need be drawn, however. Reason,
Kant insists, has an influence on the human heart. It is not without its
resources. Quiet, unnoticed amid the maelstrom of human desirings, it
nonetheless whispers in your mind's ear. Insofar as it can get your attention, to that degree it can begin to exercise its capacity for mastery,
for calming and controlling the other influences upon your will. The
question becomes: how fares reason in getting the attention of persons and communities of persons? Is reason as a final cause actually a
force in your life, in my life, in human history: a force making for
change? If so, the ideal of Self and of the kingdom of Selves is not an
impossibility, an external empty norm. If reason is at work drawing us
toward it, holding its ideal up as a banner for us to follow, then its
realization is a task, perhaps an individual task but more fundamentally
a collective task.

The books of Daniel and Revelation held out an ideal of human fulfillment as providing the ultimately constitutive principles of existence
for those faithful to its inevitability. They saw history as having a re-
gressive structure, one that actualized in each new epoch less and less
of the ideal. But the Moment would come, *deus ex machina,* for those
who endured to the end the onslaught of a thousand different denials
of its ideality. And yet the calculations of its coming proved to be in
error and needed to be recalculated, again and again. The Endtime was
always at the horizon, its glory contrasting with the never-ending, day-
by-day suffering of the faithful, a suffering that was increasingly demor-
alizing. How long, O Lord, must we cry out to Thee, our prayers
unanswered, Thy promise still unfulfilled?

Augustine introduced an educative dimension to the terrors of history: its trials and tribulations were how faith is tested, tempered, made

ready for the reward assured it everlastingly. Here too, however, the ideal remained external to history. Because there are no signs by which to mark the progress of its coming, history for Augustine cannot be understood as a ship that slowly but inexorably bears faithful passengers toward a safe harbor. Instead, history is the storm that obscures the harbor from our sight. The Endtime will come with the calming of the storm, by the destruction of historical vicissitude, by the substitution of a new heaven and a new earth for the ones that now contextualize human existence. As with Moments in any lesser sense, so too this ultimate Moment lay beyond praxis rather than being in some sense its constitutive ideal.

A thirteenth-century Christian monk, Joachim of Fiore, seems to have been the first Western thinker to reinterpret the ideal as an outgrowth of historical change rather than its negation. Judge William claimed that through the decisions that make each moment concrete you can come to incarnate your proper human nature as a lived temporal reality. Parallel to this, Joachim claims that the events of human history can come in the course of time to incarnate true human community as a properly historical reality. For Joachim, the ideal is realized in history, not beyond it; as its culmination, not its repudiation.

Joachim's views are expressed in obscure texts and in multicolored drawings of perplexing complexity,[1] but his basic vision is quite intelligible [see Illustration 5.1]. He organizes the past into two "epochs," one encompassing the period of the Old Testament and one the Christian era. The epoch of the Father comprises 42 generations divided into three sets of 14 generations each, preceded by an additional preparatory period of 21 generations, the whole of it stretching from Adam to the time of Christ. The epoch of the Son overlaps with this, its

**Illustration 5.1 Joachim of Fiore: Three Epochs of Human History**

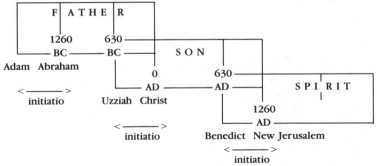

preparatory period extending from Uzziah to Christ, its period of ascendancy running 42 generations to a time in Joachim's immediate future. As each generation is calculated to be 30 years, the duration of an epoch's flourishing is 1,260 years. Thus the endpoint for the epoch of the Son is a.d. 1260. It is to be followed by a third epoch, that of the Holy Spirit, the preparation for which has overlapped the current epoch, the flourishing of which will begin imminently.

The numerology is reminiscent of apocalyptic literature. A rigid, extensional order is imposed upon the dynamic, organic flow of human interactions in a way that strikes you immediately as artificial and problematic. But Joachim's predominant metaphors are organic. The procession of the epochs is likened to human maturation, to the sequence of seasons, to qualities of flora, and to other natural developmental processes:

The first the age of children, the second the age of youth, the third that of the old. The first in starlight, the second in moonlight, the third in full daylight. The first in winter, the second in spring, the third in summer. The first the seedling of a plant, the second roses, the third lilies. The first producing grass, the second stalks, the third wheat. The first water, the second wine, the third oil. [JF 17]

The three epochs are represented in one drawing as the differing ways in which Jewish and Gentile vines intertwine as they grow upward as though on a trellis to their full blooming in the third epoch.

More important than these nature metaphors, however, is Joachim's notion of an epoch's womb-time. A period of gestation, lasting half as long as the extent of the subsequent flourishing of the epoch, precedes its emergence into historical dominance. For the epoch of the Father, this *initiatio* is from Adam to Abraham, from creation to the calling forth of Israel as a special people. The epoch of the Son gestates during the time of the prophets who from Isaiah on foresaw the coming of the Messiah. The epoch of the Holy Spirit is quickened in the womb of Christianity with Benedict and is marked by the development of the monastic orders which anticipate the ideal community soon to be actualized.

This organicism is crucial, for it means that the new depends upon the old, grows out of it, rather than merely supplanting it. The kingdoms in the book of Daniel were military hegemonies. Babylonia was overthrown by Persia and Persia by Assyria, each kingdom starting afresh upon the ruins of the vanquished. Their relatedness was superimposed by means of a secret, coded chronology. Only someone who possessed the key to the code, who could interpret the dreams or the visions, could tell that the victory of one kingdom over another marked a step toward the Endtime. But where the End is a culmination, as it is for Joachim, a result that grows progressively out of beginnings pregnant with its possibility, the interpretation requires no secret code. It is there for us to read if we would but open our eyes.

As it is with children so also it was during the flourishing of Israel: in the first epoch rules of proper behavior had to be imposed in the form of an external law enforced by external authorities. But the law made grace possible, nurtured in people the capacity for living by a law written in their hearts rather than upon tablets of stone. Hence in the second epoch the children of the Father became the brothers and sisters of the Son. Yet even during this epoch, the era of Christianity, external laws have remained necessary. Spiritual and temporal powers have had to share authority, and people are everywhere in bondage to their sins. From grace springs love, however, and the spread of love makes possible the emergence of communities based completely on love. In the forthcoming epoch of the Holy Spirit this love, immanent in the lives of all citizens then come to full maturity, will find expression in a single spiritual and monastic ordering of all human society.

Thus Joachim's characterizations of the epochs are not only in terms of organic development but also in terms of the development of personal and political freedom, the overcoming of bondages of every sort:

The first epoch was that in which we were under the law, the second when we were under grace, the third when we will live in anticipation of even richer grace.... The first epoch was in knowledge, the second in the authority of wisdom, the third in the perfection of understanding. The first in the chains of the slave, the second in the service of a son, the third in freedom.... The first in fear, the second in faith, the third in love. The first under slave bondage, the second in freedom, the third in friendship. [JF 17]

The trinitarian doctrine utilized in the naming of the epochs requires both the organic and developmental characteristics Joachim proclaims. According to Church dogma, the Son proceeds from the Father, the Holy Spirit from both Father and Son, one reality three expressions, one substance three persons. Joachim only departs from orthodoxy in giving special importance to the temporal sequencing of this trinity in human experience: that the Son is manifest through an incarnation that ushers in the Church as an historical reality, and that the Holy Spirit then comes as the agency for the spread of the Gospel to the ends of the earth. From this it follows that the Kingdom of God, the ideal Moment so fervently looked for, is to be an historical rather than a transcendent reality. The Kingdom of God comes to fulfill the law, the prophets, and the Church, not to destroy them.

The cyclical view of historical change, implicit in Augustine and clearly formulated by Ibn Khaldûn and Suzanne Langer, can be bent straight by the simple expedient of repudiating the downside of the cycle. These cyclical interpretations were as much organic as Joachim's, except that for them development was always at a price. Joachim and progressivists since him deny that this need be so. If the ideal is a completion of human nature rather than something transcending it, then if you can realize that ideal even in part the conditions of incompleteness will no longer hold absolute sway and change will begin to give way to everlasting good. The process is irreversible precisely because the perfection being actualized lacks the flaws, the disharmonies, the fault lines of evil or error or ignorance that make for disintegration. If our goal is freedom and freedom means the elimination of self-interest as a motive, then in the absence of the conditions for divisiveness there can be only unending self-autonomy and mutual caring. Where the Self has finally emerged, the laws of society will reflect, just as the laws of nature do, the Creator's unifying purpose for creation. The Kingdom of God, like Kant's kingdom of ends, is marked by respect and mutuality. All its enemies having been defeated, of that kingdom there can be no end.

The English Puritans saw this clearly. The coming of the millennium could be hastened by nurturing its necessary conditions. First individuals must be pure of heart, having freely consented to receive God's grace in the transformative experience of their own personal conversion. These saints of the Lord ought then to join together in cleansing the religious community of its impurities. The Church should have only the pure of heart as its members so that it might fulfill its mission as the paradigm for every kind of human community. The Church thus purified, thus become paradigmatic, might then itself serve as the final community of all communities, the Kingdom of God on earth. The self, the paradigmatic group, the totality: here once again are manifest the grounding principles of the completed Self.

Religious conversion may be too intense an experience, however, too nonrational a process for the development of Self, even though the Puritans were always insistent on the crucial role of reason in a conversion experience that involved, with all appropriate legal import, a covenanting agreement between the purified soul and its Creator, between the community of saints and its Founder. Gotthold Lessing offers us a less intense alternative vision, one equally religious in its inspiration but expressed, for the most part, with Enlightenment perspective and with a focus upon the pedagogy of individual and collective progress.

In *The Education of the Human Race,* Lessing sees divine revelation as coming in stages. God reveals at any one time only as much about His will, His purposes regarding individual salvation and the destiny of humankind, as people are able to comprehend. Human moral and rational understanding grows under the tutelage of divine revelation, each new, fuller disclosure coming only when human experience has matured sufficiently to grasp the truth of what has already been revealed to it. The process is the same well-ordered movement from the simple to the complex, from the partial to the complete, that goes on in a schoolroom. Therefore human beings by their own unaided reason would come eventually, given world enough and time, to a grasp of all the truths of religion. By means of revelation, however, this goal can be more quickly attained.

In the period of the Old Testament, when the Hebrews were as children with respect to their moral education, rewards and punishments "addressed to the senses" were the sources of religious motivation. Myths and allegories were "the clothing of abstract truths," told simply and poetically so as to appeal in their concreteness and vivacity to childish minds. But when a certain "portion of the human race had come so far in the exercise of its reason, as to need, and to be able to make use of, nobler and worthier motives for moral action" [EHR 55], Christ came bringing a fuller revelation. He preached the unique, immortal character of the human soul and the "inward purity of heart" that is its proper expression. The educative process ever since has been to explicate this new teaching, to effect "the development of revealed truths into truths of reason" [EHR 76].

Lessing then holds out for us a vision of the next phase in human moral maturation, when God's truth need not be taught through scripture nor through an exemplar but will be known by you and me, by everyone, directly and rationally. The purpose of schooling is to make a child into a civilized adult; the purpose of God's educating of the human species must have a similar goal, the perfecting of its moral capacities:

It will come! it will assuredly come! the time of the perfecting, when man ... will do right because it *is* right, not because arbitrary rewards are set upon it, which formerly were intended simply to fix and strengthen his unsteady gaze in recognizing the inner, better, rewards of well-doing. It will assuredly come! the time of a new eternal gospel. [EHR 85,86]

Lessing even alludes to the Joachimites, whom he faults only for thinking the "third age" would come in their own lifetime. They had
"scarcely outgrown their childhood;" they were "without enlightenment, without preparation," and so like children were impatient to see
clearly how much more the human race still must learn before attaining its goal of moral perfection. Even now, in Lessing's more enlightened age, he is not sanguine about the imminence of the perfecting.
The outcome is sure even if progress toward it may at times be difficult
to discern, may even seem to be retrograde. For "it is not true that the
shortest line is always straight." The route may well, like a set of cog-
wheels, move forward only across a complex mesh of fast-moving gears
that give rise in their interactions to the movement of that "great, slow
wheel, which brings mankind nearer to its perfection" [EHR 92].

Lessing thus combines enthusiasm for a progressive realization of the
ideal in history with uncertainty about its details and timing. The goal
is assured and the major stages of the journey are clearly demarcated,
but the specific pathways are not well marked. The Puritans also found
the developmental struggle to be far more difficult than they had anticipated. The purification of the individual self, unfortunately, was not
inheritable. The covenant the saints made with God, to exemplify in
their social interactions the ideals soon to be exemplified throughout
the whole of creation, kept being undercut by a rising generation that
lacked the requisite conversion experience. The triumphal march of
the saints found itself floundering about in the quicksand of pragmatic
expedience. Other progressivists who in their differing ways have also
sought to erect a separated communal paradigm as a tangible final
cause able to lure the rest of us to its emulation have likewise seen
their utopian hopes and their concrete efforts to realize those hopes
collapse. The American wilderness is scattered with the ruins of such
dreams, eighteenth- and nineteenth-century efforts to create communities of the Third Age in a virgin land. Their European counterparts, not
only theorists like Turgot and Herder and Condorcet, but practical
folks such as the followers of Fourier, Saint-Simon, and Comte, all fared
no better.

The progressivists would seem to be no improvement upon Daniel
after all. Apocalyptic writers claimed to possess the key for decoding
the secret meaning of history's seeming randomness. In contrast and in
keeping with its developmental character, an organic view promised
that the meaning to history could be read from the empirical evi-
dences, that the end was implicit in the means and therefore accessible
to anyone willing to take a close look at events. Joachim finds his evi-
dences in an analogical analysis of scriptural text; the Puritans turned

to their own inner experience of divine presence; more enlightened thinkers sought help from the findings of science. But all such claims have about them the odor of arbitrariness. They seem more the incense of a hope for what ought to be than the savor of predictions, based on known facts, of what will be.

Kant sought to avoid the pitfalls of empty rhetoric and unjustified prediction in his own attempt to give constitutive substance to the normative principles of the categorical imperative. Consider two of his essays: "Idea for a Universal History," which was written at about the same time as the *Grounding for the Metaphysics of Morals,* and "Is the Human Race Consistently Progressing?" which was one of the last things he wrote. The historical world, Kant acknowledges, is created by human beings who have free will, who like yourself make choices that are unique, idiosyncratic, and often or always at odds with moral rules that if followed would make their actions predictable [HRCP 83–84]. What is needed is a broad overview from which to see whatever uniformities there might be in these choices, to discern patterns and tendencies that are lost by focusing only on particular individuals. History

permits us to hope that if we attend to the play of freedom of the human will in the large, we may be able to discern a regular movement in it, and that what seems complex and chaotic in the single individual may be seen from the standpoint of the human race as a whole to be a steady and progressive though slow evolution of its original endowment. [IUH 17]

Kant was an astronomer; he knew about the need for a proper organizing principle in order to work out the trajectories of things from the confusing jumble of available data points.

Kant also notes that human behavior in the aggregate can often be predicted even when the actions of a single individual cannot. Births, marriages, and deaths follow statistical uniformities in our society even though your own or any other specific life-story cannot be predicted by reference to those uniformities. In the case of the progress of the human race, however, the problem is much worse because the known data are so few. The task is not simply to achieve a general standpoint, nor to shift in Copernican fashion from an inadequate to an adequate one. It is more like trying to predict the path of the sun across the galaxy; we know too little to be able to extrapolate with any confidence [IUH 27].

A transcendental argument can be made, nonetheless, as you would expect from a philosopher who has disdained the relevance of empirical data to a determination of how persons ought to act. "Nature does nothing in vain." The world, the result of God's creative action, shares with human praxis this much: that it is always for a purpose. Though individuals seem to seek only their own purposes, there must be a purpose for the whole species that is not reducible to the mere sum of those several desirings. Given that reason is the one distinctive capacity available to humans as an instrument for their survival and well-being (and more importantly for achieving a dignity that makes their lives and their happiness a worthwhile goal whether or not attained), it must be that the purpose of humanity is the full exercise of its rationality [IUH 19–20]. Consequently human history must be the proper arena for the unfolding of that purpose, for the completing of the human Self.

We have already agreed that individual completeness requires community. The true Self is interrelated through its autonomy with other autonomous Selves into a kingdom of Selves; Self-expression establishes commonality as well as individuation. Hence the moral development of the human species must be a shared enterprise, a history of societal maturation nurturing and nurtured by personal maturation. A "universal cosmopolitan condition," a specieswide community of Selves, is of necessity the "womb" within which alone "all the original capacities of the human race can develop" [IUH 28].

But slowly. Only slowly can the womb be formed, only slowly the fetal Self mature. It is freedom that must develop; and a free will, as you know all too well, pursues its own narrow ends more readily than the end for which it was made. Duration is therefore of the essence, an extensive extendedness,

a perhaps unreckonable series of generations, each of which passes its own enlightenment to its successor in order finally to bring the seeds of enlightenment to that degree of development in our race which is completely suitable to Nature's purpose. [IUH 19]

Kant cannot explain why this should be so, for it means that a vast multitude of individual humans, you and I included among them, will never themselves attain the perfection assured their species. Many of those who have devoted their lives to the building of the house will never have the "good fortune" to occupy it. Strange; puzzling; but necessarily the case: that short-lived individuals must die for the sake of an immortal species [IUH 20]. Maybe, Kant muses, rational beings on other planets are not of such "crooked wood" as we, may not need such a vast expanse of time to straighten their warped selves into a form usable in the constructing of ideality, and so can attain perfection in their individual lives [IUH 23]. Maybe, muses Lessing, we are born again and again until we each manage over the aeons to work our way up the levels of enlightenment to our perfected end [EHR 94–100].

So enormous, then, is the task of human perfecting that it cannot be attained during the lifespan of a single individual. It cannot even be discerned clearly in the comparatively long stretch of human history up to the present. We know only two things. First, that the goal is assured; second, that it will be attained through human beings like you and me exercising their free will, even though they are now too weak, too childish, to use that freedom other than in servitude to their passions. This is enough for us to be able to reject confidently any other claim regarding human destiny. Kant calls it "moral terrorism" to believe that humans in their freedom will utterly destroy themselves, and he is as vociferous in rejecting the opposite claim, that humanity will rapidly attain its goal. Human nature is too good to permit the former, too wicked to effect the latter [HRCP 81–82].

Nor is history the endless cycle of improvement and decline that Ibn Khaldûn and Augustine propose. Cooperation is not the original, natural condition out of which a desire for something better emerges only to be undercut by the selfishness bred of success. Kant is more attuned to Hobbes than to Rousseau on this point. It was selfish need that compelled free, unbounded individuals to accept the constraints of social order: "their passions keep them from living long together in wild freedom." But once having come together, the crooked growth of their random liberties is being pulled ever straighter by the requirements of that togetherness. Like trees in a forest,

each needs the others, since each in seeking to take the air and sunlight from others must strive upward, and thereby each realizes a beautiful, straight stature, while those that live in isolated freedom put out branches at random and grow stunted, crooked, and twisted. All culture, art which adorns mankind, and the finest social order are fruits of unsociableness, which forces itself to discipline itself and so, by a contrived art, to develop the natural seeds of perfection. [IUH 22]

Humanity has a destiny that gives meaning to its existence. This is the necessary condition for its existence: that humanity have a purpose and that the fulfillment of that purpose be assured. And there is progress toward that end, although we have found it to be empirically indiscernible. Nature works by a "secret art," a "secret plan" hidden from human view that is unfolding and in which you should place your confidence [IUH 25,27].

It is too much, however, to ask for your commitment to this ideal solely on the basis of its rational necessity. Kant thought that you would need an expectation that the kingdom of ends was a constitutive principle of human nature in order to accept fully its regulative authority. Now he thinks that you need some empirical evidence to support your belief that the principle is constitutive. You seem to require some "subjective incentive" to complement the rational incentive of the value of the ideal as such. Empirical evidence is precisely what is not available, however, for the reasons just explored. So Kant settles for a "sign": a concrete indication that what is *permitted* by the history of humankind is also *supported* by it, some tangible corroboration of reason's claim.

There must be some experience in the human race which, as an event, points to the disposition and capacity of the human race to be the cause of its own advance toward the better.... That event would have to be considered not itself as the cause of history, but only as an intimation, an historical sign ... demonstrating the tendency of the human race viewed in its entirety. [HRCP 84]

Kant proposes that this sign might be found, in a very general and sketchy way, by attending to the "regular progress" that has been made since the Greeks in the creation of national political constitutions based more and more explicitly on just and equitable laws [IUH 29–30]. This "guiding thread" he later calls "the evolution of a constitution in accordance with natural law" [HRCP 87]. It is the slow but persistent emergence into historical actuality of *respublica noumenon,* "the eternal norm for all civil organization in general" [HRCP 91]. It is the kingdom of ends clothed at last in the solid flesh of human history.

But this guiding thread is as abstract as the transcendental deduction it is supposed to buttress. A scholarly analysis of constitutional development is every bit as softspoken an expression of progress as is the whisper of reason. Kant wants a louder sign, one that speaks more directly to the will. He finds it in the reaction of people outside France to the events of the French Revolution. Like spectators at a game, their sympathies attach to one of the sides in the controversy, that of the insurgents, and they enthusiastically give that side their support, wishful even that they might themselves be able to do something on its behalf. Their sympathy is "disinterested" in Kant's sense: they favor the revolutionary forces over the Ancien Régime even though they are distant from it and have nothing to gain one way or the other. Indeed, their sympathies if made known to their own local authorities might conceivably work to their disadvantage [HRCP 85].

Enthusiastic, empathic preference for something is a passion. But because in this instance it is aroused in a situation where the person who feels it has no stake in the outcome, it is a moral passion, an expression of the "moral character of humanity." Reason, Kant had said, commands categorically that you do what a good will would have done spontaneously: to act without consulting your interests and in a manner that actively respects the infinite worth of individuals within a just and equitable community. Here, confronted by the spectacle of a people attempting to assert their right to provide themselves with a civil constitution that is "just and and morally good in itself," you respond spontaneously by applauding the ideals for which they struggle, identifying with them, hoping for their success. You, and people everywhere whose responses are not distorted by prospects of gain or loss, react as a good will would have reacted. In that moment, the "moral disposition in the human race" toward the good finds concrete expression. The good will, which is the true essence of human nature, is fleetingly actualized. What has been the regulative principle of your praxis is for a brief shining moment made constitutive.

It is as though the empirical flux of things that veils experience from its principles had been pulled back just for an instant, giving a glimpse of underlying truths. It is as though the *noumenon* had for that moment been seen within the *phenomena,* as when the theatrical backlighting is turned on and the scrim dissolves to reveal what lies beyond it. Just a glimpse; no more than that. But it is enough, says Kant, for to know that human beings are fundamentally good, that they are predisposed to this sort of moral character, "not only permits people to hope for progress toward the better, but is already itself progress insofar as its capacity is sufficient for the present" [HRCP 85]. You have a right to believe in human progress, in the perfecting of the human soul, because there are no rational or empirical grounds for denying such a belief. But now, knowing that this belief rests upon a rational knowledge of its inevitability and having also an empirical glimpse of its presence as a human disposition, your will to believe grows strong. Your hope that the human race has a purpose, that its history has a meaning, gains a resoluteness that is historically efficacious. The capacity to hope resolutely for progress, to really believe in the perfecting of the human spirit, is a small contribution, sufficient "for the present," toward the attaining of that far-off goal.

"For such a phenomenon in human history *is not to be forgotten.*" Once brought to consciousness, its force as an ideal will not dissipate even if the political events that were its expression should fail utterly in their effort to realize it. The French Revolution may miscarry, the

Bourbons may return to power and the course of events run once more in its "former rut." But what was once only an implicit possibility, a dream of prophets, an hypothesis of philosophers, you now know to be within the capacity of the human race to realize. You and everyone else are now aware that it is a practical possibility. And so it is now "too important, too much interwoven with the interest of humanity, and its influence too widely propagated in all areas of the world to not be recalled on any favorable occasion by the nations which would then be roused to a repetition of new efforts of this kind" [HRCP 88].

The ideal at work inchoately, whispering to humanity the promise of the realization of its inherent dignity, works exceedingly slow against the counterweight of selfish desire and willful inconstancy. It is so elusively inchoate, indeed, so softly whispered, as to go undetected: a secret plan known only to nature and nature's God. Yet its workings are progressive and eventually the inchoate begins to flicker into full consciousness, to become articulate, even to be articulated in the reflective purposes of human agents, and to be actualized in some fragmentary and momentary way in the institutions and constitutions of human communities. The ideal, once conscious of itself, thence forward speaks in more than whispers. It speaks not only to the rational faculty but to the will and through the passions; its lure henceforth engages the whole person. Although still hidden from the eyes of scientific proof, this ideal of Self has become an active belief. No longer is narrow self-interest the sole vehicle for progress. Aware of their more noble destiny as Selves, individuals such as you or I now sometimes and to some degree act for the sake of the ideal of *respublica* and of the peaceable kingdom of persons whose value is beyond all price. The pace of progress accelerates when the end it seeks comes to self-consciousness.

You have earlier agreed with Kant that ultimate value, that which gives life meaning, must be attainable or else the meaning is lost. Ought implies can. Were you to locate value in what is beyond your control to realize because dependent upon the accidents of history, you would be basing your life on a goal that renders your actions essentially meaningless. You would have been victimized by a new version of the flaw fatal to every form of hedonism. But if value is the development of an excellent praxis rather than of excellent results, then it must be possible for excellent selves to be concretely realized. A properly developed self, as you have seen, is definitely a good that is within your control. It is a task that every person has, to become a Self, to realize our nature in all three of its dimensions: as uniquely individuated, as interdependent, as generically human.

By the very nature of this task, however, no individual can become a Self except amid a community of other Selves. The logic of Kant's analysis, as also the logic of Judge William, Sartre, and Fromm, requires him to look to the transformation of the whole of humanity as a condition of, and as an expression of, the transformation of each particular person. The development of the species cannot be a matter of good fortune, for then Selfhood would be essentially contingent, realizable only if what need not be realized were by happenstance actually realized. But that is the hedonist's dead end, now appearing at the collective rather than individual level. Consequently, says Kant, the perfection of the human race is the necessary condition of human freedom because the task of becoming a Self can be meaningful only if the conditions for its realization are in place. It is not just that the species must have a purpose alongside the purposes individuals have; this would be an instance of the fallacy of composition. For Kant, rather, the fulfillment of the species-purpose is the condition for the realization of the purposes of individuals. For the kingdom of Selves, just as for the solitary Self: ought implies can.

Kant had postulated in his second *Critique* that eternal life might suffice as a way for giving completion to those who in this life serve faithfully an imperative they cannot fully embody. Yet this reduces the moral ideal to a sort of transcendental hedonism, rewarding in an eternal Moment what cannot be gained in the Moments of temporal life. It also means redeeming individuals but not the communities with which they are inextricably bound. Kant, however, cannot avoid the fact that his arguments entail the claim that a self must become a Self in community and in history. You must by your own free powers realize the ideal if that ideal is to be something actually within your control, a meaning you can create and be held responsible for because it is a meaning that expresses your essence, a meaning you essentially *are*. What you must freely realize is not just your autonomy but the necessary expression of that autonomy as a member of a community of autonomous selves. Short of Lessing's reincarnational solution or a foolish sanguineness concerning the present depth and extent of human selfishness, Kant and his philosophic compatriots have no choice except to see human history as the receptacle for the realization in the species of the ideality that defines its meaning and its destiny. That all cannot share in this destiny is perplexing to Kant. We might prefer him to have said, rather, that it is a terrible and tragic fact. Which surely he would have, had he recognized that his solution, the idea of eternal life, is meaningless in the context of his own insistence that the ideal of developmental Selfhood is of something essentially communal.

The American pragmatists took very seriously the importance of the communal dimension of Self. No individual is genuinely free except within a social order that fosters freedom; genuinely human values cannot be realized except under cultural conditions that are conducive to their continued realization. Thus, for instance, Dewey sees the goal of any individual seeking fulfillment to be "the search for values to be secured and shared by all, because buttressed in the foundations of social life" [QC 311].

Real values are for Dewey, as we have seen, those possibilities which you have shown experimentally to satisfy human need when realized, which you have related to other possibilities and actualities in ways that promise an expansion in the scope of such realization, and the conditions for which you know how to control so that they can recur. This means that the environment in which a value is actualized should be reasonably likely to support it; in turn this means that the societal aspects of that environment need to be designed to be supportive. But human needs are always specific; the problems that arise in their pursuit are always specific as well. Social structures must be capable of constant redesign. Their worth as instruments or as occasions for fulfillment must be open to constant reassessment and improvement. A value is a judgment about the future and the past regarding their relevance to a specific, present, concrete fulfillment.

Dewey therefore rejects out of hand the notion of an ideal situation in which value would be universally secured. First, it presumes an absolute goal, a final end that when realized would be the attainment of a perfection beyond which no more problem-solving needs to be done. But this is just another redaction of the "quest for certainty." It presupposes a timeless realm beyond the flux of coming-to-be and perishing, and then imagines it as somehow established amid that flux. Yet the temporal world is the only reality there is. Our goal is to secure as best we can the methods that seem most likely to realize value, but to recognize that "the attainment of every specific good merges insensibly into a new condition of maladjustment with its need of a new end and a renewed effort" [HNC 287]. Second, the notion of an ideal human condition posits a goal so far off, so vague, so beyond the possibility of present realization as to be debilitating. Unrealizable ideals both disclose the present as inadequate and discourage any effort to do something about it. Just as with any scientific approach: the tasks should be doable; their accomplishment and the accompanying satisfaction, real possibilities.

Yet Dewey's meliorism is not quite so piecemeal as these arguments imply that it should be. What works cannot be known in advance because it involves formulating specific hypotheses and then testing each one of them. For an experimental approach to problem-solving, answers are always specific, and context-dependent responses are designed for and only appropriate to the specific questions that they validate or refute. But even though the question of what works can have no universal answer, Dewey claims that there are "generic lines" that can be sketched regarding the ideal conditions for the "creation of a better world of daily experience" [QC 271–76]. As might be expected, Dewey's sketch is in terms of process not product. An ideal situation is one in which the experimental method is used just as routinely to find answers to societal problems as already it is used to answer questions posed by the natural sciences.

Dewey goes on, nonetheless, to acknowledge the pragamatic usefulness of the symbol of "a community of life in which continuities of existence are consummated" [HNC 330]. Such a substantive ideal offers men and women, alone and as groups, a glimpse of what they hold in common: hope for a better life, the struggle toward its attainment. "Within the flickering inconsequential acts of separate selves dwells a sense of the whole which claims and dignifies them" [HNC 331]. To heighten this sense of their shared venture by giving it an articulated content, heightens in people the importance they attribute to their various tasks and to themselves as agents.

A Common Faith is Dewey's one clear explication of what this symbol might mean. Your own ideals are a function of your particular situation and needs. As possibilities to be realized, they have stirred your imagination and impelled your efforts to make them existing tangible realities. These ideals are multiple, vastly different from one situation in which you find yourself to another, but the emotion in which they are clothed, the desire for their realization, the power of their allure, is in each instance the same. Your sense of self-identity grows up through the nurture of these recurrent factors in your experiences.

Likewise this "unity of loyalty and effort evoked by the fact that many ends are one in the power of their ideal, or imaginative, quality to stir and hold us" [CF 43] draws you together with other selves into a community of shared purposes. You also work with these others in attempting to realize your equally felt ideals. You share with them the same milieu needing to be changed, similar proximate goals, complementary methods, and an equally energetic commitment to getting the job done. The essential unity of your ideals is thus given "coherence and solidity" by your shared efforts to attain their realization [CF 51]. As your several differing praxes harmonize in this manner, you and these others take yourselves as part of a single ongoing community.

Yet beyond this you also project imaginatively the ideal of a "comprehensive community," one that is a product of "the cooperative and communicative operations of human beings living together" [CF 86] without any exclusions or subjugations imposed upon some of them by others. This

community of causes and consequences in which we, together with those not born, are enmeshed is the widest and deepest symbol of the mysterious totality of being the imagination calls the universe.... We who now live are parts of a humanity that extends into the remote past, a humanity that has interacted with nature. The things in civilization we most prize are not of ourselves. They exist by grace of the doings and sufferings of the continuous human community in which we are a link. Ours is the responsibility of conserving, transmitting, rectifying and expanding the heritage of values we have received that those who come after us may receive it more solid and secure, more widely accessible and more generously shared than we have received it [CF 85,87]

Dewey offers this interpretation of the religious in experience as an alternative to traditional religions, for he is sure that it is crucial for people to be committed to ideals that can unify momentary actions into extended selves, selves into enduring communities, and communities into the belief in a common humanity. Without such a conviction your praxis becomes dispersed, your interactions with others increasingly divisive, and your ideals degenerate into mere fantasies or into backward-looking rejections of change and novelty.

So Kant's kingdom of ends reappears in Dewey as an ideal of human unity and fulfillment. Although he resists letting such an ultimate ideal distract us from the more immediate ideals relevant to the problems of the day, Dewey nonetheless recognizes that it is this ultimate ideal, not the proximate ones, that gives persons both the dignity and the motivation required for their ends-in-view to be realized effectively. Dewey's comprehensive community thus comes very close to functioning both as what Kant calls a subjective incentive and as what he calls a rational incentive. It is the infinite worth of human being, made vivid by the symbol of a shared destiny, that captures your commitment to work for human good. It is the hope that this destiny can be approached, made "more solid and secure" for your children and their children after them, that gives the struggle for human good significance.

In *A Common Faith* Dewey never refers to William James's essay on "The Will to Believe," but in its arguments James anticipates Dewey

and makes far more clear than Dewey ever does the influence of expectation on outcome. As a pragmatist, says James, you judge claims to
truth by their ability to lead you effectively from old to new empirically specific experiences. Short of such verification, you suspend judgment. In the case of theories and other generalizations, you remain
suspicious enough to call them hypotheses, claims that you will act
on as true only insofar as they continue to be confirmed by further
experience.

This is all good scientific method. But James then notes "cases
where a fact cannot come at all unless a preliminary faith exists in its
coming" [WB 209]. So James proposes his famous definition of a "genuine option": a situation where you are presented with a choice that is
live, momentous, and forced. The beliefs among which you are to
choose are plausible, the consequences one way or the other are considerable, and there is no way to postpone the choice nor, having made
it, to reverse your decision later. In such matters, James argues, you
have a right to believe that one of the choices is correct, that what it
claims is true, even though confirming evidence is meager, ambiguous,
inconclusive, and even though the alternative seems likely to be
equally as effective in leading you from old truths to new.

These are choices of the sort Judge William talked about: ones that
do not merely play at life but make a real difference in how things are,
ones by which you become a person of character and purpose. It is not
that genuine options are dramatic choices made in a moment of crisis,
everything riding on the yes or no of it. Rather they are sequences of
choices that, persisted in, make a genuine difference in yourself and
your world. The choice at the crossroads to take one path or the other
is a forced choice, but not so much in the first step taken as in the
striding off that soon has carried you a long way down the one route
and left the other far behind. James's examples are of love and trust.
Your belief that she loves you is a conviction built up of countless decisions no one of which could fairly be called the first nor the crucial
one. You trust your compatriots in a group not by one act but by the
pattern of your actions, by a disposition that does not immediately leap
forth from your interactions like Athena but instead grows up out of
them as any proper offspring would.

The beliefs James is especially concerned about are those that answer that most momentous of all questions: what is the ultimate nature
and destiny of the whole universe? The religious answer is that "perfection" will be triumphant over imperfection, good over evil, harmony
over divisiveness. The ideal good shall "throw the last stone." But
James's version of religious belief is not just this claim about the End-

time but the further claim that the outcome is as yet unsettled. According to Augustine you may not know the hour or the day of the final victory, but you know the victor. For James the uncertainty of your belief is due not only to your ignorance but also to the openness of the future. Even Perfection cannot pre-determine what actual temporal choices alone will make determinate. So the ideal good is like your love of that woman and your trust of that colleague: its realization is to some degree a function of what you do. It is a goal for you to help actualize. Such belief is not passive; it is a course of action.

"In truths dependent on our personal action, then, faith based on desire is certainly a lawful and possibly an indespensable thing" [WB 209]. Because you want the ideal good to be made actual, the suffering and incompleteness of human existence to be overcome, and because it is an open question whether it will be or not, you have a right to believe that it will. But more than that: your belief could well be indispensable to realizing the ideal, so you have an obligation to believe it will. James's incipient hedonism is thus transformed into a Kantian duty. The object of your desire, if we are to take it seriously, if it meets Dewey's criteria for being a genuine value, is desired for what it offers not merely yourself but anyone. Your desire is founded on a sense of human worth, founded, indeed, on your sense of the intrinsic worth of the whole vast pluralistic universe of entities. And you envision that value, that worth, as realized in the form that overcomes imperfections, that completes and fulfills what is now partial and perishing. Your will to believe, in short, is the belief appropriate to a Kantian good will.

James extends his profile of the religious claim to include a belief that this Perfection has personal form, that it is a Thou and not an it. The ideal thus addresses you as Thou to thou. Insofar as your religious desires are less than those appropriate to a good will, the belief comes to you in the form of a command: believe thou as a good will would believe. And because beliefs "are measured by [our] willingness to act" [WB 194], act thou as a good will would act, which is to act so as to contribute to the realization of Perfection in time. Because it is the qualities of personhood, of dignity and caring and mutual empathy, that compose the nature of that Perfection, your actions seek the realization of what can appropriately be called a kingdom of ends.

James makes no explicit mention of actual human communities in his characterization of the ideal good, but he is very clear that attaining the ideal calls for commitment in the form of beliefs that make a difference to the world. Such beliefs must therefore be ones that shape your own character and the character of your society, consequently beliefs that make you a better person and your country a better nation. These beliefs then have some kind of salutary effect on your sense of what it is to be human and beyond that on your sense of how even our world, our ecosphere, our universe should be. For James, the ideal good is more than an ideal for human nature: it is an ideal encompassing all of reality in the ideal cosmic community he calls Perfection. Persons of good will, communities of like-minded adventurers, the divine Thou: such a harmony of self, other, and God in a common effort to make this a better world is James's version of the Kantian hope. For James the sign that the human spirit has an affinity with the cosmic is not something to behold but to exhibit. The zest in life, the experience of life's significance, is the cash value of your belief that the Good will ultimately triumph.

For Dewey, the character of a community clearly sets conditions, positively and negatively, for the realization of your personal character. Therefore the "comprehensive community" as an ultimate ideal implies norms for you to strive to realize as constituting the quality of your own character. Your worth as an individual derives from your role as agent and as product of the groups that find their worth in a vision of human beings as composing a single all-inclusive community. Dewey speaks of that community in quasi-religious terms, but James, in contrast, is willing to use the religious symbols for divinity in naming that ideal, thereby implying a congruence of cosmic and human ideals. The perfect reality is one in which the intrinsic worth—the dignity, freedom, and interdependence—of all entities is together realized. The crooked wood of human existence can be straightened only by human intelligence, but that very fact lends grandeur to the task because it means that human consciousness, so far the highest expression of nature, is in harmony with the ultimate ideal of a perfected reality.

Dewey has emphasized the societal dimension of ideal realization, the comprehensive community that you should seek in the creation of every actual community to which you contribute and by which their worth is measured. James has emphasized the individual dimension, the way in which your own individual choices are necessary contributions to realizing a goal that has no preestablished sufficient condition. Dewey's community can therefore also be taken as a final cause, the content of the ideal, and James's believers as its efficient cause, the agents of its realization. The dimensions of human nature and of formal causation remain to be considered.

Henry Nelson Wieman argues that there is a power at work in the world that, if we cooperate with it, will make possible the realization of the ideals of James and Dewey. Wieman calls this the "creative event."

You can do by yourself only what it lies within your power to do; the limits of your imagination, rationality, and interpretive insight set a boundary to the improvements in your condition that you can accomplish by yourself. The same is true for you working in consort with others. Human beings singly or collectively can improve only insofar as a creative power works in them to carry them beyond their former capacities:

Man can do only what lies within the scope of the imagination that he has; he can seek only the good that he, to date, is able to appreciate. To do what lies beyond the reach of his imagination, a greater imagination must be created in him. To seek a good beyond what he can appreciate, a greater appreciation must be developed in him. The creative event, not man himself, creates this greater imagination and this more profound and discriminating appreciation.... The creative event is suprahuman, not in the sense that it works outside of human life, but in the sense that it creates the good of the world in a way that man cannot do. [SHG 76]

The greater good is whatever leads to an increase in "qualitative meaning," whatever increases your and my and others' experiences of the harmony of contrastive elements within a given qualitative unity, along with the web of relationships into which that unity enters. Wieman thus speaks of four "subevents" or phases composing the creative event. The first is experiencing new qualitive meaning, especially as this is communicated to you by another; second, integrating this with the meanings of which you are already aware; third, appreciating the world thereby in a manner more sensitive to the richness of its accomplishments and possibilities; and fourth, developing more profound relationships, through this enlarged appreciation, extending and strengthening your community with other persons [SHG chap. 3].

Like James, Wieman thinks of the positive forces in the universe as engaged in a struggle against negativities, with the outcome at issue. The created goods made possible by openness to the creative good can be destroyed by human willfulness. But the power making for good is irrepressible; even where it fails in a given instance, or indeed even when its failures stretch out across the millennia, it nonetheless is always present in each new moment as a resource that when tapped releases the kind of problem-solving rational energy celebrated by Dewey. "We have no knowledge of any evil that can destroy creativity. It can be obstructed.... But all available evidence indicates that it can begin anew at any level and construct again the good toward higher levels" [SHG 90].

Wieman's creative event is thus a standard against which you must measure your own activities and those of your community. A fully human nature would be one fully open to the meliorative power of the creative event. Thus the evil in the world is whatever blocks such openness. Wieman attempts to find in biological, psychological, and social development empirical evidence of how the source of human good works and of the distorting, truncating consequences of denying it, closing its transformative power out of your life.[2]

There is empirical evidence to justify your dedicating your life to the goal of improving the human condition, and by doing so you may actually be contributing to the ultimate triumph of the good. But for Wieman more is at stake than this Jamesian invitation. Wieman argues that the way to act on behalf of the good is by opening yourself to the creative power of that goodness. The Thou is not a voice of an ideal end calling you to rally to its cause, but a presence at work in you. The harmony of self and Perfection is not a congruence of purposes but, rather, your capacities transformed by a power of creativity into increasingly effective instruments for the realization of good. Your openness to the creative event, and therefore your commitment to it, is the only way by which you can achieve the fulfillment and dignity worthy of your human potential. It is only through such achievement that what makes for good in the cosmos will be able to accumulate progressively the proximate goods by which the ultimate ideal good can be realized.

Wieman thus explicitly links human nature with a dynamic tendency at the heart of reality. The source of human good is the source also of cosmic good, and so you are a Self by acting creatively, by permitting the heart of reality to express itself through your actions. This openness to the power of the ideal is the way of its realization, transforming your character and your communities into selves and societies of increasing qualitative meaning, of ever-widening and ever-deepening integrated unities.

Sandra Rosenthal comes by another route to similar conclusions. Her initial concerns are epistemological, trying to avoid the relativism seemingly entailed by pragmatism's insistence that all things are temporal and that therefore you always must take the world from within a perspective that is an historical artifact. Rosenthal argues that there is a "foundationally real world, the spatio-temporally real world," which "is ontologically one with the independently real processive concreteness of the natural universe" [SP 157]. But this reality is real for us by being known, and it is known only from within the perspective of the meaning system of some human community. Rosenthal attempts to avoid having to claim either that this reality is absolutely independent of human experience or that it is absolutely dependent: "Truth is agreement of belief with reality, but it is agreement with worldly reality, a reality that we have partially made" [SP 160]. Truth is always *within* an interpretive context but it is always *of* reality.

The members of a given community each have their own individual perspective from which they approach matters, in terms of which they pursue their own ends and interact with others. Given any particular situation, they will each see it differently, find it problematic or not for divergent reasons, propose variant responses. Conflict is endemic where there are as many points of view as people, where the perspectival character of experience individualizes everything, including what counts as factual truth. But these perspectives are interpretations of reality and not its invention. They therefore need not be arbitrary; to attempt their reconciliation is not a useless passion.

Any community, argues Rosenthal, is an ongoing dynamic effort to change the perspectives of individuals, singly or in bunches, by persuasion rather than by force, so as to effect some relevant coordinated social praxis. For this dynamic to be workable, however, some differences must already have been resolved: those required for believing in the further possibility of resolving actual or potential conflict. Thus a functioning social order implies, or rather entails, says Rosenthal, that there is a "basic world interpretation" shared by all or significant portions of the humans who compose that social order.

Pluralism within the world emerges from the backdrop of a common world, for in its deepest sense, the questioning and doubting that changed the world could only occur within a context that did not change, but lent the prereflective constancy and communality of its meaning to the meaningfulness of both the problem and its resolution. [SP 163]

The point is akin to Habermas's notion of the lifeworld as the background necessary for the communicative activities by which the members of a community discursively achieve agreement on the conditions of their common life.

So perspectives are everywhere: your viewpoint and mine, that of the group to which we both belong, those of groups encompassing our group, nested viewpoints and overlapping ones, ones seemingly incommensurable and ones that seem to dissolve into an undifferentiated unity. You act within this complex of perspectives, some of them found gladly by you as pre-forming the orientation of your own praxis, creating your needs, delineating the possibilities for their fulfillment, defining means and ends for realizing them. Other perspectives are foisted upon you; others you create or share in creating; some you nurture, some you betray or destroy.

But a community can function as a community only so far as all of these differences are constructively related. Hence Rosenthal arrives at this norm: "True community requires... myself as both partially constituted by and partially constitutive of the generalized other. Further, it requires this in the dynamic and changing manner of socializing adjustment" [SP 166]. Unless you are a self constituted by orientations that transcend the idiosyncratic limitations of your individual experience, community is not possible. The remembered and anticipated views of others, of ancestors, of far-flung contemporaries, of generations yet unborn, generalized into the agendas, ideologies, and traditions of groups, are necessary ingredients in any kind of enduring social order. But unless you are at the same time an individual with a unique, irreducible perspective, community will lose the dynamism that results from an ever-recurrent need for new forms of reconciliation. Therefore a workable community can be neither a static totality nor a disconnected plurality. The tension among perspectives, the whole confusing complexity of those perspectives interactively related, is the necessary condition for community. The preservation of that tension is thus normative.

So far as all of us work together within a viable social order, the differing perspectives out of which we severally work are set within a constraining framework of shared meaning. Rosenthal's strategy follows the approach proposed by Lucas: the minimal conditions for a community must be respected by the praxis of individuals whose sense of self depends upon it. If through the sorts of unrepeatable, responsible choices of which Judge William spoke, you are someone whose essence it is to be an American, then the conditions necessary for the flourishing of American culture are inviolate for you. You cannot do violence to who you essentially are in pursuing purposes expressive of that selfhood. This is Sartre's point about the Terror, except expressed in the soothing tones of Burke rather than those of Robespierre: the condition for the continuance of a group lies in its mutual commitment to the authority of its traditions.

These traditions, these communal frameworks or practices within which individual actions are constrained, are themselves in turn set within a preconceptual, prelinguistic constraining horizon. This most basic of frameworks, or rather this condition for any framework whatsoever, is, for Rosenthal, felt rather than known. She used the term "anteception" to refer to the experiencing of what our interpretive experiences presuppose; hence an "anteceptive field" is the "indefinitely rich matrix" of "primordial processive activity within, or upon, which we project the meaningful background for the delineation of objects" and the other constituents of a worldview [SP 68–69].

As with Wieman, Rosenthal's appeal is to experience, and what is experienced is dynamic: "processive." It is marked by what Whitehead called "causal efficacy," your experience of the constraint of inheritance, the power of the past as creating the channels within which your praxis will function. But it is therefore also marked by "anticipatory flow" because the channels concentrate what they delimit; they shape inheritance into a force that overruns the present into which it is being poured, that presses toward some realization beyond itself. Rosenthal calls this "impulsion": "that ongoing advance of an ontological density that manifests itself in the actualizations of tendencies" [SP 186–87].

Notice how Rosenthal has characterized this experience of an anteceptive reality. It is active; but the activity is processive, a directional thrust; the thrust is an impulsion, which means that it impels change; the change is temporal, from the past causally toward the future anticipatorily and creatively; the temporal change is from a tendency to an actuality, from processive activity to settled outcome. You experience this anteceptively: not as a set of qualities conceived of and articulated in the manner just done, but as an emotional intensity, a feeling of transforming accomplishment, of the in-the-making-now-made of things. You feel drawn into it, its power becomes yours, its outcome-making inventiveness a truth about a reality of which you are intimately a part. Dewey argued that emotion is what unifies situational experience into *a* situation and transforms multiple ends into a single ideal. Here also for Rosenthal, it is anteceptive feeling that identifies the self with the ontological power of the underlying processive activity of the world, relates it root to ground, expression to expressed, instance to whole. Wieman uses almost the indentical language in discussing the noncognitive experience of the creative event.

Hence our individual creativity takes its cue from what is at the heart of our essential nature; that the anteceptive field makes for realized value assures us that our own particular efforts to do so are in harmony with the nature of reality. Because it is ideals that are achieved, always some harmonization of what was previously discordant, you also feel that the impulsion of the processive world is toward the better and that your impulses should be similarly oriented. This is true both of your solo efforts and of group efforts in which you participate. The whole of what you do gains strength from your sense of taking part in some way in a striving shared by the whole of what is. In sum,

The drive toward betterment through creative growth in the dynamics of socializing adjustment is a natural offspring of the anteceptive sense of creativity, of ontological density, and of being with. The anteceptive sense of creativity, of efficacy, is the motivating force for meliorism: one *can* make things better; one *can* increase the value-ladenness of the universe. [SP 191]

This is all a matter of feeling, however. Its conscious articulation, as Rosenthal has already argued, must be within an interpretive framework, a worldview that is historically derived and therefore unavoidably inadequate. Your world is always a worldview, a point of view as distinct from that of which it is a view. Yet this very relativism implies its ideal: a "foundationally real world" that is the perfect interpretation of the felt processive reality. Because the various worlds are expressions of the diverse human communities that have over generations developed different ways of seeing and doing things, so likewise the foundationally real world must be an expression of an ideal social order, a "community of communities," which is "that foundational community upon which the horizonal dimensions of all other communities ultimately open" [SP 171]. The salient feature of this ideal community is the diversity of its member communities, each with its differing perspectives, each composed of individuals with their own differing perspectives. Differences are constantly arising because persons are free. They constantly reinterpret themselves and their relationships through newly fashioned beliefs and practices. But these differences are also constantly being adjudicated, used for mutual enrichment instead of divisiveness, building up the foundation of shared meaning from which new differences are constantly impelled.

So the concept of a "foundational community" bespeaks the ideal felt in anteceptive experience: it is the standard by which all actual communities are to be judged because as realized it is the outcome toward which they all tend; it alone is the outcome which can fulfill them all. Most pertinently, this ideal of community is the end you as a human being must seek insofar as you would seek your natural end, insofar as you would seek to realize your essential human nature. The way of your seeking, accordingly, must be to exemplify the practices appropriate to that end, practices exemplarily human: acting so as to enhance individual freedom, to strengthen ties of interdependence, and to fashion practices of empathy and love. It is by living as a genuine human being that you give a genuinely human shape to history. And thus is the formal cause of the kingdom of ends the human perfection it alone makes actual.

Pragmatists and radical empiricists such as Dewey, James, Wieman, and Rosenthal are typically most comfortable when their attention is directed toward the practical problems of everyday existence. They came to rescue philosophy from the ballet of ghostly abstractions by which they thought it had been mesmerized. They try to play tunes by which the dance of practical human living might be performed. Life turns out to be more than practical activities, however, more than milking cows and building viaducts. It has to do with habits and traditions, with dreams and predictions. It has to do with interpretations and not just facts, with values and not just needs, with ideals and not just ideas. In their struggle to be adequate to concrete experience these pragmatists are led in a direction that finds its fullest expression in the "absolute pragmatism" of Josiah Royce.

In *The Problem of Christianity,* Royce uses a theory of interpretation he borrows from Peirce to build up a portrait of the individual self as essentially social. You grow up within a community, learning what to do and believe by unthinking imitation of those around you. Were your imitations always successful, the customs of your society being well entrenched within a stable natural environment, you would presumably live out your life merely exemplifying general practices and thereby contributing to their perpetuation.

This bucolic idyll of an unself-conscious existence lived in perfect harmony with others and with nature is for Royce no human ideal, however romantic its attractions might be. It might remind you of the insipid "chautauqua" way of life James castigated and to which he contrasted the adventuresome, zestful style of those who have found a moral equivalent to war.[3] It is also reminiscent of the Epicurean trap into which hedonism falls when the Moment is defined less by pleasure attained than by pain avoided. Individual self-awareness and critical reflection, and thus personal development, arise only out of conflict. The source of conflict is others, whose actions are at variance with yours.

When you forget to imitate accustomed ways, perhaps due to the lure of some novel possibility, others in the name of your community chastise your errancy. This social discipline returns your behavior to normalcy, but the momentary contrast, the comparison you are afforded between what you did and what others do, marks your birth as a self distinct from other selves. Indeed, it marks your birth as a moral self: what others do is what you were expected to do as well, and so your actual self is known by you henceforth in contrast to a better Self.

But such a self can be its own critic. Your conscience need not be the voice of a collective Other demanding your conformity to its traditional ways. It could just as well be a voice appealing to an ought rooted in your own sense of Self and thrusting itself up in defiance of traditional ways. This defiance will call down a more intense chastisement by the communal authorities of your deviance, and the chastisement is likely to stimulate a further growth in your sense of difference from society. Self-will and social will can thus grow ever more antagonistic. A community of free, genuinely autonomous individuals would in this way become oxymoronic, forcing an impossible oscillation between anarchy and tyranny, were it not for the service provided by interpretation.

Anarchy and tyranny are precisely what has been haunting our inquiry up to this point. The hedonist's voracious desiring turned community into Hobbes's war of each against all, and our attempts to damp down this raging fire handed the firebrand over to the agents of the social whole who, not being gods, predictably tended to brandish it tyrannically. Our quest for a moral standard transcendent enough to constrain the hedonism of such rulers and of the ruled as well led us to an ideal vision of a realm where individual freedom freely expressed itself in actions respecting and enhancing all other selves. But we have been having difficulty finding a way from our actual situation to any realistic expectation that its ideal might be realized in history. This formidable conundrum is what Royce seeks to resolve.

You are interpreting your own actions when you see them as needing to conform to what you had done earlier. You look at your present action in terms of certain of its qualities; you compare them to your previous actions taken as constituting recurrent instances of an enduring quality, and then defend that present action against its critics on the grounds that it too instances that same enduring quality. This is precisely the notion of character we have been elaborating. You refuse to offer incense to Caesar today because it would be out of character to do so. You have opposed this absolutist claim by the tyrant in the past, done so with such consistency that your defiance has come to describe you in a fundamental way. To act otherwise now would be to repudiate all that you have stood for over these past years. You would be acting out of character in the sense of betraying yourself, denying what is most important to you because essential to who you have been and have expected yourself to be. You are a person of character, someone with personal integrity, because you are loyal to the best in yourself. As Royce puts it, "The self comes down to us from its own past. It needs and is a history. . . . My idea of myself is an interpretation of my past—linked also with an interpretation of my hopes and intentions as to my future" [POC-2 40, 42].

Character, as we have seen, is more than interpreting your actual or proposed actions in terms of your own individuating purposes. It involves not only being true to your self but also being true to your community and to humanity, or rather to what you take to be the ideal expression of each. Thus a Self is a triadic affirmation of loyalties. Royce confirms all of this and then asks a question we have been so far avoiding: suppose you are not true to these norms? Suppose you prove disloyal to your sense of Self, become your own Self's quisling. The dimensions of Self are standards you have made your own, values that you have come to in coming to selfhood. They are the heart of the way in which you are free, the form your autonomy has taken, the foundation of your sense of worth, of dignity. To betray them is to betray your whole world.

Royce calls this the "hell of the irrevocable" [POC-1 263] because no matter how hard you might strive henceforth to conform to the norms you have denied, you remain and know yourself to remain a traitor. When the request yesterday to bow down to Caesar was accompanied by a drawn weapon, you had become frightened and so did as you were told. You could, of course, cope with this bit of cowardice by slipping off into some form of Sartrean bad faith, denying that you were really responsible for what you did. But Royce is not so sanguine as to think that honestly acknowledging your failure, repenting it, seeking and receiving forgiveness, will suffice to put your failure behind you. Sartre's depiction of the citizens of Argos, haunted and hunted by the Furies for their complicity in the death of Agamemnon, makes this plain: the repentance only exacerbates the guilt. The choice is not a pleasant one. You can deny your Self by fleeing into forgetfulness of self, or you can deny your Self by guiltily remembering the deeds of self.

From the horns of this dilemma you can be saved only by acts of self-reinterpretation, says Royce. Interpretation is always triadic: A is related to B by means of C. You identified your prior actions, A, with your present ones, B, by means of certain qualities, C, which you saw as salient features of them both. What you took to be important about B was its similarity to A and hence the continuity between them. Your gesture today had many features; it could have been described a thousand ways for a thousand differing purposes. But you chose to emphasize certain of its features and to construe them as supporting a particular meaning: you took your actions as a gesture of defiance. As Davidson might put it: by interpreting your behavior as an action with defiance as its reason, you fused it with your earlier actions, those already interpreted as defiant deeds. An anti-authoritarian attitude has emerged as the enduring quality actualized through a series of particular beliefs that those gestures then and this one now are its proper instantiations.

Is it possible, then, for you to reinterpret your act of self-betrayal so that it has a different meaning? Yes, says Royce; by doing something that makes amends for your negative act, turning it into an event that has positive results. "Atonement" is "the creation by somebody of a definite individual good on the basis of a definite previous evil" [POC-1 372]. You have learned your lesson; you now realize the need for greater resolve in remaining true to your convictions. The proof lies in this pudding: that today you met a challenge you might never have managed without the deepened convictions that grew from yesterday's cowardice. Repenting was not enough, although it may have helped. You needed to do something with the act of denial itself. You needed to take what had only the negative significance of being a repudiation of your character and, giving it a new, instrumental value, thereby to weave it back into the extended fabric of your character. Atonement is a praxis in which discordant elements are made into a new harmony. It involves a fresh interpretation of events but, in order to avoid the pit- falls of bad faith, it requires a reconciling deed as well. You cannot wish your fault away, Royce insists, but you can redeem it.

Shift now to the level of communities and what we have said of in- dividuals applies here also. You have interpreted your earlier activities as exemplifying an enduring character that is who you essentially are. Now enlarge the scope of your interpretation so that it encompasses deeds done by your predecessors in the community of which you are a member. Do the same regarding expectations: expand these to include what you know or can imagine to be the unfulfilled plans and hopes of your ancestors, and also those of your children and of the generations that will come after them. In finding an interpretation able to express enduring strands of quality that extend over such immense spans of time, you do more than stretch the duration of your selfhood. You also entwine yourself with whomever else has those same ancestors and en- visions those same hopes. You and this other person share a common past insofar as the same recurrent qualities of past actions are taken as characterizing the same people, characterizing her as aspects of the self you have become and hope yet to be. Like you, she also defies Caesar today as a gesture of solidarity with those who only last summer died as martyrs for the sake of this nation's ancient and inalienable free- doms. She and you are essentially children of those martyrs and their principles. Offspring of the same parenting past, your hopes for the future also merge into the same vision of a newborn world devoid of tyranny.

Any viable community, thus, is for Royce a "community of memory and of hope." But as it is only under some interpretation that our remembrances and expectations are merged, any such community is also a "community of interpretation." The practices that give such a way of life its consistency, its character, are standards to be exemplified in each individual's character and activities, standards that include interpretive traditions for reconciling conflicts and healing disparities.

Here also atonement is required: when individuals betray their own best sense of responsible citizenship and make themselves the enemy of that to which they have offered their highest allegiance. A betrayal of the community can only be overcome by someone other than the betrayer, for it is the betrayer whose antisocial deeds must be reinterpreted positively to the rest of the community. Again, this reinterpretation requires more than words, more than a fine speech about the erring individual's good qualities or a passionate confession combined with a promise never to do wrong again. It requires doing something in which the rejected person and that person's negative behavior become means for accomplishing some social good that otherwise might not have been possible. It requires "atoning deeds, deeds that, through sacrifices, win again the lost causes of the moral world ... by creating new good out of ancient ill" [POC-1 377–78].

A community is sustained, therefore, by actions in which one member or all the other members are reconciled to an alienated second member through the praxis of a third who does something that gives a positive social value to the alienated person's life. The members may be groups as well as individuals, communities at war with one another whose disputes are mediated by the intervention of a third. The healing deeds may bind up wounds that stretch across the years or centuries, meliorating a generational dispute or reconciling a people to the barbaric slaughters that marked their origin. But always the dynamic is from disputation to resolution, from warfare to peace, from adversaries to comrades; *e pluribus unum.*

You are loyal to a community so far as your actions support interpretations that build up that community; your failure so to act and so to understand is nonetheless, through the atoning work of others, built back into its unity. Loyalty to a community thus transforms your self from its "natural narrowness" to a self as vast as that community. Nor is your self lost as it expands and deepens its ties with the collectivity; your relationship to it is neither passive nor interchangeable. You are dependent on others for treating you as a member of the group, for appreciating your place within its social ecology, for seeing you as a part of an ongoing tradition. But they are equally dependent on your treating, appreciating, and seeing them in like fashion. You contribute your interpretive and atoning work from your distinctive location within the community, your very individuality thus being the instrument for your commonality with others.

Royce is convinced that there is no praxis so irrevocably negative that its ruptures cannot be repaired, no evil so great that love and loyalty cannot make it an instrument for some atoning good. The communities that can be built then have no necessary outer limit short of encompassing all human reality. What Royce calls the "Universal Community" is precisely that ideal culmination in which all persons, living and dead, are united in a single human community stretching from the origin of the species to the end of time:

The universe is a community of interpretation whose life comprises and unifies all the social varieties and all the social communities which, for any reason, we know to be real in the empirical world which our social and our historical sciences study. The history of the universe, the whole order of time, is the history and the order and the expression of this Universal Community. [POC-2 272–73]

This entails an ethic very similar to Kant's. Consider this ideal: in which every individual is reconciling all the possible disharmonies among others, as a wise legislator would seek to frame laws that everyone obeys; in which the dignity of each person is manifest by his autonomy, by his unique ability freely to create this realm of mutuality; in which each does for others what he would wish done for him, lifting them from isolation into participation in what is universal in scope and worth. Royce talks of love and Kant of law, but Royce's love is no mere hedonistic passion and Kantian disinterest is evenhanded interest rather than indifference. Consider the ideal they have both proposed, and hear what the very consideration of a Universal Community commands: "Act so as to hasten its coming" [POC-1 360].

Royce joins in the pragmatist insistence that ideals, both proximate and ultimate, are something that can be realized only by human effort. A community of interpretation requires its interpreters. It is a pragmatic community in that its truth is its results; the ideal must have cash value or its claim upon us is fraudulent. But Royce is an "absolute pragmatist" because this claim is not merely a human invention, the dream of some single visionary or the hope of some ancient tradition. The foundation of the ideal is not persons or communities but the universe, the one infinite reality of which all finite communities are but partial expressions.

Remember, though, that absolute pragmatism is not absolute idealism. This reality for Royce is not an eternal unchanging Ground, a transcendent One of which all temporal things are merely passing reflections. Time as Royce interprets it is as real as any reality can be. As we affirmed when hedonism had led us to a similar notion, to deny the ultimacy of the world of becoming and perishing is a self-contradictory praxis, an instance of temporality struggling to hide what its very struggle makes manifest.

That time is real, that reality is temporal, is not, however, a mantra you are required to chant lest you be cast out from the community of absolute pragmatists. That would be to confront one transcendent One with its dynamic alter ego. Royce's point is that reality is an interpretation. It is the way in which the members of a community take their experiences, their memories and hopes, lift certain of their features into prominence, and then fashion enduring strands of coherence, weaving them together into the enduring fabric that those members experience as that meaningful order of things in which they live and move and have their being. This is what happens in science; the Ptolemaic world, the Newtonian world, the world of quanta and relativity are all realities taken as such by an interpretive community of scientists. Likewise, the cultural world is a function of the citizens of a society, a civilization, a tradition. They weave that world around them as the meaningful context for their actions. Hence "the real" in an absolute sense can *be* only concomitantly with an absolute community.

Kant asked for a sign[4] that would stiffen his resolve to act now that the kingdom of ends might through his action become a nearer reality. He needed more than James's permission to believe; he wanted evidence, although he was content to forgo proof. Royce offers both evidence and proof: a world in which interpretation is everywhere the truth of things is a world the "impulsion" of which is everywhere toward the realization of value. Your self-identity is an achievement of value, the creation of an enduring order that integrates a breadth of experience into an intensity of reiterated, developing enjoyment. The communities in which you share are similar instances of sustained unities triumphant over the diffuse anarchy of solitariness. Your experience of the wider environment as a universe is of a solid, persisting accomplishment awesome to behold. All these achievements perish, but we and all creation keep coming to be again and in ever-changing ways, transforming what perishes into the stuff of new realities. The evidence is everywhere that time is through and through interpretive, and that interpretation has unity as its goal.

But what of that goal? The Universal Community, according to Royce, is an interpretation of all of time and space as composing a single reality, a single complex harmony of past and future, memory and expectation, manifest in a living present of differing entities whose interdependencies compose one integral whole. Such an interpretation is beyond the capacity of any single human mind to comprehend much less create. Such a reality could not ever be completely realized in some one place or time. But even though you are unable to grasp the realized content of such an ultimate reconciliation of all things, you can nonetheless know enough to know that such is indeed what would result were each limited interpretation to be built up from its predecessors, were the process of seeking unity from diversity to be cumulative until all its possible goals were realized.

Is this unity really possible? Yes, says Royce, for what it requires is an interpreter as great as the task required of it, a viewpoint and a reconciling activity as universal as the Universal Community it makes possible, as real as the universe it makes a reality. Such an interpreter would itself need to grow into its role along with the communities of interpretation in which it dwells. Humanity itself is precisely that power, growing as its integrative capacities grow, atoning for its own failures, finding no evil of its doing so irrevocable as not to be salvageable within the context of a newborn good, no wood so crooked that it cannot be made straight. Given its memory of redemptive acts of old, and given the creative tasks that give present meaning to their lives, members of the human community also share a common expectation: "The sense of life, the very being of the time process itself, consists in the progressive realization of the Universal Community in and through the longings, the vicissitudes, the tragedies, and the triumphs of this process of the temporal world" [POC-2 387].

Illustration 5.2 summarizes the various pragmatic views of community that find their richest expression in Royce's notion of the Universal Community. Royce has transformed Kant's subjective incentive into an objective reality. The coming of the moral ideal is not a pious wish, a hope against hope that what deserves to be realized in fact will be. Kantians go into their closets and pray that the kingdom might come. But an absolute pragmatist lives within a functional community that is at work in the midst of the becoming and perishing of things trying to overcome negativities, to redeem suffering, to transform hate into love and swords into plowshares. Within that struggling community the expectation of the ultimate triumph of the ideal is part and parcel of its members' lifeworld. It is woven into the very meaning of what they do, a regulative principle for judging their labors but one that also lures forth atoning acts that turn the worst into the acceptable and the good into the better. And so the ideal is constitutive of their common reality even now. It is what they are together each day realizing brokenly, and

**Illustration 5.2 Pragmatist Modes and Conditions of Societal Dynamics**

|  | James<br>individual | Dewey<br>societal | Wieman<br>cosmic | Rosenthal<br>cosmic | Royce |
|---|---|---|---|---|---|
| material<br>cause | empirical<br>experience | problem<br>situations | empirical<br>events | anteceptive<br>field | self-will<br>vs. social |
| final cause | Perfection<br>[Thou] | comprehen-<br>sive com-<br>munity | human good<br>(+ cosmic) | foundational<br>community | universal<br>community |
| formal<br>cause | choice<br>free will | experimental<br>method | creative<br>event | interpreta-<br>tion | atonement<br>(interpre-<br>tation) |
| efficient<br>cause | zestful<br>belief | meliorist<br>actions | creative<br>good | impulsion | loyalty |

what they are thereby developing the skill and wisdom eventually to realize fully, more fully, most fully.

Absolute pragmatists do not go into their closets but out into the streets and fields. Their prayers are the praxis, transformed through loyalty to an ideal, by which they are emboldened to step forth and this day make themselves their kingdom come.

# Six

## THE DEVELOPING OF HISTORY

You and I have been inquiring about ideals and whether they can ever be realized. We have insisted that a possibility is a value only if it leads us toward its actualization. Although at first our values were expectations of acquired Moments of fulfillment, we came eventually to believe that this notion was inadequate. Values were not to be thought of as objects to be possessed. What is really of value is yourself become a Self. Such a Self, we saw, is emergent from a relational environment and achieves through interpretive acts of creative self-transcendence an individuated but still relational definiteness. For you to be free, therefore, meant for you to be autonomous in a manner only made possible by community and only expressible in community. Our inquiry thus was about whether human communities, as the milieu for the realizing of Selves, can be realized.

The attainment of Selfhood can be a value for praxis only if a society of Selves is an historical possibility. So far we have heard a loud chorus of voices raised to sing the praises of such a possibility, but there has been surprisingly little evidence to buttress the claim of its being manifest as a concrete temporal reality. Kant found a glimmer of support for his expectations in the emotional way people respond to a struggle for political liberty; Royce searched the entrails of interpretive actions for a clue to what they might imply; James lectured us about self-fulfilling prophecies. But by and large these are all expressions of hope rooted in emotion. They are anteceptive feelings of the deficiencies of the past projected into the future as goals to be achieved. This is as it

181

should be, for the vague, brooding materiality of inheritance is the foundation for the values praxis takes as its orienting finality. The question, then, is whether there are available as well formal and efficient conditions sufficient to the task of historical transformation.

You need more than a lump welling up in your throat when the band plays the "Marseillaise"; you need more than a flow of adrenalin as you rise up in quest of some unknown grail. If the perfecting of our selves and our communities is a categorical imperative that lies under the control of human beings and so is their duty to realize, then why are not at least some tentative results visible in history? Where are the stages on the way that mark off our progress, that you and I can show as the first fruits of our labors and that will embolden us to a renewed effort on behalf of the ideal? Joachim drew pretty pictures at his desk in the monastery seclusion of Fiore, and Lessing dreamed a pleasant dream in his gentleman's study in Saxony. But what of the life-and-death struggles of real human beings, numbered countless as the pebbles by the shore? What of the ways of their interactions, the binding customs, rituals, and institutions by means of which they struggle, live, and die? The mixing of this gravel with this cement, the process of making this concrete reality that is our history: wherein is it a coming to realization of the ideal?

Even if the case can be made that an ideal community of Selves will emerge from the sounds and fury of historical change, why must so many generations suffer and perish in the meantime? If the dignity of human beings is the one absolute value, how can it be that every human who has so far lived, and the uncountable more to come, are denied that dignity? Are they all merely means to an end, their value only instrumental and not intrinsic? This smacks too much of hedonism, of being-for-another, of cosmic forces playing battledore and shuttlecock with the whole of our existence. Is the Self only a disguise of the Moment? Is the admonition that you should strive for Selfhood only another one of Johannes's clever deceits?

So far Kant and Lessing have been the only ones to address this second question, and their answers have been notably unsuccessful. Eternal life and reincarnation are not solutions to the problem of Self-realization; they are cries of anguish at its impossibility. They are the recognition that you who want so desperately to do as a good will would do are going to fail again and again in your struggle, due to your own inadequacies and those of a cultural environment riddled with dehumanizing obstacles that block your best-laid plans and most pious intentions. These cries of anguish are the recognition that you are going to die with your deepest value, your most important goal, unrealized. The crooked wood of our lives: can it really ever be made straight?

Georg Wilhelm Friedrich Hegel is the true successor to Kant because he took very seriously this cry of anguish and the call for evidence that, because unprovided, triggers it. He recognized that the possibility of ethical life, of living your life in a positive and appropriate way, depends upon your rational conviction that history is a meaningful process and that what you do is thereby also meaningful. It should be no surprise, therefore, that Hegel's *Philosophy of History* begins by assuring us that our cries of anguish are quite appropriate. The anguish is not only to be expected, but is also already an indication of how it can be overcome.

The past, says Hegel, presents you with "a vast picture of changes and transactions; of infinitely manifold forms of peoples, states, individuals, in unresting succession" [PH 72]. What you are witnessing is hedonistic praxis, persons everywhere seeking to fulfill their varied purposes, to satisfy their needs, exercise their talents, attain happiness. Some of this activity may be on behalf of "aims of a liberal or universal kind—benevolence it may be, or noble patriotism"; but overwhelmingly what you find is narrow "passions, private aims, and the satisfaction of selfish desires" [PH 20]. It is more than likely, you conclude, that even the "finest exemplars of private virtue" act from essentially selfish motives. The result of such rampant selfishness is quite predictable: disagreement, violence, immorality, leading to failed purposes, the death of accomplishment, the collapse of aspiration and hope. What is true of individuals is all the more true of nations and civilizations. The ruins of Carthage, Palmyra, Persepolis, and Rome offer mute testimony to the narrow-visioned ways by which even values of the greatest importance are all too soon sacrificed "to an infinite complication of trifling circumstances" [PH 72].

How does the past appear to you? A cacophony, a clash of ignorant armies in the night, a confusion of conflicting values that simultaneously demand your allegiance and threaten your survival. In Hegel's account of it, your reaction to the historical evidence is deeply emotional, just as it was for Kant and the pragmatists. But unlike them, it is also deeply negative because no positive sign worth taking seriously can be found in it. History is not something you can approach indifferently. It catches you up immediately because it is a story of human beings like yourself or like me, persons with whose actions you can identify. It is a story redolent with the most central of our ideals, with the "goodness, beauty, and greatness" to which you yourself aspire and which you imagine might be someday exemplified in the groups from family to nation that mean so much to you. You see in the struggles of ancient people, in the lives and deaths of historical figures, an urge toward some version of the Universal Community. This spectacle lures forth your empathy for those who in ages past gave that ideal some modicum of presence in their lives. But Hegel forces you to stare squarely into the face of these ancestors and to recognize that their striving has come to naught, and that the cause of the failure was themselves.

Hegel then leads you down the pathway of anguish that is the only reasonable response to the evidence provided. You experience "sorrow at this universal taint of corruption," to be sure; but beyond that, "a disinterested sorrow" at the resulting decay of so many good accomplishments. Yet you recognize that none of this had to be: it is human will and not Nature which is the source of it all, persons doing what they need not and ought not to have been doing, yet learning nothing from their own sins and failures much less those of their predecessors. You are consequently filled with "moral embitterment," with "the profoundest and most hopeless sadness, counterbalanced by no consolatory result" [PH 21]. There can be no exonerating excuses by which to brighten the sad tale history tells. We humans are responsible for what has happened and our selfish desires, our willingness to sacrifice others to further our own gain, shows no sign of ever changing for the better.

Such powerfully negative emotions require relief. Your response is therefore obvious. You withdraw into your own subjectivity, seeking the "quiet shore" of your private aims and interests, finding in them a refuge from the dolorous vistas provided by your inheritance. This self-indulgence is a balm that eases the pain of such endless public tragedy. But it is a counsel of despair, a form of fatalism; it incarnates the very selfishness it decries. You have made a separate peace with human history, on terms that give you some momentary personal happiness but that do nothing to arrest the widespread and ongoing social decline that had called forth your anguish.

This inward-turning response is what Hegel calls "natural death," and as it is reiterated from individual to individual, generation to generation, it becomes culturally entropic. An original "fulness and zest" for some ideal end having been lost because shown to be impossible, life loses its significance. In the absence of ideals, you are content with the actual and so, as Dewey suggests would happen, your activities become routine; inquiry gives way to habit, and old ways no longer are able to adapt themselves creatively to the relentless change constituting the natural flow of things. "Thus perish individuals, thus perish peoples by a natural death" [PH 75].

But stop. Such an anguished attitude is not the whole story of how you approach history, nor of how I do. We also have a deeply felt conviction that the world is fundamentally rational, that "Reason governs the world, and has consequently governed its history" [PH 25]. We believe that each and every thing is a part of a meaningful order of things and that its purpose is disclosed by reference to that order. Kant relied upon such a belief; it is the pre-condition for his argument regarding the necessity that a kingdom of ends be historically realized. Hegel assumes that you and I share this faith, and that we are troubled that it should seemingly be denied by the historical evidence. But it would be foolish simply to make some kind of arbitrary choice between your faith in reason and the evidence of your senses. Hegel proposes, instead, that you take the rationality of things as a point of departure, as an hypothesis. Set about systematically testing the grounds for your faith in reason, because it is only through an actual inquiry into history that your belief in history's rationality can ever be proved or disproved. "It is only an inference from the history of the World, that its development has been a rational process" [PH 10]; it is not something merely to be settled *a priori.*

To be sure, a philosopher or historian

brings his categories with him, and sees the phenomena presented to his mental vision, exclusively through these media. And, especially in all that pretends to the name of science, it is indispensable that Reason should not sleep—that reflection should be in full play. To him who looks upon the world rationally, the world in its turn presents a rational aspect. The relation is mutual. [PH 11]

But an hypothesis brought to bear upon the phenomena, tested for its adequacy to the facts, clarified and corrected by those facts, in turn exposing previously unnoted relationships among the facts and disclosing new facts, is a process that if rigorously pursued will yield a convincing proof or disproof in place of the initial hypothesis.

Hegel rejects "a priori inventions" imposed arbitrarily upon the data of history. He is also dismissive of vague, indefinite theories that make the claim that there is a rational order to things but then fail to test their claim by showing what it means specifically, that is, by providing "its determinate application, and concrete development." Hegel takes to task especially those, presumably like Kant, who give this hypothesis a religious twist while continuing to leave its expression vague. Such people talk of a Providence that "presides over the events of the World," but then assert that its workings are "concealed from our view." This is not only unsatisfying, but to be content with such pious platitudes is immoral. If inanimate Nature can be said to give ample evidence for the existence of a divine purpose, then surely all the more should human history provide such evidence. If so, it is our duty to seek it out.

If all you do is to proclaim that your life, all lives, are caught up into a providential but hidden plan, then you have given yourself a "convenient license of wandering as far as [you] list, in the direction of [your] own fancies" [PH 14]. An abstract Providence supplies no norm by which to judge whether any particular thing you do is wrong, is out of harmony with God's purposes. Or, Hegel might have added, if you claim to know the providential norm because of some special authority vested in you by revelation or tradition, there is no way to distinguish your claim from a merely arbitrary pronouncement. Thus "vanity and egotism" have free play in a world where God's purposes, even though affirmed, are nonetheless unknown. This is why the *Philosophy of History* is a theodicy: not only, as Hegel emphasizes, because it reconciles the existence of evil with the presence of a beneficent deity, but more importantly because it exhibits, as at work in history, the standards for individual and communal praxis without which morality is not possible.

You fail to improve upon this understanding of Providence when you proclaim that it can be glimpsed at work in the lives of specific individuals, attempting thereby to provide edifying examples of divine succor as guides to the perplexed or comfort for the needy. It is a "peddling" view of God that finds divinity retailing its grace to assist people in fulfilling their specific desires. The God who answers your prayers for victory in a football match or for a high grade on the upcoming examination, the God who responds to a community's supplication for rain or for success in battle, is a creature of its hedonistic desirings. It is not the God of history.

Hegel is thus prepared to answer the first of the two questions left unanswered by Kant. The plan of Providence can in fact be known, for "what was *intended* by eternal wisdom, is actually *accomplished* in the domain of existent, active Spirit" [PH 15]. In coming to understand the essential character of historical change, you will come to understand how God works in history to the realization of ideal good. But if the ideal good is what you are commanded categorically to seek, then the ethical rules governing your behavior are there in history for you to see insofar as you are able to grasp the essential structure of that history. The moral standard defining your duty is what history is in the process of realizing. The relative goods and evils of any particular time and place are discerned as such only by reference to the ideal good implicit in them and being realized through them, a final good of which they are the momentary, partial expressions.

It is thus your duty to know the ideal good so that you might do some concrete good. It is your faith that you should seek to know God so that you might be saved. It is your rational task to understand the character of the whole sweep of human history so that you might know yourself through knowing the essence of reality. Ethical, religious, and philosophical mandates are thus coordinate expressions of the selfsame truth: that in this praxis only is the attainment of Self.

"The very essence of Spirit," says Hegel, "is activity" [PH 73]: the essence of the essence of things is processive. It is what Rosenthal called an "impulsion" toward determinate outcomes marked by the realization of value. Likewise, the "Spirit of a people" is essentially dynamic, the working out in historical time of the characteristics which give that people its distinctiveness. This *Volksgeist* is a matter of customs and constitutions, "the whole complex of its institutions" as these come to be fashioned by the members of a community through their transactions with one another, with nature, and with other communities. This that they make of themselves is what they *are*: "nations are what their deeds are" [PH 74]. By appropriating this national Spirit as your own, you gain the "character and capability" to do something meaningful with your own life, to make for yourself "a definite place in the world": your job, your calling, your comradeship all find their value in the way they function within the environing social order.

This is a familiar triad. You gain self-identity by choices that instantiate a cultural norm in some individuating mode; this is your character, taken both as a partially realized accomplishment and as an ideal criterion of evaluation. The community to which you are thereby acculturated realizes its distinctive institutional shape as an embodiment of yet more fundamental norms. Its government and other forms of interacting, its traditions and its sense of destiny, are taken as historical accomplishments that accord to some extent with transcendent values regarding what is just, fair, and humane, and by appeal to which it can be found to deserve praise or to need reform. Hence Hegel can say that a society is "moral—virtuous—vigorous" so far as its members think themselves to be, and actually are, participants in such a dynamic triadic structure.

You participate in this structure and discover that it involves the harmony of self, society, and human nature, aligned by their normative orientations like planets in conjunction. You also discover that the structure is dynamic, that you are oriented within it teleologically, toward the realization of values implicit in your situation. You experience this dynamic structure by living toward the realization of what, to your best ability to grasp it, is the ideal character that defines you as an individual, a member of a community, and a representative of your species. It is a character you incarnate sufficiently to be able to know as ideal, but it is a character you incarnate insufficiently to realize easily. Its more adequate realization is a task requiring your deepest loyalty, your categorical commitment. A people so aligned is what Hegel calls "world-historical": its efforts are one of the ways by which the overall ideal that is the essence of the world, the "universal principle" that is the end for which history is the accomplishing, grows up toward its full, matured realization.

If you do things that are out of character, if your character is not commensurate with social practices, if your society is not concerned to provide for the common weal; if, in short, these three dimensions of praxis are not aligned, then "mere desires" motivate your actions. When the normative webbing that connects self, society, and human nature is stripped away, all that remains is desire desiring. It is these hedonistic strivings that come to nought, that "pass over without leaving a trace" because what they accomplish has no significance beyond the momentary quelling of some momentary need. These are the children of Chronos, spawned by the flux of time and soon devoured by it.

When you survey the history of the human race and find only individuals struggling for their brief moment in the sun, find only the rise and fall of empires, the coming to be and soon perishing of one purpose or another, then it is understandable that you should suffer anguish. Kierkegaard only echoed what Hegel is saying by having Judge William proclaim a life lived in terms of ethical norms as the only antidote to the poisoning despair of an aesthete's dependence on contingency. Whoever looks at the world solely in hedonistic terms sees there only the wreckage of unrealized desire. Whoever acts solely in pursuit of the Moment realizes ends that have no meaning beyond the moment of their realization and so are quickly consumed by the inevitable press of things toward new ends, new meanings. Not to be world-historical is to be normless, and to be normless is to have neither self-identity nor communal identity, to have no place within the scheme of things.

An interpretation, in Royce's sense, is a normative pattern by which an identity is woven for a sequence of actions or a collection of persons. Through acts of interpretation, the disintegrative, dispersive processes of time are overcome. This norm, as we have been arguing, is always triadic. First, sustaining the weave of your own self-identity requires seeing each of your particular actions as occurring within the framework of your character, deciding, for instance, that even though an action has transgressed that framework, you can find a way to use it nonetheless to reconfirm your character or improve upon its relevance. To be guided in what you do by a sense of how you should act, and to take whatever you do, even where it negates your guidelines, as contributing to an eventual increase in its concrete realization, is how your actions come to exemplify a consistent quality, a character that constitutes the essence of who you are. Your normative sense of self is the constant warp to the flying shuttlecock of your ever-changing actions. But the incessant back and forth weaves weft onto warp, and thereby creates a reality in which the warp is no longer abstract but has become integral to what was realized.

Likewise, at a second level of normativeness, even though individuals are born and die, if they are seen as embodying certain ideal cultural standards and if that culture's practices are able to find a place even for their critique within its dynamic ongoingness, then the culture endures and the felt promise of its significance takes on objective solidity. The third dimension of the triad is the ideal of the whole of humanity integrated into what Royce calls a Universal Community by means of practices guided by the sense individuals and nations have of their common human nature and their common human destiny.

When you look at history rationally, when you see not only the weft threads but the warp as well, then not only do you see the conditions that make possible responsible selves, enduring peoples, and the seamless web of human history, but you have available the resources for being yourself more responsible, for contributing more effectively to your nation's security and well-being, for becoming a more vital part of the struggle of our species to realize its special destiny. It is as your actions are constrained by the hope of exemplifying valued characteristics partially exemplified in your prior actions and in those of others that what you accomplish becomes worthwhile. It was Zeus who "put a limit to the devouring agency of Time," who "set a bound to its principle of decadence" by establishing "something inherently and independently durable" [PH 77, 76]. It is he who does the "moral work" of providing the permanent strands of ideality that discipline the shuttlecock of desire so that its efforts will turn out to weave meaningful historical cloth. Thus Zeus triumphs over his father Chronos by introducing normative measure into the flux of time.

The actions of each successive moment still perish; you perish; the kingdoms of this world perish. But if there is awareness that something worthwhile can be rescued from the perishing and then reborn within the milieu of subsequent accomplishments, then your deed perishes but you endure. You grow old and die but your people flourish. The glories of elder races are long forgot but the immense journey of the human species continues on. Not only onward but upward, for each renewed achievement of character is the occasion for improvement. The negative aspect of change is the perishing, but the positive aspect is that it makes room for fresh accomplishment. Hegel gives Lessing's desperate notion of reincarnation a transformative twist: it can happen in history that what must perish makes what about itself need not perish into some new and better reality:

Spirit—consuming the envelope of its existence—does not merely pass into another envelope, nor rise rejuvenescent from the ashes of its previous form; it comes forth exalted, glorified, a purer spirit. It certainly makes war upon itself—consumes its own existence; but in this very destruction it works up that existence into a new form, and each successive phase becomes in its turn a material, working on which it exalts itself to a new grade. [PH 73]

Perpetuation, yes; the new a recovery of the old, handing it on as a sacred treasure from one generation to the next. But why better?

Hegel's answer is the one underlying our interpretation of praxis. Reason is the order, the form, the structure of reality. To understand it, to explain its workings, requires appeal to its four conditions. "Reason is the *substance* of the Universe; viz., that by which and in which all reality has its being and subsistence"; it is "its own *Infinite Material* underlying all the natural and spiritual life which it originates," including the possibilities for realization from which arises its "absolute final aim." Reason is also the "energizing power realizing this aim," the *"Infinite Form"* or *"Infinite Energy* of the Universe; since Reason is not so powerless as to be incapable of producing anything but a mere ideal, a mere intention" [PH 9]. The substance, form, and power of the universe are correlates of a final aim the realization of which they condition. The flux of things has an absolute end just as the flux of any specific thing has a relative end.

You are a rational creature because your actions can be explained by reference to how the content, purpose, manner, and energy of your praxis interrelate as you go about doing the things you do. The cultural ethos of a people is rational if it can be accounted for in terms of the interplay of tradition, belief, practice, and commitment. To say that the world is rational is to say the same thing of it: that what explains why things transpire as they do is found in an examination of the relationship among givens, possibles, patterns, and impulsions. So it is appropriate that Hegel should turn to the structure of praxis for his hypothesis regarding the structure of all forms of reality. A human self can be explained only by referring beyond its immediacy to more encompassing actual and ideal contexts with which it strives to be in harmony. Similarly, a culture can be understood only by taking into account ideal possibilities that constitute its sense of its place in history. What it means to be a human being is found to involve understandings not reducible to the sum of human or societal practices. These differing domains of self, society, and human nature are themselves harmonized by the common ideal character they variously strive to exemplify. Consistent with this, the universe of which these domains are constituent must share that same character with them, harmonizing the human triadic harmony with that of its other constitutive harmonies, organic and inorganic, intramundane and intergalactic. At all levels of reality there ought to be and is manifest an impulsion toward the realization of ideals, including the ideal of a harmony among all those ideals and realizations.[1]

Let us limit our inquiry, however, to the human harmonies, those having to do with reality insofar as it is coming to self-consciousness. Reason so manifest is Spirit and the essence of Spirit is Freedom. History, then, is an interpretation of the world as the way by which the ideal of human freedom comes to characterize human relationships. It is the story of how human dignity, taken as a value, as the aim of all human striving because it is the condition of its very striving, is through those strivings made a determinate quality of the important enduring achievements of humanity. Kant's ethical imperative supplies the "ought" for which Hegel's account of history supplies the "is."

Kant was at a loss to figure out how an actual will could be brought to do what a good will would do, since attempting to determine its commitments by offering incentives, rational as well as hedonistic, only compromises the freedom without which a good will does not exist. But Hegel sees that the mistake is to think that a person, in order to realize a higher ideal, must first be motivated by it. A change in your standard of Selfhood, an aspiration to improve, to set your sights higher, may well lead to your becoming a more mature individual, more your own person, more responsible for what you do and responsive to those who need you, more effectively involved in the affairs of your community. It is far more likely, however, that these results, if they occur, will do so despite your intentions, that consequences of your unrepentant selfish purposes will nonetheless, in clash and consort with the ramifications of others' purposes, arrive at the same improved result. Human praxis because it is free is of necessity disruptive, and so is always opening up fresh opportunities for realization. The implications of what it means to be free are worked out by that freedom being exercised, even if the agent be unaware that it is free.

"Passion," for Hegel, is the energy of praxis, the power it has to transform what is complete and settled into something unsettling and then newly but differently complete. "We assert then that nothing has been accomplished without interest on the part of the actors," that is, that *"nothing great in the World* has been accomplished without *passion"* [PH 23]. But passion is not merely Don Juanian desire. It involves the further characteristic of sustained commitment, a single-mindedness of will and intelligence in pursuit of some end. A passion subordinates other needs and wants to a single, orienting goal, weaving "every fiber of volition" into a web of conviction that produces the sort of consistent behavior required for nonephemeral achievement. Hegel says that he was tempted to call this "character," which is precisely our term for it. His preferred term, "passion," captures more clearly the power of this purposeful energy, but "character" retains the sense of its consistency. Hegel's reference to the "hue of resolution" is even better; to speak of your resolve is to point to your willful intent to persist, to be resolute, until a course of action has been completed. Resolve is the spine of agency.

Passion may be more than mere desire, but its root is there nonetheless. When you desire something, you want to possess it in order that you might no longer feel incomplete. Your aim is to make that object *your* object, to find your satisfaction and hence your full, completed self in it. If you are successful, it becomes not only your object but *you.* Your desiring, by striving to win for you your completed self, has thus proclaimed its own selfhood as the highest good, as an ideal. This is to have made selfhood into an ethical principle, into a standard for any praxis: "This is the absolute right of personal existence—to find *itself* satisfied in its activity and labor. If men are to interest themselves for anything, they must (so to speak) have part of their existence involved in it; find their individuality gratified by its attainment" [PH 22]. But what is pursued as a right and not just the happenstance of a transitory craving is pursued steadfastly. It has ceased to be an object to be consumed in a Moment and has become a characteristic to be exemplified as far as possible from Moment to Moment, to be sought persistently across the days and years. To exist, to be a person, to find yourself satisfied by what you do: the affirmation in action of this absolute right is what Hegel means by passion. Or as Jefferson put it: life, liberty, and the pursuit of happiness are inalienable rights because they are the necessary conditions of being human. Their violation violates your right to be human, and so justifies the absolute passion of a revolutionary praxis in defense of Self.

So passion may be narrowly selfish but it is not animalistic. There is an ideal at work in your passion that serves to organize your animal energy, to give it focus, and therefore to individuate it, to give it identity through time. "Spirit is at war with itself; it has to overcome itself as its most formidable obstacle" [PH 55], because Spirit is expressed dynamically as passion. The energy of Spirit is compacted into praxis, into individual enduring purposive entities. Because your purposes are narrow, however, and because so are everyone else's, they impede each other. Others' aims intrude upon your own and yours upon theirs; other selves become formidable obstacles for the attaining of your own selfhood. But this obstructing is only a new version of the incoordinate, dispersive flux that desiring manifested. Passion needs to extend its scope, to achieve its Moment by bringing about an effective way for the purposes of individuals to be harmonized within a collective purpose. In this manner your passion for fulfillment is attained by paying more attention to the context of its pursuit, by substituting cooperation for conflict. And so the passion rises to a higher principle, to an ideal of group solidarity. You are unswerving now in your conviction not only that you have a right to exist but that your group, as a prerequisite for that right being realized, also should exist. This calls for a greater passion than before, but you are galvanized by it and so you struggle resolutely to make its more encompassing structure into a living reality.

Recall that something has "world-historical" significance for Hegel if its ideals are in some manner a realization, however partial, of the ideal of freedom. If you lack passion or if your passion is for ends that contradict the praxis they exemplify, then it is unlikely that a rubric can be found for harmonizing your aims with those of others. Your environment will be rocky soil for your dreams; it will not nurture what you have sown until the harvest. So it is the passions that can be made compatible with other passions that will survive, that will gain in strength, that will deepen their resolve, that will see their ends embodied in the concrete practices of a group and ultimately in the actual beliefs and customs of a nation or a civilization.

Hegel's "world-historical individuals" are those whose passions effect a transformation from some form of societal order to another where the ideal at issue, the object that their passion brings to historical realization, is some modality of Freedom, some "new grade" of accomplishment in the endless effort to wrest effective order and hence fulfillment from the clash of competing interests. These culture-heroes are practical people; their aims are parochial, concerned with the problems of their own time and place. But they have had "an insight into the requirements of the time—*what was ripe for development,*" and so have grasped an ideal by which to look beyond accustomed ways of relationship to what seems to them a more effective or a broader or a more intense way. "World-historical men—the Heroes of an epoch—must, therefore, be recognized as its clear-sighted ones; *their* deeds, *their* words are the best of that time" [PH 30].

Hegel is not succumbing to romanticism in this talk of heroes. Their greatness is not in some innate "genius" they possess; they are not great souls born for the titanic roles they are called upon to play. If they have a genius it is what Hegel calls "national genius": a principle of "idiosyncrasy" that sets limits to what can be done but that within those limits works out their possibilities to the fullest, on all of the available levels of expression [PH 64]. But this is precisely what character is, an individual character or a national character: the principle that gives an enduring unity to its constituents. So a world-historical person is one whose character involves fresh, unfamiliar ideals, and whose passion for them is powerful enough to make them actual. It is a passion able to turn a group or a nation from its traditional practices to a different collective praxis: a new sense of context, new goals, new strategies, new leaders, and new accomplishments.

Some persons lack the dream who would have the energy, some dream but do not believe. But most of us have imagination enough to grasp new possibilities when they are conjured up for us, and we have resolve enough to follow when we are being led toward something better. So there are little, limited ways, perhaps, in which each one of us has been a minor hero for a group of two or ten. Even the superheroes of our race (Hegel's examples are military leaders who also were heads of state: Alexander, Caesar, Napoleon) are not heroes to their valets, are not heroes whose significance is felt absolutely everywhere. Within a culture there is a continuum of creative acts of transformation. Without the secondary and tertiary works of creativity there could be no heroes; these acts echo, fill in, and amplify those of the leaders and give them world-historical resonance. At every level it is insight and commitment that make the difference. The possibility of both is always present, brooding just below the horizon of the actual, awaiting the time for which it is the ripeness.

So there is an "impulse of perfectibility" in Spirit, in any reality that is conscious of itself, that is not evident in other forms of life; nor is it a quality of the inanimate world (although implicit even there). Self-consciousness in its most rudimentary form is individuating and idealistic. It sets you apart from the rest of things as lacking those things, and so relates you to them in the form of desiring what you lack. Ideals and the ideas for realizing them, final and formal causes, are always unavoidably the mode of self-conscious activity. This individuated pursuit of ideals means that any actual accomplishment always stands in contrast to what could have been accomplished instead. Or in ethical terms, "is" always implies some other possibility as an "ought." The impulse of perfectibility is the passion that takes those oughts seriously and so always finds itself trying to change things from what they are into what they ought to be.

Unthinking things merely grow until they perish, following a "direct, unopposed, unhindered" path. But persons seek to rearrange the world to their own advantage and so end up rearranging it for whoever, sometimes not themselves, might find advantage in what results. History is the story of the passions by which the world up to now has been arranged and rearranged. The power of the varied individual passions assures that the rearranging will go on endlessly, unless it should ever be the case that the results are to the advantage of everyone, that everyone's advantage is the same, that everyone's ought has become everywhere an is. Hegel hesitates to claim that the impulse to perfection can ever arrive at this Endtime, this point after which there is no passion and hence no history. The drive toward novel achievement in the midst of an unacceptable adversity is clearly a distinctive feature of human activity, but that the movement overall is toward making explicit the full range of ideals implicit from the first is not so obvious.

Metaphysical considerations say that such a movement is necessary, but the empirical evidence can only say to what extent such an interpretation works, how well it provides an order to the flux of things, presents them as a course of history, as a dialectical progression toward the full realization of what ought to be. You need not be detained, therefore, by the specifics of what Hegel actually says in the *Philosophy of History* regarding how Freedom has gained an ever-increasing historical concreteness. Nonetheless it would be a mistake for you to dismiss the enterprise in dismissing the result. If all you learn from Hegel is what ought to be, then you are at the same point we were with Kant. The ideal of Freedom—individual, societal, and global—would still be there as a standard of excellence by which to gauge our actions and guide our purposes. But it would only be regulative,[2] whereas we were promised a way to show that it is constitutive as well.

Hegel's metaphors are all progressive, but the progress is not open-ended and infinite. The metaphors are of developments that have a definite culmination, that move toward a highest and therefore final expression. He talks of the process by which Freedom becomes historically concrete, calling it "the great Day's work of Spirit." First of all, as a *day's* work the realization of Freedom progresses from morning through noontime into afternoon and draws to a close with the coming of the evening. Secondly, as the *work* of a day it begins in "utter aston-ishment" at the splendor of the world, moves to a recognition of its individual needs within a world that can supply them, and ends up constructing an artifact, a building in which to dwell. Freedom makes this building from the raw material of the natural world, objectifies its imagination by making its own world, a new world equally as astonish-ing as the one it had originally encountered [PH 103]. Thirdly, the ge-ography of a day is from the place where the sun first appears above the horizon to the place of its setting, so

The History of the World travels from East to West, for Europe is abso-lutely the end of History, Asia the beginning. . . . For although the Earth forms a sphere, History performs no circle round it, but has on the contrary a determinate East, viz., Asia. Here rises the outward physical Sun, and in the West it sinks down: here consentaneously rises the Sun of self-consciousness, which diffuses a nobler brilliance. [PH 103–4]

And finally, a person's work, day after day, traces a career from child-hood to adolescence to adulthood and finally to full maturity.

Utilizing all four of these metaphors at once, Hegel sketches the ways in which human self-consciousness has been expressed over time in the societal structures that are its fullest manifestation. Asia is the dawn of civilization, our childhood, when a person is still largely deter-mined by biological necessities and the world seems awesome, a time-less structure of massive importances, an overwhelming presence to which one must adjust. The Greek world is our adolescence, the noon-time of the human day, when the young self asserts its subjectivity, arrogantly conjures up in its fertile imagination a vision of the whole world bowing down to its purposes. Ever westward, the Roman state then arises, embodying the "manhood" of history, the disciplined power to impose its purposes upon a recalcitrant nature, to remake the world by reference to a plan in which individuals find their proper place within a coordinated whole. In the evening of this day, when Spirit has attained "perfect maturity and strength," a governmental form emerges in which people are ruled by law rather than by arbi-trary will, by universal principles they impose upon themselves and obey because they recognize those principles as the essential shape of their truest selfhood. This creation by human beings of their own soci-etal dwelling-place, one founded on their own free praxis and not on natural necessity, is "the ultimate result which the process of History is intended to accomplish" [PH 110]. It is what in fact has been accomplished by the nations of modern Europe.

Hegel usually collapses this four-step development into a triad, by combining the Greek and Roman cultures into a Mediterranean phase midway between those of the Orient and the modern West. Trinitarian principles of order come readily to his mind because of their predominance in Kantian logic and in the Christian religion. Hence the forms of propositional quantification suggest a sequence: "The Eastern nations knew only that *one* is free; the Greek and Roman world only that *some* are free; while *we* know that all men absolutely (man *as man*) are free" [PH 19; similarly, 104]. Each historical stage implies a different form of government and a whole cultural ethos of undergirding beliefs and practices. First there is oriental despotism with its dependence on nature and the assumption that its leaders are bestowed upon the people by natural mandate. The limitations of this narrow sense of freedom finally become the soil for a world to emerge governed by a privileged group that functions internally as a democracy of equals but which as a group is dependent upon the subjugation of slaves and the ostracization of barbarians. Only when the weaknesses inherent in this form of freedom have fully manifested themselves is it possible for there to arise a wider freedom, one in which all members of a society are governed by law embodied in a constitution and administered by a rationally structured government.

In the fashion of Joachim, Hegel also proposes thinking about the three phases of the culminating stage of human history, the stage comprising the era of the European peoples, as kingdoms of the Father, Son, and Spirit [PH 343–5; see Illustration 6.1]. Its initial phase is equivalent to an *initiatio,* a time of incipience, of gestation. What will become the highest known form of free human association is at first hidden by the Roman Empire and by its later manifestation under Charlemagne: divinity not yet explicit in the world.

Then comes the emergence of this religion as a sociopolitical force, a feudal theocracy in which the sanctity of the individual is incarnate in history but in the dualistic form of narrow, fixed private fealties in contrast to vague, general ideals. The third period, the kingdom of the Spirit, begins with Charles V and the Reformation. Thereafter "the principle of Free Spirit" is made "the banner of the World," Reason comes consciously to regulate political life, and the antithesis between the spiritual and the secular is at last "harmonized."

Immediately upon proposing this approach to an interpretation of the nature and significance of European history, Hegel suggests that the

**Illustration 6.1: Hegel's History: The Dialectic of the Nations**

x: substantive          y: subjective          z: synthesis

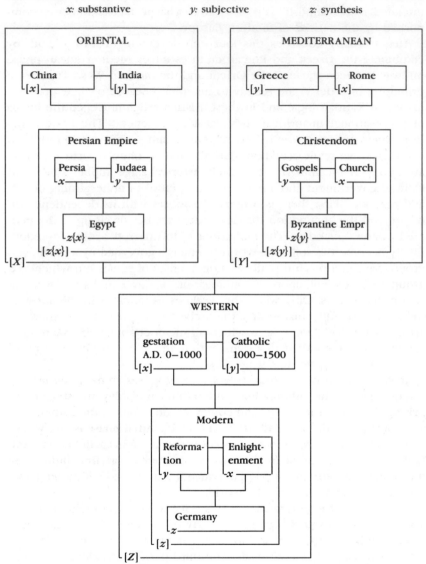

same triune progression could be found in a comparison of the Persian, Greek, and Roman worlds. The movement from Persia's "substantial unity" to the Hellenic "ideal unity" to the "universal" unity which marks the "Hegemony of self-cognizant Thought" as institutionalized by the Roman Empire [PH 345–6] is the same as the movement through the phases of European self-realization. Indeed, Hegel's dialectical trinities are like mathematical fractals: each element of a trinity reflects the structure of the whole. The relationship between the overarching Oriental, Mediterranean, and European periodization of history reappears as three distinctive phases in the history of each period, which in turn is reflected in the subdivisions of each period.

The recurrent relationship is a movement from undifferentiated unity to a polarity between the concrete particulars and an abstract universal, this tension impelling the emergence of a new, reconciling form of unification. This is the familiar Hegelian dialectic, of course. But if we attend to its fractal character we will be saved from thinking of the dialectic as a ghost in the world-machine, as an external impetus bending events to its purpose, a sacred ark borne on the backs of suffering individuals who unwittingly bring it to its intended destination. Praxis itself has an Hegelian structure. Hence selves, societies, the whole human species, and the very Universe should be fundamentally dialectical, each manifesting that selfsame structure in some distinctive, context-relevant way.

In this sense, Hegel's actual account of the place of the worldviews and achievements of various peoples in the development of constitutional government and of its artistic, religious, and philosophical analogues is not what is important. Whether you will find his story adequate or not is an empirical matter; his account is a test of the hypothesis that the world is rational. If this hypothesis can explain the evidence, then your confidence in it grows from mere belief toward knowledge. If not, then you need to revise the hypothesis or take fresh stock of your facts, attempting once more to tell the story. If reason is indeed the dynamic structure of our lives, manifested recurrently and fractal-like in all the praxes of our history, you will come eventually to get the story right and to know how Freedom has come at last into its kingdom.

Hegel's answer then to the first of Kant's unanswered questions is yes, there is a developmental pattern to history and it is one in which the ought implicit from the first in the very nature of human being becomes an is, comes to determinate realization in social institutions and practices. History has a purpose; a story can be told of it, an explanation concretely deployed that shows why things have transpired as they have. Ideals do not only govern the human world as aloof magistrates, judging the value of our intentions and accomplishments. They also govern it by leading us to strive to make them characteristics of our own character and of our own accomplishments, to make them into the genius of our nation and of its history, to existentialize them as the essence of human nature and of its destiny.

The accounting made at any given time will suffer from the limitations of the society providing it. The history of Spirit needs to be constantly rewritten as the dialogue between theory and practice, philosophical understanding and particular accomplishment, alters and deepens.[3] That this is so, that Hegel's *Philosophy of History* needs to be rewritten for an age quite different than his own, casts no disparagement on his claim but instead confirms its point. So let me tell you afresh this story of our liberties. Let me tell you how it has come about that through us the ideal of human Selfhood has achieved its finest historical expression ever.

For in the beginning, when the peoples of China were already old, the government of Yao arose. . . .

For in the beginning, your Father Abraham heard the voice of Yahweh and took up his tents and journeyed out from Ur of the Chaldees, he knew not where. . . .

For in the beginning, when the hills of Rome were still a wilderness, then from the ravages of Troy came bold Aeneas to that distant shore. . . .

For in the beginning, England was an insignificant nation, an island people interested in farming and fishing, in trading with the European nations across the channel, and in defending its shores against foreign intrusion. It was not a nation given to commerce or warfare that might carry it far from home. Its efforts eastwardly to consolidate feudal holdings in France and its constant campaigns to control the Celtic peoples surrounding it to the west sufficed to fulfill its aspirations. So England played no role in the early phases of modern European overseas exploration. Spain and Portugal had divided the New World between themselves and projected their power along the coast of Africa and as far as India while England slumbered, turned in upon itself first by the dynastic struggles of Lancaster and York, then by the religious controversies of the Tudor period.

Until Elizabeth. At the time of Elizabeth's ascension to the throne in 1558 England was at long last turning to the sea; the queen's murky policy of encouraging private adventure without acknowledging it gave English seamen and merchants an opportunity to fulfill simultaneously their greed, religious fervor, and patriotism. As early as 1432, a poet would admonish the adolescent Henry VI, while turning in his hands a coin, the noble, which carried the image of one of Henry's great predecessors:

For foure things our Noble showeth to me,
King, Ship, and Swerd, and power of the see ...
Put to good will for to keepe the see,
First for worship and profite also,
And to rebuke of eche evill willed foe.[4]

Drawn on by the lure of "profite," the propagation of Protestant "worship," and a hatred of all manner of "evill willed foe," England slowly became first a maritime power, cautiously extending the scope of its fishing and trading. By the end of Elizabeth's reign it had become a naval power as well, dominating the Atlantic and protecting its merchants as they sought to expand their commercial hegemony around the globe. Finally it became a colonial power, an empire upon which by the nineteenth century the sun would never set.

As Hegel remarks, "Nations are what their deeds are. Every Englishman will say: We are the men who navigate the ocean, and have the commerce of the world; to whom the East Indies belong and their riches; who have a parliament, juries, etc" [PH 74]. The record of the deeds that made this England what it was are contained in volumes edited by Richard Hakluyt, first published in 1589 and reissued in a greatly expanded version in 1598–1600 under the title *The Principal Navigations, Voiages, Traffiques, and Discoveries of the English Nation, made by Sea or over-land, to the remote and farthest distant quarters of the Earth, at any time within the compasse of these 1500 yeeres.* Hakluyt was an archivist, not an historian. His volumes are for the most part compilations of primary sources, what he calls a *peregrinationis historia:* firsthand accounts of the people who actually took part in the adventures rather than summaries made by an author whose pretensions are to write a "universal cosmography."

The result is a story of people "mooved with desire to advance Gods glory and to seeke the good of their native Countrey" [PN-7 381] in their exploration of new lands and their search for a sea route to Asia, yet people also seeking "to plant, possesse, and subdue" [PN-8 101] whatever they might encounter. It is powerful reading even today. The bare accounting of his adventures by a sea captain or a gentleman knight, sometimes by a scholar who had accompanied the expedition, occasionally by a sole surviving sailor, expresses on every page the courage, or the foolhardiness, of men willing to run enormous risks in order to make their fortunes, win fame, satisfy their scientific curiosity, or wreak vengeance on an enemy. No wonder that Hakluyt's book soon became a standard part of the cabin supplies for any English ship of exploration and commerce. Indeed, use of his volumes was credited by the East India Company with saving a fleet of ships from having to turn back to England when delays had required them either to do so or to find fresh supplies of food and water along an unknown shore. The *Principal Navigations* contained an account of that area, enabling the captain to find safe harbor, and profits from the voyage were eventually a quarter again what they would otherwise have been [HP-2 502].

Adventure, yes, but more as well. For "there is no sea innavigable, no land unhabitable," they said, no place where an English ship cannot go. And so no place where the Gospel could not go as well. As Hakluyt says in his "Epistle Dedicatorie" to the 1589 edition, the success of English ships lay not only in their having journeyed to distant lands and returned with great wealth, but also in their having been well received both by the strange savages they found in the New World and by the mighty princes and kings they met in the courts of Asian nations. This happy response of the local populations was to be taken as a "pledge of Gods further favor" on England, if it would use this opportunity to carry "the incomparable treasure of the trueth of Christianity, and of the Gospell, while we use and exercise common trade with their merchants" [PN-1 xxi].

Nothing should take precedence over the "planting" of the Christian faith, argue the adventurers. But as the knight and gentleman George Peckham makes clear, conversion of the heathen involves more than baptizing them in the faith. It means also taking "such competent quantity of Land" from them "as every way shall be correspondent to the Christians expectation and contentation," especially since the natives are making no agricultural use of their lands. Moreover, this is what God's people have done from the beginning. Peckham expostulates at considerable length about Moses and Joshua conquering the Canaanites, about how the Apostles, "being inspired with the holy Ghost, and the knowledge of all strange languages, did immediately disperse themselves to sundry parts of the world," and about what Constantine did in vanquishing enemies and spreading his faith throughout the Roman Empire, then beyond it to "all such remote Barbarous and Heathen nations, as then inhabited the foure quarters of the worlde," even including "the Island of Britaines" [PN-8 98–105].

Hakluyt entreats Queen Elizabeth to do no less than her heroic predecessors did: extend the Christian religion by extending her political hegemony until it has encompassed the known world. Her loyal subjects, the flame of those past "woorthy actes" burning "in their noble breasts," would then be bold to carry forward their efforts "untill such time as their owne valure had equalled the fame and glory of their progenitors" [PN-1 lxvi].

These arguments are echoed by Edward Haye in his report on Humphrey Gilbert's 1583 voyage to Newfoundland. Although only a remnant of the group returned safely, although their booty was minimal, and although Gilbert himself perished when his ship foundered off the Azores, an English presence had nevertheless been established in the New World and the Gospel preached among the savages. The significance of this is considerable, for "in this last age of the world" the time is "compleat" that the Gospel should be spread to the ends of the earth, and if so then "God will raise him an instrument to effect the same." Clearly neither Spain nor Portugal, nor even France, is that instrument; they have all suffered defeats that can only be taken as evidence that God is not pleased with them and so has banned them from playing any further crucial role in world history. England has come late on the scene, and alone has had success in the temperate regions north of Florida. It seems probable, therefore, that "God hath reserved these last new lands," these last of the "Gentiles," to be "reduced unto Christian civility by the English nation." As further proof, Hayes adds,

Which also is very probable by the revolution and course of Gods word and religion, which from the beginning hath moved from the East, towards, & at last unto the West, where it is like to end, unless the same begin againe where it did in the East, which were to expect a like world againe. But we are assured of the contrary by the prophesie of Christ, whereby we gather, that after his word preached thorowout the world shallbe the end. [PN-8 36–38]

Gilbert's rival in the search for a northwest passage, John Davis, makes a similar argument. Scripture is clear that "there shall be one shepherd and one flock," that the Gentile nations shall someday all be united. So

what hindereth us of England (being by God's mercy for the same purpose at this present moment most aptly prepared) not to attempt that which God himself hath appointed to be performed? There is no doubt but that we of England are this saved people, by the eternal and infallible presence of the Lord predestined to be sent unto these Gentiles in the sea, there to preach the peace of the Lord: for are not we only set upon Mount Zion to give light to all the rest of the world? ... It is only we, therefore, that must be these shining messengers of the Lord, and none but we. [PN-12 31]

These are not merely the rhetorical flourishes of clergymen attempting to further their own self-interests, although there was certainly plenty of such preaching heard. Nor are they arguments that realistic adventurers have cast cynically in an argot they know would appeal to the queen and her counsellors, although both realism and cynicism were abundant commodities in such transactions. Amid all the practical arguments for granting commercial patents, for quietly supporting piratical adventure, and for enlarging English power, were the recurrent themes of purification and mission. Too long, warns Hakluyt, have the English been busy at "those soft unprofitable pleasures wherein they now too much consume their time and patrimonie" [PN-1 lxvii]. But insofar as they have taken to the sea, the desire for "sluggish security" and "idleness" has given way to what Haye calls "a vertuous and heroycall minde." The nation has been purified, renewed; under the leadership of her Elizabeth, this latter-day "handmaid of the Lord," is now ready to be God's shining messenger to the farthest reaches of the globe. Why else would God have kept these heathen people in ignorance of his truth, except that through their conversion the world might at last be made ready for the coming of his kingdom.

Hakluyt's self-appointed successor as editor of the growing volume of reports on England's work was Samuel Purchas. Elizabeth's Stuart successor, James I, says he read and reread *Purchas His Pilgrimage, or Relations of the World and the Religions observed in all Ages and Places discovered from the Creation unto this Present.* This 800-page tome published by Purchas in 1613 aims to display the world as an arena in which the "workes of God" can be seen in the "Justice and Providence" by which the "mightiest Empires" have been pulled down because they have forsaken God's will or by which individuals and whole nations have fallen into the delusion of false belief. Thus the heathen are not ignorant; they are sinners being punished for their sin.

Yet, says Purchas, his royal readership very much in mind,

*God hath shewed his Word unto our* IACOB (THE Defender Of His Faith) his Statutes and his iudgements unto this Israel of Great Britaine. *He hath not dealt so with every Nation, neither have the Heathen,* nor scarsely, if scarsly, any other Christian Nation, so much *knowledge of his iudgments.* [PHP "To The Reader"]

Even though England's people have not always been so quick as Purchas would wish in heeding what has been revealed to them, their godliness is enough for him to close his book by imagining that he has returned to England after this "pilgrimage" around the world. He knows no better sights anywhere than in England: "Christian Churches, without Heathenish, Jewish, or Antichristian pollutions"; a land that is, indeed, a "Map of Heaven and Earth," a place so pure in its freedoms and its piety as to be the "Suburbs of the true heaven" [PHP 918].

Purchas was read by more than the king. Two further editions of his book were published within two years and a subsequent book on human sin and salvation was equally popular. But it was not until 1625, when he published an expansion and update of Hakluyt's volumes, that Purchas states explicitly the import of the confidence he and his countrymen have come to have in England's purity and mission. Twenty volumes in length, this new work is called *Hakluytus Posthumus or Purchas His Pilgrimes; Contayning a History of the World, in Sea Voyages & lande Travells, by Englishmen & others*. In it Purchas argues that all these tales of adventure, trade, and religious conversion are part of the process by which God is restoring to mankind a lost unity. In Adam's fall, our race was scattered across the world into separate and warring peoples. Slowly but steadily over the generations they have grown aware of their original condition and of how God has used even their sinful desires to create increasingly the possibility for its restoration. So the discoveries and commerce of these latter days, even when pursued for selfish ends, have made us increasingly interdependent and brought us to realize that we could again be one people under one God. England, as God's special nation, now leads this venture as it enters its closing chapter.

The claim that England should be destined to be the harbinger of the millennium needed to rest not only on her present virtue and vitality but also on the character of her beginnings. Hakluyt opens the first volume of the *Principal Navigations* with king Arthur, excerpting from histories that relate his supposed sixth-century conquests, including ventures to Lapland and the annexation of Norway. Arthur's great successor, Edgar, the "Saxonal Alexander," is said to have defined the ancient boundaries of the British kingdom. Hakluyt's second volume, turning from the Northeast to the Mediterranean and southern routes of exploration, reports on "Brittons" who played a role in the histories of Greece and pre-Christian Rome; he points out that the daughter of Coelus, king of Britain, was mother of the Emperor Constantine. But Hakluyt and Purchas focus on the more recent and more interesting explorations, so their account is spare concerning the genealogy of England's intimate connection with God's purposes.

John Foxe had already filled in the gaps. His *Actes and Monuments of These Latter and Perillous Dayes* first appeared in 1563 with an expanded edition in 1570, reprinted almost yearly thereafter.[5] The work obviously influenced the thinking of Hakluyt and Purchas; they were only giving an extended meaning to Foxe's insistence on England's special place in God's plan of redemption. The focus of Foxe's book is on Protestants martyred during the reign of Elizabeth's sister Mary, but their sacrifice is set in a context of Christian martyrs from "the primitive beginning" to "these our days" [FBM-1 2]. It is made clear that Britain received the Gospel directly from Joseph of Arimathea in the year 63, and that Lucius was made king of the Britons in 180 with the blessing of the Bishop of Rome. It is further asserted that the daughter of the sixth successor to Lucius married the Roman Constantius. Their son, Constantine the Great, was not only born and raised on British soil but also gained the imperial crown with the help of three legions of British soldiers [FBM-1 306–12]. So "this realm of Britain" is both the first of the Christian nations and the homeland of the emperor who made Christianity the religion of Europe. Moreover, "religion remained in Britain uncorrupt, the word of Christ truly preached," from the very first. Britain's kings run in continuous succession from Lucius to Elizabeth, and its people under their leadership remained steadfast over the centuries in preserving a "doctrine of Faith without mens traditions" [FBM-1 xx]. In contrast, the Church of Rome, "so visible and glorious in the eies of the world, so shining in outward beauty," has grown more wayward, "preaching of mens Decrees, Dreams, and idle Traditions" [FMB-1 xix, xxi].

Foxe organizes the history of Europe into epochs based on his interpretation of the book of Revelation [see Illustration 6.2].

The first 300 years of the Church are a time of persecution, closing in the year 324 with the victory of Constantine and the binding of Satan. For a thousand years the Church is free to preach the Gospel. Beginning with Lucius in 180 and running through four 300-year periods, England resists various threats to its preservation of the faith. The Roman kings reign for the first 300 years and are succeeded by seven Saxon kingdoms that flourish for another three centuries; with Egbert's consolidation of West Saxon hegemony about the year 800, another 300-year period begins that culminates in the reign of William the Conqueror. The next trinity of centuries is marked by increasing tribulation and by the loosing of Satan in the form of an arrogant and corrupt papacy [FBM-2]. This apostasy of the Church of Rome has Gregory VII, Innocent III, and Boniface VIII as its exemplars; by the fifteenth century and on into the sixteenth, things have become so bad that Foxe brands all the popes Antichrist. Meantime, with John Wickliff, the countervailing forces of the Reformation emerge. Nonetheless the false Church waxes stronger and with the coming of Mary Tudor to the throne of England reaches its climax.

**Illustration 6.2: Foxe's Chronologies**

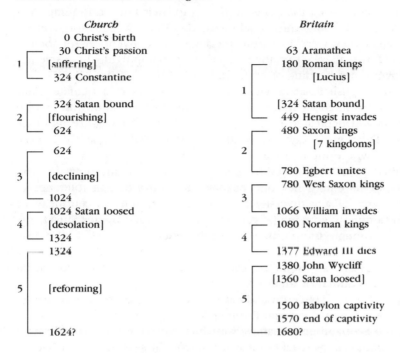

| Church | | Britain | |
|---|---|---|---|
| | 0 Christ's birth | | |
| | 30 Christ's passion | | 63 Aramathea |
| 1 [suffering] | | | 180 Roman kings |
| | 324 Constantine | | [Lucius] |
| | | 1 | |
| 2 [flourishing] | 324 Satan bound | | [324 Satan bound] |
| | 624 | | 449 Hengist invades |
| | | | 480 Saxon kings |
| | | 2 | [7 kingdoms] |
| 3 [declining] | 624 | | 780 Egbert unites |
| | 1024 | | 780 West Saxon kings |
| | | 3 | |
| 4 [desolation] | 1024 Satan loosed | | 1066 William invades |
| | 1324 | | 1080 Norman kings |
| | | 4 | |
| | 1324 | | 1377 Edward III dies |
| | | | 1380 John Wycliff |
| | | | [1360 Satan loosed] |
| 5 [reforming] | | 5 | |
| | | | 1500 Babylon captivity |
| | | | 1570 end of captivity |
| | 1624? | | 1680? |

This tribulation, this "Babilonicall captivitie" of the true Church of God, is seen as coming to a close with the triumph of Protestantism in England. These latter and perilous days are a time, then, to prepare for the end of history and the coming of the second Millennium by purifying the English Church of its papistical influence and its sloth. The English men and women who have remained faithful through so many years of persecution are, strengthened by those persecutions, now ready to meet this final challenge.

Puritanism encouraged self-examination. The reform of the Church could proceed only through the reform of individuals, who were exhorted to be critical about their own shortcomings as well as those of others so that the inner sources of sin might be ferreted out, confessed to God, and purged from the soul. Those whom God granted the grace to purify themselves were his elect, the saints who would alone comprise the membership of a pure Church. They need not be educated, these saints, but they ought to be learned enough to be able to read scripture for themselves and have the good common sense needed to interpret it correctly. They needed to explain themselves constantly to others, confessing their sins, testifying to their faith, critiquing their neighbors, defending their reading of the Holy Word. Moreover, as God's elect they were free from the laws and conventions of society, expected instead to act on the basis of their own individual conscience, their own inner heeding of what God would want of their lives.

So the English Puritans were self-aware, educated, articulate. They were optimistic about the future, expectant that the end of the world was near and dedicated to doing what they could to assure its quick arrival. They were convinced that England and England's Church would be where the end would begin, that they were the vanguard of the Kingdom of God, called by grace to create here and now the conditions for its emergence into history. Elizabeth's benign tolerance of the Puritans, of any diversity that did not threaten her authority or England's quietly growing power, was not continued by her Stuart successor. Although the Puritans were harassed by James I, the pre-Elizabethan persecutions and martyrings were not resumed, and the Puritans became all the more resolute in their commitment to the divine work required of them.

England in the sixteenth and early seventeenth century, and greater Britain beginning to emerge through the uniting of the crowns of England and Scotland under James, was thus everything that Hegel says a nation should be as it takes on world-historical significance. It had an ideal to which its people were dedicated, one that involved a new way of doing things, a new way of thinking and acting. Individuals and groups were filled with passion, with the persistence and energy that are the prerequisites for realizing a new level of Spirit, a new form of the principle of Freedom. The Spirit of the English-speaking peoples was marked distinctively by self-awareness, by a high level of individuation. It would be called entrepreneurial by the traders, self-reliant by the sailors, saintly by the religious; but in each case it was their way of naming what Kant called autonomy. Far more than Hegel's Germanic Spirit of the peoples ever was, the English national spirit was characterized by a collective self-consciousness of its special place in history, its eschatological mission as an instrument of divine purpose in the final, climactic moments of the world's history.

As Hegel also insists, this Spirit found expression in all aspects of British life. The Elizabethan age celebrated the imagination. The new overseas discoveries spurred Elizabethan writers to a golden age of poetry, and the soaring wonder of their words encouraged the optimism and self-confidence so crucial for adventuring into the unknown. If Raleigh's attempted planting at Roanoke could inspire Shakespeare to create *The Tempest,* how many nameless "lovely boies" sallied forth into the unknown for God and country, power and pelf, with the dying words of Marlowe's Tamberlane on their lips:

> Give me a Map, then let me see how much
> Is left for me to conquer all the world,
> That these, my boies, may finish all my wantes. . . .
> Looke here, my boies, see what a world of ground,
> Lies westward from the midst of *Cancers* line,
> Unto the rising of this earthly globe,
> Whereas the Sun, declining from our sight,
> Begins the day with our Antypodes:
> And shall I die, and this unconquered? . . .
> Here, lovely boies, what death forbids my life,
> That let your lives command in spight of death.[6]

Behold a new praxis of world-historical significance. Its material cause is an island people at the fringe of the civilized world; its final cause, a vision of a planet in which the vast congeries of the nations would be united into a single realm of citizens able to exercise their own free conscience in loyalty to God and king. The formal cause of this achievement can be found in a commerce spreading interdependence to the remotest corners of the globe; its efficient cause, in an urgency flowing from the confidence that God has called that people forth to be His shining messenger proclaiming the good news of the end of history.

James's son was no sooner crowned than he began to curb the Puritans and return England to absolute monarchy and the Roman liturgy. In the two decades following Charles I's dissolution of Parliament in 1629, nearly 80,000 Puritans, 2 percent of the nation's total population, emigrated to the New World. For those who founded the Massachusetts Bay colony, the emigration was not a flight from persecution. They were not refugees dispossessed of one homeland and searching for another. England was home, and their journey to this new England across the sea was in order to make it possible for their homeland to be purged of the Stuart Antichrist.

Their new-world colony, as Winthrop argued, was to be "a Citty upon a Hill" to which "the eies of all people" would be turned. The saints who had withdrawn to that rocky shore were to form there a social order that would be a perfect expression of what they were convinced England had to become if it were to serve as the vanguard of the imminent Millennium. The arduous passage over the north Atlantic and the difficult conditions in Massachusetts were the wilderness through which they had to pass, by which they were being tested, on their journey toward a redeemed homeland. Like Israel, they were obeying a call from God to suffer deprivation, to wander in a wilderness, in order to be strengthened to the task for which God had chosen them.

Winthrop's intrepid band made a covenant with God, therefore, that they would create a community governed by God's laws and composed exclusively of his saints. This relationship was chosen by them, a decision they made in full awareness of its significance. Their community was not an inheritance deriving from ancient loyalties to a land planted deep with the bones and memories of their ancestors; it was newly and freely made, a covenant. It was their responsibility to live up to their promise to be a "modell of Christian Charity," and as they did so or did not God would reward or punish them accordingly. Chastised by the divine retributions visited upon them for their collective sins, and encouraged by the signs of providential blessing that came as a consequence of their public repentances, Winthrop's saints confidently awaited an indication that the time was ripe for them to return to England bearing the first fruits of the kingdom which would then break forth into history.

But God never called them back to England. Cromwell had a government to run and the New Model Army needed not saints but soldiers; differences in religious belief and practice could be tolerated as long as a person's loyalties were anti-Stuart and pro-Protestant. Indeed, the penchant of the New Englanders to banish dissenters into the swamps of Rhode Island was an embarrassment to Roundheads trying to reassure would-be supporters skeptical of the tolerance they were being promised. The Massachusetts Puritans had to contend with their own pressures for toleration as well: growing numbers of settlers, as many as 80 percent of the Bay colony, who were not saints; and children of the saints who, although baptized into the covenant, never became self-confessed communicants.

If God's elect had not been sent to New England to form a working model of the society that England and then the world were soon to emulate, for what use were their lives? Slowly and painfully the answer began to formulate itself. They were not just God's people but God's people in New England, not pilgrims trekking through this wilderness on the way to a journey's end on English soil but settlers whose mission had to do with that wilderness. These new-world Puritans had been given a western Canaan to claim as their own, a wilderness it was now their task to make into a garden. They were to drive out the savage, cultivate the land, build their communities: it was their God-given destiny to create in America a new Promised Land. It is said that in 1640 the good citizens of Milford, Connecticut, debated at a town meeting whether it was right for them, as they were already quite actively doing, to seize land from the Indians for their own use. The following resolutions summarized the results of the debate:

1. The earth is the Lord's and the fullness thereof. Voted.
2. The Lord can dispose of the earth to his saints. Voted.
3. We are his saints. Voted.[7]

Puritan beliefs energized an American version of the "Protestant work ethic" that transformed the middle latitudes of North America from an inhospitable and unknown vastness into a nation that by the end of the nineteenth century was on the verge of attaining world-historical significance.[8] But the continent transformed by those beliefs transformed them in turn. George Santayana, in a 1911 talk on "The Genteel Tradition in American Philosophy," characterized the beliefs of the American Puritans as those of an "agonized conscience" which asserts "that sin exists, that sin is punished, and that it is beautiful that sin should exist and be punished" [GT 187]. This is an "old world" view, says Santayana, marked by a self-concerned mindset appropriate only for an embattled people "on the verge of ruin, ecstatic and distressful, . . . that paints life in sharp and violent chiaroscuro, all pure righteousness and black abominations" [GT 190]. He contrasts this with "impassioned empiricism" such as found in William James's pragmatism, an aggressive, life-affirming, active viewpoint, one far more appropriate to a "young country" set in the midst of "a virgin and prodigious world." The new wine needed for America's new bottle is one that teaches "the vanity and superficiality of all logic, the needlessness of argument, the relativity of morals, the strength of time, the fertility of matter, the variety, the unspeakable variety, of possible life" [GT 213].

But Santayana misses the way in which the new bottle made the old wine itself new, so that pragmatism and the entrepreneurial vitality exploding out of post–Civil War America could be seen as an expression rather than a denial of its Puritan heritage, fulfilling in a different but equally dramatic way the eschatological hope of Winthrop that his colony might be the shining messenger destined to lead the whole world into an earthly Paradise.

Puritanism, after all, could be said to have provided the American character with four salient qualities: *individualism*, the belief that through self-discipline and effort sin could be controlled and sainthood attained; *egalitarianism,* a conviction that the community of saints are an elect all of whom are equally worthy of that status; *patriotism,* the confidence that this community is elected to play a special role in the working out of God's purposes within history; and *optimism,* the assurance that therefore the world is fundamentally on the side of Americans, both as individual persons and as a people. These beliefs, become habits of mind ramified throughout the triadic dimensions of Selfhood, adapt well to the challenges of a vast, untamed continent with its endless possibilities.

When pragmatism argues therefore that ideas, including moral beliefs, are not timeless mirrors of Truth but rather tools, weapons for achieving your purposes, it nestles its claim in the arms of a long-standing conviction that the cash value of hard work is individual fulfillment. You need self-discipline not because you want to avoid sin but so that you can develop an eye for the opportune, can engineer the real-world construction of your dreams. The narrow equality of a saintly band easily becomes a wide egalitarianism to which, as Whitman remarked, nothing that is human is alien. In America pragmatism has long held that there are, deep down and essentially, no sinners at all; we are, everyone of us, saints. For these descendants of the Puritans, the chosen people have a mission still: as the world's youth they own its future, taking over from a tired, decadent Europe the mantle of world leadership. The very universe itself is on America's side; there is an evolution to nations just as there is to nature. This newest of the nations, this fullest flowering of the English-speaking peoples, embraces the whole development of human history, the whole long maturation process of the human species. The United States of America, say these latter-day Puritans, is the end for which the first was made, the omega of Creation itself.

John Fiske, a popular Harvard historian and social philosopher, published his *Outlines of Cosmic Philosophy* in 1874. Inspired by Darwinian biology and drawing heavily from Herbert Spencer's evolutionist theories, Fiske makes American culture the culmination of processes begun when the universe began. Every natural process transforms indefinite, incoherent, homogeneous matter into an increasingly definite, integrated, heterogeneously structured complexity. What is true in the formation of galaxies, planetary systems, Earth's ecology, and the evolution of species is also true in the development of humanity.

*Homo sapiens,* Fiske continues, has developed most strikingly in terms of increases in the size of the brain and in the degree of its convolutions. The larger the brain, the greater the capacity for intelligence.

The results of the human evolutionary process are preserved in the varieties of human beings still extant, and these results are dramatic. Primitive peoples such as the Australian bushman or the African Hottentot are small-brained, the volume of their crania averaging 70 cubic inches or about double that of the chimpanzee. In contrast, the cranial capacity of an Aryan Englishman is 114 cubic inches.[9] The difference between the savage and the civilized European is thus greater than that between the savage and the higher primates. Therefore, claims Fiske, it is not merely that primitive cultures lag far behind those of the great civilizations. "In the presence of the Aryan, even under the most favourable circumstances," uncivilized peoples "tend to become extinguished, rather than to appropriate the results of a civilization which there is not reason to suppose they could ever have originated" [OCP-4 53]. The more advanced races, having developed capacities for adaptation and control far exceeding those of their less evolved fellows, are more fit to survive. Unable to grasp the complexities requisite for civilized life, the savage peoples languish in the backwaters of evolutionary progress and will eventually perish.

A larger brain, Fiske tells us, has meant the ability to represent in consciousness what is not present to the senses, to abstract from experience and explore relationships among those abstractions, to anticipate and predict. These reasoning powers come to replace instinct as the instruments for adaptation and survival, but they mean that the human infant no longer possesses automatic response mechanisms. It is dependent upon adults until it has managed to learn the habits it will need in order to survive. Thus the development of the family as the basic mode of human relationship marks a fundamental turning point in human evolution. Thereafter human progress would be based on social rather than physical transformations. Moreover, a family depends upon and fosters nonegoistic attitudes required by interdependence. So the gradual spread of altruistic rather than selfish feelings accompanies the spread of civilization.

Fiske sees cultural evolution as the shift from hedonism to morality, from actions motivated solely by a desire for personal gratification to those based on conscience and empathy.

As the sympathetic feelings are extended over wider and wider areas, no longer needing the stimulus of present pains and pleasures to call them forth, they generate at last an abstract moral sense, so free from the element of personality that to grosser minds it is unintelligible.... Conscious devotion to ends conducive to the happiness of society is the latest and highest product of social evolution. [OCP-4 151, 153]

The institutional expression of this is the shift from "first order aggregates" in which the family, clan, or tribe is the sole unit of social organization to a "second order aggregate" in which loyalties based on nonbiological relationships emerge, integrating families into village and city communities. A further degree of aggregation is then possible: the integration of such communities into a nation, with a nation encompassing the whole of the known world as the highest form.

Fiske argues that this evolution in levels of social aggregation can be seen clearly in European history. The shift from clan-based war bands to the settled civic communities of ancient Greece, and then to Rome and eventually to the modern nation-state, is the story of the emergence of Western civilization. Unique to this development is the invention of federalism. An expanding political hegemony is self-defeating when it is accomplished simply by eradicating the conquered peoples. This is the approach taken by the Oriental empires, and the results were uniformly stultifying. The suppression of individuality for the sake of overall unity chokes off creativity and so destroys the prerequisites for continued development. Rome incorporated the communities it conquered in a way that permitted them to retain their distinctive cultural and political forms, but the actual practice of the Roman Empire was too repressive and soon degenerated into a version of the eastern despotisms.

It has been the special accomplishment of the Teutonic peoples, the Germans and the English, to build up their nations on the firm foundation of the principles of federalism. At the core of these societies, Fiske argues, were small local governance structures based on the full participation of all citizens: the ancient Germanic mark, the English parish, the New England town-meeting. This "stubborn mass of old Aryan liberties" is then preserved within the wider social order because federalism coordinates local differences to the extent required in order to carry out its specific functions. It manages to "secure permanent concert of action without sacrificing independence of action" [API 94]. Federalism is, to Fiske, the golden mean: not too much individual autonomy and clannish freedom, lest it lead to disintegrative anarchy, but not too much coordination and uniformity, which might lead to despotic tyranny. The result is optimal flexibility, the capacity to adapt rapidly and constantly to an ever-changing environment. It is such societal forms that are most fit and thus most likely to survive.

The Roman Empire had attained an approximation to a humanity-embracing social order but fell too quickly into despotism. In the medieval period, Fiske contends, efforts to revive Rome's universalism took a similarly despotic form. The aspirations of the Catholic Church and the Holy Roman Emperors would have meant, had they been realized, the "Asiaticization" of Europe; Byzantium, indeed, succumbed precisely to that danger. But in the West neither Church nor Empire could ever triumph over the other, until with the rise of the first modern nation-states the goal of a single social order seemed likely to be realized through the reconciliation of the two. Initially Spain, then France, blended absolute monarchy with absolute Catholic Christianity and so threatened once more to erect a single despotic empire dominating the civilized world. The northern Germanic Protestant peoples resisted, but were then crippled by the exhausting sixteenth- and seventeenth-century religious wars against the southerly Catholics. Only England survived, having "the rare good fortune" to possess "a territorial position so readily defensible against the assaults of despotic powers" [API 122]. Fiske points to the defeat of the Spanish Armada as a further sign of how the force at work in evolution worked also to protect during its vulnerable infancy the people who would soon become its greatest offspring.

One of the features of evolutionary development, according to Fiske, is a shift from the physical to the social environment as providing the primary stimuli for change. Since a society is more heterogeneous, more complexly integrated, than any natural order of things, as societies become more advanced they become more dynamic. Success increasingly is a function of the inventiveness and boldness required to keep control of a situation, to avoid becoming obsolete and hence being overwhelmed by new, unfamiliar realities. It took 800,000 years from the appearance of the first human creatures to the emergence of civilization; it took only another 20,000 years for those civilizations to break free from despotic immobility into the progressive form of social order represented by the Aryan and Semitic races [OCP-3 61–65]. This exponential acceleration of change has thus put a premium on individuals and cultures that are adventurous, that seek new challenges and are creative in meeting them.

Among all the historic civilizations, the European is the one of which we can most decidedly assert that it is not autochthonous. The Aryans who conquered Europe in successive Keltic, Italo-Hellenic, Teutonic, and Slavic swarms, were not the quiet, conservative, stay-at-home people of prehistoric antiquity, but were rather the elect of all the most adventurous and flexible minded portions of the tribally organized population of Central Asia.... They were the pioneers or Yankees of prehistoric antiquity, in whom unusual flexibleness of mind was the natural result of continual change in the sets of relations to which they were obliged to make their theories and actions conform. [OCP-4 32–33]

It was the most adventurous of these adventurers who then crossed the stormy sea to the western island they called Angle-land and there preserved their freedoms from the encroachments of a continent steadily being overwhelmed by Roman despotism. The most daring among these daring people then braved the wild Atlantic, made the New World they found into a second England, and defeated the efforts of Spain and France to dominate them. Fiske says that "the triumph of Wolfe [at Quebec] marks the greatest turning-point as yet discernible in modern history" [API 56] because it assured that the North American continent would be English, thereby proving that the Teutonic-Protestant peoples are indeed a higher evolutionary development than the Mediterranean-Catholic peoples.

The mission of the "two Englands" is to bring about the moral and political regeneration of humanity. Fiske celebrates capitalism and federalism as providing the models for an ultimate integration of all of humanity. "Dollar-loving" industrial entrepreneurs may be pursuing selfish interests, but their actions are peaceful, they foster individuation, they demand cooperation among those producing and marketing a product, and they presuppose the value of mutual adaptation between buyers and sellers. Federalism is the political analogue to this: Fiske envisions a single worldwide federal government based on the American model to be in place, perhaps by the end of the twentieth century, as the complement of a single worldwide free-trade market.

Fiske is not always so sanguine about the timing of such an ideal attainment, however. He recognizes in the first place that evolution in any form is never linear. It proceeds in a treelike fashion, with particular branches leading to dead ends or even bending back regressively toward the ground. But the general tendency is upward and the ultimate result is the full realization of what initially was only a capacity. So "an absolutely perfect state of society" can be "only gradually, relatively, and approximately realized," and then only by persons attaining in their own lives the altruism, the sympathetic concern for others, that is the necessary condition of that ideal of individual liberty and collective coordination for which humanity yearns. As a coral reef is built up by millions upon millions of "polyps," so the kingdom of heaven made real on Earth "will be the result of myriads of individual efforts toward greater completeness of life" [OCP-4 359–66].

Fiske betrays his basic principles, however, when he limits the activities that realize the ideal to those of separate individuals. Just as the family makes possible the sympathetic feelings out of which wider communities and eventually federal nation-states are constituted, so those nations provide the world-historical vision and power necessary to achieve the global community he is so confident will someday arise. Others of Fiske's contemporaries recognize this necessary function of social groups and governments. They argue more forcefully than he for America's special responsibility in leading the nations toward this final goal.

Some turn-of-the-century activist thinkers saw America's role as that of the city on a hill, providing an example so powerful that it would lure the world to its emulation. Washington Gladden, one of the most influential clergymen of his day, speaks in physical and biological metaphors. The United States need only be true to its own highest ideals of what a human social order should entail:

Such a society as this would be a magnet that would draw to itself, all the children of men. . . . Righteousness and truth, justice and fair play, kindness and friendship are what the world needs, and when the world sees them organized into society and bringing forth their natural fruits in society, the world will lay hold on them, and cleave unto them. That is the way the kingdom of God is coming, by the mighty contagion of social justice. . . . I believe that the people of all the nations are beginning to discern something of the loftiness of our national ideals, and to turn with wistful hope to America for leadership.[10]

But there were others who would not settle for such a passive role. The shining messenger of the kingdom must create what it proclaims, and it must do so using fully its instrumentalities of state. For the unification of the world is a work that only a nation can do, and it is for this work that America was made. The junior senator from Indiana, Albert J. Beveridge, speaking in 1898, just prior to America's declaration of war against Spain, makes it clear what this entails. Beveridge quotes Ulysses S. Grant when he envisions all of humanity as citizens of a single nation, speaking a single language, no longer requiring armies and navies with which to fight each other. "The dawning of the day of that dream's fulfilment is at hand," says Beveridge, and the United States is to be its agent:

Fate has written our policy for us. . . . We shall establish trading-posts throughout the world. . . . We shall cover the oceans with our merchant marine. We shall build a navy to the measure of our greatness. . . . Our institutions will follow our flag on the wings of our commerce. And American law, American order, American civilization and the American flag will plant themselves on shores, hitherto bloody and benighted, but, by those agencies of God, henceforth to be made beautiful and bright. . . . For liberty and order and civilization are not planted by speeches, nor essays, nor editorials; their seed are borne in the talons of Trade and planted by the fingers of Might.... Events, which are the arguments of God, are stronger than words, which are the arguments of man. We are the allies of Events and the comrades of Tendency in the great day of which the dawn is breaking.[11]

Beveridge could be just as strident in a 1900 speech made on behalf of the Republican Party during the election campaign and printed by it for general distribution. After making many of the same points regarding the character of America's role as a world power, Beveridge concludes with a diatribe against those, the Democratic candidate in particular, who would argue for a less activist, even isolationist, approach. Sincere and earnest though they be, the tide of history runs against them:

They were resisting the onward forces which were making of the American people the master Nation of the world—the forces that established us first as a separate political body, then welded us into a national unit, indivisible; then extended our dominion from ocean to ocean over unexplored wilderness; and now in the ripeness of time fling our authority and unfurl our flag almost around the globe. It is the "divine event" of American principles among the governments of men for which these forces have been working since the Pilgrims landed on the red man's soil.

The old, unforgotten sounds of a people's sense of its destiny reverberate in Beveridge's sonorous phrases. The Elizabethan "King, ship, and swerd, and power of the see," in league with "profite" and the "rebuke of eche evill willed foe," are the instruments by which the twentieth-century United States will become the "master Nation" of a federated, peaceful world. America's "talons of trade" and "fingers of Might" are how it will fulfill now in "these latter and perillous dayes" the eschatological task of bringing to completion the "great Day's work of Spirit."

More recent voices tend to speak cautiously of America's role in bringing about an ideal social order, chastened perhaps by the sour taste of turn-of-the-century jingoism and the tragic collapse of Woodrow Wilson's dream that the United States might lead free peoples everywhere in creating a peaceful, federalized world-community under the auspices of the League of Nations. But the dream, however much chastened, seemed more a necessity dictated by realism than merely an idle dream when the failure of the League soon plunged the nations once more into devastating war. Reinhold Niebuhr, a realistic theologian if ever there was one, could predict in 1943 that Great Britain and America would emerge from the war as providing together "the cornerstone of any durable world order."[12] Niebuhr took the need for Anglo-American cooperation in this task as being "of such tremendous significance" as to require expression in religious terms:

Only those who have no sense of the profundities of history would deny that various nations and classes, various social groups and races are at various times placed in such a position that a special measure of the divine mission in history falls upon them. In that sense God has chosen us in this fateful period of world history.

World community is desperately needed. The Anglo-Saxon peoples are not only uniquely positioned by the fortunes of war to possess the power needed to fashion such a world-order, but they possess also political ideals needed to restrain its arbitrary, unjust imposition. Those ideals, "woven into the texture" of British and American history, "are less incompatible with international justice" than has been true for "any other previous power in history." Niebuhr then goes on at considerable length to warn against the pitfalls of overweening pride and similar sins that are the concomitance of power and opportunity; he talks about the effort as not likely to be realized fully but only "with relative success." Nonetheless, "the world community cannot be realized if the Anglo-Saxon world fails in its historic mission." Destiny for Niebuhr is not a predetermined role nor is success in carrying it out assured. But it is the English-speaking peoples who bear this burden in a perilous time, with the future of the human race once more hanging in the balance.

These concepts of America's destiny still have enough resonance among its citizens for them to be used regularly in the speeches of a recent United States president. The following is from Ronald Reagan's closing remarks at a debate with John Anderson during one of the 1980 campaign debates. President Reagan thereafter continued to espouse similar views, using the same imagery, up through his farewell address in 1989:

I have always believed that this land was placed here between the two great oceans by some divine plan. It was placed here to be found by a special kind of people—people with a special love for freedom and who had the courage to uproot themselves and leave hearth and homeland and come to what in the beginning was the most undeveloped wilderness possible. . . . We built a new breed of human called an American—a proud, an independent and a most compassionate individual for the most part.... For 200 years we've lived in the future, believing that tomorrow would be better than today and today would be better than yesterday.... I believe I can solve the problems we've discussed tonight. I believe the people of this country can. And together we can begin the world over again. We can meet our destiny and that destiny can build a land here that will be for all mankind a shining city on a hill. I think we ought to get at it.

Here in these more recent American voices Puritan millennialism is expressed in a secular and, in Fiske's case, a scientific vocabulary. Whatever their language for expressing it, however, these various speakers all claim that there is a direction to history, a struggle toward an ultimate triumph over all forms of negativity. Because of their special attunement to this direction of things, the English-speaking peoples are asked to perform a special praxis: they are to be a model to the rest of humanity regarding the way by which this final triumph can be achieved. In the New World especially, those elect from among the nations, pilgrims sent into a wilderness, nonautochthonous wanderers drawn to the greatest of all challenges, have an opportunity first to create and then to disseminate a way of life that permits the fullest flourishing of the human Self. Nor will their task be finished until all the world shall be united, until the kingdom of heaven, the utopia of rational imagination, is made flesh to dwell among us full of grace and redolent with glory.

Here also is the Hegelian dialectic, where history is taken as the climactic stage in a process of cosmic realization (see Illustration 6.3). If human being is the highest expression of that cosmos, the point at which it comes to consciousness of itself, there are nonetheless some among those humans too primitive, too unaware of self, even to have composed their own narrow-focused histories. But rising out of them after long centuries are the historical civilizations, distinguishable from primitive cultures, the nonhuman environment, and autochthonous realities, only by the glimmerings they have of themselves as free, autonomous, world-creating selves. From out of Asia this glimmer moves ever further west, its light growing progressively brighter, until it finds its noontime brilliance in modern Europe, in people consciously able and willing to make choices and accept responsibilities. The culmination of this growing development of human potential comes with the formation of a culture in which free, responsible selfhood finds expression in all of its dimensions, whether aesthetic, political, scientific, religious, or philosophical.

For both Puritan and Hegelian, and likewise for Fiske, history is a story of how hedonism is made an instrument of its own overcoming. The pursuit of narrow ends can have unintended consequences if there is an essence to things, to praxis in particular, of which history is the manifestation. The difference between our selfish efforts to satisfy a momentary desire and our selfless concern for another's dignity is developmental. Both express the same essential structure of human praxis, but the one minimally and the other fully. When you desire some Moment of personal fulfillment, you are not acting in a debased fashion; you are acting blindly. You lack sufficient awareness of what is involved in the tension between your desire and its object. Your striving needs to be rationalized by being put into the social and historical context that discloses to you its full complexity. In doing so, you recognize that your striving has qualities that make it more than a feeling of the moment, that make it into an expression of enduring values of self-identity, mutuality, and humanity. Desiring when directed toward this wider, deeper goal finds its meaning and motive no longer in an ephemeral satisfaction but in the contribution it makes to the realization of something of permanent significance. Your desire to find a Moment that does not perish, that is completely satisfying, and that is not corrupted by the demands of a settled past or by the partiality of unrealized hopes, is thus always a desire to make the given world over into something better. Each effort in some fashion works out that aim toward a relative ideal, and in so doing the newly made world discloses a new and more profound ideal relative to its changed conditions. Thus it is only through realizing limited ideals that less limited ideals can come into view as possibilities for being desired. The realization of an ideal that embodies without limit the full implications of your desiring self amid its desired world comes about only through efforts intending less than what they achieve.

**Illustration 6.3: Hegel's Modes and Conditions of Praxis**

|         | material                  | final                      | formal               | efficient       |
|---------|---------------------------|----------------------------|----------------------|-----------------|
| self    | biological individuals    | perfection [fulfillment]   | resolve [character]  | heroic passion  |
| society | primitive societies       | world-histor significance  | national genius      | national spirit |
| world   | Nature [Substance]        | Freedom [realized]         | History [Zeus]       | Spirit [Idea]   |

It takes time for selfish desire to mature into mutual care. A temporal sequence is required: an end aimed for, striven for, in some fashion realized as the new platform from which a new aim can then be raised up. Sequentiality is essential to praxis. History is the account of how the aims and strivings and realizings of human beings manifest an essence that involves the process of that manifestation as one of its constituent aspects. Either the sequence of historical happenings has no character, human desire always entrapping itself in some momentary Don Juanian enterprise; or it has a character that is the work of desire. If the latter is so, the work is one that no single person can accomplish nor all persons acting separately. The character of human being, its ideal for realization, involves an interdependency without limit and so entails a work that must go on until the species has attained the sort of ultimate unity glimpsed in the utopian notion of a kingdom of ends.

Hegel's argument is that history tells precisely this tale. You as an individual recapitulate in your own development into full adult self-consciousness the development of your culture with its institutionalized self-consciousness about its place within the scheme of things. The highest extant cultures recapitulate in turn the developing awareness of the destiny of the human species in general, a destiny that constitutes the historical course of empire and of civilization. This sequence need not be linear, perhaps not even dialectical, nor need it be in the form of Fiske's somewhat stochastic branchings. But it is progressive and discernible. Insight into the shape of historical development is part of the struggle for self-consciousness that is the content of that shape.

So Hegel offers one pattern and points to Germany as its culminating expression; you and I have traced a related but somewhat different pattern and pointed to the United States of America as its fullest flowering. Both approaches agree on this: that there is a developmental pattern and a final apotheosis to be realized in history, that our ability to recognize that final outcome is a function of the degree of its development, and that therefore our effort to discern how and toward what end history is developing contributes in some small way to its eventual realization. The apocalyptic writers asked you to await the kingdom of God, offering signs of its approach to give you the courage to believe in its coming despite all evidence to the contrary. Joachim claimed that the kingdom could not simply come but had to emerge, so he offered a trinitarian justification for this idea and pointed to signs of the growing presence of the Kingdom of the Holy Spirit, asking that you believe in its eventual arrival on the basis of the abundant supporting evidence. Kant provided a rational argument for the necessity that the Kingdom must be realized, that a value definitional of human essence and thus normative for human behavior must be capable of actually being attained by human beings. Hegel agreed, insisting that the arena for that realization must therefore exhibit its progress from mere idea to concrete actualization.

Consequently you and I can affirm that there are essential realities and a course of things by means of which those essential realities work themselves out in time. We can affirm that there is a human nature and that the course of the nations traces the developing objectification of that nature in history. We can affirm that the dignity of free individuals, the forms of mutuality shaped through representative government, and the human solidarity expressed in a worldwide federation of nations, are to be found partially but persistently realized in the practices and ideals of the English-speaking peoples, and are for this modern age of ours the highest manifestation of that final realization for which "every creature groneth with us also, and travayleth in payne together unto this present."[13]

# Seven

## THE PERFECTING OF HISTORY

Even if the case can be made that an ideal community of Selves will eventually emerge from the sounds and fury of historical change, why in the meantime must so many generations suffer and perish? This was the second question we asked at the beginning of Chapter 6, but through all our concern with world-historical developments and the destiny of the English-speaking peoples it has gone unanswered. Our talk concerning a peaceable kingdom in which everyone is treated as an end and never merely as a means is edifying to others only if they pretend not to hear the agonizing cries of those from whose suffering we and they benefit. Yes, of course: we shall all celebrate their glorious sacrifice in an annual Memorial Day parade, affirming and reaffirming that our honored dead shall not have died in vain. But they suffered and died nonetheless, and not voluntarily, without themselves ever enjoying what we now endlessly enjoy.

Does the end justify the means? William James gives this age-old question a piquant turn when he argues that if you and all humankind were offered the most perfect of utopias in which everyone were

kept permanently happy on the one simple condition that a certain lost soul on the far-off edge of things should lead a life of lonely torture, what except a specific and independent sort of emotion can it be which would make us immediately feel, even though an impulse arose within us to clutch at the happiness so offered, how hideous a thing would be its enjoyment when deliberately accepted as the fruit of such a bargain?[1]

225

The very idea of that lonely lost soul being tormented eternally in order that you might be happy is repugnant. No matter how much you and I might desire the Moment it makes possible, no matter how much a kingdom of Selves might be served by it, you should repudiate the bargain, says James, as morally unacceptable. Kant was correct: human life has a dignity that is beyond price, so that even an infinite benefit cannot outweigh the dehumanization of one solitary human self. How much less justified, then, is the sacrifice of thousands of generations of human beings for the sake of perpetual peace or the classless society or, even, the Kingdom of God?

Hegel's reply seems at first to be brutally pragmatic. Real, concrete human freedom is a goal worth paying any price to attain. It is the god for whose birth "the sacrifices that have ever and anon been laid on the vast altar of the earth, through the long lapse of ages, have been offered" [PH 19]. In order that your future harvests might be good, you would go to the temple and offer some of your precious resources as a sacrifice to the gods. Their favor thus secured, they succor your planting and tilling until the fields and orchards are ripe and you are able to glean a harvest more than sufficient to replenish what you have sacrificed, enough to assure the survival and well-being of yourself and those dependent upon you. In similar fashion, Earth is a vast altar upon which the human race has offered the precious resource of its early generations so that those who have come afterwards might flourish, one generation sacrificing itself that its successor might know freedom a bit more fully, all the generations until now contributing their propitiatory sufferings so that Spirit might reap finally the harvest of a world secured against any further suffering.

But there is no intended nobility in this sacrifice. Those who are "the means and instruments of the World-Spirit" do not understand their role any more than do the sheaves of grain or the firstborn child. The wheat grows upward in search of sun, the baby cries lustily for its mother's breast; neither understands the knife that turns the results of their striving into a higher good. As they "seek and satisfy their own purposes," they at the same time serve "a higher and broader purpose of which they know nothing—which they realize unconsciously" [PH 25]. Spirit is "cunning" to arrange things thusly, so that selfish passion "pays the penalty, and suffers loss" while Spirit "develops its existence" so as to draw itself ever closer to perfection [PH 33]. This is not the cunning of a trickster, however, the deceptions of a cosmic Johannes. Spirit is not a clever demon getting others to take the blame while it escapes unscathed. There is simply no other way than the sacrifice of the generations for any abstract principle, even the highest one of them all, to be turned into a concrete reality.

Consider, says Hegel, what happens when you build a house. Your architectural drawings are an abstract possibility that will be made tangibly concrete by utilizing the available natural resources. The walls of your house will be made, for instance, by taking earthly clay, mixing it with water to a specified consistency, forming molds, baking them in an oven whose fire is regulated by appropriate applications of an air bellows, letting them cool, and finally turning their contents out as bricks. By this and similar utilizations of the elements, a house is eventually completed the purpose of which is to exclude those elements, to form a sanctuary protected against the ravages of earth, wind, fire, and water. Likewise,

the passions of men are gratified; they develop themselves and their aims in accordance with their natural tendencies, and build up the edifice of human society; thus fortifying a position for Right and Order *against themselves.* . . . They gratify their own interest; but something further is thereby accomplished, latent in the actions in question, though not present to their consciousness, and not included in their design. [PH 27]

The purpose of building a house is to exclude the untamed powers of the natural elements; there is no way to do this except to use those powers against themselves. The purpose of history is to exclude selfish passions from human praxis, to develop Selves who are genuinely free. There is no way to attain this purpose except to use people's selfish passions against themselves. What you can learn only from experience requires that you begin by making ignorant mistakes that will then serve as the occasions for that learning. You must suffer the painfulness of your mistakes in order to overcome your ignorance. It would be preferable, perhaps, were it possible straight off to have knowledge, to acquire Selfhood, to enter the kingdom of ends. But such is not possible. Selfish people such as Johannes (and the innocent Cordelia as well) must suffer the consequences of their hedonism before duty and compassion can become possible traits of human character. Vast populations must bear the yoke of tyranny and nations perish in the flames of revolution before the rule of law can become a viable form of political organization.

Individual moral development, at least as Judge William explained it to us, involves a self-transcendence that leads to self-fulfillment. You who begin in ignorance of your duty to work, to specialize, and to share will be the ultimate beneficiary of the sufferings by which you are goaded upward. The despair that is the grave of your hedonistic strivings is at the same time the womb for your rebirth as an ethicist. But life is short and, Lessing's views to the contrary, there is not time enough for you to undergo sufficient despairings and rejuvenations to attain final perfection, to be born along with everyone else into a utopian world. How pitiful, this individual fate of yours. The journey is terribly long, and your strength will prove to be no match for its rigors. Eventually you fall exhausted by the side of the road; others, strangers who did not begin so far back as you, will take up your burdens, not even acknowledging them as yours, and carry them on down that road a further mile or so, far beyond your desiring, around the bend and on beyond your knowing.

Hegel argues, however, that life is not merely pathetic; it is tragic. Our very strengths are our undoing. Desire focuses your energies and so makes possible your achievements, but the narrowness required by that focus blinds you to its limitations. You develop a character and live out its ideals of selfhood as fully as you can manage, but your loyalty to that sense of self prevents you from realizing that you have excluded other and greater loyalties as irrelevant. So it is for a nation. A nation's cultural ideal, the *Volksgeist* that is its principle of unity, gets worked out in the form of institutional structures and revered traditions, the taken-for-granted customary beliefs and practices of a people. Having brought that limited ideal to fruition, however, the people are too caught up in its goodness to take seriously its faults. They are unable to see in it the seed of something yet even better. The fruit of a nation's efforts is a "poison-draught it cannot let alone, for it has an insatiable thirst for it." But "the taste of the draught is its annihilation" even though it contains also the potency for "the rise of a new principle" [PH 78].

Biology prefigures history in this respect. The very achievement of complexity in an individual organism, the differentiation of its cellular components, means that it is relatively short-lived. But chromosomal transmission from individual to individual makes it possible for new individuals to replicate that same achievement, to adapt it to changing environments, to refresh and improve it constantly so that it effectively serves as the means by which the gene pool will be perpetuated. Individuals perish that the species might endure. Indeed, species perish when they serve as protective environments for new chromosomal configurations that generate organic forms better able than they to survive and flourish in that environment. Species perish that species of a more adaptive complexity might emerge.

These are not Hegelian ideas, of course, but they provide suitable analogues to his views on the dialectic of history. The struggle toward self-consciousness has extended over a long period, most of it marked by the existence of human communities that lack any viable collective memory. It is not enough, Hegel argues, that there be human beings, nor that they have formed for themselves a social order. What is required in addition is that they know themselves as constituting a society with an origin in the past and a story to tell of the events which have led from that origin up to the present, a story that gives meaning to their lives by creating their sense of unity and purpose, their distinctiveness as a people, their place within a greater scheme of things. Lacking such a memory, embodied in tales told around campfires or sung by bards at tribal celebrations, these people can play no role in the development of freedom. Their actions and interactions are "nothing but wild arbitrariness—transient activity—or rather the play of violent emotion without any goal of advancement or development" [PH 62].

Pre-history is not the only expanse of time in which human beings have lived lives devoid of world-historical significance. There are the geographic backwaters, for instance. The tropics and polar regions are unfit places for self-consciousness to thrive, and the need for large land masses excludes the whole of the southern hemisphere from ever contributing to the realization of freedom. Also, the good times in any nation's history are also relatively insignificant; they are static times, not progressive ones. Hegel sounds like Dewey in noting how crucial problematic situations are to the deployment and improvement of consciousness. "The History of the World is not the theatre of happiness. Periods of happiness are blank pages in it, for they are periods of harmony" [PH 26–27]. Even for those peoples whose self-consciousness develops sufficiently, who shun Chronos and adopt Zeus as their father, the extent of their relevance is limited. China first and each world-historical people thereafter have their brief moment on the stage of history, decked out in one of the personae of Spirit. But for centuries before and forever after that hour of their glory, they have no role to play.

Hegel is impatient with such complaints, however. The hedonistic morality of Don Juan or John Stuart Mill and the ethical norms prescribed by Judge William or Kant only apply to individuals. It is simply not appropriate for you or me to use them to make judgments about history. Mill may insist that the good of society and of the whole of humanity be taken into account, through a judicious application of sanctions, in determining your greatest happiness. Kant certainly insists that the dignity of others, alone and in community, is a universal and necessary ground for your good intentions. But these matters are introduced only as considerations relevant to your individual praxis. The deeds of persons are what is judged. Such judgments, insists Hegel, are simply inapplicable to persons whose actions serve as catalysts bringing about historically significant transformations. "The Litany of private virtues—modesty, humility, philanthropy and forbearance—must not be raised against them" [PH 67]. World-historical heroes do despicable things, using and abusing others in complete disregard of the categorical imperative and the greatest happiness for the greatest number. Their worth lies not in such matters but in one thing only: whether or not what they did served either to bring a nation to fuller realization of its distinctive purposes or to make possible the emergence from its ruins of a new nation bearing the promise of a higher purpose.

"The claim of the World-Spirit rises above all special claims" [PH 37]. Hegel's answer to James's question is, first of all, that it should not be repugnant to acknowledge what is necessary. It is better to suffer for the sake of a greater good than simply to suffer. At least your pain and anguish have a meaning that gives them value. You can enjoy the value, the ideal which you envision, even though you cannot enjoy the concrete reality of that value realized. Hegel's answer recalls Augustine's comment about the pagan virtues of Roman heroes. Our selfish purposes bring their own momentary satisfactions; the greater good they serve lies beyond our comprehension anyway. But Hegel's answer also involves the appeal to a higher morality. It is one of the ways of Nature, a way become predominant at the organic level, that it projects itself through time by the reiteration of individuals, and at the level of self-consciousness that it does so by the same medium of freedom that is the goal toward which it strives. You do not bewail the wasting of a thousand seeds for each one that takes root, nor do you take pity on the lower members of a food chain whose sacrifice makes possible the survival of the higher members. Nor therefore should you complain that billions of human beings perish, either having wasted their lives as members of irrelevant societies or having found their significance as burnt offerings on the vast altar of history, if because of this the apotheosis of humanity shall one day be attained.

Yet this answer is still inadequate. Insofar as you remain merely a stepping-stone, contributing to but not participating in what is eventually to be realized, your life has no essential worth. The scale of action may have expanded awesomely, but its shape seems to have remained very hedonistic: the Moment is the only intrinsic good, all else is good to the extent that it enhances the Moment or helps secure access to it.

As with Cordelia, so also with yourself: once having served your purpose you are no longer of any value and can be expediently discarded.

Suppose, however, the Moment is not external to the process of its
realization. Then its essence extends from its origin to its completion.
All of the phases of its becoming constitute its essential worth. Yet this
is precisely what a Self is, an identity of purpose that organizes possibilities into patterns for actualization and then over time brings them
to realization. Hegel agrees: "The individual traverses as a unity various
grades of development, and remains the same individual." Moreover, as
we have argued, this same structure of purpose, pattern, and activity
applies at a societal level as well: "In like manner also does a people,
till the Spirit which it embodies reaches the grade of universality." Hegel then makes the same third move we made, although where we had
spoken of human nature he speaks of history:

This is the soul—the essential consideration—of the philosophical
comprehension of History. . . . The principles of the successive phases
of Spirit that animate the Nations in a necessitated gradation, are themselves only steps in the development of the one universal Spirit, which
through them elevates and completes itself to a self-comprehending *totality*. [PH 78]

The individual, a nation, humanity as a whole: each in their differing
ways "traverses as a unity various grades of development" yet in doing
so "remains the same."

You are essentially the same person from birth to death, although
initially that essence is very abstract and generic. Over the course of
your life you give it an actual characterization rooted in the conditions
and choices composing your history. What can be said about who you
are essentially is, at the end, concrete and unique. This was Judge
William's point: bringing a universal into history individuates it, turning
"one's" duty into "my" duty. So far as your life is your own creation, it
is individuated; but because your life is a human life as well, it individuates a universal essence. The individuating realities that are your self
and all other human selves is what the universal essence of humanity is.
It is one reality, one universal essence. But what that essence is, concretely, is those many individual lives spread out across space and time
from the origins to the demise of the species.

When Hegel asserts that "Spirit is immortal; with it there is no past,
no future, but an essential *now,*" he speaks, at the very least, misleadingly. He implies a denial of time, as though a focus on what is essential
would abstract from the passage of things and concentrate upon a time-

less now. But a timeless now is an oxymoron; if it is timeless there is
no now and if it is now then it is linked essentially with what is now
past and what is now future. So Hegel immediately attempts to clarify
himself:

This necessarily implies that the present form of Spirit comprehends
within it all earlier steps. These have indeed unfolded themselves in
succession independently; but what Spirit is it has already been essentially; distinctions are only the development of this essential nature. . . .
The grades which Spirit seems to have left behind it, it still possesses in
the depths of its present. [PH 79]

Historical distinctions are not "only" the development of the world's
essence: they are gloriously that development. The successive, independent, individuating work of the nations, and the heroic and mundane
work of each of the persons composing those nations, is how human
nature is what it essentially is. History is the *how* of the human essence: its form, its shape, the technique by which what it is abstractly,
its aim, becomes what it is actually. There is no determinate human
achievement external to that essence, nor any genuinely human possibilities. The totality of what it is to be human is the whole of the ways
in which that abstract notion is displayed in the praxis of the species.
     There is no two-realmed mysticism in this, nothing of Eliade's sacred
that finds historical expression in a space cordoned off from the profane, "cosmicized" to be a mirror image, an homologous refraction, of
the timeless. Rather, the profane is the manner of the sacred. Conscious
of your surrounding environment, therefore aware of yourself in contrast to it, desiring some object within that environment, able to assess
the success of your efforts and to try out new approaches or take up
new purposes, you actualize freedom unceasingly. The *how* of your activity is the freedom: consciously, reflexively, evaluatively, persistently.
All the adverbs of activity are what constitute the difference between
yourself and other realities: they exude your humanity, your culture,
your individuality. They are the freedom that you are unfolding temporally. The manner of the timeless is temporal, which is to say that the
timeless is not a realm apart from the temporal but rather its unity or,
in Hegel's language, its principle.
     Insofar as you are human you live your freedom, and so your choice
to do this or that, your purposes, your desire for happiness and your
effort to do as a good will would do, *is* Spirit manifest in time. You are
not "used up" by Freedom, an external implement it avails itself of and
then discards. Freedom is not the agent and you the instrument; you

are the agency that is Freedom at work here and now. It is a vast totality, stretching from origin to end, from Alpha to Omega, and you are an
integral aspect of that stretch.

In *The Reality of Time,* Errol Harris argues Hegel's point in a way
that underscores the importance of individuation to the process of
temporal development. Any totality is so by virtue of some organizing
principle. That principle could be what you have chosen arbitrarily to
impute to things, with some personal or momentarily useful end in
mind. For example, you might sort people into two groups, those to
your left and those to your right, when asking them to leave a room
with two doors. But where your way of grouping things makes sense
not only for you but for others, not on a particular occasion but recurrently, then the principle at work would seem to be more immanent
than imputed. Where this principle creates an order that is stable and
enduring, we are justified in claiming that the relevant ordering principle is not our invention at all but rather defines a natural structure
constituting a distinctive region of reality.

Harris then turns to some of these natural regions—the physical
universe, the biosphere, mentality, and human history—and argues
that in each case the principle that provides their unity is one that has
necessarily a temporal dimension.

Every whole is a unity of differences. It cannot be a whole unless it
unites within itself a multiplicity of diverse elements. As a structural
unity, it is dominated by a principle of order regulating the relation
between these elements, and for this reason no such whole can be posited all at once in a single point-instant. Its principle of unity must par-
ticularize itself by setting out its differences in the proper order . . .
[i.e.,] this self-differentiation of the whole will take the form of a serial
unfolding. [RT 153, 154].

Just as your knowledge of some integral whole moves sequentially from
a vague grasp of its integrity to a precise articulation of the pattern and
content of the relationships composing it, so also that whole itself,
when it is a natural region of the universe, proceeds from vague homo-
geneity to differentiated complexity. The movement is serial; its accomplishment is what is meant by time.

Harris refers to the serial order, which is how these natural principles of order are ordered, as an "ascending scale of forms" because
each stage in the process increases the distinctions among its elements,
thereby requiring a more complex and subtle web of relationships in
order to sustain the integrity of the whole. In other words, the tempo-

ral realization of a principle of natural order is hierarchical in a developmental or evolutionary sense, progressively achieving ever more completely determinate articulations. The process, however, is dialectical rather than linear. There are negations that seem to lead away from higher levels of attainment into devastating forms of conflict, breakdown, and devolutionary collapse. But the negations are eventually and inevitably themselves negated, and the several principles of natural order are themselves ordered. The universe is itself a totality, a whole manifesting a principle of the whole. Therefore the natural regions of reality compose a scale of forms that ascends, temporally as well as logically, from least to most differentiated, from the unformed energy underlying the Big Bang to the self-conscious, societally structured, human beings that are currently the most highly developed of the forms of reality.

Harris draws three conclusions—he calls them "corollaries"—from this understanding of temporal development. First, because each new phase in a process more adequately realizes its principle than have prior phases, the present phase is "key" to understanding the whole of the process up to that point. Second, each new phase thus "encapsulates" its predecessors; insofar as the old has produced the new, the new "incorporates" what it has inherited into itself. Third, the phases of a development are not infinite and so must in some way culminate. That final outcome is "prefigured" in each intermediate phase: each "gives persistent evidence of the reality of the completed system which its phases portend" [RT 155].

Hegel was reticent about the future. A philosophy of history is, after all, about the past, about what has been accomplished and the principles therein revealed. Practical activity casts you forward into the unknown, creating determinate structures that only thereafter can be known, made sense of, their principle of organization disclosed. The owl of Minerva takes flight only after the completion of some day's great work: yours, that of a *Volksgeist*, or, ultimately, that of Spirit Itself. Harris departs from Hegel, therefore, in this notion of prefigurement. You might argue that he is perhaps too sanguine about his ability, the ability of a mind formed and delimited by the distortive biases of the Spirit of the English-speaking peoples, to reach through the principles manifest in the present world to those that only the culmination of history and time will make accessible. Surely he sees darkly through the glass of this age, not face to face.

Harris's response is that of Teilhard de Chardin, with whom he is in close agreement. The developmental direction of evolution is clear enough. It is toward the harmonizing of differences in complex, comprehensive unities. The culmination, therefore, must be an ultimate unity of all differences, an Omega to match the Alpha of origination. As for the content of the Omega, it cannot be less than the content manifest in the highest form of development so far attained, which is that of the human being. To say more is, to be sure, speculative. But these are rational not gratuitous speculations, reasonable projections from what is known. They are ideal and normative because not yet made historically determinate, but their ideality is organically related to that from which it is thought their actuality will grow. As Joachim pointed out, you have confidence that the Kingdom of God will come if you can see its conditions already sprouting around you. You may not know the whole of what Omega will be, but you know an "at least." The adult will be more than what you can now see in the child, but not less.

At the Omega, it can therefore be said, characteristics of human personality will surely flourish. Personality, for Harris, means self-consciousness: the ability of an entity to "grasp together, and in mutual relation, the different elements of its objective experience, as one systematic whole" [RT 160]. His reference is to the systematic whole grasped in understanding, but Harris means to refer equally to the unifications achieved through practical activities. You as a person stand apart from that of which you are conscious, interpreting it, judging it to exemplify certain principles, to be capable of transformations that would result in its measuring up to certain standards of worth or relevance. But you also stand apart from yourself, recognize your limitations and potential, your finitude and your possibilities for development, and so you interpret and judge yourself by reference to an implicit standard of infinite worth and relevance. You are thus akin to the ordering principle of the whole, the Omega, because you also create worlds in thought and action. But what you do imperfectly it accomplishes normatively. In this sense, Selves are made in the image of God.

But personality, as we have seen, is interpersonal as well as individual; the Omega if it is to be a time and place where persons flourish must be social. Harris argues that a genuinely integrative community would need to achieve integration at the level of consciousness. If the single conscious self were primary and its relationship with others secondary, social order would be derivative rather than essential, a value for personhood but not of its essence. Community, however, on certain occasions functions as more than a derivative phenomenon. For instance, cooperative activity for the sake of a common end can only be carried out by individual human beings, but the techniques and information required to achieve that end typically transcend any single individual's skill or knowledge. "In all these corporate actions each member of the community is aware of (and is activated by) the purpose and guided by the knowledge and the skill of all" [RT 161]. Harris's examples are a symphony orchestra or a football team (appropriately, we might add, for it is metaphors from exactly these realms of endeavor that abound wherever members of functioning groups talk about their collective activities: the value of teamwork, everyone playing their part, orchestrating the results, knowing the score, not letting down the side). The whole in these instances has become more, cognitively and practically, than the sum of its constituents.

Teilhard is especially insistent that this notion of an emergent corporate mind, what he calls the "Hyper-Personal," not be understood as a fusion of individual minds. The Omega is not a single superconsciousness surpassing and negating all individual consciousnesses. Rather, as the multitude of individual minds draw closer they become more clearly distinct from one another.

In any domain—whether it be the cells of a body, the members of a society or the elements of a spiritual synthesis—*union differentiates.* In every organized whole, the parts perfect themselves and fulfil themselves.... Thus it would be mistaken to represent Omega to ourselves simply as a centre born of the fusion of elements which it collects, or annihilating them in itself. By its structure Omega, in its ultimate principle, can only be a *distinct Centre radiating at the core of a system of centres;* a grouping in which personalisation of the All and personalisations of the elements reach their maximum, simultaneously and without merging, under the influence of a supremely autonomous focus of union. [PM 262]

This is as fine a description of Kant's kingdom of ends as you could ask. Harris immediately identifies it with the Kingdom of God, the "perfected human community," the communion of saints.

You are a citizen in Kant's ideal kingdom so far as you freely acknowledge yourself as subject to its laws. You are sovereign so far as you legislate those laws and hence are "subject to the will of no other." A sovereign's position, therefore, says Kant, "can be maintained not merely through the maxims of his will but only if he is a completely independent being without needs and with unlimited power adequate to his will" [GMM 434]. The law that is the ordering principle of the kingdom of ends is the objective will of a sovereign whose attributes are those of perfection: not only moral autonomy but also unlimited self-fulfillment and power. The sovereign must be, as Sartre would put it, an *ens causa sui* in creating the law by which the ideal society is ordered. You or I, so far as we are sovereigns as well as citizens in that kingdom, are divine as well as human.

Kant thus adumbrates what Teilhard calls the Omega Point in the Omega. The perfected community is not a democracy; such would make it merely a compilation of individuals, a multiplicity of petty sovereignties. It is the principle of their unity as well: the law or constitution or monarch or god, the Center at the core of their centers. The Center is that which makes possible the unity of the centers, hence makes possible the perfecting of their differing unique personalities— we have called it their character—through the intimacy and interdependency that unity provides. As Harris keeps insisting, the principle of a unity transcends what in gathering together it also fulfills.

Harris and Teilhard speak of love whereas Kant and Hegel emphasize rational understanding in describing how the principle of unity unites its constituent members. But the reality meant would seem to be the same. Harris parses love as "genuine felt concern for the true welfare of its object," and in Roycean fashion goes on to speak of loyalty and honor, mutual respect and trust. He then extends love beyond concern for other persons and groups of persons to include the embrace of sun and sky, a "yearning for unity with nature," and "aesthetic ecstasy of all kinds." This is very much what Fromm does, affirming that erotic love and brotherly love overflow into a love of all reality that is "the act of experiencing the oneness with God" [AL 78]. When you love fully and not partially, you seek harmony with others and with the whole of reality; you come to recognize that love of your neighbor and love of God are the same love. And you who create and are created by those neighbors, you who are godlike and a creature of God, thereby are loved by God, by others, and by yourself.

Harris summarizes:

This then is Omega, a transcendent suprapersonality uniting in itself all other persons, while maintaining their several individualities in mutual interdependence and love, and bringing to final fruition its own self-manifestation in a world as an evolving hierarchical scale of physical, biological, psychological, intelligent, moral, and spiritual forms. [RT 164]

That "final fruition," the end of time, is not its cessation but its perfection, a "continuing condition, not a termination." Harris envisions the Omega as an ongoing community in which the limitations of need, self, relationship, and world are all overcome, in which suffering and evil, separation and subjugation are abolished. It is a fully functioning community in which ideals are actualities forevermore. The Omega is "a temporally continuing activity of living directed by conscious identification with and devotion to a transcendent Idea" [RT 159].

Teilhard criticizes "modern thought" for its halfhearted recognition of the presence in history of evolutionary synthesis. Such processes are acknowledged, but they are said to arise by chance, to be always vulnerable to reversal, and to bring about a totalizing unity only, if at all, in some "extremely distant future." But Omega is not a far-off endpoint. It is the power of love right now at work in the yearning of all things for unity. "Neither an ideal centre, nor a potential centre could possibly suffice. A present and real noosphere goes with a real and present centre. To be supremely attractive, Omega must be supremely present" [PM 269]. But if this power were itself only temporal, it and thus its achievements would be essentially fragile. A progress that does not "eliminate death" is only a limited power. Omega must be independent of what perishes. It must "escape from the time and space which it gathers together" in order to assure that its accomplishments will not be lost but constantly built upon. The "ultimate earth," says Teilhard, is the irreversible destiny of our actual earth.

The author of the book of Revelation turns, at the end of his story, from an account of the struggle between agencies of good and evil to the final defeat by the good of the evil hosts of Gog and Magog. Fire comes down from heaven to consume the enemies of God; and Satan, Death, and Hell are destroyed forevermore. Then, says this storyteller of the Omega,

I saw a new heaven and a new earth, for the first heaven and the first earth had vanished, and there was no longer any sea. I saw the holy city, new Jerusalem, coming down out of heaven from God, made ready like a bride adorned for her husband. I heard a loud voice proclaiming from the throne: "Now at last God has his dwelling among men! He will dwell among them and they shall be his people, and God himself will be with them. He will wipe every tear from their eyes; there shall be an end to death, and to mourning and crying and pain; for the old order has passed away!" [Rev. 21: 1–3].

What this apocalyptic visionary expresses in terms of cataclysmic substitution, a new earth for the old, a new Jerusalem to replace the irredeemable cities of the old earth and the terrors of its history, Harris and Teilhard express developmentally. The new earth has become an ultimate earth, emerging from its struggles as fulfillment rather than repudiation. But for both evolutionist and apocalypticist, it is indeed a new earth that is realized, one that lies beyond history, one in which there is no longer any sea. The dangers of the sea, its recalcitrance to human purpose, its retention of the primordial chaos that had once been tamed in order for the first heaven and first earth to be created, shall now finally be overcome.

Yet the repudiation of the sea would seem to be a repudiation of our humanity as well. If Selfhood can be completely realized only in a community that transcends history, isn't this just the hedonist's Moment in yet another one of its disguises? The nature of praxis is that it seeks to realize the future, but that future is essentially at risk; else the quest for its realization would be merely a charade. The final cause of action is a vaguely felt import of value tincturing the given, and the form of its pursuit is a schema of possibilities for giving that feeling voice and relevance, thereby empowering the desire that it might be realized. The essence of praxis, which is the essence of the human person, is freedom: the projection of the determinate into the indeterminate, of the settled past into an unsettled, unsettling future. Can the sons of Adam and the daughters of Eve ever attain the final completeness of the aboriginal paradise they think they once possessed, except by ceasing to be human?

Bernard Loomer, in "The Size of God," answers this question along lines that provide a helpful antidote to the confident promises we have been offered concerning the world's ultimate perfection. Whitehead took a strongly empirical stance in *Process and Reality* when he argued that "actual entities are the only *reasons*" [PR 24]. The character of any individual praxis, he said, can be explained only by looking to the character of what it inherits and, derived therefrom, the value it then seeks to realize. Concrete particular actualities are the source of the power, the vision, and the resources that make and constantly remake the world. Abstract principles, even immanent ones such as Hegel or Harris or Teilhard propose, are neither concrete, particular, nor active and so cannot be the causative foundation of anything. Whitehead calls this the "ontological principle" to which any metaphysical truth must conform. Loomer prefers to call it the "naturalistic principle": "The reasons why things are the way they are and behave as they do are to be found within the things themselves and their relationships (including the factors of chance) to each other" [SG 25].

These "things themselves" are radically multifarious; they compose James's buzzing, blooming world. The plurality in the universe is so vast as to escape our comprehension and our control. Loomer thus proposes as a second fundamental truth about the universe the "principle of ambiguity"; that is, the claim that reality is too varied ever to be encompassed by any single interpretation or principle of organization.

But the reason for ambiguity is not just quantitative, not only a matter of the immensity and variety of what must be included in any single world order. In addition, the recalcitrance of persons, of their societies, of the whole world, is endemic to the very process by which they create and sustain themselves.[2] The material conditions on the basis of which you act are ambiguous because they involve achievements arising from other perspectives, ones not privy to your own concerns and ones concerned with matters no longer relevant. These compete for your attention, and so tend to fracture the clear lens by which you would hope to perceive what might best be sought. The ambiguity of your situation ambiguates your intentions as well; accordingly faults develop also in the character of what you do and the single-mindedness with which you commit yourself to do it.

But confusion and conflict are not the only sources of ambiguity. Clarity and effectiveness are sources as well. The more sharp-eyed you are about the ends you have in view and the more cogent your strategies, the more you will be able to distinguish trivial possibilities from important ones, to get your priorities straight, and then to act upon them incisively, excluding whatever proves to be incompatible or irrelevant. So the new unity in being successful also creates a new contrast. This is what Whitehead means in remarking that although a concrescent process unites the whole of its past within itself, thereby making the many one, the result is also to increase the many things there are by one [PR 21]. Because the denial of any possibility is also a possibility, every inclusion within a coherent whole entails the exclusion of its denial. What you neglect or eradicate is not only a denial of any pretensions you might have had about achieving totality, but may also set in motion consequences that will eventually come back to haunt your enterprise, undermining what in fact you have accomplished.

Ambiguity and vagueness are quite different qualities. When something is vague it is ill-defined, undifferentiated. In contrast, something is ambiguous because it has an excess of definition, because it has more than one meaning, participates in more than one system of relationships. You would never confuse an instrument for swatting baseballs with a sonar-guided winged mouse, but you call them both a "bat." Loomer would accept Teilhard's claims about the present vagueness of the world. Insofar as it has not yet fully realized the principles immanent in it, a person or a people is partially indeterminate and the universe is still in mid-course in its evolution from Alpha to Omega. But the world also suffers a surfeit of omegas; it is ambiguous. Its indeterminacy, indeed, results from the clash of unreconciled determinants, from incompatible networks of relatedness more than from the absence of networks.

In celebrating ambiguity, therefore, Loomer celebrates what he calls the "web of life," although he hardly means to restrict the web to living entities. "Process exists for the sake of relationships" [SG 31]. Interconnections of the sort that weave actions together into persons with character and that weave persons together into societies with traditions, that weave the nations together into a history of the species, are going on incessantly. The effort to form relationships is "indigenous" to the world. In arguing that ambiguity is a metaphysical principle, Loomer argues in the same fashion as Harris that ordering principles are required for processes to be productive, for the flux of things to issue in something meaningful. It is only through relatedness that anything actual can come to be.

The "stature" or "size" of persons has to do with how extensive the web of their relationships is. These terms are evaluative: it is good to enter into relationships, you are more fully a human the wider their scope and the richer their intensity, and the best of all worlds would be a single interdependent human community. Love is not the power that binds you and me into a relationship. It is the other way around: because we are related, love can emerge as a quality of that relationship, an augmentation of its intensity and duration. Similarly, individual and political freedoms are what relatedness makes possible. They are augmentations of community not its prerequisites. The "concrete processes of life" involve the formation, deformation, and decay of structures that link events and patterns of events together. Seeking the increase of those linkages in our own life-processes, and thereby seeking them for others also, you and I commit ourselves to fostering "the relational life in its deepest meaning." This "commitment of attachment," this Roycean loyalty, is the measure of our stature. Generalized, it is the measure of the realized value of the universe.

All of this is quite compatible with Hegelian arguments, and with those of Harris or Teilhard as well; as reality increases in stature it resolves vagueness into ambiguity and then weaves ambiguity into unity. For Hegel, the relational life "in its deepest meaning" is the concrete universal, the web of the world woven on the loom of time into a determinate, fully complete totality. Loomer, however, rejects this final step in the Hegelian argument. Totality is neither a necessary nor a desirable outcome to the processes of evolution and history. The idea of a single overarching principle of order is an abstract idealization derived from the concrete plurality of what is actually achieved. If by

Loomer's naturalistic principle there are no powers at work in history except those that create fresh unities from a problematic inheritance, and if by his principle of ambiguity those achievements entail selection and hence exclusion, then it is ontologically impossible for there ever to be a single absolute realized perspective, a universally inclusive concrete totality.

"The tragic richness of the concretely actual can never be redeemed by the poverty of abstractions, however purified they may be" [SG 45]. If you insist upon an absolute principle of order, a God that overcomes discord and conflict, that incorporates into itself everything compatible with its essence, then all else will have to be banished to historical or eternal oblivion. Evil, understood as whatever is at war with the one real order of things, whatever is inconsistent with the real meaning of things, would have to be fundamentally unreal, its reality only temporary, its importance at most penultimate. This would provide a theodicy, just as Hegel proclaimed: the perfection of the divine is its power to transform primordial chaotic vagueness into an everlasting order in which all things have their proper place and their appropriate significance. Good is necessarily triumphant over evil. The suffering and striving of persons and nations are the birth pangs of a final unity limitless in space and time; they are therefore meaningful elements within a totality of meaning. Because it is an order which finds a place for everything that actually was achieved, whatever was not actualized must never have been possible. So there are no possibilities, realized or otherwise, that an Hegelian ultimate totality excludes. The rational and the real, necessity and actuality, are one comprehensive, coherent, consistent whole.

But, Loomer protests, don't we see that this is only an idea and that to achieve it would be to destroy the open, vital, risk-filled, dynamic world in which human beings live out their lives?

The creative advance of the web of life is not to be understood as an adventure toward perfection. Given the nature of the world as we experience it, the adventure toward perfection is a movement toward the vacuity of abstraction. The passion for perfection is a protest against the unmanageable vitalities of concrete life. It is a yearning for the bloodless existence of clean-cut, orderly abstractions. It is, in short, a yearning for death. [SG 51]

For Loomer, any given order of things is an emergent accomplishment. It is brought to experience by the mind seeking to understand and by the practical self attempting to control. Either activity tries to make sense of what until then lacked that sense. Hegel and Harris presume that the sense was there all along, immanent in the given; only as it is uncovered by pursuits initially unaware of it does anything of lasting value get realized. Order to be real must be timeless even though the form of that reality is temporal. Any organizing principles that are not timeless lack objectivity; they are essentially ephemeral and therefore unreal. But, argues Loomer, if to be objective is to be the realization of some possibilities by the exclusion of others, if ambiguity is primordial and every actual order an invention, something contingent made up out of what has been given, then ideas of timeless principles are what lack objectivity and what is ephemeral is what is essentially real.

The thesis of Loomer's essay is that "God should be identified with the totality of the world, with whatever unity the totality possesses" [SG 20]. God as the unity of a totality seems a very Hegelian notion, but the principle of that unity is for Loomer an abstraction, derived after the fact from an emergent accomplishment, whereas for Hegel it is that without which there could have been no accomplishment. Both divinities are immanent; both are identified with the dialectical process by which the future is realized. Hegel's divine reality, however, embodies a definite goal, which is its essence. Since it itself only becomes aware of that goal by the temporalization of its essence, Hegel's God struggles and even suffers as it works out its story. But the perfection is there throughout. The form of temporality is, after all, just that essence seen concretely rather than abstractly. Harris shows solid Hegelian credentials when he quotes Plato to summarize his own version of this argument: time, indeed, is the moving image of eternity.

For Loomer, in contrast, there can be no perfection except as an ideal valued from a limited perspective, and so divinity is not only unclear of its goal but has no single goal. The cacophony of the actually realized goals encompassed in its endemic ambiguity sets conditions on whatever further goals might be imagined and then embraced by newly emerging realities. But the conditions have no necessary trajectory nor point of culmination; the goals are contingently derived, and whatever clarity might emerge will not be recognized as having been all along implicit and essential. Time is the moving image only of itself.

Loomer, however, is not making the mistake Harris warns against. He recognizes that if God is the world in the reductive sense of merely being the sum of the occurrences composing it, then there will be no unity at all, no sense to the world, nothing to be made of its goings-on. An organizing principle is required, but not of the sort Harris proposes, or Hegel. Loomer is attempting to make the structure of praxis the organizing principle of reality. He speaks in traditional terms of God as the "divine eros," the "persuasive and permissive lure" drawing entities toward greater "stature." God provides for the world's creatures a "conceptual appetition toward the good" that is evidenced as a persisting "restlessness," a "tropism not only to live, but to live well and to live better." But Loomer's criticism of Hegelian-like views of God, as well as of orthodox Judeo-Christian views, is that they overemphasize these final-cause aspects of divinity. By conceiving God primarily or exclusively in terms of value, in terms of an ideal goal toward which the whole creation moves, all else is degraded in importance. The ambiguating complications introduced by the other causative aspects of God are consequently overlooked.

To correct this one-sidedness, Loomer gives equal emphasis to the "body" of God, divinity's material aspect. He denies that God is an eternal reality. God is the "stuff of existence," a unity of the totality of the world's ongoing processes, but that actual totality just as much as its unity. God is also the shape of that "stuff," the physical and conceptual webs of relationship that are how actions go together to form selves and to become aspects of wider unities, including the unity that is the whole of it. With bold consistency, Loomer insists that God also includes the "discontent" of the world, the unfocused "organic restlessness" that drives it toward both "greater good" and "greater evil."

Thus God for Loomer "includes all modes of temporality," "operates through all the Aristotelian causes," and is therefore a wholeness "to be identified with the concrete interconnected totality of this struggling, imperfect, unfinished, and evolving societal web" [SG 41]. We have understood the nature of praxis in terms of Aristotelian causes and the three modalities of time, and have argued that persons, societies, and human history compose an interconnected dynamic totality. I propose therefore that we interpret Loomer's God as the structure recurrently manifest in each specific praxis, unifying them all in a total relational webbing.

The moral ideal of "attachment to the concrete" thus means placing value not in the goals pursued by the various praxes but in praxis itself. As Sartre asks in the enigmatic closing paragraphs of *Being and Nothingness*, "What will become of freedom if it turns its back upon this value?" that is, turns its back upon the goal of completion, of attaining Godhood, becoming an *ens causa sui*. "In particular, is it possible for freedom to take itself for a value, as the source of all value?" [BN 797, 798]. If so, then the primacy of history, of the world of becoming and perishing, would no longer be in question. The course of things is the concreteness of praxis, and its principle is an abstraction from the bubbling plurality of that concreteness which reveals the unity immanent in it. But the unity is formal rather than final: it has to do with how the world is made and not with the results. Praxis as an ordering principle defines a process that is ongoing rather than culminating. The kingdom of ends is a style of relationship, one that respects and enhances praxis but that defines no particular outcomes. God and the Kingdom of God so understood thus have to do with life rather than death, with realities in the making, with the journey and not the journey's end.

But there is a steep price to be paid. The praxis we are talking about is not a superpraxis with its own achievements, its own further overarching purposes, its own strategies, and its own drive for their realization. A transcending praxis of that sort would be no different than the God of Augustine, building the heavenly city amid the wreckage of earthly empire. Or, the structure made properly immanent, it would be no different than Spirit's overarching purpose of building up the concrete universal out of the conflicting achievements of particular purposes. Loomer's totality lacks these characteristics; it lacks what Whitehead calls "personal order." There is no central organizing thread of inheritance, no sequence of actualizations that coordinate and control the pluralism of achievement and possibilities constituting a society. Were there such, this sequence of occasions would serve the same role as an Hegelian organizing principle but without violating Loomer's and Whitehead's ontological principle. Teilhard, indeed, might be interpreted as claiming that the Center of the centers evolving toward the ultimate unity of Omega is more person than principle. Whitehead, however, attributes a controlling personal order only to a very limited region of the cosmos: the higher forms of organic life. Loomer agrees with this, rejecting even the indirect control of the wider world provided in Whitehead by a God whose praxis is a nonomnipotent superpraxis, luring but not compelling all worldly processes toward finer forms of accomplishment.

But if there is no Center to the centers, no primordial seed in the form of an abstract essence or implicate order that time necessarily explicates, how can ideal totalities of any sort ever emerge? Loomer's position would seem to require that they can emerge only by chance. There is nothing in the nature of praxis, understanding this as in some sense the pattern of creativity found throughout the natural order rather than being solely the structure of human action, that forecloses such developments and that imagines them building upon one another until they begin to approach integrations of nearly universal stature. Indeed, these developments should be expected. If everything comes to be what it is by resolving a problematic situation, fashioning it into a settled unity, then a quest for wider, better, more richly integrated unities should be a likely consequence. But not a necessary one.

Only the achievements of a particular moment express the structure of praxis necessarily. The more enduring achievements take their creators beyond natural necessity into artful activity, into works of freedom and therefore of contingency. Your character, your culture, your human destiny are inventions. They endure by leaning on one another; some of them take on a permanence, and hence an importance, that makes them seem necessary. But they are not necessary, and so their trajectories can be diverted from an enhancement of praxis to its degradation. Progress need not be linear; it need not be dialectical; it can have been both and still not be so any longer. Loomer is content with this. As Frankenberry puts it: Loomer "affirms the risk and adventure of an unfinished universe." She interprets him as gladly forgoing a belief in inevitability, divine control, immanent necessity, and all the other stultifying, deadening attempts you and I make to escape from life. We should be content to aim at achieving greater stature, to work diligently for an increase in the quality of the relatedness of things. It is enough for us to live in terms of "hope, trusting expectation, and covenantal faithfulness—in the face of no assurances."[3]

Yet this is too much contingency even for Loomer. Hoping for a better world is fine, presuming you take hope in an activist sense, as James recommended, translating it into commitment, working steadfastly for an ideal you hope will eventually be realized. But in what are you trusting, with what are you covenanting? Frankenberry's call for zestful loyalty is a gloss on the last sentence of Loomer's essay: "The conception of the stature of God that is presupposed in this essay may be indicated by the speculative suggestion that the world is an interconnected web endeavoring to become a vast socialized unit of experience with its own processive subjectivity" [SG 51]. There is an ultimate goal after all: an end of history, which the creatures are groaning and travailing to bring forth. The "processive subject" is the unifying Center of the all-encompassing society, the ultimate earth, the new earth along with its new heaven, into which our world is endeavoring to make itself.

Loomer's processive subject is thus just another avatar of Hegel's Spirit or of the "vast socialized unit of experience" that is Teilhard's Omega. But if it is not an essential structure of reality, if it is only a power that might emerge from the flux of things and an end that might be brought about if that power manages to endure, then hope is no more than wishful thinking and faithfulness akin to foolishness. The sacrifice of so many generations of humanity on the hope, the outside chance, of some eventual success makes the injustice of the sacrifice intolerable. The absence of any concrete evidence that progress is being made toward actualizing the ideal weakens confidence that it is re-

alizable at all. Loomer has rescued the openness, the mystery and
contingency, of the future from the dead clutch of necessity. In doing
so, however, he has opened up once again the gulf between the actual
and the ideal. We are back with Kant, knowing what a good will should
do, knowing it as our duty so to act, but finding that we fail constantly
and that there is no indication that things can or will be otherwise. The
ideal is once more only a regulative principle. Illustration 7.1 offers a
summation of the views of the ideal presented so far.

Whitehead finds a way off the horns of this dilemma through the
notion of "Peace." His theory of concrescence as the structure of all
becoming can be interpreted, as you remember from Chapter 1, in
terms of the Aristotelian four causes: an inherited plurality of objective
data, oriented by a subjective aim and guided by subjective forms, con-
cresce to become a new unified actuality. He closes *Adventures of
Ideas* by discussing these same four factors as they are manifest in human societies. His rhetorical strategy utilizes abstract universals for
names instead of talking about data, aims, forms, and creativity, but
their functions are the same. Truth comprises the given reality of past
accomplishment; Beauty is the ideal that arises in contrast to it; Adventure is the urge toward the realization of that ideal, and Art is the technique by which that urge is effected.

But, says Whitehead, were human actions only constituted by the
interplay of this fourfold, the resulting praxis would be "ruthless, hard,
cruel." It would lack "some essential quality of civilization" [AI 284].

**Illustration 7.1: Conditions of Perfection**

|  | material | final | formal | efficient |
|---|---|---|---|---|
| Harris | homologous matter | differentiated complexity | ascending scale: forms | time |
| Teilhard | Primordial Earth: Alpha | Ultimate Earth: Omega | Center, system of centers | Omega as love |
| Revelation | old heaven, old earth | new heaven, new earth | cataclysmic substitution | God: Ancient of Years |
| Loomer | body, total of processes | maximal size stature | webs of relatedness | discontent good/evil |
| Whitehead [AI] | Truth | Beauty | Art | Adventure |
| Whitehead [PR] | actualizing occasions | everlasting significance | perfective harmonization | consequent nature of God |

What is missing is Peace. Its emergence as an explicit quality in experience is crucial to the process by which individuals become mature adults and barbaric cultures become civilized.[4] What Peace means will alter as those who experience it grow in their awareness of its potency and come therefore to be nurtured by it. Whitehead's comments, I want to argue, sketch this developmental progression in a way that can be seen as recapitulating the pathways by which you and I have come in our search for an adequate ethic.

In your youth, you are exuberantly Don Juanian: full of yourself and pursuing your own Moments of fulfillment with shortsighted abandon. You seek vivid, intense experiences; what is important is novelty, not happiness. This seeking opens you, however, to the appeal of ideals beyond immediate fulfillment, grandiose aspirations and lost causes that sweep you up into their magnificence. It is thus a natural extension of your brashly exuberant aims to develop a Rotation Method that actively involves you with a world you have imaginatively revalued to support your dreams of grandeur. In practicing this sort of hedonism, your praxis is a relentless desire for the satisfaction of your own ego; nonetheless there are moments when you can lose yourself in "ideal aims that lie beyond any personal satisfaction" [AI 288], even though your ideals be superficial and your self-forgetfulness fleeting.

The hunger for fame requires more substantive satisfactions. Your underlying egoism seeks objective evidence of its importance. You want to be assured that you are a "central reality" to whose deeds and person all else is subservient. This is Johannes's point of view: delighting in your own powers and insisting upon your primacy. Your actions betray an unspoken craving to "stand conspicuous in this scheme of things" [AI 289], to be great not by virtue of your ego as such but by virtue rather of a greater reality into which you fit and which gives you your special significance. Fame requires others to bestow it; a central reality is aware that it needs a wider world of which to be the center.

Your hedonistic selfishness thus becomes aware that there are values other than itself required for its own value to be realized. The emergence of your self as a Self then involves transmuting those other values from instrumental to intrinsic goods, recognizing that your own worth is an expression of the same qualities of humanity as is the worth of others. Love is how that truth is lived and, as Fromm indicated, its first and most intense form is exclusive: "the love of particular individual things" and especially the love of individual persons. When you love someone, you desire another's "perfection" rather than solely your own. This is not simply a matter of esteem. Your love for an individual means that "the potentialities of the loved object are felt passionately as a claim that it find itself in a friendly Universe" [AI

289]. The world for a lover should be such that its harmonies do not exclude, nor even merely tolerate, but instead sustain and nurture the loved one's achievements and possibilities. You demand of the world that it be a place in which your child can grow up to become a fully functioning, fulfilled adult. You are thus taken by love beyond your ego not only to the object of your love but to the wider context situating that object and securing its reality.

As Aristotle understood so well, love of others leads to love of the *polis,* for the state provides the fundamental environment for securing the reality of loved ones and for assuring their proper development. Well-educated citizens develop habits of loyalty to the state. As they mature they love it not because it serves as a necessary means to the fulfillment of themselves and those they love; they come to love their tribe or clan, their city or nation, as having its own intrinsic worth. Whitehead takes the farmers of the Roman republic as an example of what he means: their patriotism meant a passionate commitment to the idea of the republic, an idea for which they were ready to die and in the service of which they found a meaning that transcended their own brief lives. "Such conformation of purpose to ideals beyond personal limitations is the conception of that Peace with which the wise man can face his fate, master of his soul" [AI 291]. When you take up a "calling" in the manner suggested by Judge William, seeing your humanity expressed in actions that serve the well-being of your society, you do neither more nor less than what those Roman farmers did. You find in such a praxis that your distinctive individuality has transcendent worth.

For this sense of Peace, of a worth beyond any Moment of your own attaining, to be brought to reflective, self-critical awareness is for it to measure off yet a further progression in its civilizing potency. You now have become aware that the quality of the society to which you belong depends upon individuals who are not self-regarding, who are motivated by ideals other than personal gain. Ibn Khaldûn turned this insight into a philosophy of history: societies arise from barbarism, attaining and sustaining the highest qualities of civilized existence, so far as their citizens are motivated by "group feelings." When self-interest crowds this aside, the social order loses its vital unity, fractures, and soon fragments into lesser forms of community. These sober truths strengthen your resolve to remain loyal to the ideals of your society, and your society harvests the fruit of this in the form of institutions and traditions that support such high-mindedness.

An enduring social order is a self-fulfilling prophecy: it will endure if it can continue to raise up citizens who think it deserves to endure and are willing to devote their lives to that end. The stability is a result of the deference given by the present to its past. Your aim now is to make some specific good "appear" concretely in the world. If what appears conforms in its fundamentals to what has previously appeared, if it is in effective continuity with the past, then it will strengthen the social order, reinforcing, deepening its hold upon reality. At the same time this strengthening reinforces and deepens the qualities that you most value, qualities that define your sense of your own enduring worth [AI 293]. By your traditions you are saved.

But the "indefinite repetition of a perfected ideal" is a form of suicide. Without the "surprise" of new challenges, new ideals to discern or new obstacles to overcome, your passion for realization grows stale. The characteristics of what endures lose their importance for you; they are taken for granted. A "slow paralysis of surprise," a stultifying indifference, sets in until "intensity of feeling collapses" and the social group to which you belong finds itself "gradually sinking towards nothingness" [AI 286]. So Whitehead finds an even higher expression of Peace in your recognition of the value of the "exceptional." What is now tradition was once an exception to accustomed practices. Devotion to the ideals found in past achievement should not be uncritical; commitment to their continued realization should not be blind. Modes of achievement that "stand above the average level" thus point to an even higher patriotism than that of conformity to the past [AI 294]. In seeking the improvement of society by attempting to lift it beyond what it is, attempting to make actual what it ought to be, you serve it best, even though the ordinary people will reject your efforts as disruptive. This is what Kantian duty and Royce's loyalty are all about. You are guided in your actions by a rational ideal, not by an empirical actuality, by normative measures not Gallup's polls. Because without adaptability there can be no endurance, it is those who seek to create a better world, not those who seek only to perpetuate the given world, to whom the future belongs.

This brings us to Whitehead's notion of Tragic Beauty. Beauty, remember, refers to final causes, the perfections you and I seek to realize in our individual and collective praxes. Your goal is to accomplish these tasks, to possess fully the Moment or express completely the Self. You fail to do so, or you succeed, but your success is fragile and soon perishes. How tragic it is, this inevitable loss of "so much beauty, so much heroism, so much daring." Nonetheless, without such tragedy there could be no novelty, no development, no replacement of lesser goods with higher ones. This Hegelian thought is somewhat comforting: "pain, frustration, loss, tragedy" are the price that must be paid for progress. Yet the loss is still lost, the suffering still a brute fact of life. It would be a "gross evil" were the passing of all the world's achievement to be the final truth. Even were some "perfected ideal" somehow able indefinitely to repeat itself without thereby destroying itself, the irrevocable passing of all prior achievement would remain an unjust evil, tainting its claims both to perfectedness and to ideality.

Peace is the transmutation of gross evil into "tragic evil":

Peace is then the intuition of permanence. It keeps vivid the sensitiveness to the tragedy; and it sees the tragedy as a living agent persuading the world to aim at fineness beyond the faded level of surrounding fact. Each tragedy is the disclosure of an ideal: —What might have been and was not: What can be. The tragedy was not in vain. [AI 286]

The evil remains; your lost opportunities can never be recovered and all your achievements will eventually perish. But your efforts need not be in vain. First of all, the ideal you struggled to realize is still there to be realized. Indeed, your struggle on its behalf may have been the occasion by which it was first taken to be a possibility worth seeking. Times change and your past accomplishments may no longer have relevance for the modern age. But the ideal of which they are the realization may still be worthwhile, although requiring fresh shape and substance. What is needed is sufficient sensitivity to the tragic nature of the perishing, so that you see actual occurrences in comparison to what they could have been and then recognize that what could have been can yet still be in some new way.

Peace is thus the recognition of Tragic Beauty: what perishes discloses ideals worth striving for, and hence discloses efforts that are paradigms of how humans should live their lives. If all you experienced was the effort, you would find life a constant struggle to survive, a battle against uneven odds in which you often lose and even when you win soon find the spoils of victory to be ephemeral. Your way of living could hardly be other than self-concerned, cynically realistic, devoid of hope. Yet if all you experienced was the ideal, your active life would be a dream, a fantasy about worlds unconnected to the actual world. You would be turned in upon yourself, living a practical life devoid of any hope that your ideals might ever find a home there. An "aim at fineness beyond the faded level of surrounding fact" is motivated by a recognition that dreams can be ideals for realization, that they can actually become incarnate in historical fact, and that the failure to have done so then or there or even now does not diminish the value of the ideal nor of the effort, but rather makes all the more reasonable your own obligation to take up that ideal and make it tomorrow's reality.

The "aim at fineness" is always situational: it is a goal for a particular praxis within its particular context. As Whitehead says, "all realization of the Good is finite, and necessarily excludes certain other types" of Good [AI 291]. Not only are your attainments momentary, they are also partial; and so "tragic issues" are "essential in the nature of things" [AI 286]. There can be no hope that Beauty and Truth, the rational and the real, will ever coincide, that praxis will pass beyond its dynamic fourfoldness into a structure of absolute completeness. What Hegel finds necessary, Whitehead finds impossible.

So the ultimate sense of Peace for Whitehead is not confidence that the essence of the world is a principle unfolding in the mode of concreteness what it is timelessly. Peace is the experience of what he calls the "Unity of Adventure," the sense of your own ideal aims and actual efforts as not occurring in isolation but taking their place within a community of other adventurers, other aims, other efforts, other situations (see Illustration 7.2 for a summary of Whitehead's modes of Peace). The unity that is realized is this: the awareness we each have that all of us are striving, to some extent and with some degree of self-awareness, to realize what we think is the best future that is possible for ourselves and those we love, for our society, for humanity and for all creation. We also realize, each of us, that we have failed or soon will, and that in doing so we are joined by every other agency, past, present, or future, human or otherwise. So we are all striving, all failing, and all disclosing ideals that call us back to renew the strife once more. This is "the final Beauty with which the Universe achieves its justification" [AI 295]. It is the ideal of a dignity that entities have which lies beyond all price: the oneness of all things in the everlasting rhythms of their reach toward the better. "In this way the World receives its persuasion toward such perfections as are possible for its diverse individual occasions" [AI 296].

**Illustration 7.2: Whitehead: Modes of Peace**

|  | particular | general | universal |
|---|---|---|---|
| self | self-centered egoism | romance about lofty ideals | fame |
| society (others) | exclusive and erotic love | patriotism | self-aware loyalty |
| world | tragic realizing of ideal | Tragic Beauty | Unity of Adventure |

Charles Hartshorne argues that this is not enough. A shared adventure is not a sufficient motive for attempting to create value if what is ventured has no lasting significance. Whitehead correctly sees that it is a mistake to make all temporal accomplishment depend upon some single eventual result. Hegel is really no improvement over Johannes or the apocalypticists. For all three the product is what justifies the process, the value of individual achievement is only found in the achievement of the whole to which it contributes. There can be no ontological room for the chance that the Endtime might not come, because without it everything would have been in vain. As Johannes says so poignantly, "How much I have gathered into this one moment which now draws nigh. Damnation—if I should fail!" [E/O-1 439]. But Hartshorne will not accept what seems to be Whitehead's solution as well as that of Sartre: to extol the process in disregard of the product.

Individuals create goods in situations that constrain what can possibly be achieved and that influence the manner of its perpetuation. It takes courage in such a world to dedicate your efforts to preserving traditional accomplishments, much less to aspire to improve upon what you have inherited. The courage that is needed, says Hartshorne, can be sustained only by optimism. Not an optimism about the future, about the chances for the Kingdom to come, but rather an optimism about the intrinsic significance of what you have done now. Hartshorne advocates an understanding of reality that

does not explain away risk or opportunity; rather, it tries to show why the risks and opportunities for action that confront us are at least significant, even in view of all the future, including our death, and the presumptive death of the human species. This is the only "security" it asks for.[5]

He insists that achieved value be "significant," that the labor, the suffering and the imagination, expended for the sake of any accomplished end remain meaningful no matter what might happen to its author or what sort of influence it might have upon its successors.

Hartshorne is as ready as you or I would be to accept the fact that the negative achievements of praxis fade quickly into oblivion, but he is not prepared to see the good that has been fashioned by the exercise of creative effort perish irrevocably. What good is it to do some good, to be loyal to a tradition or aspire to an ideal, if ultimately that achievement comes to nought? What use is it to work to bring to fruition some "definite matter if the universe has no way to retain that definiteness?" [IO 360]. Tragic evil is still too great an evil. It is not enough to treasure the lost ideal; the unique, genuine achievements actualized along the way toward that final loss must be treasured as well. Were you to know that your life's achievements, including the whole of your life as itself a unique accomplishment, had no significance enduring beyond the brief moments of their creation, you would have no reason, no motive, for trying to go on doing worthwhile things, for continuing to live at all. Hence, says Hartshorne, the very fact that you cling to life, that you are not overcome by despair, indicates that you believe that what you do matters, that it has some sort of lasting worth.

Influencing the future is one way for your actions to matter. You can tolerate the thought of your own death if you believe that what you have achieved will have significance through its influence upon the persons and institutions that succeed you. Yet your successors will also die and the institutions that are monuments to your purposes will eventually crumble. Something more enduring than this is required. If our planet and galaxy and even the universe itself cannot claim exemption from eventual dissolution, then what is required to preserve and honor your accomplishments must be like no other actuality. It must be imperishable as well as actual. It must be "a form of life that includes all lives and survives all deaths" [IO 115], a "cosmic awareness" capable despite our world's destruction of preserving "the already actualized experiences of animals through billions of years" [IO 336], able in the collapse of the temporal ordering of the cosmos itself to nonetheless preserve without loss the achievement of that cosmos in all its manifoldness.

"Significance," for Hartshorne, thus has three conditions. In order to be worthwhile an achievement must have an influence that never perishes, that influence must be integrated into a coherent whole that is itself fully actual and immune to loss. Further, the achievement given such enduring value must be the work of a determinate individual and must be created in time as a contingent realization, a concreteness that need not have become actual yet in fact did. Your efforts as an individual human being are meaningful, and so lure forth and justify the creative energy required for you to succeed, so far as you know that they meet all three of these significance conditions.

For a finite life such as your own to be meaningful it needs to have a beginning, middle, and end. Death as such is not an evil; mortality may even be a necessary condition for the existence of entities with the capacity for genuinely creative activity. The issue is not longevity but the creation of value, of determinate complex actualities. Even if such activity does not require timeless opportunity, it nonetheless will never occur, claims Hartshorne, unless its results are believed to endure. "The book of a person's life has a last chapter, but the book, though created is not destroyed; it is permanent, everlasting, though not eternal" [IO 326–27]. With such assurance, finite mortals like you and I can live meaningful, creative lives of the kind claimed by ethics and religion to be both the duty and the glory of being human: doing good, obeying God, pursuing some dimly perceived vision of the Kingdom of God.

Because the ontological principle requires that there be some actual entity in order for there to be any power to preserve accomplishment, Hartshorne says that it is ontologically necessary that there must be such an entity, and its name is God. He develops his ideas along lines sketched by Whitehead in the concluding pages of *Process and Reality.* Whitehead takes the goal of complete fulfillment, the notion of a concrete universal that we have been attempting to identify as the final outcome of all temporal endeavor, and turns it on its head. "The perfect realization is not merely the exemplification of what in abstraction is timeless. It does more: it implants timelessness on what in its essence is passing. The perfect moment is fadeless in the lapse of time" [PR 338]. For Hegel or Harris, the apotheosis of cosmos and history is that they finally become exemplifications in the concrete of a timeless principle. Loomer protested that this gives primacy to the principle and hence makes an abstraction more significant than the individuals who struggle, suffer, and die on its behalf. Hartshorne agreed that concrete achievement is what is fundamental, but argued that therefore it is not sufficient that the abstract ideal of the realized perfection of the cosmos be all that remains after the deaths of all the attempts to actualize it. Despite what seems in *Adventures of Ideas* to be his agreement with Loomer, Whitehead here provides what Hartshorne wants: a way to affirm that multiple temporal perishing achievements are primary but that their significance is everlasting.

God has a consequent nature, says Whitehead. Just as any praxis involves an appropriation of the determinate past as the material which it is given to determine afresh, so God appropriates that past as the content of divine actuality. Whatever you achieve on some occasion is experienced not only by your successors but also by God who, being an actuality enduring without end, preserves without end its objective content. God's relation to the world as thus preserved can be said to be one of "a tender care that nothing be lost," an "infinite patience" with the tumultuous, disputatious cacophony of things [PR 346]. Both metaphors suggest sensitivity to the nuances of unsuspected value, finding importance even in what seems trivial and perceiving harmonies even in what seems unalterably contradictory.

In this sense God's consequent nature "perfects" the several accomplishments of the world's individuals by mediating their differences, weaving a multiplicity into a unity. What each individual must do within its limited situation in order for it to achieve some result, God does with all situational results in order to achieve the reconciliation of a cosmic multitude into a unity from which nothing has been excluded. Or rather, it is a unity from which "nothing that could be saved" has been lost; for whatever is so "self-regarding" as to lack relational compatibilities must be "dismissed" from the divine harmony. The evil of any achievement is that which in no way can contribute to the good which is the interdependence of elements in a whole. When you act out of character or a new practice is attempted that is at odds with tradition, that praxis will be thought absurd and perish without a trace unless made relevant to the established character or tradition, reforming or refreshing it, testing its mettle or foreshadowing its decline. Royce talked of atonement as the redemptive act of finding a way to use what has fractured a community as the vehicle for re-creating it in some improved fashion. So Whitehead's God is continually redeeming the objectified world by finding ways to turn its discordance into elements of a passage in the fugue of the world, to transmute its stubborn multiplicity into the voices of a cosmic madrigal.

My musical metaphors are temporal analogues to the kingdom of ends in which the quality of the unity requires and is required by the quality of its many members. Autonomous persons of infinite worth perfect their freedom by harmonizing its several expressions in one ordered totality; without the differing voices of the several singers there could be no chordal harmony. The "final end of creation," as realized in God's consequent nature, is "the perfect unity of adjustment as means" and "the perfect multiplicity of the attainment of individual types of self-existence." Ends and means have become reciprocal. "The sense of worth beyond itself is immediately enjoyed as an overpowering element in the individual self-attainment" [PR 350]. Kant's hope, Teilhard's dream, is fulfilled not in history nor in time. But in consequence of the labors of time's creatures, it comes to be concretely and everlastingly in God.

The "objective immortality" of your achievements in the endless concreteness of God is nonetheless still not enough. Gross evil is not the only thing dismissed into the nothing of divine forgetfulness; your subjective immediacy is as well. For if evil is whatever is self-regarding in achievement, the process that brings about any achievement is self-regarding. It is an absolute processive uniqueness, a potency driving toward the realization of a singular Moment or Self. The radical disjunctiveness of these centers of creativity must be eliminated if the actualities they have created are to be woven together into worldly and divine harmonies. The process must perish that the product might endure. It would seem then that "the best that we can say" of the turbulence of creative subjectivity is, in the words of a religious liturgy, "'For so he giveth his beloved—sleep.'" [PR 342]. Hartshorne affirms the nobility of this, the profound piety in a life lived for the sake not of self but of God: "My goal is to contribute to, rather than to attain for myself after death, the absolute Telos.... Apart from my (direct and indirect) contributions to God I am indeed literally nothing of any value whatever" [IO 217].

But why, asks Whitehead, should creativity in all its vast plurality of upsurging inventiveness be merely a means to ends that lie beyond its immediacy? "Why should there not be novelty without loss of this direct unity of immediacy among things?" [PR 340]. If the unity of God's consequent nature, as from moment to moment God experiences the creatures of the world, is "an ever more complete unity of life in a chain of elements for which succession does not mean loss of immediate unison" [PR 350], then immediacy need not be the functional equivalent of evil. The consequent nature of God is surely not a mausoleum for our honored dead, an everlasting memorial created to assure you that only those arguments are still to be believed which say that their deaths were not in vain. Were it only this, God would walk its marbled halls alone and the echoes of the divine footsteps would reverberate in the everlasting silence. But the experience of God is "an ever more complete unity of life." It is the kingdom of heaven in which the beloved are not consigned to eternal sleep but sing their hosannas in robust and everlasting enjoyment of what together they have wrought.

And so "the insistent craving is justified—the insistent craving that zest for existence be refreshed by the ever-present, unfading importance of our immediate actions, which perish and yet live for evermore" [PR 351]. That it should be the objectified products of our actions, rather than those immediate actions themselves, that have unfading importance is the necessity imposed by Whitehead's formal system. Like Sartre's, it requires that to be known is to be an object of experience. Subjects must be transformed into objects in order to enter into relationships, to have influence, and therefore to be a part of any transcending totality. But the "realized perfection" of the world is the presence in one unity of all that is good. It is the unity of a love that tenderly saves whatever is of worth. Including, surely, what has an infinite worth for which no price could ever justify the sacrifice.

This is the metaphysical understanding to which we have been led in our long inquiry regarding human praxis and its meaning. The kingdom of ends, the beloved community, preserving infinities of unmediated freedom in the realized perfection of its togetherness, is an "exception" to Whitehead's metaphysical principles and not "their chief exemplification." It is an oxymoronic impossibility that "the Apotheosis of the World" should be a divine everlastingness defined as that wherein "immediacy is reconciled with objective immortality." Nevertheless we affirm with Whitehead: "The concept of 'God' is the way in which we understand this incredible fact—that what cannot be, yet is" [PR 350].

# Eight

## THE DESTINY OF PRAXIS

An inquiry into the nature of praxis is itself a praxis. You and I undertook this inquiry because we wondered about our lives. How might we best go about developing a way of acting and thinking that would lead to our feeling satisfied with who we are and what we do, confident of our significance within a vast and seemingly indifferent universe? We agreed to inquire together into the sources and, we hoped, the remedy of our unease. It was fitting that we should have begun by assembling a wide range of ideas and arguments from the Western intellectual tradition as our resource materials. They proved to be as recalcitrant as they were helpful, but we struggled with them as best we could. Eventually a thread of interpretation began to emerge, a way to make sense out of the conflicting ideas swirling around us. Following this thread, we were led along labyrinthine pathways toward our goal and finally into the open air provided by its promise. The fourfold dynamic causality of any praxis was thus exemplified in the inquiry we have pursued.

We were told to transmute our desire for immediate gratification into strategies for identifying and then securing satisfactions of enduring worth. We were told this meant attending not only to the external world where the objects of our desiring reside but also to ourselves; the development of our own enduring worth as persons was more important than any desires we might fulfill. This inward turn, however, led us back once more into the world when we came to realize that we could be fully ourselves only within the supporting context of other

259

selves. Our quest for community proved to have no boundary short of the whole expanse of human history and the evolution of our species. Indeed, we were told, our restless hearts could find no rest except within a universal cosmic harmony. We had discovered that praxis is not only a causal structure but a relational hierarchy, stretching from microcosm to macrocosm, from momentary actions to the everlasting-ness of God.

Our nature as essentially free persons, we have learned, also has a destiny. We began, ill at ease, facing an unknown and seemingly hostile future in which we had to find whatever fulfillment we could. Alone and desiring, we had to realize our own future. We have ended up facing that same future, still needing to realize it in some appropriate way. But we have a better grasp now of what we need, where we should be looking, and what resources we have available. We have been told to be confident in the enduring significance of ourselves and our achieve-ments, the worth they will have even when the futures being realized are no longer ours to know or to share in making.

You have been with me throughout all of this adventure. It was not only your inquiry nor only mine; together we worked our way up from the crudest kind of egoism to the most subtle kind of self-forgetfulness. Together we now find ourselves enmeshed within a vast horizontal and vertical matrix of relationships, a synchronic and diachronic spiderweb of our own making. A spiderweb of our own making, yes; but one in which the spider has herself been caught. For it is our understanding of self and world that has made the very world we are trying to under-stand. Our praxis accounts for itself by its account of us.

Doubt plucks at the edges of what we have woven so laboriously. Do we really have confidence that this web can account for itself? It is, after all, our own account. No matter how widespread the web may be, it still has a center from which it began. And, unavoidably, this center in the beginning was blind to what it might realize as it spun itself outward toward the stars. As our web grew in awareness of its work and of itself, we tried to correct for the limitations imposed by that initial unseeing finitude. But the center can never completely be wo-ven out of the web. The spider's world is necessarily from a perspec-tive, and only through the interweaving of all the webs of all the spiders there ever were would it be possible for us to make a whole that leaves nothing out. Yet even that would be a web of many, many centers and not one that has passed beyond centeredness to a neutral, seamless objectivity.

You and I are very much aware of this with respect to other world-views. We know, for instance, that the philosophical positions we have been exploring are human artifacts, expressions of one or another situated praxis. We have assembled them for our use, aware of their limitations. They were the work of persons who were products of their own culture, hemmed in by its parochial constraints at the same time as they were liberated by the meanings and possibilities it disclosed. Even though the sounds and odors of Athenian continuities and Macedonian innovations are more apparent to us in reading Aristotle than are the English traditions and post–World War II disruptions in reading Oakeshott, the space–time boundedness of both discloses itself because of our distance from them. Obviously these philosophies are not confined to the relevance they had for their contemporaries, however. They have escaped their cultural limitations insofar as we have found a use for them now in our own quite different time, as we have also used what others over the intervening years have found useful about them. But we are no better off than they; there is no privileged insight into truth or justice afforded us by our location as their successors. The result of our usage of past philosophies is to have made yet another philosophy, one that like all the others is also parochial, although in ways neither you nor I will ever fully appreciate, and that is rich with what others will find liberating in ways we also will fail fully to appreciate. In making a philosophy, the many previous philosophies become one, but thereby they are also increased by one.

So we have not arrived at any final truth nor even approached it asymptotically. How can either of us believe that we have done more than add yet another voice to the myriad voices composing what Oakeshott calls "the conversation of mankind"? I am suspicious that our efforts have not done at all what they intended to do, that we have not found a way, after all, that will lead us to some future realization of the Moment or Selfhood or the Kingdom of Ends or Omega.

Perhaps you recall poor Mrs. Moore's experience in the caves of Marabar:

There are some exquisite echoes in India; there is the whisper round the dome at Bijapur; there are the long, solid sentences that voyage through the air at Mandu, and return unbroken to their creator. The echo in a Marabar cave is not like these, it is entirely devoid of distinction. Whatever is said, the same monotonous noise replies, and quivers up and down the walls until it is absorbed into the roof. "Boum" is the sound as far as the human alphabet can express it, or "bou-oum," or "ou-boum,"—utterly dull. Hope, politeness, the blowing of a nose, the squeak of a boot, all produce "boum." . . . Pathos, piety, courage—they exist, but are identical, and so is filth. Everything exists, nothing has value. If one had spoken vileness in that place, or quoted lofty poetry, the comment would have been the same—"ou-boum." If one had spoken with the tongues of angels and pleaded for all the unhappiness and misunderstanding in the world, past, present, and to come, for all the misery men must undergo whatever their opinion and position, and however much they dodge or bluff—it would amount to the same.[1]

Each of us shouts out our own perspectival truths. But they are not reconciled in some integrated whole that preserves the individuality of each within a complex harmony. Instead, our truths meld together, their distinctive achievements lost in the unending drone that the cave returns. "Boum" or "Om" may be a sacred sound for those who would try to convince us that individuals and temporality are illusions and that what alone is real is the timeless undifferentiated One. But were that so, then the sacred sound itself would have no reality because it also is only an acoustic event propagated fleetingly in time. You and I have been insisting that if there is any meaning and worth to be found at all it must include the strivings and achievements of time-bound creatures; the echoes that fill the Marabar with "Om" cannot but fill us with despair.

This may seem harsh, but I do not think it is an overreaction. We have been after completeness, some way to be rescued from the partiality which defined us initially as a desiring that lacked something it did not possess in order to be fully itself. We found that the quest for what we were missing, the quest for ourselves, could culminate only in an affirmation of the unity of all things. We began with the dyadic relatedness of desiring and desired; we ended with the infinite relatedness of the Kingdom of Heaven. But the problem with our conclusions is that they are not believable. Those putative Moments of absolute fulfillment again and again prove themselves quite perishable commodities. Our transcendental Selves time after time betray themselves as mundane and mendacious. Our kingdoms with a human face turn out to mask the grim visage of imposed authority. Slowly it dawns upon us that Omega will never dawn upon the world. We have been dreaming about the future but we have not been realizing it.

Yet this should cause us no surprise. Of course we disbelieve such things; we live, after all, in an age of disbelief. If, just like everyone whom we have studied, you and I are also limited by the world in which we find ourselves, then what is that world like? What are the horizons beyond which we cannot see? Arnold Toynbee argues in *A Study of History* that the latter decades of the twentieth century are for us, the denizens of Western civilization, a time of crisis. The society that has made us who we are, that has given us the resources and purposes, the methods and commitments, by which we live, has lost its vitality. It is passing from centuries of growth into a phase of break-down and disintegration. In such times, people lose their belief in objective truths and foundational purposes. They begin to see every-thing as stamped with the imprint of their own or someone else's praxis. Everything, they believe, is relative to some human perspective, and so no claim to truth or call to action has any more authority than that of the person or persons making it.

Toynbee says that this unrelenting critique of all forms of authority is both symptom and cause of civilizational breakdown. No longer hold-ing the beliefs that have long united them, people also become trou-bled by the actions that are expressions of those beliefs. Both the beliefs and the actions are attacked as unwarranted and self-serving. The smooth functioning of things therefore turns rough; the engines of social order get out of tune. Reforms are needed in order to repair the damage and restore the civilization to its former effectiveness. But the beliefs that governed the old smoothness are now in disarray. Des-peration, the stepmother of invention, evokes a variety of make-do re-storative responses, all of which are faltering and ultimately inadequate attempts to find a substitute for the beliefs and practices that had for so long served the people well.

I propose that you and I take a look at what Toynbee has to say. Perhaps we will find ourselves depicted in his analysis, see profiled there our convictions and the skepticism eroding them. Perhaps we can find with his help a way to shore up the conclusions we have been at such pains to construct but which seem nonetheless to have been built on the shifting sands of a civilization in decline.

An effective social praxis, according to Toynbee, emerges in re-sponse to some challenge threatening the ongoing routine course of things. The challenge involves some sort of departure from how the world has traditionally been ordered, some intrusive novelty that alters how things work. Accordingly, the response must also be a departure from traditional practices. It must have an element of novelty to it, pro-vide some new and different way of doing things. But inventiveness is a rare quality; we live for the most part by the reiteration of long-established strategies that have served us well. Few are willing and even fewer able to see that the times have changed and that some of the old and self-evident truths have become uncouth and opaque. A civilization manages an effective response to a new challenge only if the few who are creative enough to develop that response can then secure the allegiance of the rest of society to it and to themselves.

Thus in a time of growth, a "creative minority" provides society with the beliefs and practices it needs in order to survive. The majority of society takes its cue from the minority, vesting it with authority to set the norms to which by "mimesis" the majority then conforms. The solution to one challenge becomes the context for the next challenge. A society flourishes as long as it can continue to meet this never-ending sequence of fresh challenges. Each subsequent challenge is not only different, Toynbee argues, but also more "ethereal." At first the problems that must be solved are physical and require a physical re-sponse. A drought has stretched on for years and threatens agriculture; marauders on the frontier steal the harvest and slaughter the innocent. Irrigation methods must be devised and implemented; retributive raids must be organized and a line of forts constructed along the frontier. But as the civilization matures, the challenges become primarily inter-nal and the solutions required become far more subtle and intangible. Problems in the flow of communication replace problems with the flow of water, and citizens demanding the right to peaceful dissent re-place foreigners demanding control of the borderlands. The soldier king is succeeded by the persuasive politician.

Creativity is a fragile accomplishment. Those able to provide the so-lution required by a given set of problematic circumstances may not be suited to do so when the next challenge comes along. They may be good civil engineers but poor at civic engineering. They may simply have grown tired, worn down by their responsibilities. Or they may have been spoiled by their success, thinking themselves more fit to lead than is actually the case. They can become blinded by the adulation of their followers so that they fail to perceive a newly emerging challenge until it is too late, thinking that an old solution will do quite well, or assuming that they are impervious to failure. This "nemesis of creativ-ity" is overcome in a developing society by a shift in who composes the creative minority. A group outside the centers of authority, unbur-dened by nemesis and brimming with untapped potential, gains a hear-ing when it warns about the need to take this new danger seriously. Soon its offer to provide new leadership is gratefully accepted. The mi-mesis of the majority shifts allegiance; social purposes are redirected; the new response proves successful. The civilization thus continues to flourish, adapting in this way to whatever further challenges an unpre-dictable world might throw in its path.

Social breakdown results when these functional relationships go awry. The old minority may not relinquish its authority, thereby pre-venting a new creative leadership from emerging when it is needed. The old order continues to rule, but force rather than mimesis be-comes the basis of obedience. Or, the majority may become so en-thralled with the habit of doing things in ways hallowed by custom that they lose their willingness to chase after new gods, to adapt to new ways. The creative practices they are asked to follow are ignored or followed halfheartedly. If so, says Toynbee, the creative minority degenerates into a "dominant minority"; the submission forced upon the majority turns it into a "proletariat."

Consequently, a challenge goes unanswered, or the answer is a stop-gap solution that only puts off the problem for a time. As a result, the challenge eventually reappears: not a new, etherealized challenge, but the same old unanswered one. The society, aware of its failure to rise to the occasion earlier, responds more defensively than innovatively. The results are again inadequate; the challenge once more presents itself. Losing confidence in its leaders, its cohesiveness, and its sense of common destiny, the society becomes increasingly desperate to solve its problems and increasingly inept at doing so.

Toynbee identifies twelve different kinds of response, all of them inadequate. Some of the responses are active in character, some passive. Some are efforts initiated by the minority, faint echoes of creativity, while others are substitutes for mimesis initiated by the majority. I would suggest that the responses can also be seen as reflecting the efficient, final, and formal dimensions of praxis. This results in a double array of the modalities of strategy by which a society struggles to reverse the increasing evidence of its collapse. [See Illustration 8.1].

Toynbee's analysis offers a fresh perspective on the limitations of the various philosophical positions we have been exploring. These positions, along with some others that I shall introduce, can be seen to illustrate the several failed responses that are symptomatic of civilizational breakdown. Perhaps it is another symptom of that breakdown that I am only proposing you take Toynbee's analysis as a heuristic device, as a model we can use to organize our reflections. That Toynbee might be offering us an objective description of the breakdown and disintegration of civilizations, or that such a description might even be possible, is a claim which I as a child of these doubt-plagued times would never think of making.

One of the responses to a growing threat of social disintegration is "abandon." You might attempt to restore creativity to your failing leadership by returning to what you think to be its wellspring. "By giving free rein to [your] own spontaneous appetites and aversions [you] will be 'living according to Nature' and will automatically be receiving back, from the cornucopia of this mysterious and therefore possibly puissant goddess, the precious gift of creativity" which you have lost [SH-5 377]. Toynbee takes Alcibiades, "the slave of his own passion," and Thrasymachus, advocate of the thesis that might makes right, as

**Illustration 8.1: Toynbee: Schisms of the Soul**

|  |  | efficient | final | formal |
|---|---|---|---|---|
|  |  | creativity | feeling | external |
| minority | passive | abandon 1 | sense drift 5 | archaism 9 |
|  | active | self control 2 | sense sin 6 | futurism 10 |

|  |  | efficient | final | formal |
|---|---|---|---|---|
|  |  | mimesis | style | internal |
| majority | passive | truancy 3 | promiscuity 7 | detachment 11 |
|  | active | martyrdom 4 | sense unity 8 | transfigur 12 |

classical exemplars of abandon [SH-5 400], but he obscures his point by doing so. Your act of abandon is an attempt to recover a lost capacity for fresh problem-solving ideas by cutting yourself free from the old, worn-out, constrictive ways. You plunge into spontaneous, uninhibited activities on the presumption that they will bring you in touch with the primordial powers that can rekindle the dying fire of your creativity. Hedonists like Alcibiades are merely Don Juanian: they are spontaneously spontaneous. A return-to-nature strategy is artful, an attempt to be spontaneous by schedule, to trick the "puissant goddess" into believing that you are one of her devotees. Ironically, however, your attempt to repudiate the traditions and trappings of office, those things that set you aside from the masses whose leader you purport to be, only blurs the distinction between them and yourself. It increases your unfitness to rule.

The alternative is "self-control." You apply yourself to a regimen of physical, mental, and spiritual discipline in the belief that "Nature is the bane of creativity and not its source, and that to 'gain the mastery over Nature' is the only way of recovering the lost creative faculty" [SH-5 377]. Your asceticism may run to the extreme of monastic withdrawal or, like the Stoic, you may cultivate a serene indifference to things that are beyond your control. Taking Marcus Aurelius as one of the exemplars of this approach, Toynbee describes his writings as marked by "melancholy" because his stoicism "never could quite brace" the emperor "to bear on his lonely shoulders the Atlantean load of a collapsing world" [SH-5 400]. But a Sartrean hero hardly seems stooped by melancholy as he celebrates what his self-control makes possible. Orestes takes the burden of the Argive people upon his own shoulders, thereby overcoming it through his authentic refusal to bow down to Nature and to Zeus its god. But even were a steely stoic will enough to give you courage and steadfastness, it would not necessarily increase your powers of inventiveness. Neither Nature nor its denial are sufficient conditions for a recovery of the smooth mesh between ends and means that is the source and fruit of genuinely creative praxis.

Were you a follower rather than a leader, you would experience social breakdown as a loss of mimesis, a waning both of your spontaneous identification with the purposes of the group and of your belief that its leaders deserve your loyalty. An obvious response to this is "truancy," the escapist strategy of withdrawing "from an irreparably ruined real world to the Utopia of some Lotus Eaters' Land or Calypso's Isle" [SH-5 406]. The Rotation Method is escapist in this sense, but so is any withdrawal of allegiance to the values and persons who have guided your society. Toynbee is especially incensed by the "betrayal of the intellectuals," their repudiation of the religious basis of Western civilization, their key role in its growing secularization. The point of truancy is that it is essentially negative: you step away from your commitments, lose faith in them, trivialize their significance. Were you doing so because of the attractive pull of some fresh vision of how things might be, your shift of allegiances could well be part of a creative transformation of the social order. But the truant opts out without having any where else to go.

"Martyrdom" is the inverse of truancy. "A martyr is primarily a soldier who takes it upon himself to bear witness to the supreme value and the absolute obligation of the military virtues in a situation in which his only means of giving his testimony is to sacrifice his own life on a forlorn hope" [SH-5 378]. As you sense familiar values slipping away, you respond by doubling your efforts on their behalf. You attempt to convince yourself of a loyalty you know is no longer unquestioned by the increasing intensity of your words and deeds. Your obedience becomes blind, even fanatical; self-surrender is made into an absolute virtue. You martyr your independence of mind, your ability to think for yourself, sacrificing your own values for the sake of a cause or group that in your eyes can do no wrong. Toynbee's examples are all military and religious, but they need not be. Judge William's defense of

duty can easily be taken as a portrait of the perfect bureaucrat, following the rules woodenly, without questioning them, without any sensitivity to their limits or to changing circumstance. Mimesis requires its
own mode of creativity; when this mode is squeezed out by blind loyalty the resulting rigidity is of no help to a society in need of reform.
The fanatic, just as surely as the cynic, accelerates decline by driving
mimesis to an extreme.

Abandon and truancy are passive responses whereas self-control and
martyrdom are active. They are ineffective, polarized alternatives to
the creativity and mimesis that are the efficient causes, the motive
force, of civilization. They are what social praxis looks like when it has
lost its *élan vital.* Breakdown, when it occurs, is manifest in all of the
causal dimensions of praxis, however. Thus when Toynbee talks about
responses of "feeling," he seems to have final causes in mind. Here, too,
the orientation first of leaders and then of followers goes awry; their
sense of mission, of their own purposes and their peoples' destiny, fal-
ters. The responses are polarized and, once again, inadequate.

The first of these is a "sense of drift." Although you are one of the
leaders in your society, you have lost confidence that the governing
elite knows where it is going, that it has some consensus about itself
which is being translated into the particular aims and aspirations of its
citizens. The process by which the whole is individuated into the various callings that provide diversity and hence specialized effectiveness
no longer seems to be working. You might respond passively by feeling
overwhelmed, believing that you and your comrades are no longer able
to "master and control" your situation. You have come to think of yourself as "at the mercy of a power which is as irrational as it is invincible:
the ungodly goddess with the double face who is propitiated under the
name of Chance or is endured under the name of Necessity" [SH-5
380]. Your sense of drift is of someone tossed about on a rudderless
boat, a piece of flotsam or jetsam at the mercy of arbitrary and unpre-
dictable forces. It would do no good to plan ahead, to set your course
toward some distant goal, as the world is far too chaotic a place, far too
chancy, to support organizing principles of such specificity. But you
might think these forces are unpredictable because unknown to you;
you might believe it foolish to set a course of your own because that
course has been already set. If so, it is necessity not chance that you
think rules the world. Whichever face the "ungodly goddess" turns to
you, your feeling is that human efforts are of no avail. Such attitudes,
however, find no obvious counterpart in the philosophers whose help
we have sought. Even Machiavelli carves out a place for human choice
in a world devoid of objective values, arguing that it would be achieve-

ment enough for you to keep your ship afloat amid such storms, without having to worry about what ports of call you might initially have wished to reach.

The nihilism implicit in a sense of drift is countered by a "sense of sin," the conviction that you and your comrades are the real reason for civilization's lack of direction. You are the cause and not the victim of the social malaise engulfing everyone. What has not been mastered and controlled is yourself. Self-control is discipline utilized as an instrument for recovering the creative energy needed to achieve social ends; the self-discipline that comes in response to a sense of sin is taken as an instrument for recovering those ends themselves. In Kant's terms, it is your awareness of the contrast between the unworthiness of what you actually have done and the infinite value of what you ought to be doing that stiffens your moral resolve. The passions becloud your reason; the discipline of passion is what will free reason to function as the guide of your intentions. Even though repenting your sins is an active response, however, it is primarily negative. Its aim is to cleanse not to create. It turns you in upon yourself rather than outward toward the societal challenges it is incumbent upon your leadership to address.

The mimesis of creative leadership instills in the general population a sense of style, a repertoire of attitudes and values thought to be properly expressive of the society's distinctive purposes. The members of society, united in their common endeavor, exhibit that unity of expectation in the similarity of their taken-for-granted assumptions, their common sense regarding what is right or worthwhile. A "sense of promiscuity" is "an acquiescence in the total loss of all sense of form," which arises when these stylistic confidences begin to collapse [SH-5 381]. Without an ideal to rank possibilities on a scale of significance, all of them seem of equal value. A Benthamite calculus of subjective preferences reduces public purposes to a survey of constituent desires, each desire weighted the same as all the others. Indeed, the dominant minority begins to take its cues in taste and morals from the proletariat, copying the crude ways of the external barbarian and the vulgar practices of its own internal masses. The political franchise is universalized, syncretic religions and philosophies abound, superstitions and oddities of all sorts are tolerated, and the grammar and pronunciation of cultured speech succumbs to the common polyglot language of the streets. This tropism toward the lowest common denominator preserves the unity of an increasingly pluralistic society, but at the expense of focus.

The other way to retain social unity in the face of a growing pluralism is to see the differences as trivial. A "sense of unity," says Toynbee, is the conviction that "the flickering film of a phenomenal world in which the forms of outward things take shape only to disappear again is an illusion which cannot for ever obscure the everlasting unity that lies behind" [SH-6 1]. This somewhat Hindu way of expressing the sense of unity is misleading, however, because what Toynbee has in mind is any belief that moves beyond parochial loyalties. A "pan-barbarian comradeship" in which group solidarity is a matter of shared purpose rather than shared ancestry is one example of this sense of unity. Indeed, this unity finds its best expression in the attempt of Alexander the Great to impose "the compelling spiritual power of his humanitarian gospel" of *homonoia* upon "the recalcitrance of his Macedonian companions" by having them take Persian wives and by creating an army in which soldiers from the various subjugated peoples were all accepted on equal terms into a single fighting unit [SH-6 5–7]. This notion of an "oecumenical commonwealth" always becomes the ideal and ideology of empire. We have seen this, for instance, in tracing the way in which the English-speaking peoples found both a purpose worthy of their loyalties and a convenient rationalization for their exploits in the dream of a united world. As Hegel argued, conflict and chaos may abound in human history, but its essential principle is by means of that very conflict moving inexorably toward the full realization of peace and harmony. The divisive pluralism that seems so rampant is in fact merely temporary, transitional, incomplete. It rests upon something more fundamental.

A sense of unity is thus a device for overcoming the disintegrative tendencies rampant during a time of social breakdown by looking for an underlying unity. Whereas through a sense of promiscuity you try to find this in the lowest common denominator, a sense of unity proposes that you reach for a highest common denominator. But both strategies denigrate the actual pluralism that arose initially through processes of individuation, which are the hallmark of civilizational development. It is when a society has lost control of the diversity it is nurturing, when its leaders are no longer able to fashion an actual, dynamic, functionally effective unity out of the motley beliefs and practices of its citizens, that those citizens, desperate for an object upon which to focus their mimesis, turn to forms of unity too superficial or too abstract to serve the functional needs of a growing society. Here also, therefore, the response to breakdown is an ineffective substitute for creative vision and the steadfast commitments it alone can invoke.

Toynbee next turns to the third set of responses to breakdown, those having to do with what he calls "alternative ways of life." I would interpret these as constituting suggested changes in the formal conditions of a social praxis, proposals regarding the general shapes of the organization that should be put into place if the society is to regain its former effectiveness. These have to do with beliefs and practices: the schemata of acceptable ideas and techniques that the people draw upon in their mundane activities, that monarchs and politicians also draw upon to orient their ambitions and justify their accomplishments.

"Archaism" is defined by Toynbee as "a reversion from the mimesis of contemporary creative personalities to a mimesis of the ancestors of the tribe" [SH-5 384]. If you take this, however, to mean advocating some ancient moral code in place of the one currently in place, then archaism is only a quixotic atavism, asking you to tilt at the windmills of a past long since lost beyond recovering. It is a different matter if you turn to the past in order to find there the origins of your present accomplishments, to discern the continuities that tie the old together with the new. Ever since Judge William first spoke to us of self-identity as a continuity among choices, you have appreciated how important it is for the present to be rooted in and nurtured by its antecedents. Don Juan's denial of the time-boundedness of Moments of fulfillment was not only futile but also foolish. As Johannes was quick to point out, fulfillment requires infusing the present with the past instead of cutting yourself off from it.

One way of establishing these continuities is by conforming your purposes and practices to those already established. As I have argued in *The Importances of the Past,* the historical density of a structure of societal relationships gives that structure significance. The meaning it exemplifies has endured, has resisted the encroachment of alternatives, and has done so because based upon values as old as the society, as old as humanity, as old as time itself. If such importances exist, then it is crucial that you conform your beliefs and practices to them through ritual practices, link up with them by being in the places where they have already been manifest, and express your loyalty to them in your identification with the heroes whose great deeds have confirmed the destiny of this relationship. Should these current times be out of joint, a recovery of intimacy with the ancient importances is possible through acts of propitiation, a physical and spiritual homecoming, a renewed dedication to the founding gods and heroes and to the cause for which they stand.

Another way of establishing these continuities is the one suggested by Hegel: to look to the past not for its intrinsic value but for the historical principle immanent within it. The actual achievements of the past are never worth emulating. They were the result of ideals and efforts that, from the perspective we have attained because of them, are obviously inadequate and distorting. You need to look through the actual to the ideal implicit in it, to the ground of its significance. The importance of the past is not a matter of the givenness it has brought to birth but rather of the future with which it is pregnant.

What do we do when both of these beliefs have eroded away? Neither you nor I believe there are any laws of the nations to complement the laws of nature. We weave our fabrics now without an objective warp, without either importances or principles to give them permanence. So how can the past be of any help to us? Hannah Arendt offers an answer in her *Lectures on Kant's Political Philosophy,* suggesting that we take another look at Kant.[2] It would seem unlikely that we could be helped by the philosopher who has been insisting that there must be a transcendental basis for the continuities of choice by which we fashion our moral character. Kant said that you were to make yourself a self whose rectitude is measured by the timeless norms of Self. But you doubt that there is any essential, normative humanity to be realized either in your own life or as a collective historical destiny. You are unsure that reason has the power to disclose an essence even were there such, for you no longer have confidence in claims about synthetic *a priori* truths, about truths untarnished by the desires of self and the prejudices of culture. Granting the validity of your skepticism, says Arendt, Kant is nonetheless an invaluable resource for finding a way to fashion the historical continuities needed for your life and work to be meaningful.

In the *Critique of Judgment,* Kant argues that there is a "common sense," the *sensus communis,* possessed by all human beings. This sense refers not only to the uncultivated, roughly reliable grasp of how things work that people everywhere have, but also to

a faculty of judgment which, in its reflection, takes account (*a priori*) of the mode of representation of all other men in thought, in order, as it were, to compare its judgment with the collective reason of humanity, and thus to escape the illusion arising from the private conditions that could be so easily taken for objective, which would injuriously affect the judgment. [CJ §40]

When you make a commonsense judgment, you are attempting to free yourself of the biases that normally inform your actions. Concerns rooted in your selfish interests and familiar habits, for instance, will tempt you to judge a particular event good simply because it furthers your purposes or plays up to your prejudices. You find satisfaction in the news of the revolution going on in France because it means higher profits for your business or because you have never forgiven the Bourbons for their supercilious attitude toward all Prussians.

You often act on such subjective considerations, but there are times when prudence cautions you to pause and ask yourself if your views are sensible, if they are the sort anyone in your situation might be expected to hold. You wonder if you might be too blinded by the intensity of your emotions or prejudices to see what everyone else sees: the silliness of your intent or the unfortunate consequences that are likely to result if you act unthinkingly. As a check on yourself you compare your judgment with what you think anyone else would likely feel was appropriate, with "the collective reason of humanity." This move is somewhat similar to what would be required by the categorical imperative, locating yourself in terms of a principle that treats everyone equally. But in a commonsense judgment you do so without appealing to any principle. It is a judgment of sense, of feelings, and does not in any way involve reason. It is "aesthetical" rather than intellectual, a judgment of taste not of cognition.

Nor does common sense involve taking account of the actual judgments others make; there are no empirical surveys or opinion polls involved. Your judgment is compared to "the possible rather than the actual judgments of others." You imaginatively put yourself in the place of any other person, although not any particular individual whom you might actually know and whose specific responses or style of response might thus become a factor in what you envision. You think how this hypothetical person would probably judge the situation. Because this person is no one in particular, the judgment he or she is imagined making is generic. If anyone would make it, everyone would; yourself included. Taste is thus the conviction that your judgment about the appropriateness of your feelings toward something is a "universally communicable" judgment, one that is shared by you and your fellow human beings generally. You feel yourself in agreement with them even though no concept has been introduced, no unifying principle enunciated for which their judgments and yours are instantiations.

Arendt argues that there are two "operations" in the exercise of such aesthetic taste judgments. The first is imagination. You step back from your involvement in things, your business dealings with émigré Bourbons for instance, and you see in your mind's eye the impact the events of the revolution might have on the feelings of anyone who might become aware of them. The second operation is reflection, your judgment about the harmony between your personal feelings and what you have imagined would be the common reaction of people. The double operation of taste establishes the most important condition for all judgments, the condition of impartiality, of "disinterested delight." By closing one's eyes one becomes an impartial, not a directly affected, spectator of visible things. [Like] the blind poet . . . one is in a position to "see" by the eyes of the mind, i.e., to see the whole that gives meaning to the particulars. [KPP 68]

And Arendt then draws this conclusion:

The advantage the spectator has is that he sees the play as a whole, while each of the actors knows only his part or, if he should judge from the perspective of acting, only the part of the whole that concerns him. The actor is partial by definition. [KPP 68–69]

When you are busily pursuing your interests, you see things in terms of their relevance to whatever ends you have in view. You are caught up in the practical requirements of praxis, working toward a resolution of some problematic, anticipating its consequences, preparing your next strategies. You are too close to things, too involved in their shaping, to be able to see them whole and dispassionately. As a spectator, however, you are able to step back from events, put them in context, see things as they have come to be, complete and determinate, rather than as still in the making. A spectator makes an aesthetic judgment. In witnessing an event you are already at a distance from it. It is an object for you to inspect if you should choose; it demands nothing of you, neither threatens nor lures a response from you. So you remove the event from its actional context, hold it before your mind's eye, and give it a place within the world of your remembrances. The Jacobins, in your opinion, were unusually frenetic in their recent debates; probably, you note, in frustration over the failure of their recent attempts to silence the complaints of the Languedoc farmers; their extremism is not likely to breed the stability you feel France now so desperately needs.

Like the blind poet, you see with your imagination instead of with your eyes. You take what you have learned and make it part of a story, locate it within a dynamic context of relationships that determine its meaning and the meaning to which it in turn contributes. Homer's epic weaves its tale without a preestablished principle as its warp. The temporal sequence of the events he recounts and the cadences of his poetry are warp enough to give direction and coherence to the seamless fabric fashioned by the sightless bard. What is seen through his story as it unfolds for you is seen from an objective point of view, from the perspective you would have had were it to have been your luck or fate to have been present with Achilles when he was sulking in his tent and to have stood beside Odysseus when he glimpsed once more the beloved hills of home.

Arendt agrees with Kant in making a sharp distinction between ethical and aesthetic judgments. As an agent of historical change, you engage your interests and freedom in a praxis that seeks to make the given into something new or to restore it to what it was. Your actions are to be guided and evaluated by the injunctions of the categorical imperative. Your reason tells you the moral maxim; the judgment is whether a particular action accords with it or not. The meaning of your action is an ethical one; judgment is concentrated solely on your intentions, on the will that determined your action and on whether it was heteronomous or autonomous. Clearly, for instance, no act of insurrection against the established government would ever be morally acceptable. It involves conspiracy and so cannot be universalized; it treats those it would displace in power as a means only; and its aim is to legislate a partisan interest.

But Kant as a spectator of the successful French insurrection against the Bourbon monarchy can applaud its achievement as evidence that the kingdom of ends is not an idle dream, that its realization is the destiny of human history. A spectator, in contrast to an ethicist, makes a judgment about accomplishments, about results rather than intentions, about the work of agents as these find their place within an ongoing historical context. Here the meaning of your deed is an aesthetic one and so is concentrated solely on the relationships fashioned by what you did, their coherence with what had been previously done and their import for what might come next. An aesthetic judgment is a matter of taste rather than morality. It is an assessment of the significance of what has happened, not of the right or wrong of its doing. Though founded on common sense rather than reason, this judgment is nonetheless unbounded in scope and so is as legitimate, well-grounded, and objective as is an ethical judgment.

Moreover, says Arendt, "it seemed to Kant that the spectator's view carried the ultimate meaning of the event, although this view yielded no maxim for acting" [KPP 52]. Whereas ethical judgments are about individuals, aesthetic ones are about the whole of humanity. You rebel against the chains of this oppressive social order, proclaim the infinite worth of every human being, and with your comrades carry on to victory: *liberté, égalité, fraternité*. But what does all this mean? Is it a blow struck for human freedom, a defeat for tyranny, or is it a violent form of the circulation of elites, one tyrant's yoke being replaced by another's? That depends on the verdict of history. It depends on what account is given of the relationship between those revolutionary events and the conditions that preceded them. A story will need to be told, the threads of this new praxis woven into the fabric of the old. The meaning this story tells will explain what happened, provide its causes, show how and why it came to be inevitable. It will determine the ultimate meaning of what you did. For Arendt, "The freedom to initiate fundamental political change imposes a responsibility—the need to legitimate the new order—that can only be accomplished by situating the founding act within a historical narrative connecting it to a prior foundation in the past."[3]

The legitimation comes not only because the spectator-historian is able to provide the needed connective narrative, but also because the historian's judgment is aesthetic, hence rooted in the *sensus communis* of a people. The historian has imaginatively occupied all our points of view and so speaks for us all in assessing the meaning of what has transpired. An historian arguing a special interest, pleading for your support of one side or the other, is merely a propagandist. The disinterested voice of the genuine historian tells a story that transcends partisanship, that gives the endless clash of purposes a meaning, that speaks of the ultimate significance of human deeds.

It is instructive to compare Arendt with Errol Harris[4] regarding this role of the historian. An historical account, Harris notes, is based upon evidence, upon artifacts interpreted as providing access to the purposes and presuppositions of once-living human agents. What cannot be directly provided by such evidence, however, must be supplied by the historian's imagination. But what sort of evidence the artifacts are interpreted to be, how imagination is able to supplement that interpretation, and by what criteria the resulting webwork of relationships are judged plausible, draws from and depends very much upon context. The historian's imagination "is steeped in social tradition, and must necessarily be molded by the outlook and prejudices of the historical period and the society in which the historian has been nurtured" [RT 115]. For Harris, thus, imagination is central to historical judgment but is limited by the limitations of its social context.

Historians do their best to overcome this constraint. They try to make sense out of the welter of their data by finding principles of organization by which those facts can be related in temporally sequential ways. What counts as the relevant facts is, in turn, a function of those organizing principles. But if the principles are merely subjective preferences, arbitrary inventions by the historian, the data will be equally subjective. The result will be historical fiction, not history. Consequently, a historian's account can correct for this subjectivity, can be said to be objective, only to the extent that the principles utilized permit a narrative to be woven around them that is as comprehensive and coherent as possible. In this sense, says Harris, "the only criterion of historical truth is history itself" [RT 113].

The more completely integrative an activity is, the more effective and enduring its results. An individual's rational action realizes objective purposes insofar as it takes account of the complete context of the ongoing social tradition of which it is an expression. The same criteria of rationality and objectivity hold for groups. Their policies are realistic if consonant with traditional practices and for the benefit of all their members. Similarly, historians write objective histories insofar as their narratives take into account the whole complex of cultural beliefs, practices, and structures, along with the conditions of the natural environment, that have influenced the events being interpreted. These criteria of rationality and objectivity are the same, no matter what the form of action by which they are expressed.

Notice that for Harris, as for Kant and Hegel, the ordering principle in a historical account is not a covering law. A principle of order for interpreting a particular set of historical events is articulated in terms of a story, a sequence of actions that trace out reasonable attempts by persons or social groups to achieve reasonable goals within the context provided by their reasonable beliefs about the world. The recurrent criterion of reasonableness is in each usage an appeal to perspectives ordering experience in some coherent and comprehensive manner. The historical narrative collects these perspectives into a new perspective, one ideally more coherent and comprehensive than any one of them. Even where the goals, practices, or beliefs being integrated are not reasonable, they are judged so by reference to what it would have been reasonable to do. No story, individual or collective, can simply be predicted, deduced from the principle it realizes temporally. Nor can what happens be translated into general statements except by losing everything that makes the historically concrete story important. A historical narrative hangs together, or its failure to do so comes to your attention, because you have judged its subject matter to be a whole of which the story told, the interpretation offered, is the unfolding.

The more clearly you know your own story, can make sense out of why you believe as you do, why you are committed to certain ends rather than others, why you pursue them by one means rather than another, the better you are able to accomplish what you have set out to do. Self-understanding is how you make progress toward self-fulfillment. The historian, Harris argues, plays a similar role with respect to society, helping it understand better its collective story, helping its members make sense out of the ends toward which their

explicit policies and customary practices, and those of their predecessors, point. "History is the self-awareness of the civilized mind" [RT
133] because it provides the basis for actions that move a community
toward a more complete realization of the ideal of a social order able
to fulfill the essential capacities of its citizens.

The broader the consensus among the storytellers, the less the principles at work are idiosyncratic ones. But for Harris more than this is
needed. Consensus is only an approximation to objectivity, a second-
best solution to the problem of subjective and cultural bias. Intersubjective agreement is ultimately no substitute for objectivity. Thus, argues
Harris, unless a historian's narrative can be shown to be based upon an
objective principle, shown to trace intrinsic relations among actions,
persons, and societies, it cannot be judged to be true. Harris, however,
cannot provide proof that any specific narrative principle deployed by
a historian is an objective one. Such an objective principle is discover-
able, but its actual discovery is exceedingly difficult because only at
the time when it has become fully actualized can it be fully known.

Hence the historian's existential situation as interpreted by Harris is
very similar to what Arendt says it is. You are located willy-nilly in a
temporal context and can see only from a standpoint that is partial and
unavoidably distortive. You attempt to correct for this by drawing on
something that transcends your limited perspective, a criterion of coherence or of consensus, extended as comprehensively or as commu-
nicatively as possible. This criterion gives you confidence that the
historical interpretation you are attempting to articulate has an objective basis. Coherence and comprehensiveness in narrative accounts are
necessary even though not sufficient conditions for the story they
characterize as being objectively rational.

The difference between Harris and Arendt, nonetheless, is more fundamental than their similarities. Harris, like Hegel, expresses the self-
confidence of a culture in its halcyon days, believing in itself and in the
importance of the role it has to play in the unfolding drama of history.
Harris's eyes are on the future; he probes into the nature of the past
and present in order to find clues for when time will disgorge its still-
unrealized treasures. Arendt has suffered the death of that belief and
that confidence. Her eyes are intent upon the present task of making
whatever sense she can of things by showing their continuities to a
meaningful past. She puts on a brave face, indeed a noble one:

If judgment is our faculty for dealing with the past, the historian is the
inquiring man who by relating it sits in judgment over it. If that is so,
we may reclaim our human dignity, win it back, as it were, from the

pseudo-divinity named History of the modern age, without denying history's importance but denying its right to be the ultimate judge. [KPP 5]

There is no principle at work in history that gives it its significance, no God whose purpose is its essence. There are only men and women who make their own sense of significance out of what they have done. Gods and absolute principles are masks of authority behind which tyrants lurk, charlatans attempting to impose their own limited perspective on the rest of us. Arendt's appeal to Kant's aesthetic judgment, to the *sensus communis* that is its key, is her way to protect us against such totalitarian propensities by appealing to something radically egalitarian. Aesthetic judgments are the way we tell to one another the story of who we are. It is a story to which when you hear it you nod assent, for it speaks as you yourselves would have spoken had you the skill. Only what all of humanity judges for itself to be its truth can compose the intersubjective substitute for objectivity.

But when a civilization's confidences break down, the halfway house of archaism will not suffice. Arendt is not successful in her attempt to replace the judgment of history with the judgment of historians. Kant required of the "common human understanding" that it conform to three maxims: that you should think for yourself, that you should put yourself in the place of others, and that you should think consistently. The first requires you to be "enlightened"; it is

the maxim of a never *passive* reason. The tendency to such passivity, and therefore to heteronomy of the reason, is called *prejudice.* . . . The blindness in which superstition places us, which it even imposes on us as an obligation, makes the need of being guided by others, and the consequent passive state of our reason, peculiarly noticeable. [CG §40]

But the possibility of enlightenment, of unprejudiced clarity, is precisely what has been called into question when the possibility for objective rationality is rejected. Similarly, the second maxim to which Kant says common sense must conform asks you to reflect upon matters from a "universal standpoint." The possibility of "enlarged thought," the capacity for giving all perspectives equal weight, for spinning a web without a center, is impossible unless preceded by the evenhandedness of enlightenment. The third maxim, that of "consecutive thought," is, according to Kant, a consequence of the other two.

Consequently, the claim to speak for humanity is no less a mask of tyranny than the claim to speak for history. Commonsense judgment depends on an act of imagination that boasts of having occupied a generically human perspective. But there can be none if we share no common humanity, if you and I are only what we have interpreted ourselves to be. The very skepticism that erodes our confidence in reason reduces our confidence in common sense. A general human taste is as much a will-o'-the-wisp as a universal rational morality. There is no way to adjudicate the rival claims of the historians, nor any basis for Arendt's contention that the judgment of the dispassionate historian is better than that of the passionate agent. Indeed, is not the clash of rival claims, the struggle among committed agents for change, the only genuine way by which a question of truth can ever be settled?

There is something about archaism, says Toynbee, "that drives it into self-defeat in frustration of its conscious purpose" [SH-6 95]. It impales itself on a dilemma. On the one horn, it would attempt to do justice to its inheritance, to a tradition of beliefs and practices that find little room for innovation much less for radical change or revolution. The newly emerging realities will not be stopped by the archaist's condemnations, however; the force of change "will shatter into fragments the brittle shell" that the archaist is "bent on retrieving." On the other horn, archaism would seek to make the present meaningful, but can do so only by ignoring or trivializing the old ways, "introducing so much new masonry to reinforce the remnant" that this "pious work of 'reconstruction' will be difficult to distinguish from the Vandalism of naked demolition and replacement." Either way, the result is a destruction of the continuities. Into the resulting vacuum, says Toynbee, will come "some ruthless innovation that has been lying in wait outside for this very opportunity of forcing an entry" [SH-6 97]. Hence archaism gives way to "futurism."

The futurist is a revolutionary who thinks that the best way to deal with existing problems is to start all over again. The established order of things is fraught with injustices, with social surds and historical anomalies. Reforming them will produce only marginal improvements. The problem is with the order of things itself, which must perish utterly if something better is ever to succeed it.

In the political sphere Futurism may express itself either geographically in the deliberate obliteration of existing landmarks and boundaries or socially in the forcible dissolution of existing corporations, parties, and sects or "liquidation" of existing classes or abolition of existing organs or offices of state. [SH-6 107]

Jean-François Lyotard is a futurist, attacking all efforts to achieve unity in the beliefs and practices of a society. These efforts, he says, are all servants of totalitarianism, of practical hegemonies justified by "metanarratives" that celebrate the rightness of a single political order and proclaim the truth of a single conceptual order. For instance, Lyotard argues that consensus is the touchstone of capitalist bourgeois society. The legitimacy of a government is said to be based on the consensus of its citizens as arrived at through public debate, and the legitimacy of an abstract idea is supposed to be founded on a consensus of thinkers who have deliberated rationally about its claims. Disagreement is good but only as a means for finally attaining agreement. Communist societies work from metanarratives that differ from these in no important way.

One of the two basic forms of the justificatory metanarratives of societal unity is primarily cognitive. It argues that a satisfactory society can only be achieved by first devising an adequate "discursive ordering," a systematic conceptual framework of understanding that includes an ethical theory and hence provides well-grounded norms of what is good or right or just. This ideal model can then be compared with the actual societal situation; the contrast generates a "prescriptive" ordering which specifies "the measures to be taken in social reality to bring it into conformity with the representation of justice that was worked out in the theoretical discourse" [JG 21]. Correct practices are a mimesis of true theories and ultimately of a single, coherent, and comprehensive Truth.

The other important metanarrative justifying social unity is practical. It claims that the people must express their collective will in the form of "emancipatory" actions, gaining mastery over persons, institutions, and traditions that would attempt to constrain them in the expression of their rightful freedoms. The value of anything is its relevance to this ideal. Even knowledge "has no final legitimacy outside of serving the goals envisioned by the practical subject, the autonomous collectivity" [PC 36]. True theories are those that improve the efficiency of correct practices, that contribute ultimately to the practice of a single, harmonically integrated realm of free persons.

In contemporary Western civilization where both of these "grand narratives" have become problematic, a third approach to justifying the social order has developed, one that has neither a theoretical nor a practical ideal undergirding it. With no goal to orient it, society justifies itself by criteria of efficiency or "performativity": success is a matter of maintaining the system, of continually engineering a functional integration of its component parts. Technocracy is the triumph of means become their own self-justifying ends.

Lyotard rejects all of this. The hallmark of the "postmodernism" he advocates is "incredulity toward metanarrative," a belief in the irreducible "heterogeneity of elements" comprising any societal complex. A single norm of any sort is abhorrent, not only timeless ideal models and immanent Hegelian principles but also even the sense of a shared condition to which Arendt had turned.

There cannot be a *sensus communis*.... We judge without criteria. We are in the position of Aristotle's prudent individual, who makes judgments about the just and the unjust without the least criterion.... We are dealing with judgments that are not regulated by categories. [JG 14]

This means that choices and evaluations are always made in a radically specific context. The skill required is not mimetic, finding the general rule for which the decision to be made or the action to be evaluated is an instance. But neither is the requisite skill a matter of autonomy, of self-expression; such would merely replace the authority of a general rule with the authority of the will of the decider/evaluator. The Aristotelian judge makes prescriptive decisions without appealing to either an absolute truth or an absolute will.

Lyotard insists that we abandon both these "totalizing" narratives for one devoid of absolutes. He proposes the storyteller in a South American jungle tribe as exemplary: the story this person recounts to others is said to have been told to him by another. It is a story about themselves, its being told is more important than the specifics of its content, and the listeners are expected in turn to tell that story to others. The story is thus not a transcendental truth or a sacred tradition made present by the telling, a normative measure brought to the people as a criterion of propriety to which they must conform. Nor is the storyteller himself a god or a speaker for the gods, a shaman who enunciates prescriptions that the people must obey. There is only the group, their roles interdependent and interchangeable, who are struggling to make some sense out of their actions. Their story arises from and is for themselves.

The emphasis in this exemplary activity is on the process and not the results. The value of the story is its attempt to make sense of things. What is important is the telling of the story and not what sense was actually made at this time or at some other time. The story is a creation made in this context for this context. All that can and need be done subsequently is to carry on the storytelling, to contribute to the ongoing of the group and its sense of itself.

We are always within opinion, and there is no possible discourse of truth on the situation. And there is no such discourse because one is caught up in a story, and one cannot get out of this story to take up a metalinguistic position from which the whole could be dominated. We are always immanent to stories in the making, even when we are the ones telling the story to the other.... There is no outside; there is no place from which one could photograph the whole thing. [JG 43]

Because of the Greek and primitive tribal roots of this attitude, Lyotard thus becomes an advocate for "paganism." Pagans are those "who do any telling only inasmuch as it has been told, and who, themselves, are told in what they tell" [JG 38]. They reject all hegemonies and all absolutes, all Gods and Goods. There is only the multiplicity of the perspectives created by a multiplicity of particular situations and their particular stories.

Arendt would not disagree with this denigration of absolutes. Her interpretation of Kant's *sensus communis* avoids the rationality and hence the conceptual normativeness that Lyotard abhors. But Arendt's narratives, although parochial and incomplete, are always aspiring to be metanarratives. Their aim is to weave the same seamless fabric of the realization of an ideal community as was aimed at by Royce or Hegel or Fiske. Arendt's problem is that the only transcendence she has available is that of reflective distance. It is a relative, ever-shifting absolute; its weavings are only momentarily authoritative.

Lyotard dismisses even this, however, as an arbitrary, unjustifiable endeavor.[5] A reflective weaving is never a neutral assessment. It is every bit as much a moral action as a revolutionary praxis. It may contribute to the revolution by explaining how it is an inevitable development out of the previous social conditions, thus making the new an integral part of an ongoing totality. Or, the historian's narrative may be counterrevolutionary, rejecting the new as alien, as incommensurable, as evil. Arendt seeks hegemonic victory by means of aesthetic judgments rather than ethical acts of will or intellectual system-building. Her claims may be more modest than those of Kant or Robbespierre, but they are equally imperialist. She practices a form of the Terror, attempting to blackmail us into accepting what she prescribes lest in failing to do so we lose the meaning that we each need in order to live fulfilling lives and that our society needs in order to survive. See things my way, Arendt insinuates; do things my way—or perish!

But you can survive quite well without global meanings. A regional meaning will do, if it works for you in the situation where you find yourself. Lyotard borrows Wittgenstein's notion of language games to talk about these regional meanings, these "small narratives," by which we live. They are human creations; they spring up in endless profusion in response to differing and changing needs; their value is limited but genuine. You play them as you choose, obeying their local rules so far as you find doing so useful or satisfying, opting out when other opportunities arise. You play many games all at once, take on a variety of roles and pursue a variety of ends: emotional, sexual, familial, professional, political, cultural ones. Any one of them is authoritative only because "agreed on by its present players." It is a "temporary contract" to act or think or otherwise behave in consort, under the aegis of some common rules for the sake of some limited purpose. The agreement is "subject to eventual cancellation" when your needs change or it suits you to try something new [PC 66].

Toynbee argues, however, that the exemplary gesture of the futurist is not really tribal storytelling. It is book burning. As the caliph 'Umar is supposed to have argued when asked what his victorious generals should do about the library at conquered Alexandria: "If these writings of the Greeks agree with the Book of God, they are useless and need not be preserved; if they disagree, they are pernicious and ought to be destroyed." Useless or pernicious, irrelevant to our new freedom or else its enemy: in either case, 900 years of scholarship put to its last and best use as fuel for heating the public baths.[6] Lyotard's reasons are the inverse of the caliph's. If the writings favor God or Law or some other unifying principle, they are pernicious; if they attack such absolutes they are useless except in the moment that inspired them. In either case, libraries are irrelevant. No objective, general, enduring knowledge about the natural world and human history exists and so no books and hence no libraries are needed to preserve it. We would be better off to save the trees for shade.

Paganistic pluralism is stridently anti-intellectual, because according to Lyotard the whole point of intellectual activity is to develop hegemonic justifications:

To establish a derivation between the two [descriptives and prescriptives] is to tie in with the tradition of the intellectual, with the tradition of a form of thought that is there to try to justify imperatives whatever they may be. And the fact that they may be imperatives in keeping with dominant morality (inasmuch as there is one) or in keeping with the dominant political power, or, to the contrary, that they are oppositional imperatives, does not change one iota to the fact that this is the thinking of an intellectual, that is, of someone who is there to derive prescriptions. [JG 45]

As Toynbee notes, in sorrow and in anger, "the triumph of Futurism" comes when the heirs of the intellectual tradition of a once creative but now merely dominant minority proclaim their own mental bankruptcy by positively repudiating the cultural heritage which they have failed to defend against the futurist attack and voluntarily embracing the anti-intellectual faith which has been the deadliest weapon of their futurist assailants. [SH-6 115]

Toynbee is thinking of the fascism growing to a frenzy in Germany and Italy as he was writing, political and cultural movements adept at the uses of the hegemonic terrors of police power and propaganda to obtain a desired social consensus. But Lyotard's critique of all modes of justification that claim authority over some general range of time or territory—his critique therefore of the normativeness of reason and of tradition—leaves him with no recourse against the aggrandizement of one language game at the expense of another. Except, that is, the use of the very police power and propaganda he rightly disparages.

Lyotard is aware of this nihilistic implication in his thought, and he tries to avoid it by the notion of an "empty" transcendence. You are playing the "game of the just" when you make any moves that alter the distribution of goods and resources within a social order. You prescribe that the distribution should be thus and I counter with a different prescription. We are like opponents in a chess game, successes and failures resulting from the reiterative interaction of our competing strategies. It would be incorrect to say that your aims are just and mine unjust, or vice versa. We clash because we have two differing but equally valid viewpoints regarding how society should be ordered. We both act justly, therefore: which is to say, we join together in playing the game of the just, and in playing it we both obey its rules. The only unjust action is one that denies those rules: when one of us cuts the other off from the "possibility of continuing to play the game of the just." [JG 66].

But how do you justify your judgment that I have deliberately violated the rules of that game and so have forfeited my right to participate? How do you make your case that playing the game of the just is a condition of membership in a given society? When I do something and you call it unjust, says Lyotard, you cannot defend your judgment against such questions. Why is that unjust? I say; you are unable to answer. But nonetheless, Lyotard goes on, you think: "here I feel a prescription to oppose a given thing, and I think that it is a just one." You can provide no descriptive narrative from which to derive a justification of your feeling, but your feeling is not felt to be merely a private emotional response. You are not making a move within the game of justice but appealing instead to the conditions of the game. It is a move characteristic of transcendence. "Except," says Lyotard, "that the transcendence is empty." That is, "it does not say what it says, what it prescribes" [JG 69].

More accurately: there is no sayer who says it. The position of authoritative enunciator of the prescriptive statement directed against my praxis is "neutralized." There is no voice of God, no teaching of the ancestors, in whose name you are issuing your "thou shalt not." Nor is the prescription itself authoritative in the sense of being self-grounding, a claim the rightness of which is carried on its face, a categorical imperative embedded in your command as its necessary condition. But precisely because your statement has been stripped of all these esoteric supporting devices, I am able to feel the full force of its prescriptive character, to appreciate its prescriptiveness without being distracted by the why and wherefore of its putative justification. Yet if you are not permitted to provide authority for your claim, neither am I nor anyone else. The game of justice has no author nor any authoritative content. This lack is no accident: it is the essence of the game that no one playing it be able to assume a privileged position within it, nor that anyone not a player have standing with respect to it. In the games of the just there are no umpires.

Lyotard utilizes two other images in trying to allude to this idea of an empty transcendence. He speaks of the "horizon of justice" as the "horizon of a multiplicity or of a diversity" in contrast to the "horizon of a social totality" [JG 87]. The ideal, in other words, toward which the game of justice is oriented and in terms of which it is played is not one that values "convergence" or "congruence" but one that favors "discrepancy" instead. Its goal is openness rather than closure, ongoingness rather than completion. Its categorical imperative, were it possible to have one, would be:

"Always act in such a way that the maxim of your will may" I won't say "not be erected", but it is almost that, "into a principle of universal legislation." Into a principle of a multiplicity. [JG 94]

Lyotard's other image is of the sea, the medium linking together a myriad of islands into an "archipelago."[7] An admiral sails from island to island, proposing to the inhabitants of each some ways they might do things differently. The admiral intervenes in the practices of the island, but his intervention "hasn't any object, it has no island of its own" the benefit of which would be the purpose and hence the justification for what he does. The sea and the admiral who sails upon it are a reality transcendent to the islands, uniting them without violating their several integrities, framing and even influencing what they do but without imposing itself upon them.

It is as though our language games were a jumble of "minority groups," of "territories of language," each insisting on its ethnic irreducibility. You should deal with them under a "rule of divergence," not seeking to create a melting pot but instead letting them all flourish on the single condition that they all retain their minority status. "Every one of us belongs to several minorities, and what is very important, none of them prevails. It is only then that we can say that the society is just" [JG 95]. Should one language game attempt to prevail, to utter prescriptions that terrorize another game into submission, that claim authority over it, then the rule of justice would be interventive. It would prescribe a restoration of "purity": commanding that there be no excess, no overreaching of the authority granted each game by the rule of divergence. All the games at play within the community must be kept in their "proper" place; they must be maintained as minorities, as "different games that cannot have the value of sources of universal obligation" [JG 97]. Thus, although the rules of each game are at the will of the players, there is also a game of games that has a rule the players cannot violate.

If you listen closely to the voiceless voice of Lyotard's empty transcendental, you cannot fail to note the cadences of Jeremy Bentham. As an individual you do as your nature inclines you, and you cooperate in temporary compacts with others in order to achieve the fulfillment of your desires. You are your own best judge of pain and pleasure; there are no criteria except your own feelings to be appealed to. The greater the divergences among individuals, the more shifting their alliances, the better. Such divergence creates a pure market of interactions, and the consequence of the unfettered opportunity it permits is in the long run to the benefit of all. Government operates best where it intervenes least, except that it should apply whatever sanctions are required to assure the continued purity of the system; that is, no operation within the system may become predominant nor any enduring confederation of them. Lyotard's "patchwork" of incommensurable language games "that vibrate at all times" without being woven together into any substantive whole is the pure classical theory of the capitalist free-market economy. It is a version of the Utilitarian argument that each individual *conatus,* if prevented from violating the freedom of any other *conatus,* will eventually achieve its own happiness and thereby help to assure the greatest happiness for the greatest number.

But we have seen that Bentham's ethic presumes a genuinely neutral government, one invulnerable to control by a faction arising from those it would purport to regulate. Lyotard would reject the only form of intervention guaranteed to function in a manner absolutely neutral among the players: an Unseen Hand or Preestablished Harmony as the source of an impersonal principle of order. Consequently he has to call upon instrumentalities of enforcement. The admirals who sail the archipelago will need on occasion to call in the marines. This action then gives the admiral a stake in the islands' practices, and soon justice begins to speak in a factional accent. Its interventions cease to be disinterested; its prescriptions are soon "assisted by the sword." Futurism like archaism not only fails to prevent the disintegration of societal accomplishment, it hastens it. Anarchy is always and inevitably the parent of tyranny.

Confronted by such frightening alternatives, the one remaining viable response would seem to be "detachment." Lyotard admits as much: the "bad side of the pagan line I am trying to trace" is the danger of falling back into "indifferentism" [JG 96]. Faced by a pluralism without purpose, the meaningless back and forth of a social order sliding toward the war of all against all or stumbling into the submission of all to a few or to one, you would be sensible to withdraw your commitment to the games of life. Detachment, says Toynbee, "is a way that leads out of This World; its goal is an asylum" [SH-5 394]. We try to detach ourselves from the endless and seemingly hopeless struggle required to achieve an ideal, to sustain a character, to devise an atoning praxis, to rule an empire, to rise up against oppression, to usher in the classless society or the kingdom of ends. Toynbee's exemplars are Lucretius and A. E. Housman, and expressions of the disengagement from worldly concerns found in such attitudes as Stoic "invulnerability," Epicurean "imperturbability," or Buddhist "Nirvana."

Or, as Macbeth mused:

> Tomorrow and tomorrow and tomorrow
> Creeps in this petty pace from day to day
> To the last syllable of recorded time;
> And all our yesterdays have lighted fools
> The way to dusty Death. Out, out, brief candle!
> Life's but a walking shadow, a poor player
> That struts and frets his hour upon the stage
> And then is heard no more: it is a tale
> Told by an idiot, full of sound and fury,
> Signifying nothing.[8]

The game of the just has been judged to be a game of fools and its players creatures of self-delusion. The storyteller has become a pathetic

voice reduced to mumbling incomprehensible nonsense, and the pathway into the bright hope of our tomorrows turns out to lead on only to dusty death. Macbeth had been an active player in the game of the just. His moves, however, had been terroristic and those who countered with antagonistic strategies have managed to prevail over him. His speech is thus understandably filled with regret and bitterness. But he is striving for a properly detached stance, one that has overcome his remaining nostalgia for ultimate meaning, for metanarratives that promise the world-historical significance of human praxis.

John Caputo points out that Martin Heidegger is usually counted among the bards whose stories make totalizing claims, except that whereas our inquiry has focused on those who find the key to their story in its ending, Heidegger finds that key in its beginning. Caputo writes an essay entitled "Demythologizing Heidegger" because he doubts the veracity of Heidegger's story.[9] This tale is about how a primordial, pre-Platonic, awareness of truth was the disclosure of Being and about how it was distorted, covered over, made over into a notion of truth as correctness and Being as a generic label for the collection of beings that compose reality. But, argues Caputo, there is no genuinely historical evidence to support this account of things. Heidegger has made up an interesting story, presumably motivated by the belief that his discovery of the difference between an adequate and an inadequate awareness of reality requires some sort of historical explanation of how the latter awareness came to be the ascendant one. Heidegger has provided "a myth of origins, of a great beginning, of a great founding act back at the beginning of the tradition, which gives flesh and blood—mythic form—to a philosophical insight" [DH 535]. But this is merely an "a priori history," a "marvelous yarn," a "mythological gesture."

Heidegger's insight must be demythologized, purged of its mythic overlay, its metanarrative. We must renounce the narrative ploy, become indifferent to its allure, and articulate in its stead a "more austere, more radicalized" account of reality. Indeed, says Caputo, this is precisely what Heidegger himself has done in his later writings: overcome his own earlier surrender to narrational temptation. More fundamental than Being, more fundamental than the beings and *Dasein* that it discloses, is the making present of that Being and its disclosures. This that grants, that unconceals Being, is itself concealed by that very granting. It is *a-letheia*, an unconcealing power not identifiable with any particular moment of the unconcealing of Being it effects. It is that of which these moments are modes.

The history of the West is the history of successive epochs of Being and presence and *a-letheia* is the element within which that history unfolds, the open space in which a clearing is made for the various epochs of presence—from Anaximander to the present. But *a-letheia*, in virtue of its very structure as *a-letheia*, remains out of sight, and is in a certain way always overlooked—even as it is implicitly at work, functioning. [DH 533]

The mistake is in presuming that any one of these "epochs of presence" is in a privileged position with respect to that which discloses it. Not the early Greeks because they were the first to become aware of Being, nor some eschatological generation because they are to be the culminating perfect awareness of Being. Both the Alpha of Being, if there was one, and the Omega, should there be such, are only modes of Being, two among the indefinite number that have and will or might appear insofar as what gives them manifestation continues to be at work. "The truth of Being is the delimitation of truth and the proliferation of truths across the epochs" [DH 538]. Each epoch is a unique disclosure of Being, different in its content but equivalent to all the others in its epochal structure. There can be no hierarchy of the epochs, no making one absolute or ranking them from best to worst. They are incommensurable worlds. Each has its own "transient authority" and no more. There is, in short, no "master name" for Being. Heidegger, says Caputo, is "engaged in underlining the historical contingency and dissolubility of all the master names for Being which have been forthcoming in the history of the West" [DH 540].

For Caputo's Heidegger, justice, *dike*, is the one overarching rule that the succeeding epochs must obey. In Lyotard's game of the just this rule functioned as an umpire, assuring the players that the limits of the game would not be breached by someone hoping to gain an unfair advantage by becoming an exception to the rule. But for *dike* the players are not individuals. They are the epochs themselves, the language games and not the persons playing them. Fairness is assured by preventing any epoch from lingering beyond its allotted span. "The epochs of presence are but temporary ways of filling the clearing with the brush strokes of presence, subject to the *dike* which finally commits it back to the flux" [DH 540–41]. Heidegger is thus made to speak like Spengler, for whom cultures arise one after the other out of the fecundity of a Power that is only present through its modalities. Each culture has an epochal structure that it lives out in its own distinctive way, the Apollonian no better nor any worse than the Magian or the Faustian. And each culture after flourishing for a time becomes a civiliza-

tion, transmutes its dynamic qualities into rigid formalities, and suffers the deathblow of *dike* so that a new and different culture might then be disclosed.[10]

The task of the philosopher, says Caputo, your task and mine, is to do whatever we can to undermine those understandings that becloud this view of history by attempting to render absolute an epoch or an interpretation. The "violence of hierarchy" and the "idols of presence" must be combated by being exposed for what they are, "contingent and mutable structures which metaphysics stretches across the abyss" [DH 546]. Stripped of their pretensions, of the false authority to which they lay claim, these myths, these metanarratives and hegemonic practices, lose their bewitching power.

Caputo thus employs the same strategy used by Descartes: he does violence to hierarchy by denuding reality of its gradations of importance.[11] Some of these gradations may well be arbitrary and repressive, but others might be expressions of natural internal relationships or of historical, enduring stabilities. Caputo and Descartes turn a deaf ear to such pleas, however, prejudging them to be idolatrous. Everything is put in doubt; everything is reduced to the same flat plain of insignificance. Relationships are only external, contingent creations of a subject and not essential aspects of its organic complexity. Descartes speaks of ideas, Caputo of epochs. Descartes's approach ends up in solipsism of the present moment and a Hobbesian state of nature; Caputo's approach ends up with self-contained epochs and an anarchic history in which they are related only through a common remorseless fate.

The purpose of the demythologizing of praxis, argues Caputo, is in order to "preserve and shelter the mystery of what withdraws, of the clearing which, while itself never named, is that which grants the names of presence" [DH 540]. It is "to shelter what withdraws and to preserve it in the mystery of its play" [DH 546]. Caputo invites us

into the place of the unfolding of the play, of the rising up and passing away of the epochs. There remain only the coming-to-be and passing away of the epochal formations.... Here the only *arche* is a child-king who rules without why. It plays because it plays, Heidegger says, without ground and without why. [DH 545]

Macbeth was correct, it would seem, although according to Heidegger and Caputo the teller of our tale is not an idiot but a child. The stories it tells have a very simple plot. The sounds and fury made by you and me, made by any of us as we strut and fret our hour upon the stage, signify some epochal coming-to-be and then its passing away. The child plays for a moment with one of these epochs, unfolds its distinctive shadow-plot for no reason except the doing, then casts it aside and unfolds another one, and thusly and thusly to the last syllable of recorded time.

We are supposed to find this an edifying spectacle. It is to be our highest wisdom: knowing ourselves to be the whimsical playthings of a king who rules over us for no reason at all. The truth of Being, it would seem, is calmly, in detachment and resignation, to acknowledge that:

> We are no other than a moving row
> Of Magic Shadow-shapes that come and go
>    Round with the Sun-illumined Lantern held
> In Midnight by the Master of the Show;

> But helpless Pieces of the Game He plays
> Upon this Chequer-board of Nights and Days;
>    Hither and thither moves and checks, and slays,
> And one by one back in the Closet lays.[12]

The poetry is glorious and the stoicism ennobling, but the way of detachment, says Toynbee, is ultimately "self-stultifying." It offers no solution to the problem of a decaying civilization, to a loss of conviction that there are ideals worth struggling to realize. Its only recommendation invites us to indulge the very skepticism that is the bane of any possible remedy. Toynbee, therefore, proposes one final mode of response, which he calls "transfiguration." He means by this a rekindled conviction in values that are integrative and perfecting, and that express themselves in the creation of something better than the beliefs and practices currently in disarray. But all Toynbee can come up with is a version of the old, anemic idea of the Kingdom of God realized in the hearts of everyone.

You and I began our conversation wondering how we best might weave a story for our lives that would realize in its telling as well as in its end our most important aspirations. You will recall how natural it seemed to turn to others and involve them in our inquiry. Your concerns had been essentially the same as mine; they were in some fundamental sense the concerns that any human being would have. The voices in our conversation grew in number and in diversity. We were pleased to find ourselves with so many friends to help us, but we were often overwhelmed by the bewildering variety of the tales we heard from them about what had been done or what we would be well ad-

vised to do. Our conversation began as a tête-à-tête but soon seemed
more like a gathering of the clan. The intimate accounts of our personal
adventures mushroomed into epic narratives and histories of global
significance.

We puzzled over who each of us really was and what our situation
was like; we wondered how that situation might be improved and what
sort of person we could each become; we wrestled with the question
of how best we might individually or together accomplish such a transformation; we questioned one another's motives and pried into each
other's dedication to the task. It was natural for us to do so, we realized, for it was our nature to think and act in terms of origins and
endings, of methods and motives. The nature of praxis was our human
nature, and its fourfold structure was thus manifest wherever we were
being human in the world amid the ongoing course of things.

You did not hesitate, nor I, to engage ourselves fully with our inter-
locutors, to wonder with them, to puzzle and wrestle and query and
pry with them regarding the most appropriate answer to our question,
the truest way to tell the story of our lives. With praxis as our model
we were confident that the process of inquiry would come to some
eventual resolution. All adventures begin somewhere with some end in
view and somehow arrive eventually at somewhere else, even if it was
not where or what they had originally intended. But we were optimistic enough to think that the more carefully we listened to what others
had to say, the more likely the endpoint of our venture would be a
place well worth the effort required to reach it. We were confident that
thought and practice were, both separately and conjunctively, dialogi-
cal. They fed on the contributions of others; the cacophony, if dealt
with sensitively and imaginatively, would almost certainly have a
worthwhile yield. An appreciative and critical appropriation of the past
meant unavoidable present conflict, but such would be the way that
leads through atonement and reconciliation to the realization of an improved future. A dialectic of human conversation was, we were sure,
the driving force of individual fulfillment and social progress.

Our journey was an arduous one, you will admit. But our confidence
only grew stronger as we found ourselves driven on from each apparent goal we had attained to another whose new vantage point seemed
far more adequate. Our story was a *Bildungsroman,* a developmental
tale of the progress of our moral sensibility from childish, narrow-
visioned egoism to the mature embrace of a boundless community. As
we progressed along our route, the voices in our conversation became
less and less advisory comments from the outside; more and more they
were the voices of our comrades, our own speech echoed and echoing

in the voices of all humanity. Our several praxes, we came to realize, had a common destiny. It was the nature of praxis that it achieve the final reconciliation of all its instances in an ultimate realized totality, that the many voices become one voice, the many stories a single history.

But there was something fabulous about this account of where we had come and where we might be headed. It seemed contradictory to the very nature of praxis that it should have a totalizing destiny. The objective situation in which we found ourselves did not bear out the claim that some ultimate unity was near at hand or even well on the way toward being realized. Our purposes seemed intractably incommensurable. Our strategies seemed far too vulnerable to misuse, serving again and again to exacerbate rather than mediate conflicting purposes. Our confidences were waning instead of waxing. Toynbee's model of an age of civilizational breakdown and collapse seemed to provide a devastatingly relevant analysis of our world.

And so the threads of our common tale began to unravel. We came to the conclusion that we do not argue and compromise in order that there might emerge a clear and accurate articulation of who we are and what we ought someday to become. Our conversation is all there is. In talking we create ourselves, stipulate the conditions of our communality and then build generation after generation our own sense of shared significance. Soon we were questioning the validity of even this. Our storytelling was not taken to be the way we make rules governing the world in which we dwell but rather as the way we rationalize, after the fact, our world-makings. Yet there are as many ways to tell that tale as there are standpoints from which to tell it, nor can the voice of the activist be slighted, nor favored, over that of the reflective interpreter. Our conversations were breaking up into huddles of the like-minded, sameness replacing difference as a value within any particular group at the same time as it was celebrated as the sole value governing the relationship among groups. A plurality of separated cliques was replacing a plurality of interacting perspectives as the highest good. Our conversations had once more become tête-à-têtes, our community a gigantic cocktail party of a thousand unrelated, unrelatable confabulations.

The outcome could be foreseen; the logical consequence of the unravelling was predictable. We came in the end to vaudeville, to a sequence of single acts, each spinning its own tale, narrating its own beginning, middle, and end, strutting its wares upon the stage of history until forced to make way for the next activity. The pageantry of it all, we were sure, was organized by an unknown impresario: not for our momentary edification, nor for reasons beyond our poor powers to comprehend, but for no reason at all. The single acts in this endless pageant we took to be whole historical epochs, but they could just as well have been solo voices. Mine, yours; each in our turn.

First me, now you. Strutting out there all alone, each of us conversing only with ourself. Shouting out our private, cherished story. Bravely, boldly, shouting it into the night. Hoping that we might be heard over the wind that blows toward us steadily, indifferently, from off the darkling plain of time.

# CODA[1]

Look at this mess! Such a shame, isn't it? We promised we'd do
something about it. We said we would definitely repair the dikes and
clear out the wells. We asked them to believe us, that the raw sewage
could be treated and the dumping stopped. But as far as I can tell it's
been all talk. We've only made things worse, I'd guess. Well, don't lecture me about it; don't lecture me. You're right, the place has gone
from bad to worse. It's nothing more than a wasteland now. So I suppose it's not likely you'll be wanting to build here after all. Can't say I
blame you.

But look who I see. Over there. There, down by the water's edge.
That old fellow, the fisher king. I take it you've tried to talk with him.
He never seems to have much to say. Just sits there all the time. It looks
like he's fishing, but what's he fishing for? He never seems to catch a
thing. He seems, in fact, to spend most of his time gazing out across the
sea. Looking for his ship to come in, do you suppose? Perhaps. Yes,
that's it; perhaps he's expecting something. Or maybe not. Maybe he's
looking for his ship to go out instead. I mean, suppose he wants to go
somewhere. Suppose he's longing for some distant shore, for the place
where he was born or the place where he will die. His place of memories or his place of hope. Do you ever wonder why he waits and why
he fishes? Do you ever wonder that?

Here, put it there right next to him. Alongside those fragments that
look to me like something he brought with him into this ruined land
of ours, this swamp of our desolation. Put it there, alongside those
ancient, rusting assurances of an impending spring, and right beside
the utopian stories I left for him to read. Add this further thought. The

297

thought of Ithaca, of home. No, not first of all nor most importantly, not Ithaca of blessed memory, our place of birth, the whence by which we live. And no, not last of all nor most realized, not Ithaca of our desires, our destination and our destiny, the thence by which we live. But Ithaca our home. Its shores, its hills, the now of it. Put that thought there, beside his wounded side.

A philosopher named Wittgenstein once looked at our language and saw it was an ancient city. He pictured a bunch of twisted, narrow lanes running in and out of crowded piazzas, begun long ago, built up and torn down, remodeled and restored, changed a thousand times but remaining through it all a city, a place where people dwell. At the edges of the city the newer neighborhoods, the surrounding suburbs with boulevards straight as measuring sticks and houses freshly painted, full of all the more recent conveniences. He saw it was our city, this language surrounding us, our home. We know the trick of negotiating its unmarked curving roads; and we can find our way around the crisp gridwork of its vast uniformities. Even when the place we are is unfamiliar and we have lost our way, we know the place of which it is a part. We know that any way we turn, any place we look, there will be people who know the way, whom we can ask for help. We know that this is no empty wilderness through which we stumble confusedly. It is our home; our way, our life, our truth.

We are a city to our cells, and some part of us is simply patterns replicated a billion-fold while some part of us is convoluted, involuted, unique and irreplaceable, a labyrinth of obscure side streets and quiet neighborhoods that seem far older than the self who is their home. Our cells are cities too, and the alleys and avenues constringe to molecules of immense complexity. But so are we cells for cities sprawling outward to the stars. All of them are languages in which we dwell, patterns by which we live and which are lived through us.

There, put that down, these thoughts of Ithaca. And then despair of this wasteland, this ruined city that never was nor could ever be. Poor blind Tiresias. If he could only see what we can see, would he still sit there, patiently fishing in the sea?

# Abbreviations

[This is an alphabetical list of works referred to in the text by abbreviation; see *Works Cited* section for full bibliographical information]

AI      Alfred North Whitehead, *Adventures of Ideas*
AL      Erich Fromm, *The Art of Loving*
API     John Fiske, *American Political Ideas*
BN      Jean-Paul Sartre, *Being and Nothingness*
CDR     Jean-Paul Sartre, *Critique of Dialectical Reason*
CF      John Dewey, *A Common Faith*
CG      Augustine, *The City of God*
CJ      Immanuel Kant, *Critique of Judgment*
CL      Walter Miller, *A Canticle for Leibowitz*
D       Niccolò Machiavelli, *Discourses*
DH      John D. Caputo, "Demythologizing Heidegger"
E       Jean-Paul Sartre, "Existentialism"
E/O     Søren Kierkegaard, *Either/Or*
EAE     Donald Davidson, *Essays on Actions and Events*
EHR     Gotthold Lessing, *The Education of the Human Race*
EN      Aristotle, *Ethica Nicomachea* (Nicomachian Ethics)
FBM     John Foxe, *The Acts and Monuments of John Foxe*
GMM     Immanuel Kant, *Grounding for the Metaphysics of Morals*
GT      George Santayana, "The Genteel Tradition in American Philosophy"
HAL     Charles Taylor, *Human Agency and Language*
HC      Michael Oakeshott, *On Human Conduct*

HNC    John Dewey, *Human Nature and Conduct*
HP     Samuel Purchas, *Hakluytus Posthumus*, 20 vol.
HRCP  Immanuel Kant, "Is the Human Race Consistently Progressing?"
IO      Charles Hartshorne, *Insights and Oversights of Great Thinkers*
IP      George Allan, *The Importances of the Past*
IUH   Immanuel Kant, "Idea for a Universal History"
JF      *Joachim of Fiore: A Study in Spiritual Perception and History*
JG     Jean-François Lyotard, *Just Gaming*
KPP   Hannah Arendt, *Lectures on Kant's Political Philosophy*
LTI    John Dewey, *Logic: The Theory of Inquiry*
M      Ibn Khaldûn, *The Maquaddimah*
OCP   John Fiske, *Outlines of Cosmic Philosophy*, 4 vol.
PC     Jean-François Lyotard, *The Postmodern Condition*
PH     G. W. F. Hegel, *The Philosophy of History*
PHP   Samuel Purchas, *Purchas His Pilgrimage*
PM    Pierre Teilhard de Chardin, *The Phenomenon of Man*
PML   Jeremy Bentham, *Principles of Morals and Legislation*
PN     Richard Hakluyt, *The Principal Navigations*, 12 vol.
PNK   Susanne Langer, *Philosophy in a New Key*
POC   Josiah Royce, *The Problem of Christianity*, 2 vol.
PR     Alfred North Whitehead, *Process and Reality*
QC     John Dewey, *The Quest for Certainty*
RT     Errol Harris, *The Reality of Time*
SAP    Mircea Eliade, *The Sacred and the Profane*
SG     Bernard Loomer, "The Size of God"
SH     Arnold Toynbee, *A Study of History*, 12 vol.
SHG   Henry Nelson Wieman, *The Source of Human Good*
SP     Sandra Rosenthal, *Speculative Pragmatism*
U      John Stuart Mill, *Utilitarianism*
WB    William James, "The Will to Believe"

# NOTES

## Chapter One

1. This is the burden of my argument in *The Importances of the Past*.

2. The Greek and Marxist meanings of "praxis" that I briefly mention here are explicated within their historical contexts in Nicholas Lobkowicz, *Theory and Practice: History of a Concept from Aristotle to Marx* (Notre Dame: University of Notre Dame Press, 1967). See especially pp. 9–15 regarding Greek meanings, and pp. 419–22 for his best summary of Marx's meanings. See also David Hall, *Eros and Irony* (Albany: State University of New York Press, 1982) for an interpretation of the relation between *theoria* and *praxis* that differs from mine in subtle but important ways.

3. See H. H. Joachim, *Aristotle: The Nicomachean Ethics: A Commentary* (Oxford: Clarendon Press, 1951), pp. 188–89.

4. Marion Leathers Kuntz and Paul Grimley Kuntz, "Naming the Categories," *Journal of Speculative Philosophy* 2:30–47 (1988). The professors Kuntz call this the W.H.Y. method. Their claim that both Aristotle and Whitehead use categories as tools of interrogation, "the interrogative-pronominal-adverbial method," is taken from John Herman Randall, Jr., *Aristotle* (New York: Columbia University Press, 1960), pp. 123–29; this method has influenced the strategy of this whole chapter. Aristotle's discussion of the four causes is somewhat elusive; the primary texts are *Metaphysics* A.3 983a24–983b6 and *Physics* II.3,7 194b16–195b30, 198a14–198b9.

5. Clifford Geertz, *The Interpretation of Cultures* (New York: Basic Books, 1973), especially chap. 1: "Thick Description: Toward an Interpretive Theory of Culture."

6. This last point is nicely developed by Vincent M. Colapietro in an essay that makes creative use of some ideas in Dewey and Peirce: "Human Agency: The Habits of Our Being," *Southern Journal of Philosophy* 26:153–68 (1988).

"Reflective power," the power of the self over itself, needs to be complemented by "receptive power," the power of the self to be open to the other. Colapietro takes this especially to mean openness to what is other than the given, i.e., to ideals.

7. Jürgen Habermas, *The Theory of Communicative Action*, vol. 1: *Reason and the Rationalization of Society* (Boston: Beacon Press, 1984 [1981], pp. 335, 336.

## Chapter Two

1. Ernst Zeller, *The Stoics, Epicureans and Sceptics*, trans. Oswald J. Reichel (New York: Russell & Russell, 1962 [1879]), p. 502.

2. This interpretation is not quite accurate, according to Sandra Rosenthal [SP 178–83]. In the course of her explication of Dewey, she distinguishes "de facto terminal value" from "de facto fulfillment value" and "objective value" from "de jure value." I agree, but find this an unnecessarily fine mesh for the purpose at hand. My cruder analysis is a reasonable first approximation.

3. Mozart, *Don Giovanni*, Leporello's list aria, Act I, scene 5.

4. William James, *Pragmatism*, Lecture II: "What Pragmatism Means" (Cambridge: Harvard University Press, 1975 [1907]), p. 37.

5. Friedrich Nietzsche, *On the Genealogy of Morals*, trans. Walter Kauffman (New York: Vintage Books, 1967 [1887]); I, section 13.

6. Garrett Hardin, "Lifeboat Ethics: The Case Against Helping the Poor", *Psychology Today* 8:38–43, 123–26 (1974). The quote is from a reprint in William Aiken and Hugh La Follette, eds., *World Hunger and Moral Obligation* (Englewood Cliffs N.J.: Prentice-Hall, 1977), p. 21.

7. René Descartes, *Meditations on First Philosophy*, trans. Laurence J. Lafleur (Indianapolis: Bobbs-Merrill Co., 1951 [1641]); section 4, p. 55.

8. I am using the New English Bible translation for all citations. In this instance, I have followed the alternate translation of the last phrase.

9. D. T. Suzuki, *Zen Buddhism* (Garden City: Doubleday Anchor, 1956), p. 241.

10. Quoted in D. T. Suzuki, *Zen Buddhism*, p. 24.

## Chapter Three

1. In Aristotle's time Athenian citizenship was limited to 28,000 adult males. Assume a wife and two children for each household, and four servants. These plus a few resident aliens comprised a total population of 258,000. The adult males thus made up a scant one-ninth of the whole. My data are from the Oswald translation of *Nicomachean Ethics*, note 35 in Book IX (pp. 267–68).

2. Thomas Hobbes, *Leviathan: Or the Matter, Forme and Power of a Commonwealth Ecclesiasticall and Civil* (New York: Collier Books, 1962) [1651]); II.17, pp. 129, 132.

3. Sartre's term for the act or reality of this affirmation is *le serment*, which Sheridan-Smith translates as "pledge." I prefer a somewhat freer translation in

order to season the term's drab legal connotations with the spice of religious apocalyptic intensity. Borrowing the Puritan notion of a pledge that creates a relationship which has absolute authority over those who have committed themselves to it, I will tend to speak of making a "covenant."

4. Ibn Khaldûn was a fourteenth-century Islamic diplomat in northwest Africa and eventually a professor and judge in Cairo. Our inquiry draws from the *Maquaddimah*, which is an introduction to the *Kitâb al-'Ibar*, his universal history of the world.

## Chapter Four

1. Martin Oswald is typical of Aristotelian scholars in distinguishing "*eudaimon*" from "*makarios*": "happy" from "blessed." The latter term, says Oswald, describes "happiness insofar as it is god-given, while the latter describes happiness as attained by man through his own efforts" [p. 18, note 32 of Oswald's translation of *Nicomachean Ethics*]. My point could thus be made by saying that the development of a good character is what makes a person's life happy, that it might be more than that, that it might come to be crowned with blessedness as well, is greatly to be desired but not necessary to one's life being fully virtuous. Martha Nussbaum is *The Fragility of Goodness* (Cambridge: Cambridge University Press, 1986), however, argues that Aristotle intends no such distinction and sees happiness or blessedness as always involving an element of risk [e.g., chap. 11: p. 340].

2. The notion of an enduring self that I am developing here has affinities to, and is in part influenced by, Robert Cummings Neville's notion of "discursive harmonies" and "discursive individuals." See *The Puritan Smile* (Albany: State University of New York Press, 1987), pp. 122–35; the notion is developed much more fully in his *Recovering the Measure* (Albany: State University of New York Press, 1989).

3. George R. Lucas, Jr., "Agency After Virtue," *International Philosophical Quarterly* 28:293–311 (1988). See Lucas's related arguments in "Moral Order and the Constraints of Agency: Toward a New Metaphysics of Morals," *New Essays in Metaphysics*, ed. Robert C. Neville (Albany: State University of New York Press, 1987), pp. 117–39.

4. Lucas, "Agency After Virtue," p. 303.

5. Jean-Paul Sartre, *No Exit and Three Other Plays* (New York: Random House, 1955). Obviously, this volume also includes *No Exit* to which I will allude shortly.

6. This implies a commitment to "moderate realism" with respect to the nature of universals. See the perceptive defense of this against its alternatives, ancient and contemporary, in Donald W. Mertz, "Particularism, Exemplification, and Bradley's Regress," *Journal of Speculative Philosophy* 1:177–205 (1987). Whitehead's distinction between Creativity and actual entities implies a similar commitment.

7. John Rawls, *A Theory of Justice* (Cambridge: Cambridge University Press, 1971).

## Chapter Five

1. I have not consulted the primary unpublished texts and drawings except as they are partially reproduced in Delno C. West and Sandra Zimdars-Swartz, *Joachim of Fiore: A Study in Spiritual Perception and History* (Bloomington: Indiana University Press, 1963).

2. Nancy Frankenberry in *Religion and Radical Empiricism* (Albany: State University of New York Press, 1987) makes a telling critique of Wieman's claim that the reality of the creative event can be proven empirically. Using Hempel's arguments about the validation of scientific hypotheses, she shows that Wieman commits a "functionalist fallacy" in claiming that what functions in human experience in creatively transformative ways must be a distinctive reality and, because that is how a divine reality functions, can legitimately be called God [pp. 124–26]. This is more or less the Aristotelian fallacy of affirming the consequent: if there is divine power, it would function in creatively transforming ways; such creativity is found in human life, therefore there is a divine power at work. Frankenberry's discussion of Wieman, along with two other theistically inclined radical empiricists (Meland, Loomer), is an especially valuable part [chap. 4] of her fine book.

3. William James, "What Makes a Life Significant," from *The Will to Believe and Other Essays*, published in *Pragmatism and Other Essays* (New York: Washington Square Press, 1964 [1896]). James could castigate Lake Chautauqua's inspirational lectures as "too tame," the "culture too second-rate," and praise instead "human nature *in extremis*" and other ideals that require "fidelity, courage, and endurance" to actualize. But James was a staunch opponent of "such outbursts of the passion of mastery" as the Spanish-American War. As we shall see, the distinction is difficult to maintain.

4. Royce cannot resist the temptation to do as Kant did and give a sign. Royce notes that scientists are very successful at coming up with hypotheses that resist experimental falsification. Indeed the ratio of successful to failed hypotheses is immensely greater than the statistical probabilities would have predicted. Hence human interpretive powers must be well suited to their task of weaving coherent, comprehensive understandings [POC-2 394–418]. This "fit" of the human mind with what it interprets is very like the fit Kant sees between our spontaneous emotions and the practical good inherent in the world. It is as though they were cast against type: Royce chooses something rational as his sign, Kant choosing something emotional. Royce's sign, nonetheless, is no less problematic than Kant's.

## Chapter Six

1. This way of phrasing what I take to be the aim of Hegelian metaphysics shows its interesting affinity to the recent work of Robert Cummings Neville: to some degree his arguments in *Reconstruction of Thinking* (Albany: State University of New York Press, 1981); but more clearly in *Recovering the Mea-*

*sure* (Albany: State University of New York Press, 1989). Given how this chapter will develop, it is not surprising that another of Neville's books, closely related to this last one, is *The Puritan Smile* (Albany: State University of New York Press, 1987). How Neville's notions of self, cosmos, and the nested harmonies relating them differ from my own views is a task to which I will turn in the sequel to this book.

2. Harry Brod, for instance, calls it a "Kantian reading of Hegel" [148] for Richard Dien Winfield to reject the notion of deducing "particular events from the requirements of what must occur if justice is to come into being," as well as to reject "an interpretative application of philosophical concepts to facts that must be experienced and related to be known." Winfield argues that it is beyond the scope of philosophy to do so. He substitutes the claim that "no matter where we stand in the order of events, we have the opportunity of redeeming the transience of our practice by enacting the timeless conventions of justice" [142, 143]. See Winfield, "The Theory and Practice of the History of Freedom," and Brod's "Comment"; both in Robert L. Perkins, ed., *History and System: Hegel's Philosophy of History* (Albany: State University of New York Press, 1984), pp. 123–44 and 145–48. Klaus Hartmann is even more explicitly taking a Kantian tack by arguing that "Hegel's philosophy constitutes a developed form of *ontology* or a *theory of categories*" [70], and thus that "a move from one category to the next is *not* to be construed *genetically* or in such a way that, in time, and with mounting complexity, items take on a novel determination" [72]. See his "Types of Explanation in Hegel and Whitehead" in George R. Lucas, Jr., ed., *Hegel and Whitehead* (Albany: State University of New York Press, 1986), pp. 61–85.

3. Hegel says this explicitly in his "Preface" to *The Philosophy of Right* (trans. T. M. Knox; Oxford: Clarendon Press, 1942 [1820]): "Whatever happens, every individual is a child of his time; so philosophy too is its own time apprehended in thoughts. It is just as absurd to fancy that a philosophy can transcend its contemporary world as it is to fancy that an individual can overleap his own age, jump over Rhodes" [p. 11].

4. From "The pollicy of keeping the Sea", found in Richard Hakluyt, *Principal Navigations*, vol. 2, pp. 115, 144. The 1598–1600 edition of Hakluyt's work is reprinted in 12 volumes by James MacLehose and Sons, Glasgow, 1903–1905. Purchas's *Hakluytus Posthumus* appears in the same series as vols. 14–33; his earlier *Purchas His Pilgrimage* is available, as far as I can discover, only in seventeenth-century editions. These two collectors of English and European exploration accounts provide the basic information for this first part of an extended argument about the English-speaking peoples, which will compose the remainder of this chapter. In developing this portion of my argument I have, in addition to reading Hakluyt and Purchas, drawn from the following secondary sources: Louis B. Wright, *Religion and Empire: the Alliance between Piety and Commerce in English Expansion 1558–1625* (Chapel Hill: University of North Carolina Press, 1943); George B. Parks, *Richard Hakluyt and the English Voyages* (New York: Unger, 1961 [1928]); Edward Lynam, ed., *Richard Hakluyt and His Successors* (London: Hakluyt Society, 1946), especially J. A. William-

son's opening essay, "Richard Hakluyt"; and Walter Raleigh, "The English Voyages of the Sixteenth Century," in the MacLehose edition of Hakluyt's *Principal Navigations*, vol. 12, pp. 1–120. Ernest Lee Tuvenson, *Redeemer Nation: The Idea of America's Millennial Role* (Chicago: University of Chicago Press, 1963), is relevant not only here but for the topics discussed throughout the remainder of this chapter.

5. My quotations are from the eighth edition, published 1583, but volume and page references are to the more accessible 1848 edition, FBM, which has modernized the spelling. Most recent publications of Foxe truncate the contents, leaving out most of the history and concentrating on the stories of the sixteenth-century martyrs. In addition to Foxe, I have also been helped by William Haller, *Foxe's Book of Martyrs and the Elect Nation* (London: Jonathan Cape, 1963).

6. This link of poetry and exploration is argued with a lavish use of literary examples, especially from Shakespeare, in Walter Raleigh, "The English Voyages of the Sixteenth Century." He quotes on pp. 106–7 from Christopher Marlowe's 1588 play, *Tamburlaine*, part II, act V, scene ii; I have excerpted lines 123–25, 145–50, 159–60, restoring Marlowe's original spelling.

7. The interpretation of the transformation in Puritan mission is based on Perry Miller's arguments in *Errand into the Wilderness* (Cambridge, Mass.: Belknap Press, 1956). The "doubtless apocryphal" Milford town meeting is reported in Louis B. Wright, *Religion and Empire*, p. 158. I have also relied on William Haller, *The Rise of Puritanism* (New York: Columbia University Press, 1938); Edward S. Morgan, *Visible Saints: The History of a Puritan Idea* (New York: New York University Press, 1963); Alan Simpson, *Puritanism in Old and New England* (Chicago: University of Chicago Press, 1955); and Roderick Nash, *Wilderness and the American Mind* (New Haven: Yale University Press, 1967).

8. Nor would Hegel have been surprised; see PH 80–87. "America is therefore the land of the future, where, in the ages that lie before us, the burden of the World's History shall reveal itself" [PH 86].

9. Stephen Jay Gould in *The Mismeasure of Man* (New York: W. W. Norton, 1981), chaps. 2–3, discusses the "craniometry" underlying these arguments about the inferiority of the nonwhite races. Gould repeated some of the experiments, using the same skulls used by Broca and others in arriving at their racial averages, with quite different results. There is simply no correlation between brain size and racial or cultural background. Nor does brain size correlate with intelligence.

10. Washington Gladden, *The Nation and the Kingdom: Annual Sermon Before the American Board of Commissioners for Foreign Missions*, Boston, 1909; selections published in Conrad Cherry, ed., *God's New Israel: Religious Interpretations of American Destiny* (Englewood Cliffs, N.J.: Prentice-Hall, 1971), pp. 256, 257, 264.

11. Albert J. Beveridge, "Grant, the Practical," pp. 37–43 in *The Meaning of the Times and Other Speeches* (Indianapolis: Bobbs-Merrill, 1908); excerpts from pp. 43, 44, 46. The subsequent quote is on p. 142 from "The Star of Empire," pp. 118–43 in the same volume.

12. Reinhold Niebuhr's statements are taken from an article in *Christianity and Crisis*, 4 October 1943; reprinted in Conrad Cherry, *God's New Israel*, pp. 303–8.

13. This quote from Romans 8:22 is taken from the Geneva Bible. The gloss on this text is: "if the rest of the world looke for a restoring, groning as it were for it, and that not in vaine, let it not grieve us also to sigh, yea, let us be more certainely perswaded of our redemption to come, forasmuch as we have the first fruits of the Spirit." This translation of scripture, or the later one commissioned by the first Stuart, was always carried on English ships, both of commerce and of war, during the sixteenth and seventeenth centuries. And the Bible was almost always accompanied by Hakluyt's and Foxe's volumes. The popularity of these three accounts of Providence at work in history is both cause and effect of their English readers' sense of English destiny. See IP, the last two pages, for the enigmatic allusion explicated by this chapter.

# Chapter Seven

1. William James, "The Moral Philosopher and the Moral Life," *Pragmatism and Other Essays* (New York: Washington Square Press, 1963 [1891]), p. 217. This idea of the scapegoat whose suffering brings everyone else happiness has many literary expressions, but none more pithy than Ursula K. LeGuin's marvelous science-fiction short story, "The Ones Who Walk Away From Omelas," in *The Wind's Twelve Quarters* (New York: Harper & Row, 1976), pp. 251–59.

2. In a response to Loomer, Delwin Brown notes three sorts of ambiguity: ambiguities of condition, of character, and of intention. I am exploiting his analysis in what follows by mapping these onto the four-cause structure of praxis. Brown's essay, "The Ambiguity of Ambiguity," is found in SG, pp. 56–58.

3. Nancy Frankenberry, "Taking Measure of 'The Size of God' ", p. 83; her essay is in SG, pp. 77–84.

4. David Hall, *The Civilization of Experience: A Whiteheadian Theory of Culture* (New York: Fordham University Press, 1973), is still the best exploration of Whitehead's views about the nature, workings, and value of culture. Hall tends, however, like Hartshorne, to conflate the experience of Peace with the hope for objective immortality.

5. Charles Hartshorne, *Creativity in American Philosophy* (Albany: State University of New York Press, 1983), p. 94. Hartshorne's views on God as preserver of created value are fairly consistent throughout his long career. My comments are taken in part from my interpretive essay on Hartshorne's ethics: "The Metaphysical Axioms and Ethics of Charles Hartshorne," *Review of Metaphysics* 40: 271–304 (1986).

# Chapter Eight

1. E. M. Forster, *A Passage to India* (New York: Harcourt, Brace and Company, 1924), chap. 14.

2. My understanding of Arendt and of her interpretation of Kant is guided by David Ingram, "The Postmodern Kantianism of Arendt," *Review of Metaphysics* 42: 51–77 (1988), and by Ronald Beiner, "Hannah Arendt on Judging," in the book he edited of her lectures dealing with Kant's political philosophy [KPP 89–156].

3. Ingram, "The Postmodern Kantianism of Arendt," p. 61.

4. These comments on Harris draw from my review essay of his *The Reality of Time, History and Theory* 28:348–356 (1989).

5. Ingram's article develops the contrast between Arendt and Lyotard that I am utilizing, although he proposes that it be resolved along lines I find unconvincing.

6. Cited by Toynbee [SH-6 112] as an anecdote recounted in Gibbon's *Decline and Fall of the Roman Empire*, chap. 51.

7. Lyotard, *Le Différend* (Paris: Les Editions de Minuit, 1983), p. 190; as translated by Ingram, "The Postmodern Kantianism of Arendt," p. 72.

8. William Shakespeare, *Macbeth*, act V, scene V, lines 19–28.

9. See also Caputo's earlier and more extensive arguments in his *Radical Hermeneutics: Repetition, Deconstruction, and The Hermeneutic Project* (Bloomington/Indianapolis: Indiana University Press, 1987).

10. Oswald Spengler, *The Decline of the West*, trans. Helmut Werner (New York: Alfred A. Knopf, 1962 [1921]).

11. See IP, chap. 2, for my interpretation of Descartes.

12. Edward FitzGerald, *Rubáiyát of Omar Khayyám* (New York: Random House, 1947 [1872]), 3d ed.: stanzas 68–69.

# Coda

1. The allusions used here are to the closing section of T. S. Eliot, "The Waste Land," and to Ludwig Wittgenstein, *Philosophical Investigations*, I.18. Please see also the last two pages in IP.

# WORKS CITED

[Works listed here are all referred to in the body of the text by the initials indicated. Books and articles mentioned in the footnotes are fully cited there but not here.]

Allan, George
   IP     *The Importances of the Past: A Meditation on the Authority of Tradition*. Albany: State University of New York Press, 1986.

Arendt, Hannah
   KPP   *Lectures on Kant's Political Philosophy*, ed. Ronald Beiner. Chicago: University of Chicago Press, 1982.

Aristotle
   EN    *Ethica Nicomachea* (Nicomachian Ethics), trans. Martin Ostwald in *Aristotle: Nicomachean Ethics*. Indianapolis: Bobbs-Merrill, 1962. References are to book, chapter, page, column and line of the standard Bekker edition of the Greek text.

Augustine
   CG    *The City of God*, trans. John Healey. London: J. M. Dent & Sons, 1940. References are to book and section.

Bentham, Jeremy
PML     *An Introduction to the Principles of Morals and Legisla-tion*. Garden City, N.Y.: Doubleday, 1961 [1789]. References are to chapter and section.

Caputo, John D.
DH     "Demythologizing Heidegger: *Aletheia* and the History of Being." *Review of Metaphysics* 41: 519–46 (1988).

Davidson, Donald
EAE     *Essays on Actions and Events*. Oxford: Clarendon Press, 1980.

Dewey, John
CF     *A Common Faith*. New Haven: Yale University Press, 1934.
HNC     *Human Nature and Conduct: An Introduction To Social Psychology*. New York: The Modern Library, 1929 [1922].
LTI     *Logic: The Theory of Inquiry*. New York: Henry Holt and Company, 1938.
QC     *The Quest for Certainty: A Study of the Relation of Knowledge and Action*. New York: Capricorn Books, 1960 [1929].

Eliade, Mircea
SAP     *The Sacred and the Profane*, trans. Willard R. Trask. New York: Harper & Row, 1959 [1957].

Fiske, John
API     *American Political Ideas*. New York: Harper & Brothers, 1885.
OCP     *Outlines of Cosmic Philosophy*, 4 volumes. Boston: Houghton, Mifflin and Co., 1902 [1874].

Foxe, John
FBM     *The Acts and Monuments of John Foxe*, 8 volumes. London: Seeley, Burnside, and Seeley, 1843 [1563 et seq.].

Fromm, Erich
AL     *The Art of Loving*. New York: Harper & Row, 1974 [1956].

Hakluyt, Richard
PN     *The Principal Navigations, Voiages, Traffiques & Discoveries of the English Nation*, 12 volumes. Glasgow: James MacLehose and Sons, 1903–1905 [1598–1600].

Harris, Errol E.
RT    *The Reality of Time.* Albany: State University of New York
      Press, 1988.

Hartshorne, Charles
IO    *Insights and Oversights of Great Thinkers: An Evaluation
      of Western Philosophy.* Albany: State University of New
      York Press, 1983.

Hegel, Georg Wilhelm Friedrich
PH    *The Philosophy of History*, trans. J. Sibree, from lecture
      notes as edited by Charles Hegel. New York: Dover Pub-
      lications, 1956 [1822–1831].

Ibn Khaldûn
M     *The Maquaddimah: An Introduction to History*, one-
      volume abridgement, trans. Franz Rosenthal. London:
      Routledge & Paul, 1967 [1300s].

James, William
WB    "The Will to Believe" in *The Will to Believe and Other Es-
      says*, included in *Pragmatism and Other Essays*, pp. 193–
      213. New York: Washington Square Press, 1964 [1896].

Joachim of Fiore
JF    *Joachim of Fiore: A Study in Spiritual Perception and His-
      tory* by Delno C. West and Sandra Zimdars-Swartz.
      Bloomington: Indiana University Press, 1963.

Kant, Immanuel
CJ    *Critique of Judgment.* New York: Hafner Publishing Com-
      pany, 1951 [1790]. References are to numbered sections.
GMM   *Grounding for the Metaphysics of Morals*, trans. James W.
      Ellington. Indianapolis: Hackett, 1981 [1785]. Page refer-
      ences are to the standard German edition of Kant's
      works: the Königliche Preussische Akademic der Wissen-
      schafte edition (Berlin, 1902–1938), vol. 4.
HRCP  "An Old Question Raised Again: Is the Human Race Consis-
      tently Progressing?" trans. Robert Anchor; in *On History.*
      Indianapolis: Bobbs-Merrill, 1963 [1798], pp. 137–154.
      Page references are to the standard German edition,
      vol. 8.

IUH     "Idea for a Universal History from a Cosmopolitan Point of View," trans. Lewis White Beck; in *On History*. Indianapolis: Bobbs-Merrill, 1963 [1784], pp. 11–26. Page references are to the standard German edition, vol. 7.

Kierkegaard, Søren
E/O     *Either/Or*, trans., vol. 1, David F. Swenson and Lillian Marvin Swenson; trans., vol. 2, Walter Lowrie. Princeton: Princeton University Press, 1959 [1843].

Langer, Susanne K.
PNK     *Philosophy in a New Key*. Cambridge: Harvard University Press, 3d ed., 1957.

Lessing, Gotthold E.
EHR     *The Education of the Human Race*, trans. and ed. Henry Chadwick; in *Lessing's Theological Writings*. Stanford: Stanford University Press, 1967 [1781], pp. 82–98.

Loomer, Bernard
SG      "The Size of God"; in *The Size of God: The Theology of Bernard Loomer in Context*, eds. William Dean and Larry E. Axel. Macon, Ga.: Mercer University Press, 1987, pp. 20–51.

Lyotard, Jean-François
JG      *Just Gaming*, in conversation with Jean-Loup Thébaud, trans. Wlad Gudzich. Minneapolis: University of Minnesota Press, 1985 [1979].
PC      *The Postmodern Condition: A Report on Knowledge*, trans. Geoff Bennington and Brian Massumi. Minneapolis: University of Minnesota Press, 1984 [1979].

Machiavelli, Niccolò
D       *Discourses on the First Ten Books of Titus Livius*, trans. Leslie J. Walker, ed. Bernard Crick. New York: Penguin Books, 1974 [1531]. References are to book and section.

Mill, John Stuart
U       *Utilitarianism*. Garden City, N.Y.: Doubleday 1961 [1863].

Miller, Walter M., Jr.
CL      *A Canticle For Leibowitz*. New York: Bantam Books, 1976.

Oakeshott, Michael
HC    *On Human Conduct.* Oxford: Clarendon Press, 1975.

Purchas, Samuel
PHP   *Purchas His Pilgrimage*, 2d ed. London: William Stansby, 1614.
HP    *Hakluytus Posthumus or Purchas His Pilgrimes*, 20 volumes. Glasgow: James MacLehose and Sons, 1905–1907 [1625].

Rosenthal, Sandra
SP    *Speculative Pragmatism.* Amherst: University of Massachusetts Press, 1986.

Royce, Josiah
POC   *The Problem of Christianity*, 2 volumes. New York: Macmillan, 1913.

Santayana, George
GT    "The Genteel Tradition in American Philosophy"; in *Winds of Doctrine.* New York: Charles Scribner's Sons, 1911, pp. 186–215.

Sartre, Jean-Paul.
BN    *Being and Nothingness*, trans. Hazel Barnes. New York: Washington Square Press, 1966 [1943].
CDR   *Critique of Dialectical Reason* (vol. 1: *Theory of Practical Ensembles*), trans. Alan Sheridan-Smith. Atlantic Highlands: Humanities Press, 1976 [1960].
E     "Existentialism"; in *Existentialism and Human Emotions*, trans. Bernard Frechtman. New York: Philosophical Library, 1957 [1945], pp. 9–51.

Taylor, Charles
HAL   *Human Agency and Language* (*Philosophical Papers*, vol. 1). Cambridge: Cambridge University Press, 1985.

Teilhard de Chardin, Pierre
PM    *The Phenomenon of Man*, trans. Bernard Wall. New York: Harper & Row, 1961 [1955].

Toynbee, Arnold
SH    *A Study of History*, 12 volumes. London: Oxford University Press, 1934–1961.

Whitehead, Alfred North
  PR    *Process and Reality*, Corrected Edition, ed. David Griffin and Donald Sherburne. New York: The Free Press, 1978 [1929].
  AI    *Adventures of Ideas*. New York: The Free Press, 1967 [1933].

Wieman, Henry Nelson.
  SHG  *The Source of Human Good*. Carbondale: Southern Illinois University Press, 1946.

# INDEX

315